LOCALIZATION AND GLOBALIZATION OF RELIGIONS

THE LEGACY OF SLAVERY AND INDENTURED LABOUR
edited by
MAURITS S. HASSANKHAN AND FARZANA GOUNDER

LIST OF PLANNED PUBLICATIONS

1. *Social Aspects of Health, Medicine and Disease in the Colonial and Postcolonial Era,* edited by Henk Menke, Jane Buckingham, Farzana Gounder, Ashutosh Kumar and Maurits S. Hassankhan

2. *Women, Gender and the Legacy of Slavery and Indenture,* edited by Farzana Gounder, Kalpana Hiralal, Amba Pande and Maurits S. Hassankhan

3. *Collective Memory, Identity and Legacies of Slavery and Indenture,* edited by Farzana Gounder, Bridget Brereton, Jerome Egger and Hilde Neus

4. *Localization and Globalization of Religions,* edited by Maurits S. Hassankhan, Narinder Mohkamsingh, Goolam Vahed and Radica Mahase

5. *Ethnic Relations in Plural Societies. Social-economic and Political Dimensions,* edited by Maurits S. Hassankhan, Hans Ramsoedh, Brij V. Lal and Goolam Vahed

6. *Post-emancipation Indenture and Migration: Identities, Racialization and Transnationalism,* edited by Maurits S. Hassankhan, Kalpana Hiralal, Cristiana Bastos and Lomarsh Roopnarine

7. *Historical and Contemporary Aspects of Indian Indenture and Migration,* edited by Maurits S. Hassankhan, Rachel Kurian, Lomarsh Roopnarine and Ashutosh Kumar

8. *The Legacies of Slave Trade and Slavery in Post-Slavery Societies in the Caribbean,* edited by Michael Toussaint, Harold Sijlbing, Nicole Burrowes and Jerome Egger

9. *Slavery, Indentured Labour, Migration and their Legacies in the Americas and Africa,* edited by Karwan Fatah-Black, Michael Toussaint, Hilde Neus and Hans Ramsoedh

10. *Historiography, Theory and Philosophical Aspects of Slavery and Indenture,* edited by Maurits S. Hassankhan, Brij V. Lal, Vijaya Teelock and Goolam Vahed

Localization and Globalization of Religions

Edited by

MAURITS S. HASSANKHAN
NARINDER MOHKAMSINGH
GOOLAM VAHED
RADICA MAHASE

BOYDELL · MANOHAR

© Individual contributors, 2024

All Rights Reserved. Except as permitted under current legislation
no part of this work may be photocopied, stored in a retrieval system,
published, performed in public, adapted, broadcast,
transmitted, recorded or reproduced in any form or by any means,
without the prior permission of the copyright owner

ISBN 978-81-19139-21-7 (Manohar Publishers & Distributors)
ISBN 978-1-83765-139-9 (Boydell ◆ Manohar)

First published 2024 by
Ajay Kumar Jain for
Manohar Publishers & Distributors
4753/23 Ansari Road, Daryaganj
New Delhi 110 002

First published Worldwide excluding India, Sri Lanka, Nepal,
Bangladesh, Afghanistan, Pakistan and Bhutan, 2024 by Boydell ◆ Manohar
A joint imprint of Boydell & Brewer Ltd and
Manohar Publishers & Distributors
PO Box 9, Woodbridge, Suffolk IP12 3DF, UK
and of Boydell & Brewer Inc.
668 Mt Hope Avenue, Rochester, NY 14620–2731, USA
website: www.boydellandbrewer.com

A CIP catalogue record for this book is available
from the British Library

The publisher has no responsibility for the continued existence or accuracy of URLs for
external or third-party internet websites referred to in this book, and does not guarantee
that any content on such websites is, or will remain, accurate or appropriate

Typeset by
Kohli Print
Delhi 110 051

This publication is printed on acid-free paper

Contents

List of Figures and Tables	7
Foreword	11
Preface	13
Introduction MAURITS S. HASSANKHAN, NARINDER MOHKAMSINGH, GOOLAM VAHED and RADICA MAHASE	15

PART I: HINDUISM AND HINDUS IN THE *GIRMIT* DIASPORA

1. The Construction of Hindu Authority in Mauritius: The Case of a Tamil Priest
   MATHIEU CLAVEYROLAS — 29

2. Hinduism in South Africa, 1860-2020
   VINAY LAL and GOOLAM VAHED — 55

3. Transnational Hindu Movements and the South African Experience after Indenture
   KARTHIGASEN GOPALAN — 85

4. Pivotal Developments on Hinduism in Fiji
   PRASHNEEL R. GOUNDAR — 105

5. The Impact of the Ārya Samāj on Caribbean Hinduism
   FREEK L. BAKKER — 133

6. 'They Came to Mauritian Shores': The History and Symbolism of Ram Leela and *Ramayana* in Mauritius (1870-1950)
   SATYENDRA PEERTHUM — 159

6 CONTENTS

7. 'Beyond *Vanvaas*: Hinduism in Trinidad'
SHERRY-ANN SINGH 181

PART II: ISLAM AND MUSLIMS IN THE
GIRMIT DIASPORA

8. The *Ummah* in the Caribbean: African and Asian
Origins of Caribbean Islam
BRINSLEY SAMAROO 207

9. From Indentured Labourers to Permanent Settlers:
Muslims in Fiji
JAN A. ALI 225

10. The Muslims who Arrived in Trinidad, 1887-1891:
A Preliminary Assessment
HALIMA-SA'ADIA KASSIM and PERRY POLAR 253

PART III: INTERRELIGIOUS RELATIONS IN THE
GIRMIT DIASPORA

11. Interreligious Cooperation: Suriname and Guyana,
1950-2014
KIRTIE ALGOE 297

12. Fasting Practices of Religiously-mixed Families
in Trinidad: Evaluation of the Social-
Psychological Impact
SHALIMA MOHAMMED 325

List of Contributors 353

Index 359

Figures and Tables

FIGURES

1.1. Renovation of the Goodlands Mariammenkovil, June 2010   34
1.2. Announcement of the Govinden ceremony, with the street renamed after the *kovil*, November 2012   35
1.3. Aya Selven before walking over the fire, November 2009   37
4.1. An evening *kirtan* recitation taking place   108
4.2. A devotee with tridents on his body to fulfil his vow to the demigod   109
4.3. Hindus celebrating Holi with colours   110
4.4. Singing of *chautaal* during the Holi celebrations   111
4.5. Wedding attire of a South Indian bride and bridegroom   115
4.6. Head of Language & Literature Department at Fiji National University, Dr Mark Hewson launches academic Prashneel Goundar's *Pursuing Divinity in Paradise*   121
4.7. A devotee prays at the ISKCON Sigatoka Temple   124
5.1. Fire-offering in the Arya Dewaker Temple in Paramaribo, Suriname, June 2018   141
5.2. Two important Caribbean politicians with an originally Aryan background: Jagernath Lachmon (Suriname) and Basdeo Panday (Trinidad)   148
6.1. Immigrant Servanin   166
6.2. Immigrant Rungassamy   167
6.3. A Letter written and signed by Immigrant Rungassamy, Job Contractor, to Henri La Hausse, owner of Beau Vallon Sugar Estate, requesting that the Indian Indentured Workers be allowed to observe Deepavali in 1875   168

8 LIST OF FIGURES AND TABLES

6.4.	Immigrant Dharamsingh	169
6.5.	Immigrant Callee	170
6.6.	Immigrant Viramen	171
6.7.	An extract from a *Ramayana* text in the Kaithi script from northern India which was brought by immigrant Gopal Ram in 1871	175
9.1.	Fiji Muslim League branches, affiliates and non-affiliates	239
10.1.	Distribution of 'castes' among indentured Muslims	292
10.2.	Map of native places of India	292
10.3.	Location of estates in Trinidad	293
11.1(a).	Population by religion in Suriname in the twentieth and twenty-first century	298
11.1(b).	Population by religion in Guyana in the twentieth and twenty-first century	299
11.2.	Factors of interreligious cooperation	302
11.3.	Different religious groups on World Religion Day 2010	306
11.4.	Peace walk organized by IRO in 2006	311
11.5.	East Indians by Christian denomination in Guyana, 2006-14	313
11.6.	Christians, Hindus and Muslims in interreligious organizations in Suriname and Guyana	315
12.1.	Processing information	343

TABLES

2.1.	Christian composition of the Indian diaspora of South Africa	69
10.1.	Ships and dates of arrival between 1887 and 1891	277
A.	Muslims landed in Trinidad relative to overall indentured landing/emigranting from India between 1887 and 1891	277
B.	Percentage of Indian men, women, boys, girls and infants who landed in Trinidad between 1887 and 1891	279

LIST OF FIGURES AND TABLES

C. Percentage of Muslim males and females between 1887 and 1891	280
D. Age distribution of Muslim males and females	281
E. Height distribution of Muslim males and females	281
F1. Native places of Muslim indentured labourers, 1887-91	282
F2. Number of states—districts and number of persons originating, 1887-91	284
G. Second indenture—First place of indenture for immigrants to Trinidad, 1887-91	284
H. Muslim family accompaniments, 1887-91	285
I. Births on ships between 1887 and 1891	286
J. Deaths on ships between 1887 and 1891	287
K. Estates to which Muslims were indentured between 1887 and 1891	288
L. Number of returnees to India based on ship and year of arrival in Trinidad	291
11.1. Population by religion in Suriname and Guyana, from 1950 to 2012	324
12.1. Descriptions of respondents	349

Foreword

It gives me great pleasure to write the Foreword to this very important collection of articles on two major religions from the subcontinent of India which made their way into the former British, French and Dutch colonies and how they became localized and naturalized—Hinduism and Islam. Through extensive scholarly research one now knows the correlation between the emergence of ethnic enclaves created by the indentured Indians in the colonies and the appearance of profoundly different religious expressions there, each location presenting different challenges and opportunities. In other words, wherever indentured Indian communities were able to concentrate in closer proximity, there was a greater success of establishing temples and mosques to represent their religious and social identity. These religious centres not only expressed the flavour of the land of their origin, but most significantly, they demonstrated the ability of the diasporic community to adapt to local conditions and generate a more localized version of the religion that they practised. As such Hinduism and Islam that one finds in the diaspora of the former British colonies, vary in their customs, plantation systems, and proximity between the indentured labourers and the former slaves. So, in places like Mauritius, South Africa, Trinidad, Suriname, Fiji and to some extent Guyana, the opportunities to concentrate in large areas either outside the plantation lands or within them, enabled the indentured Indians to establish their own religious centres to put their own stamp of their own ethnic and cultural identity. But in the case of Jamaica such conditions did not exist as the former slaves there had already occupied the available free land as well as significant portions of the plantation lands after they became free, and thus forced the indentured Indians to spread thinly throughout the island. Hence, a strong expression of Indian culture is not seen in Jamaica and the French colonies in the Caribbean.

FOREWORD

While it is the varied conditions that shaped the expressions of Indian culture, be it Hinduism or Islam, with time these local expressions became normative for those communities in the different diasporic locations. So, one can speak about Mauritian Hinduism, South African Hinduism, Trinidadian, Fijian and Guyanese Hinduism and last but not the least, Surinamese Hinduism. When Indo-Fijian and South African Hindus intersect in Australia, their Hinduism is not the same, albeit they can both claim to have originated in India. East African Gujarati Hindus share their own differences with their counterparts from India. Such localization of religious expressions are seen by scholars with new challenges of how to theorize religion in general and religion in the diaspora in particular. Placing such localized versions on the global arena of scholarship offers interesting new insights into how one may conceptualize religion broadly, and Hinduism and Islam in particular, in the diasporic context.

The essays in this book offer insights into the kinds of challenges that one faces in critical and theoretical structures and classifies religions in the diaspora. Without saying how different they are in each of the locations, e.g. the Moharram festival in South Africa, African and Asian origins of Islam in the Caribbean, it would be difficult to get a handle on the concreteness of religions in these locations. Nevertheless, there seems to be some characteristic in all of them to transcend their specific locations and form transnational connections and engage with each other on a global arena. It is in this sense the collection of essays in this book offers new opportunities to expand an understanding of religion in the diaspora. I congratulate both the individual contributors as well as the editors who put them together for this wonderful addition to this collective scholarly engagement. I hope the scholars of South Asian diaspora will find this book not only interesting, but illuminating in many ways.

P. Pratap Kumar
Professor Emeritus
University of KwaZulu-Natal,
South Africa

Preface

This book is the fourth volume of ten in the series Legacies of Slavery and Indentured Labour. The series is an output of the 2018 conference, on Legacy of Slavery and Indentured Labour, organized by the Anton de Kom University of Suriname. This conference was the second of its kind organized in Suriname, with participation of scholars from all continents and different backgrounds. The aim of the conference, as stated in the Call for Papers, was: 'to connect historical specificities of slavery, indentured labour and migration to contemporary issues of globalization, diaspora, identity formation, nationalism and transnationalism' and 'to promote new perspectives and approaches in the study of forced and free migration and their impact on the society'.

Some of the questions which were addressed in the conference and the volumes of the series are:

- What are the legacies of slavery and indentured labour in social, economic, cultural, political fields?
- How did post-slavery identity formation occur in different parts of the world?
- What has been the psychological impact of slavery and indentured labour?
- How are transnational identities developing in the world today?
- How is the process of identification related to the imaginary concept of the country of origin and other 'partners in distress' in the diaspora?
- In the case of the second generation migrants or the twice migrants, what is perceived as their country of origin? In other words: What kind of homeland perspectives do people have and what impact will it have on their relationship with their former homeland?
- In which way did the various groups adapt to the new environment? What has been the policy or attitude of the receiving country or society?

14 PREFACE

- How are localizing processes ('creolization') expressed in migrant cultures?
- What kinds of transnational ties exist among descendants of immigrants in the Caribbean and other countries?
- Are alternative transnational identities in the Caribbean real or an imaginary one?
- How are transnational ties and identities recognized and institutionalized by the State in the former homelands?
- How and why are local processes of identity formation related to emotional and practical identification to the countries of origin, and how do these countries feature in these processes?

Based on these questions and related topics, there were more than 30 parallel sessions. Four of the panels were on 'Localization and Globalization of Religions', and on 'Tangible and Intangible Heritage of Slavery and Indenture'. This volume consists of revised versions of selected articles from these panels and supplemented by additional articles from persons who were not able to attend the conference. The articles in the volume have all undergone rigorous peer review and revision in order to provide high calibre discussions on the theme.

Suriname
May 2021

MAURITS S. HASSANKHAN
FARZANA GOUNDER

Introduction

MAURITS S. HASSANKHAN, NARINDER
MOHKAMSINGH, GOOLAM VAHED AND
RADICA MAHASE

This volume on *Localization and Globalization of Religions* is the fourth in the series published in connection with the international conference on 'Slavery, Indentured Labour, Migration, Diaspora and Identity Formation, in Historical and Contemporary Context', held in Paramaribo, Suriname from 19 to 23 June 2018.[1]

It consists of twelve chapters, of which seven are on Hinduism and Hindus in the *Girmit* diaspora, three on Muslims and two on interreligious relations in the *Girmit* diaspora. Seven of the articles are revised versions of papers from the above-mentioned conference in Suriname, while five of them have been written at the request of the editors of the volume. Geographically, the articles represent the Southern Pacific, the Indian Ocean and the Caribbean.

The significance of the book is that it fills a gap in the historiography of the indentured labour diaspora, because not much research has been done on the legacy of indentured labour in different aspects of religious heritage. The fact that in one volume the editors have combined the development of the Hindu and Muslim communities in different aspects, is remarkable. The articles on the relations between different religious communities and between Hindu and Muslim partners in an interreligious relationship are unique.

I. HINDUISM AND HINDUS IN THE *GIRMIT* DIASPORA

This part consists of seven articles on different aspects of Hinduism in Mauritius, South Africa, Fiji, Trinidad and Suriname. Most

[1] This conference was organized by the Institute of Graduate Studies and Research (IGSR) and the Faculty of Humanities of the Anton de Kom University of Suriname. We thank IGSR and the Vice-Chancellor, Professor Jack Menke for the support given and the Surinamese Postspaarbank (SPSB) for financial support.

of the contributors draw attention to the transformation of Hinduism into newer forms since indentureship in the Indian diaspora. All agree that Hinduism has retained important aspects of its Indian origin while simultaneously adapting to the local situation. This process is discussed from different angles, often in the broader context of Hinduism in a Creole society marked by religious and cultural plurality and interaction (Claveyrolas). This development demonstrates the ability of the diasporic community to adapt to local conditions and generate more localized and transnational versions of Hinduism.

Social or collective memory played an important role in preserving or reviving the tangible and intangible heritage of the immigrants (Peerthum). In this way, their religions, cultures and traditions were brought from India to their new homelands. Hinduism, the faith of the majority of the immigrants, accordingly arrived in the various British and Dutch colonies.

Hinduism is generally known for its diversity in terms of traditions, philosophies, doctrines and practices. Especially in India, where this religion emerged and developed, the diversity is incredible, leading some scholars to suggest that one is dealing not with one but multiple religious traditions 'conveniently' placed under one denomination. Similarly, the religious diversity of Hinduism was initially also reflected in the diaspora of indentureship. However, in the course of time, this diversity has been dissipating, as it was standardized and homogenized by the dominant orthodox Sanatan Dharma (Vertovec 1994). Many of the minor forms, such as the cults involving bloody sacrifices, possession cults, and worship of deities such as Dhih Devi and Sitala Mai, were largely marginalized, and only some of the established cults have survived, as seen in those focussed around saints such as Kabir (fourteenth century) and Swami Dayanand (nineteenth century).

The contributions in this volume show that notwithstanding inroads made by Christianity (through Pentecostal and other denominations), Hinduism continues to flourish and even show signs of prosperity in public spaces (Lal and Vahed). Notably, the transformation of Hinduism in the diaspora takes place partly due to influences from the Indian subcontinent and partly due to the local

INTRODUCTION 17

institutions in the form of Hindi schools (*patha-shala*) and the numerous cultural groups, such as those reciting the *Ramayana*, performing open air Ram Leela and making Baithakgana and Chutney music.

Transnational Hindu movements played an essential role in 'recreating and preserving' the main religious traditions in the new social setting. Visiting Hindu missionaries from India were pivotal in establishing umbrella organizations such as the orthodox Hindu Mahasabha and the reformist Arya Samaj. As the local colonial authorities were not interested in safeguarding the interests of Hindus, these institutions took the responsibility to preserve and promote Hindu culture and religion, Hindi and religious education and also to prevent conversion to other faiths (Gopalan).

The Arya Samaj had a robust missionary agenda and accordingly became quite popular during the first four decades of the twentieth century. It is interesting to look into the reasons for its upsurge and impact on the Hindustani community, as can be seen in women's education, anti-caste consciousness, and politics (Bakker). In this regard, attention is also drawn to academic developments such as language debates, publications and conferences for which the initiatives of local Hindu leaders and individual families is essential (Goundar). The personal or individual approach to the study of Hinduism throws light from a different perspective on the relationship between priests and their clients (*yajyamaan*). For example, the life story of an individual Hindu priest sheds interesting light on the construction of the religious authority of Hindu priests in Mauritius (Claveyrolas). Likewise, the performance of the Ram Leela, a tremendously popular *Ramayana* tradition, is highlighted as a popular medium for propagating *Ramayana* consciousness and heritage (Peerthum).

The Hindu diaspora discourse is often marked by notable religious notions, namely that of *vanvaas*. The migrants adapted this metaphor from the *Ramayana* to describe their own 'exile' or sojourn in foreign countries before returning to their native land. The metaphor of exile applies to the migrants who eventually return from exile, i.e. go back to India. About a quarter or third of the immigrants could literally achieve this ideal after serving their indenture:

Rama returning home! But those who stayed in the colonies got rooted in their local situations. However, at certain moments, a sizeable number of them were seized by the forces of globalization and migrated further to North America, Canada, the United Kingdom and the Netherlands. One could say that those Hindus went 'deeper' into *vanvaas*, or as argued by Sherry-Ann Singh, they went 'beyond *vanvaas*'.

Understanding how Hinduism is conceptualized and formulated in different settings, allows us to compare distant diasporic communities with each other, as well as with the 'homeland' and also understand how these communities view each other (Lal and Vahed). The localization of religious expressions, as described in this section, offers fresh material to scholarship in general and to researchers of religious studies in particular.

The first chapter by Mathieu Claveyrolas focuses on the construction of Hindu authority in Mauritius and in particular the role of Tamil priests. This article examines the evolution of Mauritian Hinduism, its religious and identity stakes, through a presentation of the life story, personality, and status of an individual priest. This life history is used to discuss the construction of the religious authority of Hindu priests in Mauritius. What emerges is the ambiguous relationship of Mauritian Hindu religious specialists and learned orthodoxy with the popular practices born in villages in India and the Mauritian plantation context and, on the other hand, with the contemporary Indian reference as a result of the rapidly changing image of India among Hindu Mauritians. This is discussed in the broader context of the Mauritian situation of a Creole society born out of the plantation and evolving in a context of religious and cultural plurality. This chapter also considers the Indian roots and Mauritian context and history of indenture and plantation life to understand the conditions in which local Hinduism was born and has evolved historically into the present.

Vinay Lal and Goolam Vahed examine the establishment and transformation of Hinduism in South Africa over the past 160 years. According to the authors, Hinduism continues to flourish and even shows signs of prosperity in public spaces, notwithstanding inroads made by Pentecostalism. If the reification of Hinduism is

INTRODUCTION 19

taking place, the faith is also opening itself up to other transformations, due in part to influences from the Indian subcontinent. Lal and Vahed state that South African Hinduism displays its own characteristic features and that it should be examined on its own terms, in the very specific social, cultural, political, and economic conditions in which it has been forged.

In his article 'Transnational Hindu Movements and the South African Experience after Indenture', Karthigasen Gopalan begins his story in 1912, just two years after the establishment of the Union of South Africa, when Hindu leaders in the country met under the leadership of a visiting Hindu missionary from India to establish the South African Hindu Mahasabha. The purpose of the Mahasabha was to unite all Hindus in the country under one umbrella organization and deal with what its leaders felt were the 'common problems' faced by Hindu South Africans. Hindu leaders were especially concerned that the conditions in which most South African Hindus lived would make them more likely to convert to other faiths. These conditions included poverty, illiteracy, lack of secular, vernacular and religious education for Hindu children, and an emphasis on ritual-oriented Hinduism at the expense of philosophical Hinduism. To preserve culture and religion, Hindu leaders formed an umbrella organization to unite and coordinate the activities of parochial Hindu associations and temples to safeguard Hindu interests. Despite their commitment to 'preserve' Hinduism, many of the missionaries that the Mahasabha invited, represented a reformist movement called the Arya Samaj, which aimed to eradicate some traditions and practices that most South African Hindus saw as part of their Hindu heritage. Some of the missionaries were also Hindu nationalist leaders in India, and their political views influenced other areas where Indians settled as indentured labourers. However, regardless of the popularity of the missionaries in South Africa, most South African Hindus continued their religious practices independently of reformers. This article also explores how South African Hindu leaders negotiated 'Hinduism' in response to changing economic, political and social conditions prevailing in the country.

Prashneel Goundar analyses crucial developments in Hinduism

in the context of Fiji. Between 1879 and 1916, 60,553 Indians were brought to Fiji as labourers to work on the sugarcane farms under the indenture system (*Girmit*). Of these, 86 per cent were Hindus and 14 per cent Muslims. The indenture system was abolished in 1920 (Lal 1983). At the end of their *Girmit*, the indentured labourers were given the option to either settle in Fiji or return to India. Many chose to begin their new life on the small island nation in the Pacific Ocean. Goundar looks at selected developments in Hinduism that have taken place in Fiji over the years, such as language debates, funeral and wedding customs, books and publications, as well as conferences on Hinduism. He also discusses some important *poojas* that are conducted by different Hindu communities and touches upon politics too. He concludes by bringing out the challenges and issues that need to be considered by the leaders of Hindu communities in Fiji and individual families to carry on the exceptional work by their forefathers.

In the next article, Freek L. Bakker analyses the impact of the Arya Samaj on Caribbean Hinduism. According to him, the Arya Samaj gained a strong foothold within Caribbean Hinduism during the first four decades of the twentieth century. This article explores the reasons for this upsurge and analyses the impact of this movement on various areas of the life of the Hindustani community, including education, rituals, the use of sacred scriptures, marriage and politics. Bakker demonstrates that the Arya Samajis had a lot of influence in the period after the introduction of universal suffrage in the Caribbean countries. Later, however, the orthodox Hindus retook the lead. Yet, their influence was confined by the ideals and efforts of the Arya Samajis.

Satyendra Peerthum's article is on the history and symbolism of Ram Leela and *Ramayana* in Mauritius. He examines the historical significance and symbolism of the Ram Leela, the tradition set by the *Ramayana*, community formation, the social and cultural life of the Indian indentured workers and their descendants in Mauritius between 1870 and 1950. Peerthum also covers the important themes of oral traditions, oral history and social practices among the descendants of Indian indentured workers during the late indenture era and the first half of the twentieth century.

INTRODUCTION   21

Peerthum demonstrates that the enactment of the Ram Leela is an essential and tangible example of the special cultural and historical bond between Mauritius and the Indian subcontinent. It also underscores the fact that the estimated 462,800 Indian and non-Indian indentured men, women and children who passed through the former Immigration Depot in Port Louis brought with them their tangible and intangible heritage, which included various languages, cultures, religions, traditional attires, culinary traditions, stories, riddles and popular games to Mauritius, a small Indian Ocean island, which most of them adopted as their new home.

The Ram Leela forms part of the 'Ramayana consciousness and heritage' which has existed in Mauritius since the mid-nineteenth century. This fact is important when looking at Mauritian history, in particular, the history of Indian indentured labourers and the Aapravasi Ghat World Heritage Site, which was inscribed under the UNESCO World Heritage Committee's *criterion vi*, which deals with the intangible heritage of a particular people, place and country (Peerthum 2018: 1-2). Ram Leela and the *Ramayana* tradition represent one of the important intangible cultural heritages.

In the final article in Section I, Sherry-Ann Singh deals with Ram Leela in Trinidad. Between 1845 and 1917, the British colony of Trinidad drew extensively on Indian indentured labour to fill the gap left by the abolition of African slavery in 1838. During this period, a total of 143,939 Indians migrated to Trinidad, approximately 88 per cent of whom practised various facets of Hinduism. Despite the trying conditions experienced under the indenture system, about four of every five Indian immigrants chose to make Trinidad their permanent home at the end of their contracted periods of indenture. This article explores the role and manifestations of the seemingly diametrically opposed processes of localization and globalization in Hinduism as it emerged and developed in this diasporic location. Fundamental processes in the formation of diaspora communities such as transformation, accretion, retention and adjustment worked to create what can be referred to as 'Trinidad Hinduism', which carried with it elements of both its Indian origin and its Caribbean location. Singh examines how and to what extent Hinduism in Trinidad was transformed by its

Caribbean location while retaining elements of its Indian origin, but many times in attenuated forms. She posits that several strands and trends in Trinidad Hinduism echo similar developments in other locations of the Indian indentured diaspora, including Fiji, Mauritius, Guyana and Suriname. Finally, the study shows that the eventual movement of Indo-Trinidadians to locations such as North America and the United Kingdom, along with the impact of the ineluctable forces of globalization, has transported elements of Trinidad Hinduism into the larger global space; thereby, seemingly, bringing the diasporic processes initiated during the period of Indian indenture coming full circle.

II. ISLAM AND MUSLIMS IN
THE *GIRMIT* DIASPORA

The second part of the book has three articles on Muslims in the (Indian) indentured diaspora, with one article on Fiji and two on the Caribbean. The articles in this section form a useful supplement to the 2016 publication *Muslims in the Indentured Diaspora*.[2]

The first article in this section is Brinsley Samaroo's 'The *Ummah* in the Caribbean: African and Asian Origins of Caribbean Islam', which argues that 'despite continuous European efforts to initially suppress and later marginalize Islam in the circum-Caribbean region, the religion has clearly demonstrated its resilience and has established a permanent presence in the region. Islam's appeal has been based on philosophical principles which resonate with mankind's basic spiritual needs' (Samaroo). Somaroo uses the term *Ummah* to mean the worldwide Islamic community, often referred to as 'the Nation of Islam'. It includes all Muslims everywhere, superseding, in theory, race, region or political affiliation.

He seeks to trace the Caribbean origins of Islam in West Africa and its transference through the slave route to the New World. European, Christian efforts to suppress this early Muslim presence

---

[2] See: Maurits S. Hassankhan and Goolam Vahed and Lomarsh Roopnarine (eds.) (2016). *Indentured Muslims in the Diaspora. Identity and Belonging of Minority Groups in Plural Societies*. Delhi/London: Manohar/Routledge.

INTRODUCTION   23

were swift and decisive, sending the faith underground. Asian indentured labour from India and Indonesia served to resuscitate Islam because of the substantial numbers of Muslims among the immigrants as well as a softening of the European attitude for tactical reasons. The fact that Asian and Indonesian (mainly Javanese) immigration was continuous from 1838 to 1939 meant that there was a continuous infusion of Islam's adherents, which served to strengthen the faith. An additional incentive was the visits by Islamic missionaries from Asia who refreshed the enthusiasm over the decades. During the twentieth century, such contacts were reinforced by access to the foundational centres of Islam in the Middle East. These later influences sought to 'cleanse' the faith of its Asiatic accretions, causing the emergence of reformists and traditionalists. From the mid-twentieth century, there has been a North American influenced revival of Islam among black West Indians, which has also added to the diversity of Islamic traditions in the region. Samaroo's finding is that Islam continues to hold a prominent place in a multicultural Caribbean space.

Jan A. Ali's article explores the evolution and development of the Muslim community and its participation in the plural Fijian society, which comprises many cultures, racial groups, and religions. Ali examines the emergence of a Muslim community in Fiji as a product of the broader processes of geographical and social mobility produced by the international labour market and social and economic growth through personal initiatives sought by Muslims in pursuit of a better existence. He discusses the intricate relationship Muslims have with each other and with other ethnic and religious groups and underscores the triumphs and challenges they face in a plural society. Further, the article exposes the schism that exists among Muslim civil society organizations in Fiji, and shows that despite this, Muslims are integral to the country's social, cultural, and political fabric. One of his conclusions is that Muslim are not sojourners but permanent members of the multicultural society of Fiji.

In the aticle that follows, 'The Muslims who Arrived in Trinidad, 1887-1891: A Preliminary Assessment', Halima-Sa'adia Kassim and Perry Polar suggest that in the historiography of the Indo-

Trinidadians, there is very little focus on the demographic and social characteristics of various religious and caste groups. This has led to inconsistency in the population data. The authors seek to rectify the gaps specific to Muslims by mining entries in the General Registers for the period 1887-91 and then corroborating it with entries from the Ship Registers/Emigration Passes, where available. The existing data on Muslims is analysed to establish trends and patterns regarding demographic and social characteristics. This examination of historical demographic data allows for more precise statistics on Muslims and places them as more central within the indentured labourer narrative. The findings suggest that the patterns for Muslims are generally consistent with the findings in the literature for the overall Indian migrants. Further research is required to determine if the patterns for Muslims continue between 1892 and 1917.

III. INTERRELIGIOUS RELATIONS IN THE *GIRMIT* DIASPORA

The two articles in this part deal with interreligious cooperation and interreligious relations among mixed couples, respectively. Kirtie Algoe compares the contribution of interreligious organizations to interreligious relations in Suriname and Guyana from 1950 to 2014. According to her, in many regions of today's world, relationships between three major religious groups—Christians, Hindus, and Muslims—show opposite trends: attempts to foster peace by focusing on theological similarities and increasing violent conflicts, which emphasize religious differences. The Caribbean is notable for the relatively harmonious relationships between religious groups. Suriname and Guyana illustrate this. She analyses the relative religious harmony in both nations, in particular, the influence of interreligious organizations. To this end, she *compares* the evolution of interreligious cooperation between Christians, Hindus, and Muslims in umbrella interreligious bodies by using a mixed method research design. She argues that the comparative perspective is necessary as it has the benefit of revealing factors that foster or hinder mutual understanding between religious

INTRODUCTION 25

groups. A conceptual framework of concerted diversity is used to explain differences and similarities in the evolution of interreligious cooperation in Suriname and Guyana. Her findings are that in Suriname, the inter-religious organization contributes more to interreligious relations between Christians, Hindus and Muslims than in Guyana. This difference is explained by the complex interplay between religious demography, government policies, and religious leadership.

Part III ends with Shalima Mohammed's study on the fasting practices of contemporary religiously-mixed families in Trinidad. She evaluates the social-psychological impact of this phenomenon and observed that opportunities and obstacles arise from the recent increase in the number of interreligious families. In those cases of non-conversion, one common practice is that of fasting to fulfil religious obligations. Based on case studies of five participants who are descendants of Indian indentured labourers, this article draws attention to the challenges that arise in the fasting period, the effects on relationships, and how members manage trust in each other and the tenets of their respective religions. The author found that in all cases there were elements of disagreement in the relationships but these disagreements were not due to one partner's fasting practices. The main themes which emerged were mutual concession, religious tolerance and behavioural change. The Theory of Reasoned Action was used to explain the findings by highlighting the interrelationship among four factors—beliefs, attitudes, intentions and overt behaviours.

REFERENCE

Lal, Brij V. (1983). 'Girmityas: The Origins of the Fiji Indians', *The Journal of Pacific History*, Canberra.

PART I

HINDUISM AND HINDUS IN THE *GIRMIT* DIASPORA

CHAPTER 1

The Construction of Hindu Authority in Mauritius: The Case of a Tamil Priest[1]

MATHIEU CLAVEYROLAS

This article analyses the evolution of Hinduism within the local Mauritian context through the case study of a priest from the Tamil community. In addition to accounting for nuances and paradoxes, such ethnographic analysis[2] identifies issues common in Mauritius well beyond the Tamil community. The state of construction (of religion and buildings), the organization into temple societies and national 'federations' maintaining ambiguous relations with the government, the complex relationship with Mauritian identity, India and Hindu orthodoxy: all such characteristics are shared by

---

[1] This is a translated and revised version of 'Un prêtre tamoul dans le chantier de l'hindouisme mauricien', in Servan-Schreiber, ed., *Indianité et créolité à l'île Maurice*. Paris: Editions de l'EHESS, 2014, pp. 139-68. Data was gathered through dozens of observations in the temple during and outside ritual activities, numerous informal exchanges with the priest from 2009 to 2019, with five more formal interviews inside the temple in March 2010 (all quotations of Selven the priest, are extracted from these interviews).

[2] It is estimated that two-thirds of the Mauritian Hindus are Bhojpuris today—a figure which matches the proportion of Bhojpuris among the indentured. The Tamil Hindu community is estimated at 6 per cent of the Mauritian population, and 12 per cent of the Hindu population of Mauritius, comparing to 2.5 and 5 per cent respectively for the Telugu community. All figures have been taken from the Mauritian 2011 *Central Statistics Office.*

30 MATHIEU CLAVEYROLAS

other Mauritian communities of Indian origin, whether Bhojpuri or Telugu.[3]

Looking at religion in terms of its evolution is far from obvious. For a long time, the approach came up against reifying external analyses. This is particularly the case for Hinduism, too often analysed as intrinsically linked to the Indian territory and incompatible with any impurity, *métissage*, or confrontation with the Other (Claveyrolas & Trouillet 2021). Emphasizing the evolution of religions also contradicts the devotees' aspiration to think of their religious tradition as an eternal truth (*sanatan dharma*). Thus the most radical shift is often justified, not as something new, but as a necessary 'adaptation' to our degenerate age, or as a 'correction', back to a lost truth (Tarabout 1997: 128).

The challenges of the evolution of Mauritian Hinduism have often been analysed in terms of the loss, preservation or recovery of Indian traits. As is often the case in the diaspora, this ideology of loss is shared by many local actors. However, such an approach neglects the weight of the local context, limiting the analysis of any evolution (identity splits, reformism) to mimicry about the Indian situation and limiting Mauritian Hinduism to the exclusive positioning (dependence, attraction, rejection) concerning Indian Hinduism.

Mauritius is a Hindu and a Creole society. Mauritian culture is, therefore, based on the rupture with roots and the encounters (through syncretism and conflict) between various cultures. Let one remember other historical dimensions that led Mauritius to become a Creole society: the absence of any indigenous population, the presence of diverse, equally uprooted people (mainly the European colonists, the African or Malagasy slaves, and the Indian indentured) and, above all, the centrality of slavery as a founding institution. Despite statutory differences, indentured labour is, to a point, an extension of slavery (Tinker 1974, Carter 1995), in particular through the permanence of the plantation structure, a

---

[3] The Arya Samaj is a Hindu reform movement active both in the social sphere (against caste hierarchies) and in the religious one (against 'idol' worship).

THE CONSTRUCTION OF HINDU AUTHORITY IN MAURITIUS 31

total and highly binding economic and socio-ideological system. Such strong specificity of local history must be integrated into the study of the evolution of Mauritian Hinduism.

The Mauritian indentured labourers and their descendants distanced themselves partially from the plantation, first through the 'Grand Morcellement' and then through national independence. The 'Grand Morcellement' refers to the sale by planters of their least profitable lands in the 1880s to those indentured migrants who had completed their original contracts (Allen 1999: 74). This process allowed some individuals to access land ownership and settle in villages, which proved favourable to the first claims of Indianness (Benoist 1989). Independence in 1968 saw some thirty years of social, economic and political advancement for the descendants of Indian labourers and most of all for the majority Bhojpuri community, thus founding their political hegemony.

In this context, the visibility of Hinduism has increased logically on the island (Claveyrolas 2010). The current construction of Hindu places of worship has evolved since the Indian indenture period. They began as stones placed under trees. Over a period of time, these places of worship took the form of straw-roofed and sheet-iron roofed shrines before turning to cement constructions with verandas. On the Tamil side, monumental temples have been appearing for the past twenty years, based on the so-called 'Dravidian' model of the great temples of Tamil Nadu, with colourful high domes (*vimana*) and entrance porches (*gopuram*).

Three significant dimensions specify the contemporary evolution of Mauritian Hinduism. First, the Mauritian landscape is punctuated by a very dense presence of places of worship, especially Hindu ones. Second, it is important to highlight the tendency for places of worship to display increasingly distinct and exclusive affiliations (Catholic, Bhojpuri Hindu, Tamil Hindu or Telugu). Finally, it should be noted that this Mauritian landscape is being continually reconfigured through new constructions, renovations and expansions.

Take the example of Goodlands, a city with a population of 20,000 in north-eastern Mauritius, surrounded by sugarcane plantations, where most of the indentured Indians and their descendants have

32   MATHIEU CLAVEYROLAS

worked and lived since the 1830s. In this rural area, the majority
of the population is Bhojpuri. In addition to several Catholic,
Protestant and Muslim places of worship, Goodlands has at least
four Bhojpuri temples (*mandir*), including one from Arya Samaj,[4]
a Telugu temple (*mandiram*) and two Tamil temples (*kovil*), as
well as three *kalimai*.[5] Most of these temples have been renovated
and/or enlarged during the past ten years.

The importation of knowledge and knowhow from India
through recruitment networks of religious specialists (priests, musi-
cians, craftsmen and architects) certainly contributes to construct-
ing the 'modernized' Hinduism in contemporary Mauritius. But
this Hinduism is also built through an institutionalization of temples
and priesthood[6] in conjunction with a process of 'modernization'
shared by other (including non-Hindu) communities and through
specifically Mauritian conditions. In this context, ethnography
makes it possible to describe the processes of production and legitimization of the Mauritian Hindu religious authority in a nuanced
way. How do the ideal reference (India), the ideal otherness
(Creoleness and Mauritian Christianity) and the local construction
(Mauritian Creole Hinduism) fit together, from the point of view
of the holder of ritual knowledge?

HINDU-MAURITIAN RELIGIOUS AUTHORITY

PROLOGUE

Varanasi, early twenty-first century. The Ganges, during the mon-
soon season, takes on brown hues. The boats are tossed around by
the current and struggle to stabilize as they seek to approach the

---

[4] A *kalimai* or 'plantation shrine' is a small structure originally devoted to Kali
and the seven sister-goddesses.

[5] Temples are more and more often affiliated to a national federation gradually
homogenizing the deities and rituals through financing new constructions and
assigning priests to temples.

[6] In Mauritius, there are no *purohits* or domestic priests who, in India, are
more prestigious than temple priests, because they choose their patrons. Mauritian
temple priests usually take care of domestic ceremonies needing a specialist.

THE CONSTRUCTION OF HINDU AUTHORITY IN MAURITIUS   33

banks. Viewed from the boat, the succession of *ghats* (stairs) gives the holy city of Hinduism its picturesque image. Here comes Assi Ghat, and then Dashaswamedha Ghat, where pilgrims flock to take one of the required purifying baths. The boat still goes down the river to the north until the first fumes of Manikarnika Cremation Ghat appear. In Varanasi, it is said, the Hindus wish to perform the last rites, in order to be liberated from the endless cycle of rebirth and attain salvation.

The wooden piles occupy most of the *ghat's* space, ready for the unremitting funeral activity. The flames and fumes indicate that two pyres are already well advanced. Pieces of human bodies can be seen between the logs. The eldest son smashes the deceased's skull. Then the remains of the body are thrown into the boisterous Ganges. Further downstream, another body floats: a deceased person who, having died of skin disease or suicide, was not entitled to cremation, or whose cremation remained incomplete due to lack of wood. One follows the body tossed by the Ganges outside the city. A naked man with hirsute dreadlocks enters the water up to mid-thigh level and recovers the body. He is an Aghori ascetic or 'those who follow the third face of Shiva'. The ascetic places the body swollen by water on the floor of his straw-roofed hut. He applies a red powder to the deceased's forehead, arms and chest and then sits cross-legged on the body. Then he cuts and saws with a machete the right arm at the elbow, without apparent effort or bloodshed and crushes it.

The scene, with its explanatory subtitles, scrolls on the mini screen of the mobile phone of Selven, a Hindu priest from Mauritius. He knows that I have previously worked on Hinduism in Varanasi and he has been keen to show me this film for several weeks. He comments for me: 'There is no such thing as ascetics in Mauritius. Here it's better, that's Varanasi: [they say] they have the right to do that there, they say they are the Lord [*bondié*].'

We are in the temple in Goodlands where Selven officiates. Our regular meetings take place in the middle of the afternoon, before the evening service. We sit in the office, inside the temple enclosure, where Selven receives the devotees who have come to discuss, seek his advice or participate in the organization of a celebration.

Selven's temple celebrated its 157th anniversary in 2008 with a partial renovation. The *souvenir magazine* published for the occasion briefly retraced the known history. While no mention was made of an official attachment to a plantation, it was noted that the land was purchased in 1906 by 'Mr Arnachellum Soobrayen, indentured labourer no. 33483'. A cyclone destroyed the wooden and straw temple in 1945, then a second cyclone (date not specified) destroyed the new stone and sheet iron building. The first fire walking ceremony at the temple was held in 1962. The renovation of the structure according to the Dravidian model dates back to 1999, and other improvements have been regularly made over the years, such as the altar of the nine planets—*navagraha*—in 2008 and a copper flagpole *kodimaram* in 2010.

Typically known as the 'Astoria Road *kovil*', after the alley's name that leads to it, the temple's recent renovation has given the opportunity to include the complete name: *Arulmigu Mariammen Tirrukovil*. According to the bills posted throughout the city to announce the ceremonies, it would now be renamed 'Mariammen Temple Road'.

Figure 1.1: Renovation of Goodlands Mariammenkovil, June 2010 (*Source:* Photograph courtesy author).

THE CONSTRUCTION OF HINDU AUTHORITY IN MAURITIUS

Figure 1.2: Announcement of the Govinden ceremony, with the street renamed after the *kovil*, November 2012 (*Source:* Photograph courtesy author).

LIFE STORY

Selven Adukhan is a Mauritian. He was 27 years old at the time of the field study. He is a stout young man with a beard and short hair, both ears pierced with a square diamond. All the Mauritius Tamil Temples Federation (MTTF) managers stress his theological and linguistic knowledge, as well as his charisma mixed with an undeniable 'sweetness': 'You can't miss Selven. He never shouts, but you always know what he wants.' Selven is mainly in-charge of the Mariammen *kovil* in Goodlands, having previously officiated in other temples in the north of the island. He is temporarily in-charge of one of them, the Draupadi Ammen *kovil* of Pavillon-Cap Malheureux, pending its renovation and the arrival of a priest from India. Finally, as a renowned specialist in Mauritius, Selven also officiates every week for one of the great Tamil trading families of Goodlands in their domestic temple.

Selven discovered his vocation as a priest very early in his life. 'I have always loved idols,' he explains. 'It was a dream to be a priest.

36 MATHIEU CLAVEYROLAS

Because this comes from the heart, we feel it like that. At 6 or 7 years old, I was playing Cavadee.'[7] He continues, imitating the attitude of the pilgrims, nodding with a smile: 'I took a coconut branch and put it sideways in my mouth [simulating the needles used by the devotees to pierce their cheeks and tongue for Cavadee].'

Selven does not know which of his ancestors arrived first in Mauritius and says he was not interested in the current trend of tracing his roots. He only knows that his ancestors came from Coimbatore, Tamil Nadu. He spoke about his grandfather, a religious specialist working on a Mauritian plantation, who 'taught him a lot' from an early age. He pointed to the space around his office and farther away, to the renovated temple and explained: 'With my grandfather, it was different: he was also a healer [*guérisseur*]. It was a 'quick prayer' [*tit priyer*] just like this; he wore a *vesti* and a white shirt, and he carried a little book with him. But he didn't know how to read it. He didn't understand Tamil either.'

At the age of 11, while still at school, Selven learned 'the basics of religion' from an Indian priest who had migrated to Mauritius many years earlier and is currently in-charge of the other *kovil* of Goodlands. Then, at the age of 13, he enrolled in the priesthood training offered by the MTTF. He only stayed there for three months 'because they do [training and prayer] only in Tamil', excluding Sanskrit. At 18, he completed his training in a Vedic school (*gurukulam*) in Tamil Nadu with a guru for six months.

In 2004, after several other assignments, the MTTF sent Selven to take over the Mariammen *kovil* in Goodlands. In 2008, Selven married the niece of the temple society's President belonging to a Nair family from Kerala. The family has been in Mauritius for three generations. 'Nair[8] is a caste name in India,' he explains. Selven travels to India every year for several weeks. In addition to

---

[7] *Kavati* (Tamil): one of the major Tamil ceremonies in Mauritius dedicated to Lord Muruga.

[8] Or Nayar, one of the main castes in Kerala, technically from the Shudra *varna*, but with numerous subcastes belonging to very various status, sometimes close to the Kshatriya *varna*.

Figure 1.3: Aya Selven before walking over fire, November 2009 (*Source:* Photograph courtesy author).

visiting his wife's distant relatives in Kerala, he visits the key sites of Tamil Hinduism. These sites include the temples of Madurai and Tanjore, Pondicherry and Kanyakumari, which, he says, is the 'only place in the world where the sun sets and rises in the same place'. He is also well integrated into a network of Indian religious specialists active in Mauritius, serving as an intermediary for Mauritian temples needing an Indian priest or architect. When he comes to India, he buys statues, flagpoles, and ritual and decorative objects locally unavailable and necessary for the renovation sites on the island.

THE PRIEST'S STATUS

Studying the priest's status in Hinduism sheds light on the crucial anthropological question of religious authority. In the Mauritian context of radical evolution and increased interference with the non-Hindu environment, what status defines Selven? What is his authority based on?

One should first look at the terminology, which is often very telling in terms of identity in the Mauritian multilingual context. Selven is called 'Aya' by devotees and on posters announcing his presence in a ceremony. Few people know that the term means 'grandfather' in Tamil, even if Selven's young age, is systematically underlined to contrast his remarkable competence. On most occasions, Selven is simply referred to as the 'priest' (*prêtre*) of the temple. It is also the term he uses when he talks about his office.

Hindu deities in Mauritius are often referred to under the generic Creole term *bondié*, from the French (catholic) 'bon dieu' (Good Lord). But the overall trend is towards Tamilization of religious vocabulary. When they talk about their place of worship, Tamils refer less and less to the 'church' (*legliz*, in Creole) or the 'chapel' (*sapel*), terms widely used during the plantation times. The Tamil term *kovil* is used orally more and more and systematically in publications and posters. In this context, it may come as a surprise that the Tamil terminology of *poosari*[9] is no longer used to refer to the religious specialist, but it is now a depreciating Tamil term, referring to plantation specialist, a non-Brahmin far removed from learned orthodoxy. 'We no longer say *poosari*. It is a bit like a *traiteur*', that is to say, a 'healer' or 'sorcerer'. Such specialists in individual and semi-secret popular practices are obstacles to the Mauritian Tamil authorities' desire for recognition, visibility and community union. Through terminological distinction, Selven testifies to his status as a national religious Gangaram Panday authority, in contrast to his predecessors in the same *kovil*, all called *poosari* and poorly integrated into any institutional structure.

Selven, a Hindu Mauritian, who uses Creole as his lingua franca, can express himself in French and is also fluent in Tamil. He is the first in his family to have learned Tamil. Yet, despite the prestige attached to this new and rare skill in a context where Tamil is hardly ever used in a non-ritual context, it is primarily the French and Catholic terminology of 'priest' that is used to designate Selven's religious office.

[9] *Poosari* is the Tamil word for the Hindi word *pujari*, designating a temple priest.

THE CONSTRUCTION OF HINDU AUTHORITY IN MAURITIUS 39

From the point of view of Hindu statutory categories, Selven calls himself a 'Brahmin' and wears the sacred thread. Like almost all Mauritians, particularly Tamils, he denies any importance to castes in Mauritius, which were supposedly abandoned when leaving India.[10] Selven claims to have been born 'from the Pillai caste', a high caste of vegetarian landowners in Tamil Nadu, classified among the Vellalars. When I suggested that Pillais are not Brahmins in Tamil Nadu, he explains:

'I became Brahmin after the initiation ceremony. You know this? *Upanayanasamskar*.'
Interviewer. When was that? And in Mauritius or India?
'It was in 2004, right here, I was 20 years old. Swami Arunachal performed the ceremony.'
Interviewer. He's a *swami*. . .
'Yes, a Brahmin priest from Tamil Nadu who has lived in Mauritius for fifteen years. . . He is a *swami*. Look, it's like this, it's a caste matter, he was born in the Brahmin caste, in the vegetarian caste, I was born in a vegetarian caste. I'm the first vegetarian in my family ever since my initiation.'
Interviewer. You too are a Brahmin now.
'Yes . . . but listen, I'm not a Brahmin like the *swami*. He is a Brahmin from India.'

First, note that more than the apparent misinterpretation of Hindu orthodoxy (being *born* in a caste), such access to Brahminhood should be understood within the traditional Mauritian association of the Brahmin with priestly functions. Then, beyond the master-disciple bond that unites the two priests, their complementarity must be emphasized. One, a Swami from India in his forties, officiates in a *kovil* dedicated to the vegetarian God, Shiv-Supramaniar. He is a Brahmin, speaks only Tamil and is a systematic and prestigious guest at many ceremonies in the north of the island. His temple, located along the Goodlands' main road, has long been associated with high caste devotees. The other priest, Selven is younger, and a Mauritian, and was initiated ('brahminized') by

---

[10] For a discussion on castes in Mauritius, see Claveyrolas, 2015.

40   MATHIEU CLAVEYROLAS

the former and in turn, transmits his knowledge: he officiates for other temples. He has 'passed everything he knows' to another Mauritian priest in-charge of a nearby temple (without having officially initiated him). Located inside the village, Selven's temple is dedicated to the traditionally carnivorous goddess Mariammen. It remains associated with lower caste devotees, even if the distinction has lost part of its significance. Through the priests, complementarity also governs the relationship between the two Tamil temples of Goodlands: the procession systematically link both places, such as when Selven's temple Timidee procession stops at the *swami*'s temple to perform crucial (piercing) rituals before fire walking. Selven, in addition, officiates for the domestic temple of the former president of the Shiv-Supramaniar *kovil* society.

In terms of his duties, Selven illustrates the essential role of Tamil priests in today's Mauritius, and the more prosaic status of an employee that he shares with many temple priests in India.

The Hindu temple priest in Mauritius is indeed mainly an employee of the society managing the temple. These Hindu temple societies are the democratic links essential in understanding the dynamics of Mauritius' current religious evolution. They are officially registered associations, generally with 40 members or so, about ten of whom are active and often share the functions of president, secretary, treasurer and so on by election and/or rotation. These societies do not receive subsidies from public authorities; only the National Temples Federation (under the name of Tamil, Telugu or Bhojpuri 'socio-cultural associations') is financed by the government who redistribute the money to their affiliated temple societies. But such public subsidies barely cover the priest's salary; most of the expenses related to the organization of a celebration or renovation are therefore met with by individual donations.

In Mauritius, the redundancy of places of worship is often explained by splits within temple societies when some members, disagreeing with this or that project, build their own temple, not far from the first one. Although the case seems less common in Tamil than in Bhojpuri temples, conflicts are not absent, and it is often the priest who is at the heart of them. The first task of a society is to recruit a competent and dedicated priest. It may ask the

THE CONSTRUCTION OF HINDU AUTHORITY IN MAURITIUS 41

Federation to send one or activate its own networks. There are not yet enough Mauritian priests to meet the demand from temples, whose numbers are exploding. And the importation of priests from India, once a guarantee of authenticity, is increasingly perceived as a second best solution, as one can see below. In this context, Selven is regularly called upon to serve as an officiating priest occasionally or over the long term, in other Mauritian *kovils*. He laughs, 'It's like the masons in Mauritius, it's not hard to find one, it's hard to find a good one! Mauritius does not lack priests, but it does lack serious priests.'

Behind derision comes the actual status of the Hindu priest, very far from a unilaterally prestigious authority impossible to criticize. Usually employed on a contractual basis for 3 to 5 years, it is not he but the temple society that decides the organization of religious life: the language used for prayer, the celebration of this or that ceremony and renovation projects. In addition, priests, especially those from India, are on probation for one year and can be dismissed or not have their contracts renewed, which often happens. A young Mauritian priest was dismissed just a few days before the beginning of the temple's renovation ceremony for which he had long prepared. His employer first reminded him of a mourning in the priest's family, prohibiting him from officiating 40 days. Then the society explained that the priest was 'not serious' and had 'abandoned his wife', 'whereas a priest must be an example of morality'. The priest replied that the temple society was not respecting his contract and was not paying him for the many extra hours he had put in the preparation for the renovation ceremony.

Selven testifies to this status of the Mauritian priest as an employee. He depends on the MTTF, which assigns to him one or the other of the island's temples at the request of the society concerned. It may be a temple dedicated to Ammen while the priest's preferred deity was Muruga, or vice versa. Selven explains that he was lucky to have been assigned to a temple dedicated to his personal divinity (*ishtadevam*). At the same time, the MTTF does not even know this special connection ('this is something personal'). Consequently, the salaried priest is not necessarily personally invested in the temple to which he is assigned. Many priests know neither the history nor even the founding legend of the temple where they have been working for several months. Thus, it is to the leading members of the society that one must turn to obtain such information.

But Selven enjoys an authority higher than the average Tamil priest in Mauritius and a greater power in managing the daily life of the temple. For example, he is both the initiator of the ongoing renovation and the foreman who organizes, supervises and decides the specifics. He certainly had to ask his 'employer' for approval, but, as Selven says, 'which society wouldn't want its temple to be enlarged and improved?'

In addition to the salaried status, the professionalization of the priest's office may also be noted. Selven, despite his position as a spiritual authority, speaks of priesthood as his 'profession'. Unlike the *poosari* of previous generations, he has no other professional activity. But to be a priest is to be responsible for the ritual techniques and success in the 'career' does not necessarily mean having exceptional faith. 'Many people are very religious and yet you don't see them in the temple or the church, do you? Isn't that right? You don't have to be a priest for that [being religious].' When we speak about the role of faith in the success of a fire walking ceremony (not to be burned), Selven tells me about his experiences before evoking one of the main devotees of his temple, a Creole: 'He is a Catholic, did you know that? He prays in the church. He participates in all the fire walking ceremonies, he believes a lot, more than I do even!'

Neither should the prerogatives and obligations of the priest be limited to the sole ritual function, as shown in the regular practice of the sermon. Selven and other priests and presidents of the society take this opportunity to remind the devotees of their shortcomings in fulfilling their obligations of the *obium* (offering) in the coming weeks. He also reminds them of their social vocation, the need to 'be present at each prayer as a citizen of the village'. In contrast, it is the occasional ceremonies that attract devotees. Finally, Selven also engages in pedagogical work by explaining the upcoming rituals: it is necessary to start early to 'return to the *kovil* before noon. That's the meaning of Cavadee, the stars and the

THE CONSTRUCTION OF HINDU AUTHORITY IN MAURITIUS 43

importance of complying with schedules. Otherwise, in the afternoon it's not Thaipoosam,[11] it's *poosai* to Muruga, but with another star, it's not good.'

Like other priests, Selven is on duty on certain days often before the prayers begin. He then behaves like an ideal house-holder, arranging the final preparations, welcoming the devotees and moving from one to the other, giving precise instructions to everyone and joking with ease. This social role does not stop at receiving and supervising the devotees. 'I am also like a psychologist, and I take care of young people.' The position, indeed, is twofold, between the confessor and the social worker. Selven welcomes the members of his parish (*paroisse* in Creole) almost every day for an hour or two and advices them. The office room where these 'consultations' take place in Creole, is closed in Selven's case, but even in the smallest temples without closed space, privacy is preserved, each taking turns while sitting on a bench even when a simple table is installed in the veranda at a distance. Another priest explains: 'This is the priest's job. Not to do only the *puja*. You have to give advice, listen to people. It is performing confession just like a Catholic priest does.' The main topic of discussion is marriage and family affairs. One mother asks the priest's approval for her daughter to get married. One young girl (most of the consultants are women) dressed in western clothes comes to him to entrust her plans for moving to her lover's place and takes advice on the best way to carry this out without hurting her family's feelings. Other topics such as educational or professional guidance or moral concerns (clothing, dancing, alcohol), also often arise.

Also a social worker, Selven mobilizes his networks to support, federate and 'raise awareness' among the members of his parish, especially the young. He explains in Creole to a devotee who came to consult him, 'we must help Tamil children in poverty, look for children with parents in prison, to pay for their school and food. We must pray, but the most important thing is: to save people from poverty so that they do not leave their religion. I'm going to call this baker [. . .] so that he gives these children work.' In this

---

[11] Name of the major Cavadee ceremony.

44 MATHIEU CLAVEYROLAS

sense, Selven and the Mauritian Tamil priests act as relays for the MTTF's 'social work', concerned with 'emancipating' the Mauritian Tamil community through the promotion of Tamil 'culture [more than religion]', and through what Selven calls 'identity awareness'.

Social investment sometimes comes to overshadow purely religious considerations. 'Religion is not my hobby,' admits a leader of Shiv-Supramaniar Temple Society of Goodlands. 'In addition,' he explains, 'with the *swami* [priest-in-charge], the ritual mechanics are well established, it's on auto pilot. We can devote ourselves to developing social and cultural activities, the service of people through spoken and written Tamil classes, but also yoga, English, French or mathematics classes, all free and open to all (the yoga teacher is not Tamil, and some Creoles indeed participate).

This is a dimension often highlighted in migration contexts where religious authorities are key intermediaries between their community (here Tamil Mauritians), local authorities (government, federations) and other communities. This role beyond technical ritual expertise requires an intimate knowledge of the local context and of the Creole language. Such relational competence being accessible only to Mauritian priests, it has become one of the major arguments those who prefer them to Indian priests and has become a central debate for the local Tamil community (Trouillet 2014: 188).

WHICH ORTHODOXIES? WHICH PRACTICES?

In order to further describe the current evolution of Mauritian Hinduism, I will analyse Selven's relations with two central and related orthodoxies, that of the Tamil learned religion (both *vs* pan-Indian Hinduism and *vs* popular practices), and that of Indian Hinduism (*vs* Mauritian Hinduism).

DRAVIDIAN ORTHODOXY

Selven takes part in the contemporary trend of Mauritian Tamil Hinduism, moving towards learned orthodoxy. This evolution is considered locally as a return to Tamil ancestral traditions. Hence,

THE CONSTRUCTION OF HINDU AUTHORITY IN MAURITIUS 45

the adoption in Mauritius of a 'Tamil religion' breaking with 'Hinduism', a category reserved to the majority Bhojpuri community (Trouillet 2014: 170). Therefore, a renovated Tamil temple will be 'Agamic' or 'Dravidian', the two terms being interchangeable. Evolution operates at two levels: purifying Hinduism from its most popular dimensions, and its pan-Indian or North-Indian (Aryan) influences.

Thus, Selven despairs the liberty taken by Creole in the identification of deities. He speaks of *gramadevangal* and not of *gardienlakour* to designate the guardian deities who protect the physical margins of the sanctuary, often in aniconic form, and whose individual identification is largely unknown to the devotees. Selven takes care to emphasize the Tamil etymology of such deities, not without irritation about being the only one who knows it. 'Muniswaran is a compound word of which the first lid Muni stands for "wise", and Isvaran for Lord Shiva. But people say *Minis Prince*! Maduraiviren is the great horse-warrior seen in Madurai temple, and the people here say *Maldeviren*. All this is rude talk.'

Generally, Selven follows the Tamil Federation in condemning animal sacrifice and the general ignorance of Mauritian devotees and priests. For example, some call the cane-straw constructions set on fire during various ceremonies, *bonhommelapaille* (straw figure). Notwithstanding their objective anthropomorphism, they are certainly not human representations, according to official discourse, but rather symbols of Agni, the fire for all sacrifices. This devaluation of popular representations perceived as erroneous and ridiculous, fosters the insistence of the elites on educating the rest of the community.

The overall temptation to Tamilize the vocabulary is still ambiguous. *Puja* (Sanskrit) and *priyer* (Creole) cohabit with *poosai* (Tamil), as do *murti* (sanskrit) and *stati* (statue, Creole) with the Tamil *sillai*. If the '*kovil*' Tamil terminology has supplanted *legliz* ('church' in French-based Creole), the temple is still often referred to as *sapel* (Creole for *chapel*). Interestingly, such Tamilization probably echoes an urge to emphasize the opposition not with Christianity, but with Bhojpuri Hinduism and its temples called *mandir* or *shivala*.

Selven and the MTTF stress the importance of Dravidian civilization, race, language and religion over the Aryan counterpart. Yet, rather than following the Federation in systematically denouncing the influence of Mauritian Bhojpuri culture on the Mauritian Tamils, Selven insists on the vitality of the Tamil community in Mauritius, which mobilizes massively, including Bhojpuris, to weekly prayers at the *kovil*, and organizes so many celebrations. In contrast, the Bhojpuri community is content with 'Hanuman in their backyard and Shivratri once a year'. Similarly, in a classic rejection of the Brahmin-Aryan-Sanskrit association, MTTF exclusively promotes Tamil prayers and does not teach Sanskrit in the priest-training programmes it organizes. This is, in fact, one of the reasons for holding such training in Mauritius: 'The problem with priests in Mauritius,' explained a senior MTTF official, 'is that those who come from India are Brahmins, they follow the Vedas and Brahmin culture, and not Tamil culture at all. They may come from India and Tamil Nadu, but they are not part of Tamil culture.'

Selven, on the other hand, is much more moderate and pragmatic. He was able to impose prayer in Tamil and Sanskrit in his temple 'because I like to speak and hear Sanskrit'. It is a personal choice for Selven, congruent with that of his prestigious Indian guru. While Selven is respected for his knowledge of Tamil, he also wished to emphasize his skill in Sanskrit, a complexity that sometimes lead to misunderstandings.

Selven: He [the Indian priest from a nearby *kovil*] only prays in Tamil.
Interviewer: But he *is* Tamil!
Selven: Me too!
Interviewer: But he is from India.
Selven: My *guru* also comes from India, and he does it in Sanskrit. In fact, [the other priest] doesn't know Sanskrit, that you have to learn, that's why he only does it in Tamil.

Despite standing as an authoritative representative of newly learned traditions, Selven accepts the popular practices of plantation times. He wouldn't dream of despising the practices of his grandfather, but even now continues to diversify his techniques: he learns

THE CONSTRUCTION OF HINDU AUTHORITY IN MAURITIUS   47

to *geter* [Creole: seek, watch out] fate in cards and *panjangam* (Tamil ritual calendar), but also to 'take out evil things' and 'make *systems*', another Creole term meaning a set of prayers in the context of magico-popular practices.

The Federation does not back such traditions, but the coexistence of learned and popular practices remains the norm, whether one considers sacred places or ritual specialists. Symbolically, on Selven's desk coexist the *Tirrukural*[12] and an English book entitled *Witchcraft and Black Magic*. Symbolic hierarchy during the temple ceremonies also jointly valorize popular and learned specialists. 'Ton Dassen', former *poosari*, now over 70 years old and standing for old times' plantation Hinduism, remains very active and respected: he assists in many ritual sequences and is the second person after Selven, to walk on fire, carrying the trident of the goddess during the annual ceremony of the *kovil*.

Some 500 metres from Selven's *kovil*, another Dravidian temple is renowned throughout the island for its fire-walking ceremony, organized by the priest in-charge. This ceremony has become a symbol of the Mauritian learned version of Tamil culture, the one that makes it visible to other Mauritian communities and, increasingly, to tourists. But the temple is also renowned for its weekly sessions of systems conducted in a hall adjacent to the *mandapam* (hall) by one of the island's leading specialists, who happens to be the priest's father and former priest in-charge.

It would also be misleading to confine popular practices to the residues of past times. Selven has a hard time differentiating himself from the practices of *traiteur* specialists: 'a *traiteur* is about looking at fate. He does this through the cards. I do it too, but through *panjangam*.' He shows the different calendars on his desk and ordinary playing cards that he takes from under his desk and quickly puts them away.' I also do cards. . ., but most of all the *panjangam*. It allows us to know the future, the destiny. You must bring the papers, the birth certificate, with the date and time. We think very deep; we touch a card and read the future. Normally it's the *traiteurs* who do that. That's *geter*. We can also see if a person is possessed, if

---

[12] One of the most widely used Tamil sacred texts.

there are evil things in them. To get out evil things, we make a system, it's like a prayer, with lemon, coconut, mustard and cloves. We sometimes give saffron-water too.'

INDIAN ORTHODOXY

The idea of an unambiguous conversion to intellectual Hinduism is resisted by the ethnography of Mauritian Tamil practices and individuals. The same is true for the relationship to Indian orthodoxy, which is increasingly supposed to represent the only possible authenticity, but which has been nuanced by Selven's study. His vision of India is representative of the most common and most relevant paradoxes.

Selven is deeply enthusiastic about Tamil Nadu, the source of his religion, religious knowledge, and the roots of his gods. Thus, he recounts, deeply moved, this key memory of his Indian stay:

I went to Trichy's Samayapuram Mariammen *kovil* on 5 September 2009. I arrived in India on August 30 with my family, in-laws, etc. There were 5,000 people in front of me queuing up to see Ammen. I wanted to return when a girl of about seven asks tells me to hold on. There were too many people there. Even if I stayed all night I don't think my turn would come. She took my hand and helped me sneak in between the people without difficulty. It was incredible. After a while, I arrived near Ammen, I went around the temple; everything was made of gold; the girl sprinkled me with saffron water. And all of a sudden, when I turned around, the girl was gone [. . .] You know, in India, everyone asks you for money for everything, so I was very surprised that she left after helping me so much without asking for anything in return. I had asked her name. She had told me Amou, which means Ammen in Sanskrit. Everyone who was with me was surprised. Near this temple, there is a river, and people do not go there at certain times of the day because they say that Ammen goes bathing there. I brought water from this river, and is some at my father-in-law's house, he has the proof.

There are many accounts of the apparitions of Hindu deities on the Mauritian soil: they can manifest through dreams or miracles such as a stone too heavy to be lifted or bleeding or emitting milk.

THE CONSTRUCTION OF HINDU AUTHORITY IN MAURITIUS 49

Such self-manifested images (*svarup*) are installed in local shrines: they bear witness to the Mauritian-made Hindu-ness (Claveyrolas 2010). But Selven's anecdote shows how crucial is the manifestation of his personal goddess in India.

On the other hand, the prologue clearly emphasizes the representation of a so-called 'barbaric' India. India is 'a lot of dust, a lot of diseases. I'm fragile, I stay in my hotel,' Selven explains. Only the French colonial city of Pondicherry really pleased him. Indian religious life is not spared by this critical Mauritian vision: 'there, even in temples, one must pay, whether it is to enter, to make an offering, to read the *panjangam*, or even to leave one's shoes.' The bad reputation of priests in India extends to Indian priests called to Mauritius. Selven regrets this recourse to Indian priests, 'because those who come are there only for business, they always ask for large sums of money for everything, while Mauritian priests don't do that.'

In addition to their widespread image as mercenaries with a questionable religious vocation, priests from Tamil Nadu do not necessarily stand as a theological reference. A temple employing a Chennai priest on a 3-year contract, recruited a Mauritian specialist to officiate at its fire-walking ceremony (peak of the ritual year) because the 'Indian[priests] do not know the prayer for Thimidee. It is true that they also do so in Tamil Nad, but they do not know how we do it.' While it is not uncommon for Indian devotees and managers to suspect their own priests of corruption and incompetence, it seems that the Mauritian priests sometimes enjoy a more solid prestige in the eyes of Mauritian devotees.

From an institutional point of view, the poor financial contribution of the Indian Tamils to the Mauritian Tamil revival does not help to counterbalance these temptations of Mauritian Tamil Hinduism to free itself from the Indian reference. 'India has not helped us much. In fact, we have to be honest, we didn't get anything from India,' explains the MTTF secretary.

In Selven's eyes, even Mauritian compromises, such as the recitation of prayer in the evening (during the week) when the morning prayer is considered more auspicious in Hinduism, only underline the poor and backwards India that he depicts: 'if "they" can pray in the morning, it is because there no one works'. More fundamentally, Indians are criticized for continuing with the caste system, which is considered politically incorrect in Mauritius and 'should have nothing to do with religion'. The Indians are also said to perpetuate somewhat wild traditions, such as those of the Aghori mentioned in the prologue. Caste and renunciation are two crucial dimensions of Indian Hinduism and two fundamental principles of the ideal legitimization of ritual knowledge and efficacy. However, their absence is perceived in Mauritius not as a loss but as an improvement. The many Mauritian low-caste priests involved in local Tamil Hinduism, indeed have little interest in promoting caste identity, as this other priest explains: 'There is casteism in India. It's not good, this is Kaliyuga. It is a question of power, wealth and materialism. Yes, there is casteism among Tamils in Mauritius, but it's hidden. My caste is God. But if some people know my true caste, they will ignore me, say I am a bad priest, do everything to destroy me.'

In fact, a genuinely Mauritian orthodoxy is emerging. For several decades now, Mauritian Tamil priests have gone to La Reunion Island, where the official references for orthodoxy are kept. But Mauritian Hindu influence did not stop there: Selven is regularly called on his mobile phone by Mauritians living in Paris, asking for advice on the rites to be performed in the event of death, etc. Selven was even invited in 2011 to officiate in Paris for the Govinden festival 'in the temple of the Mauritian Tamils'. He stayed there for three weeks and reflected: 'They were surprised, they don't know how to do it, I tried to do everything the same as here, everything good, but they're not used to it.'

The attempt to forge a unified 'Hindu religion' in India dates back to the nineteenth century in response to the challenges posed by the British colonial intrusion (Claveyrolas & Trouillet 2021) and was a response to essentially political issues related to the nationalist movement. In other words, this radical evolution was contemporary with indenture and, later, with the construction of a Mauritian nation, both equally radical contexts.

Mauritian Hinduism has always been a long-term process of

THE CONSTRUCTION OF HINDU AUTHORITY IN MAURITIUS   51

interpretation and adaptation, arguably even more than any other religion. It is still being built on the basis of multiple challenges, influences and constraints. In this sense, it is an effective antidote to the temptation to define an authentic state of religion.

Indeed, some dynamics imported from India can be recognized among the driving forces of the current religious processes. Although criticized, the constant rhetorical temptation of local actors to refer to India does indeed permeate Mauritian discourse and realities. As Vertovec (2000: 161) points out for Trinidad, the fact that this reference is often artificial and reinvented should not prevent one from studying its local efficacy. It should also be noted that the ideological orientation of the religious project is not specific to Mauritian Hinduism: the renovations serve, as in India, a lever for statutory demands through a more rewarding reformed practice (stopping violent sacrifices, replacing popular deities by Brahminic gods, installation of a priest, affiliation to a 'federation' of temples) following the sankritization path analysed by Srinivas (1966).

However, parallel with the analysis of what has been lost, preserved and found again, it is crucial to reintroduce the Mauritian specificities and the influence of local contexts (to stand out from the Bhojpuri Mauritians, but also the descendants of African and Catholic slaves), far exceeding the diaspora effect. Even tempted by Indianization, Mauritian Hinduism remains Creole: the ritual foundation of places of worship, deities and practices in residential camps and cane fields first matched the challenges of the plantation society, its territorial organization, its social hierarchy and the coexistence with other cultures and religions.

Similarly, current evolutions respond to the conditions of contemporary Mauritian society, whether in terms of the new socio-economic situation (wealth of a significant segment of the population able to invest massively in donations), land ownership (fragmentation of sugar estates), or new power games (positioning in the local communalist context). As for the actors of these evolutions in Mauritius (Claveyrolas 2021), the state subsidized temple federations play the role of the corrective and standardizing institution through increased administrative control over the temples.

In this context, the case of Selven confirms the need to study the evolution of Mauritian Hinduism both in its parallel with Indian Hinduism and concerning the rupture after leaving India, the structuring context of the plantation and the contemporary issues of Mauritius' nation-building processes (Claveyrolas 2012). Indeed, Selven's religious legitimacy is exemplary of the articulation of Indian roots and Creole roots. Selven is strategically positioned at the crossroads of learned (Indian) orthodoxy and popular (and Creole) traditions of Hinduism. Not only does he speak Creole and Tamil, but he was made a Brahmin—while still being an expert in popular practices. Trained in India and Mauritius, and backed by modern Mauritian Hindu institutions, Selven also plays on the most creolized register the magico-popular traditions. Indeed, his religious authority may well rely precisely on such links with the dimensions of Hinduism born in the Mauritian plantations.

REFERENCES

Allen, Richard (1999). *Slaves, Freedmen and Indentured Laborers in Colonial Mauritius.* Cambridge: Cambridge University Press.

Benoist, Jean (1998). *Hindouismes créoles. Mascareignes, Antilles.* Paris: Éditions du Comité des Travaux Historiques et Scientifiques (CTHS).

—— (1989). 'De l'Inde à Maurice et de Maurice à l'Inde, ou la réincarnation d'une société', *L'Inde en nous,* Fort-de-France, Carbet: pp. 185-201.

Carter, Marina (1995). *Servants, Sirdars and Settlers: Indians in Mauritius, 1834-1874.* Delhi: Oxford University Press.

Chazan, Suzanne and Ramhota, Pavitranand (2009). *L'hindouisme mauricien dans la mondialisation.* Paris: Moka, IRD/MGI.

Claveyrolas, Mathieu (2015). 'The "Land of the Vaish"? Caste, Structure and Ideology in Mauritius', *South Asia Multidisciplinary Academic Journal,* 1-18, Paris. Retrieved from https://journals.openedition.org/samaj/3886.

—— (2012). 'With or without roots: the compared and conflicting memories of slavery and indenture in the Mauritian public space', in Araujo (ed.), *Politics of Memory: Making Slavery Visible in the Public Space.* New York: Routledge: pp. 54-70.

—— (2010). 'L'ancrage de l'hindouisme dans le paysage mauricien: transfert et appropriation', in Bava and Capone (eds.), *Autrepart.* Paris: Sciences: pp. 17-38.

Claveyrolas, Mathieu and Pierre-Yves Trouillet (2020). 'L'Autre et l'ailleurs: l'altérité au cœur de l'hindouisme', in M. Claveyrolas and P-Y. Trouillet (eds.), *Les Hindous, les Autres et l'ailleurs. Relations et frontières.* Paris, Éditions de l'EHESS: collection Purusartha no. 38.

Srinivas, Narasimhachar M. (1995). *Social Change in Modern India.* Delhi: Orient Longman (1st edn. 1966, University of California Press).

Tarabout, Gilles (1997). 'L'évolution des cultes dans les temples hindous. L'exemple du Kerala', in Clémentin-Ojha (ed.), *Renouveaux religieux en Asie.* Paris: École Françaised Extrême-Orient (EFEO): pp. 127-51.

Tinker, Hugh (1974). *A New System of Slavery: The Export of Indian Labour Overseas.* London: Hansib Educational Book.

Trouillet, Pierre-Yves (2014). 'Les lances de Muruga à Maurice: trajectoires d'un hindouisme tamoul', in Servan-Schreiber (ed.), *Indianité et créolité à l'île Maurice.* Paris: Éditions de l'EHESS: pp. 169-98.

Vertovec, Steven (2000). *The Hindu Diaspora.* London: Routledge.

CHAPTER 2

Hinduism in South Africa, 1860-2020[1]

VINAY LAL AND GOOLAM VAHED

INTRODUCTION

The origin of the Hindu community in South Africa dates back to the arrival of 152,184 indentured migrants to Natal between 1860 and 1911 and the free Indian migrants who followed from the 1870s onward. Four-fifths of the indentured migrants were Hindus, with two-thirds from South Asia, including several hundred *jatis* or sub-castes, ranging from Brahmins to various low caste communities (Bhana 1991: 20). The free migrants, who were known as 'passengers' because they came at their own expense and choice, included mostly Gujaratis and a small number from South India. They numbered no more than a few thousand because of the racist immigration legislation introduced by the Natal government after it received Responsible Government in 1893. From Natal, some Indians made their way to the Cape and the Transvaal, but most Indians were concentrated in the province of Natal (now KwaZulu-Natal) due to restrictions on interprovincial migration. The Orange Free State, the fourth province of the then Union of South Africa, banned Asians from its territory (Bhana & Brain 1984).

Notwithstanding that Hindus were heterogeneous in terms of class, caste, region, and linguistic background, as well as traditions, beliefs

[1] Part of this chapter is drawn from Vinay Lal and Goolam Vahed (2013). 'Hinduism in South Africa: Caste, Ethnicity, and Invented Traditions, 1860-present', *Journal of Sociology and Social Anthropology*. 4.1-2: 1-15.

and practices, the movement of Hindus to South Africa was an important part of the process that helped transform Hinduism into a 'world religion'. As Lal and Vahed (2013: 2) point out, the history of Hinduism in South Africa acquires greater salience when viewed against the backdrop of the transformation of Hinduism into a 'world religion' and its transmission to outposts, near and remote, of what would become a far-flung diaspora, a development of considerable importance when one considers that until the seventeenth century the religion was largely confined to the Indian subcontinent, though there are remnants of Hinduism in Bali, among Vietnamese Cham and in other parts of Southeast Asia. As the German scholars Kulke and Rothermund have written, the transmission of Indian culture to distant parts of central Asia, China, Japan, and especially Southeast Asia is one of the greatest achievements of Indian history or even of the history of mankind. None of the other great civilizations— not even the Hellenic—had been able to achieve a similar success without military conquest (Kulke & Rothermund 1998: 143).

It was, ironically, European imperial expansion that created the conditions for the diffusion of Hinduism in the nineteenth century to different parts of the world. Indian indentured migrants were sent to colonies like Natal, Trinidad, Mauritius, Fiji, Guyana, and Suriname to replace former slave labour and they carried Hinduism with them. This happened at a time when Hinduism was facing a crisis in India in the wake of the British conquest. British advancement not only drained the country economically and resulted in large numbers of Indians living in wretched poverty but theirs was also a conquest of ideas and knowledge and those who followed 'Hinduism' found themselves severely challenged. The ways in which they responded to this challenge, as discussed below, impacted Hindus and Hinduism globally.

This article traces some of the major developments amongst Hindus and Hinduism in South Africa over the past 160 years, in the context of dramatically changing socio-economic and political conditions. It is divided into four chronological periods: the Colonial period (1860-1914), which ends not with the formation of the Union of South Africa in 1910 but rather with the departure of Gandhi from South Africa; the period of Segregation (1914-48); the Apartheid era

HINDUISM IN SOUTH AFRICA, 1860-2020

(1948-94); and the post-Apartheid period. This periodization is based on political developments within South Africa and does not coincide with any dramatic changes among Hindus or Hinduism, for many important religious developments overlapped these arbitrary boundaries.

THE COLONIAL PERIOD

Migration overseas was likely a very difficult decision for Hindus, perhaps for most not a decision at all, since one can reasonably assume that some among those who boarded the ships that took them beyond the 'kaalapani', the forbidden waters, were entirely unaware of their destination and moved out only because of economic necessity. Some would have been concerned about being 'polluted' by mixing with 'outsiders' and others would have experienced a particular sense of loss in reflecting on the journey, given the Hindu relationship with the sacred geography of India, with its gods, goddesses, holy rivers and places of pilgrimage. Migration shattered this 'emotional and ritual attachment to this landscape' (Warrier 2008: 89).

Despite the difficult work, health and living conditions on the plantations of Colonial Natal, which Desai and Vahed (2010), amongst others, have documented, migrants began to rebuild their cultural, religious, and social lives almost from the time of their arrival in Natal. The temples and religious rituals that they established, became important sites in diasporic cultural survival and reproduction. Generally, in diasporic settings, Warrier (2008, 94) argues, the migratory experience of the first generation Hindus included 'exclusiveness in their social interactions [and] communal self-renewal through participation at social events marking birth, marriage, and death'. This was largely true for Natal where Hindus constituted a majority amongst Indians, but they did participate in Muslim festivals and there was a degree of intermarriage between Hindus and Muslims.

Hindu practices in nineteenth-century India ranged from philosophical to popular expressions and similarly, the boundaries within various religious tendencies in Hinduism were highly porous (Jones 2017). Colonial ethnographers were at a loss to explain how, in the same household, one member of the family might be a Vaishnava

58 VINAY LAL AND GOOLAM VAHED

and another a Saivite. They used the idea of 'sectarianism', derived from the bitter religious wars that had shaped Europe, to understand the religious history of India, which was far from being akin to the religious history of Europe, even if some scholars might be inclined to point to similarities. Nothing in their experience would have prepared Europeans to understand a vast corpus of texts such as the *Puranas*, not merely because they suggest why Hinduism is more fruitfully explored as a religion of mythos rather than a religion of history. The *Vaishnava Puranas* elevate Vishnu as the Supreme Being, but they are ecumenical enough to embrace the god Shiva and the worshippers of the goddess; similarly, the *Devi Puranas* enshrine the Goddess as the Supreme Being, just as the *Saivite Puranas* accord priority to Shiva over Vishnu and the goddess traditions. One is, with all this, still within the realm of everything that is now embraced under the umbrella term 'Hinduism', but the religious boundaries between Hinduism and Islam (Mujeeb 1967), or between Hinduism and Sikhism (Oberoi 1994), were just as porous. European writers and ethnographers, as the *Imperial Gazetteer* amply documents, were bewildered by the presence of hundreds of communities that claimed to be both Hindus and Muslims. The writer M. Mujeeb, in his classic work *The Indian Muslims*, noted of the Gujarat region that it was a 'melting-pot of races and beliefs', including Muslims who worshipped the goddess of smallpox, Deshmukhs, 'who professed the Muslim religion' but 'abhorred meat-eating' and 'avoided mixing with Muslims', and communities such as the Husaini Brahmins (Mujeeb 1967: 10-23).

However, in response to the British imperial conquest, Indian nationalists in late nineteenth-century India sought to reform Hinduism, including casting it in a military mode, partly on the assumption that the supposed accent on pacifism of the religion had rendered it vulnerable to the Abrahamic faiths (Lal 2008). The early nineteenth-century reformer, Rammohun Roy, argued that Hinduism required thorough reformation: if Catholicism had to be shorn of its ritualism and superstitions, its venerations of saints, and its popery, to pave the way for Protestantism, Hinduism had to be rid of its idolatrous and obscurantist accretions before Vedic

HINDUISM IN SOUTH AFRICA, 1860-2020 59

Hinduism could once again be comprehended in its pristine form. Bankimcandra Chatterjee, who pioneered the novel in Bengali and became a widely acclaimed essayist, was among those who argued that the Hindu's attachment to the philosophy of *bhakti* (devotion) had emasculated the once vigorous race of the Aryans and made them incapable of defending themselves against the more militant and single-minded adherents of Islam and Christianity. His affirmation of a Hinduism that would at once be more masculine and possessed a semblance to the Semitic faiths won him many followers, especially among the following generation of nationalists.

Hinduism appeared to both missionaries and Hindu reformers as a chaotic faith that lacked a historical founder, a central church, even a text which all its adherents could agree upon as the ultimate source of 'canonical' authority. The reformers of 'Hinduism' sought to create a proper religion that, in time, would serve a proper nation state. The very idea of 'religion', as Tomoko Masuzawa (2005) has persuasively argued, came to be understood in the nineteenth century and not only among adherents of the Hindu faith, in the template of Protestant Christianity and henceforth the more vocal adherents of Hinduism would also attempt to transform it into a 'world religion'.

Few Hindus in South Africa would have been exposed to the reformist tendencies of emerging movements such as the Arya Samaj that were sweeping India from the late 1870s. The Hinduism practised in Natal was largely 'a non-scriptural devotional and ritualistic cult' known as Sanathanism, which operated on a popular rather than philosophical level and was closely bound to temples and festivals (Diesel & Maxwell 1993: 17). The fundamentals of Hinduism were transmitted to the young largely through priests, temples, and festivals, and orally through stories from Hindu texts such as the *Ramayana, Mahabharata,* and *Bhagavad Gita* (Naidoo et al. 1989: 153). The *African Chronicle* (23 April 1906) recorded that when indentured Indians arrived in Natal 'there was no one there to teach them [because] the learned Pandits in Natal themselves have very little formal education'. The Pandits, the newspaper went on, exploited the masses by keeping them in superstition and idolatry.

60   VINAY LAL AND GOOLAM VAHED

Financial constraints, difficulty in observing caste rules and absence of a learned priestly class made it a challenge for Hindus to reconstruct their religious life in Durban. 'Temples', which Hindus erected on sugar estates, became the centre of community life. Most early structures were tiny, roughly six feet square, and made from wattle, daub, thatch and later, corrugated iron (Henning 1993: 150). The first temples were at Umbilo (1869), Newlands (1896), Cato Manor (1882), Isipingo Rail (1870), Mount Edgecombe (1875), Somtseu Road (1880s), Umgeni Road (1885), and Sea View (1910).

These simple structures allowed Hindus to practise rituals and engage in sacrificial worship and they became the converging point of the social and cultural life of the community. The notion that the temple could serve as something of a community centre—a place for conviviality, for educating the young, sometimes in the form of the 'Sunday school' patterned after Christianity, in the norms of the Hindu faith, and as a place for communal solidarity—was beginning to take shape, a characteristic development not only in South Africa but across the growing Hindu diaspora. Over a period of time, as communities became more affluent and entrenched, temples came to have more elaborate designs, which sometimes reflected even regional variations in India (Bhana & Vahed 2005: 54).

Festivals, on the other hand, helped Hindus to increase religious devotion by reminding followers of particular deities: they served a social role as devotees joined together in a show of unity, and they provided an escape from the grind of plantation labour. During the formative decades, most indentured workers participated in the Muslim festival of Muharram, which was known in the colony as 'Coolie Christmas' (see Vahed 2002). What should perhaps be underscored here is the fact, that most Hindus partook of the festivities surrounding Muharram in most, perhaps all of the colonies where they settled, and everywhere the colonial authorities looked upon these expressions of intercommunality with disfavour. 'A noticeable feature of the Muharram', writes Singh, a historian of late nineteenth-century Trinidad, 'was the considerable involvement of Hindus and Negroes in it'. Singh has documented the keen interest of colonial officials in arguing that the Muharram celebration 'was a Muslim one and Hindus should therefore have no part in it' (Singh 1988: 6, 17). The Muharram

HINDUISM IN SOUTH AFRICA, 1860-2020

massacre of 1884 arose, in part, from colonial attempts to stamp the celebrations as illegitimate and prevent intercommunal solidarity. Colonial officials and European observers, shaped as they were, as one has previously noted, by their understanding of the history of Europe as one of interminable religious conflict and wholly persuaded by the idea that Hindus and Muslims had always existed in a relationship of unmitigated antagonism, could not countenance the thought that Hindus and Muslims might have a history of shared customs, festivals and ways of life. Doubtless, such intermingling was easier in the earlier days of migration and settlement. Initially, Hindus were observing Muslim festivals but over a period of time this was replaced by Hindu festivals, affirming a strong Hindu identity.

As the efforts of Hindu reformers in the twentieth century began to take effect, Hindu festivals such as Thai Pongal, Thaipusam (Kavadi), Draupadi (Thimithi), Mariamman, and Diwali assumed greater importance among Hindus than Muharram.

From 1890, the Shree Temple organized a festival annually in April during the Tamil New Year (Chaita Masam), the day Hindus believe Lord Brahma started creation. It marked both an occasion to atone for bad deeds and pray for a profitable new year. One of the most popular festivals was the Mariamman 'Porridge' festival, associated with the popular Goddess Mariamman who, in South India, is believed to both cause and cure infectious diseases like smallpox and measles. Devotees offer 'cooling' foods such as milk and coconut to the goddess to 'cool' her anger. In some places, a goat is sacrificed and its blood spilt to represent life and fertility (Diesel & Maxwell 1993, 49). This festival was celebrated widely in Isipingo on the south coast of Natal on Good Friday from around the turn of the twentieth century and drew crowds in excess of 10,000 (*African Chronicle*, 16 September 1916). Reformist minded Hindus were highly critical of temple proprietors whom they accused of exploiting the ignorant Hindu masses, but the masses have kept on coming in thousands year after year, to this very day, albeit at a different site.

The Draupadi (fire walking) festival was celebrated annually in March in honour of Goddess Draupadi, who is regarded by Hindus as 'the model of duty, love and devotion, who bore various trials with great fortitude' (Diesel & Maxwell 1993: 51). Kavadi was celebrated in February and May of each year in honour of the god Muruga who, devotees believe, has the power to cure people of their illness and get rid of misfortune. Kavadi remains a mass based festival in Tamil Nadu and Kerala, as well as in the Tamil diaspora in Malaysia, Singapore, Sri Lanka, and Mauritius. The mortification of the body is part of kavadi. The central component involves devotees ceremonially carrying a kavadi or 'burden' (such as a pot of milk carried on a decorated semi-circular canopy supported by a wooden rod carried on the shoulder) and walking around the temple on a set route and making an offering at the temple (Ganesh 2010: 35). Mortification of the body included devotees sticking needles and pins in their tongues and cheeks, or drawing chariots with strings knotted into large hooks protruding from the fleshy parts of the backs. Reformist minded Hindus, not unlike their counterparts in India, opposed these festivals because they regarded them as a distortion of 'authentic' of 'high' Hinduism, as well as because they did not quite comport with the idea of religion under modernity, of a religion that, Protestant like, ought to be stripped bare of unnecessary accoutrements.

Mariamman and Draupadi are South Indian goddesses who were widely worshipped in South Africa where the majority of migrants were from South India. Most lower caste Tamil-speaking Hindus in South India worship these two goddesses who play an important role in their daily lives. Worshippers walking on burning coals, animal sacrifices and religious figures going into trance to heal the sick are all features of Hinduism among the working classes in Madras and areas in its vicinity. In Natal, however, Saktas or goddess worshippers blended various traditions so that subsidiary deities of Mariamman, such as Munisvaran and Koterie, are often placed outside temples rather than Mariamman herself (Ganesh 2010: 33).

Swami Shankeranand, who spent the years between 1908 and 1912 in Natal, was instrumental in establishing Hindu institutional structures that allowed for the practice and replication of cultural and religious life. John Kelly and Martha Kaplan, in their 2001 study, *Represented Communities*, suggest that communities and nations are not just 'imagined', as Benedict Anderson (1983) argued when he wrote that 'print capitalism' fostered nations as imagined communities in a modular form that became the culture of modernity, but

HINDUISM IN SOUTH AFRICA, 1860-2020 63

rather that at critical moments individual leaders make significant interventions that have long term consequences. Swami Shankeranand was one such individual. He established Hindu Youngmen's Associations in the major urban centres of Natal, such as Durban, Springfield, and Pietermaritzburg, but his most significant legacy is undoubtedly the South African Hindu Mahasabha which he established in 1912 and which flourishes to this day. Through these actions, he raised a Hindu, as opposed to Indian consciousness and this is best appreciated through an understanding of his efforts in making Diwali the premier Hindu festival in South Africa. Among Fiji Indians, the anthropologist John Kelly has written, the two festivals of which the colonial state took any cognizance at all were Holi and Muharram; Diwali was not the 'focus of the Fiji Hindu ritual calendar' (Kelly 1988, 44). Much the same can be said about Diwali in South Africa: if in Fiji 'Holi and its transcendence of status and caste is especially popular among the low caste and low class, [and] Diwali among the urban middle class and rich' (Kelly 1988: 45), this consideration held sway in South Africa as well. In India and in diasporic locations, Holi has long been associated with the Lord Krishna, in arguing for the primacy of Diwali, which celebrates the return of Rama to Ayodhya, Swami Shankeranand was enacting that same Protestant impulse to render Hinduism into a respectable religion.

The Swami, however, also created dissension among Indians by taking issue with the political agenda of Mohandas K. Gandhi, who lived in South Africa between 1893 and 1914, and asked Hindus to dissociate from Indian Muslims and Christians. The presence of Gandhi was important in several respects. Gandhi was brought to South Africa by a Muslim trader Dada Abdoolla, and formed the Natal Indian Congress in 1894 to challenge the racial restrictions being implemented to curtail Indian trade, finance, residence and immigration (see Swan 1985). Gandhi played a crucial role in transcending religious differences and ensuring that religion did not divide Indians. He demanded of Hindus, Christians, and Muslims, of all classes and castes, to trust each other and work together against white minority rule. This would not have been possible had migrants remained in India (see Bhana and Vahed 2005).

64 VINAY LAL AND GOOLAM VAHED

THE ERA OF SEGREGATION, 1914-48

The decades following the departure of Gandhi from South Africa in 1914 were witness to the rapid urbanization of Indians, extensive urban poverty, formation of education and social welfare institutions and increasing state hostility. These changes in work patterns and geographic location impacted on religious and cultural practices. Most Indians in Natal were Hindus. According to the 1936 population census, 81 per cent of Natal's Indians were Hindus. African labour rendered Indians superfluous in farming, mining and the public sector and their numbers dropped dramatically on Natal's mines, railways, and in general and farming and on sugar estates. Most Indians moved to cities. The number of Indians in Durban, for example, increased from 17,015 in 1911 to 123,165 in 1949. As a percentage of Durban's population, Indians increased from 23 to 33 per cent (Housing Survey 1952: 35). Unemployment and low pay resulted in wide-scale poverty among Indians. A study by the University of Natal in 1943/44 reported that 70.6 per cent of Indians were living below the poverty datum line and that 40 per cent were destitutes (*Daily News*, 8 June 1944).

The main focus of the white minority government during these years was on repatriating Indians. A round table conference between the South African, Indian and Imperial governments in 1927 introduced a system of voluntary repatriation and an 'Agent' was appointed by the Indian government to oversee the upliftment of Indians who remained in South Africa (Pachai 1971: 108). The policy failed because few Indians repatriated while the government, for its part, did little to improve the condition of Indians. For the most part, Hindus and Muslims lived in harmony. While Indians largely overlooked religious distinctions, visits by overseas missionaries, both Hindu and Muslim, usually created religious discord (Gopalan 2014).

Religion may have been less divisive among Indians in South Africa than in India in the 1920s through the 1940s as they found themselves sandwiched between a white governing minority and the African masses. From the 1930s, the focus of the state was on repatriating Indians and segregating those who remained. The land struggle was protracted and culminated in a passive resistance campaign by Indians between 1946 and 1948 (Bugwandeen 1991). At the same time, the growing tension between Indians and Africans during the 1940s culminated in three days of riots between Africans and Indians in January 1949, which resulted in 142 deaths and 1,087 injuries. This was an indication of the depth of antagonism that Africans felt against Indians in a climate where they competed for scarce economic resources (Desai and Vahed 2010: 232-55). This brought Indian Hindus, Christians, and Muslims together in the public sphere and fostered the racial identity, 'Indianness', which would be cemented after the National Party (NP) came to power in 1948 and began to implement its policy of Apartheid. One very important trend among Hindus was the appearance of the Bethesda Temple in the 1930s, a form of Pentecostal Christianity that would have a powerful impact on Hindus in subsequent decades.

INSTITUTIONS AND EXEMPLARS: THE APARTHEID PERIOD, 1948-94

The coming to power of the National Party (NP) government in 1948 had paradoxical consequences for Indians. Social, political and economic segregation was intensified but Indians were finally recognized as permanent citizens. Partly because of state policy and in part because of settlement patterns in the post-indenture period, there was 91 per cent residential segregation between Indians and whites in Durban in 1951 (Davies 1963: 37). De facto segregation was consolidated after 1948 through the Group Areas Act which relocated South Africans into racially segregated townships. While Apartheid was abhorrent, this policy resulted in Indians living in racially segregated areas which made it easier for them to establish and practice their religion and culture. This period also witnessed an expansion of educational opportunities and economic mobility as a result of the rise of a professional class.

Important trends among Hindus included the growth of institutional religion, the expansion of reformist activities and the attraction of Pentecostal Christianity. The process of 'Sanskritization' involved giving up of oral-based religious practices in preference for worship forms that include the use of the Sanskrit language and its texts in worship. Reformist tendencies in India which proposed new forms of Hinduism influenced local practices in South Africa. While some Hindus converted to Christianity, others embraced new streams of Hinduism, such as the Arya Samaj from the turn of the twentieth century; neo-vedantic movements from the 1940s, as represented by, to name two, the Ramakrishna Centre and Divine Life Society and the charismatic guru-based sects and movements from the 1970s onwards, as can be seen among the followers of Satya Sai Baba and Srila Prabhupada, founder of the International Society for Krishna Consciousness (Ganesh 2010: 35).

These reformist movements in general, were characterized by regular communal religious services (*satsang*); avoidance of trance festivals such as firewalking; and a focus on inner spirituality through practices such as yoga and meditation and the reading and study of religious scriptures (Diesel & Maxwell 1993: 63). The Arya Samaj movement had its roots in the visit of Swami Shakeranand in the early twentieth century. While it failed to attract a large following, the Arya Samajists paved the way for other Neo-Vedanta reformist movements. Neo-Vedanta revolves around local ashrams. Its basic message is that God is real and can be realized in the depths of one's being by following one of a number of paths. The Ramakrishna Centre originated in 1942 when a group of young men led by M.D. Naidoo (1925-65), formed a literary group to study Hindu religion, philosophy and culture. His correspondence with the then President of the worldwide Ramakrishna Mission, Swami Virajananda, fanned his devotion. They studied books on Sri Ramakrishna, Sri Sarada Devi, Swami Vivekananda and the Cultural Heritage of India as well as the journal of the Mission (*Prabuddha Bharata* and *Vedanta Kesari*). Naidoo went to India where he stayed at the Headquarters of the Ramakrishna Mission in Kolkata and was initiated into spiritual life by Swami Virajananda in March 1949. He took his final monastic vows (*sannyasa*) under Swami Purushottamananda and returned to South Africa in 1953 as Swami Nischalananda. In his new incarnation, Nischalananda set up the Ashram, printing press and Ramakrishna Clinic on a fourteen acre property in Glen Anil,

Durban, in 1959 where the headquarters of the Ramakrishna Centre of South Africa is based.

The Divine Life Society bases its teaching on Swami Sivananda (1887-1963), who opened an ashram in Rishikesh in northern India in 1936. Swami Sahajananda (1925-2007), born in the small midlands town of Estcourt in KwaZulu, took up teaching and went on to found an ashram in Reservoir Hills. He was influenced by Swami Sivananda's book *Practice of Karma Yoga* and quit teaching in 1948 before leaving for India to meet Sivananda. He returned the following year and started a Divine Life branch in Reservoir Hills, just west of Durban, in October 1949. In 1956 Sahajananda visited Sivananda who initiated him into the Holy Order of Sanyasa. In recognition of Swami Sahajananda's work on behalf of the underprivileged, the University of KwaZulu, Natal in 2008 posthumously conferred the degree of Doctor of Theology on him. He also opened the Sivananda International Cultural Centre (SICC) at Sivananda Nagar, La Mercy, which is one of the largest Hindu spiritual centres in the southern hemisphere (http://www.sivananda.dls.org.za). Other Vedantic organizations include the Chinmaya Mission in Chatsworth; the Vedanta Mission for Eternal Religion (MER) in Isipingo Hills; and the Gita Mandir in Pietermaritzburg.

Among South Indians, the reformist Neo-Vedantic Saiva Sidhantha Sungum was formed in 1937 by Guru Subramaniya Swamikal (1910-53). The movement established the Siva Kumara Prathanay—Jothi Linga Mandalam in Derby Street, Durban, and now has branches countrywide, with the Pietermaritzburg centre opened in Northdale in 1980, one of the largest in the South Africa. Guru Swamikal had studied the classical Tamil scriptures of Saivism and was responding to the challenges of both the Arya Samaj and the Bethesda Movement (Pentecostal Christianity) among Indians. He started his religious revival work by giving outdoor lectures at the Victoria Street Market, at bus ranks in the city and at the Magazine Barracks which housed the working class of the city municipal workers, who were particularly attracted to Pentecostalism. The Sungum placed less emphasis on image worship and traditional ritualistic Tamil Dravidian festivals such as firewalking and Kavadi, while observing festivals such as Maha Shivatri and Kartigai Deepam. The Swami introduced a

68 VINAY LAL AND GOOLAM VAHED

rigid prayer at 9 a.m. every Sunday morning (see http://saiva-sithantha-sungum.org/home.html). The South African Tamil Federation was formed in 1968 to canvas for matters pertaining specifically to Tamils.

The 1970s witnessed the arrival of Hindu forms that centred around charismatic gurus and sects, resulting in a 'further loosening of ritual and dogma' and characterized by 'minimal ritual and [a] lifestyle inspired by Hinduism but coexisting with and indeed embracing modernity and technology' (Ganesh 2010, 36). Expressions of this form of Hinduism include the cult of Satya Sai Baba and the International Society for Krishna Consciousness (ISKCON). As an aside, it should be noted that whatever ISKCON's associations with Hinduism in the public imagination, many of its own adherents describe themselves, not altogether convincingly, as followers of Krishna rather than of Hinduism. ISKCON was founded in the United States in 1966 by the Bengali Bhaktivedanta Swami Prabhupada, who places himself in the direct lineage of Chaitanya Mahaprahu, a sixteenth-century social reformer and exponent of Gaudiya Vaishnavism. Its public face in South Africa is the spectacular Sri Sri Radha Radhanath Temple in Chatsworth which was opened in 1985. Chatsworth was established as an 'Indian' township south of Durban in the 1960s and is home to several hundred thousand Indians. The other township established for Indians in Durban was Phoenix, in the 1970s, where the skyline is taking on a new look, as domes have been installed at the new Hare Krishna Temple being constructed near the Phoenix Plaza. As with the temple in Chatsworth, temple organizers hope that it will draw tourists to this economically depressed area. ISKCON members tend to be more middle class than followers of other streams of Hinduism. While Hare Krishna beliefs are similar to conventional Hinduism in many respects, differences include the emphasis on congregational singing of God's names as a means to achieve Krishna consciousness, the worship of Krishna as the Supreme God, and the need for a spiritual master. Public festivals form an important part of the Hare Krishna Temple. The largest and most spectacular of these is the Ratha Yatra, a five-day festival of Chariots in honour of Lord Jagannath (Vishnu), which is held over Easter at the beachfront in Durban, KwaZulu Natal (see http://iskcondurban.net/about-us/

temple-history; see alsohttps://iskconza.com/iskcon-temples/iskcon-durban/).

Sai Baba began to emerge as a growing influence among Hindus from the late 1960s. The movement was founded by Sathya Sai Baba (1926-2011) of Puttaparthi in South India. The many Sai Baba groups in South Africa are affiliated to the Gauteng based Central Council of South Africa. Sai Baba emphasized God realization through group devotional singing (*bhajans*), prayer, spiritual meditation and service (*seva*) to the community. The figure of Sai Baba—his divinity and miracles—is important to believers. The movement has strong roots in Lenasia in Gauteng, another township established for Indians during the apartheid era, where members formed the Lenasia Sai Centre. Branch centres were subsequently opened in Laudium and Benoni and eventually countrywide. Devotees of Sai Baba gather annually in April to pray for and celebrate the life and accomplishments of this mystic (see http://www.srisathyasai.org.za).

Despite the attraction of these reformist tendencies, the Christian composition of the Indian population of South Africa has increased dramatically in the last half century, as reflected in the following census (Table 2.1).

The spread of Christianity among former Hindus is due mainly to the inroads made by Pentecostal churches. In the nineteenth century, traditional churches, such as the Roman Catholics, Methodists, Anglicans and Lutherans, had proselytized energetically but

TABLE 2.1: CHRISTIAN COMPOSITION OF THE INDIAN DIASPORA OF SOUTH AFRICA

	1950	1960	1970	1980	2001
Hindus	246,257	327,908	430,290	512,304	527,353
Muslims	78,905	98,946	126,000	154,348	274,932
Christians	22,754	35,850	53,550	102,625	269,128
Other/None	19,084	15,296	20,160	52,544	–
TOTAL	367,000	478,000	630,000	821,000	1,115,467

Source: Statistics South Africa. Census reports for 1950, 1960, 1970, 1980 and 2001.

70 VINAY LAL AND GOOLAM VAHED

unsuccessfully among Indians. The rise of Pentecostalism among Indians was connected initially to the movement from rural to urban areas among Indians in the 1920s and 1930s, and subsequently to the dislocation caused by the Group Areas Act from the 1960s. J.A. Rowlands, a Quaker from England, and more especially his son John Francis Rowlands, were instrumental in spreading Pentecostalism. J.F. Rowlands founded the Bethesda Church which is the largest single church among Indians in South Africa. Rowlands 'Indianized' his version of Christianity by calling his church a 'temple', showing photographs of his tours of India to his followers, and making healing and exorcism practices, which were important to the South Indian Hindu tradition, a part of the new Christianity (see Oosthuizen 1975).

In his presentation to the Trust and Reconciliation Commission (TRC) on behalf of the South African Hindu Mahasabha on 18 November 1999, Ashwin Trikamjee, the president of the Sabha, noted the negative consequences of the Group Areas Act for adherents of Hinduism.

The most serious and painful of legislation was the Group Areas Act passed in 1950. Settled communities who had built little schools and temples were rudely uprooted by the ruling class and relocated to some distant areas or new areas with very little facilities. Cato Manor in Durban was one of the many affected areas where Indians settled, built homes, started their own market gardening and worked as unskilled labourers. When this area was declared a white area, the Indian community received the biggest blow to its survival. To name one of many, the Arian Benevolent Home, which started as a home for the homeless in 1921, was badly affected in the grand settlement plan. It took about 15 years to find an alternative for re-settlement at a much higher cost. In the process, the old, the disabled and the affected children had to endure immeasurable hardships. In all such areas, including Johannesburg, where the Group Areas applied, temples, schools and cultural centres had to be left behind. Some such temples were never built. . . . It took the Hindu community a long time to rebuild their places of worship. Priority had to be given to providing much needed homes which were relatively small, giving birth to the dismantling of the

HINDUISM IN SOUTH AFRICA, 1860-2020

joint family system and the disruption of the traditional family life. To compound the problem, religious sites in the new areas were generally purchased by the Christian churches because they had the necessary funds. This led to many conversions to other faiths, especially Christianity.

A detailed analysis of the reasons for the spread of Pentecostal Christianity falls outside the scope of this article. One might argue that nineteenth-century Protestantism, though better positioned to win converts among a people who might have felt especially vulnerable in an alien land, alienated Hindus with its stern austerity; but Pentecostalism, which emphasizes baptism in the Holy Spirit, as evidenced by speaking in tongues, exorcism, divine healing, and the power of the miraculous, has been attractive to Hindus whose own forms of popular religiosity have dwelled on vibrant, even spectacular, displays of religious experience. One should certainly treat with caution the notion that Pentecostal Christianity has grown because of the ignorance of Hindu convertees, as is often suggested by local Hindu leaders. We have to assume that people choose something because they believe that it is better for them or because it helps them to confront certain immediate difficulties in their lives. According to Pillay:

Crisis, decision, commitment, and dedication were fundamental themes in the life and worship of the Pentecostal churches. Everyone in each congregation was called to evangelize, and clergy and laity were not readily distinguished. During the times of socio-economic crisis and cultural upheaval that was largely the result of apartheid legislation; churches like Bethesda gave succour to people caught between the old, traditional Indian life and culture, rapidly passing away, and the new, Western secular life. They gave to their members a feeling of continuity with an old culture and helped to foster their socio-psychological well-being. They provided a level of social cohesion sufficient to cope in difficult circumstances and to develop a relatively well large middle class despite their disenfranchisement. Pentecostal churches inadvertently contributed to social stability by creating surrogate communities for their members (Pillay 1997, 294).

Generally, it seems that the appeal of Pentecostalism lies in the emphasis on group participation and the loose structure of worship services. It also helped that many church ministers were charismatic

VINAY LAL AND GOOLAM VAHED

and that the liturgy was narrative with an emphasis on immediate and direct experience of God. While the founders of the early churches were whites, Pentecostal expansion from the 1960s was due almost entirely to Indian lay people. The emotional prayer, joyful singing, clapping, raising hands and dancing in the presence of God, which are features of Pentecostal liturgical accoutrements, have an appeal for many ordinary people. This was, as has already been suggested, in stark contrast to the rationalistic, written and set liturgies presided over by a clergyman that was a feature of most forms of traditional Christianity.

THE POST-APARTHEID PERIOD

The end of Apartheid redefined the world of Hindus who were part of an Indian minority that had a marginal role in determining the country's trajectory, even though some individual Indians figured prominently in the post-apartheid African National Congress (ANC) led government. Their presence in the higher echelons of government has declined over the last decade. In any case, owing to their comparatively small presence in South Africa, Indians could not play the much greater role that their significant demographic presence made possible in Trinidad, Mauritius, Suriname and Fiji. Indians are dealing with these new political realities in different ways. In general, the post-Apartheid period has been witness to increased religiosity among many South Africans, with mosque, church, and temple worship increasing. All streams of Hinduism—Sanatanism, Arya Samaj, neo-Vedanta movements, and guru-based sects—have witnessed a revival.

While Indian Muslims have come to reconstitute their identities as part of global *ummah* (see Vahed 2007) and many Christians crossed racial barriers to be part of non-racial Pentecostal churches, Hindus were faced with a larger challenge to which they responded in various ways. The uncertainties created by the demise of Apartheid in the context of globalization were compounded by globalization processes that challenged conceptions of national identity based on citizenship in a single nation state. Pentecostalism, growing poverty and rising divorce and addiction rates, are also a feature of

HINDUISM IN SOUTH AFRICA, 1860-2020 73

the Indian landscape. This period also witnessed the rise of India as an emerging economic power, as well as the emergence of political Hinduism (Lal 2009), which has resulted in greater identification among Hindus with India. Pilgrimages to India have become common as has the desire to obtain PIO (Person of Indian Origin) cards, but few have taken the plunge to return permanently to India.

South Africa has also witnessed an influx of migrants from the Indian subcontinent in the past two decades. Included in this flow of migrants are the Kurukkal (traditional Brahmin priests) who arrived mainly from Sri Lanka. This is an indication of the continued value of customary rituals among local devotees. Locals, however, found that some Kurukkal families were monopolizing the priesthood and that some were using the position for personal financial gain. The move back to local priests can also be seen as a move to reclaim the local from the global (canonical), and not rely on mantras by learned specialists. This has been implemented at some temples but at others Kurukkal continue to officiate as priests (Ganesh 2010: 37).

The Hindu presence is much more visible in larger cities outside of Durban, such as Pretoria, Johannesburg and Cape Town. A city like Cape Town, where the first temple was established only in 1976, has seen an exceptional growth of Hindu organizations and temples since the 1990s, in part due to the movement of Indians from other provinces of South Africa, but more especially the arrival of migrants from India. The Bengali Hindu Community of Cape Town, which was established only in 2014, organizes the Durga Puja during Navaratri; the Gurudwara Sahib, established in 2010, is the first Sikh temple in the city and was established by post-Apartheid Sikh migrants from India, Kenya and Botswana, while post-Apartheid Telugu-speaking migrants established the Sai Darshan Trust to minister to their spiritual and social needs. Recent Sikh migrants have also established temples in Durban (2000) and Johannesburg (2006).

Johannesburg has seen the establishment of the Chinmaya Mission in the Midrand in 2015; the Kali Amman Temple was opened in Malvern, Johannesburg, in 2006 when Sarojini Pillay (Tilla) had a calling from the Divine Mother Kali to serve the

Hindu Community and a Gauteng Hindu Facebook group (https:/
/en-gb.facebook.com/groups/GautengHindus/about/) has around
7,000 members and announcements of all kinds, ranging from
prayer meetings to social welfare activities. A perusal of the page at
the end of March 2019, for example, revealed a call by the Valliama
Social Justice Interim Committee for unveiling a prayer for Valliama
who was martyred during Gandhi's 1913 passive resistance march;
the Shree Benoni Gujarati Hindu Samaj Shree Radha Krishna
Mandir invited devotees for recital of the 108 Shree Hanuman
Chalisa; and there were announcement of job offers, need of caterers,
talks on aspects of Hinduism, and a card playing competition,
thunee, which is unique to Indian South Africans. The Broader
Hindu Community Business Network South Africa Facebook
account is aimed at showcasing Hindu owned businesses in South
Africa (see https://fi-fi.facebook.com/groups/8639346 83742569/
permalink/1178540138948687/).

BROADER HINDU COMMUNITY BUSINESS
NETWORK IN SOUTH AFRICA

The South African Hindu Mahasabha (SAHMS), formed in 1912,
continues to provide a forum for Hindus to discuss common
problems and share ideas. The Mahasabha has tried to become an
umbrella organization of Hindus. It purports to be an umbrella
group, sheltering anyone who may subscribe to one of Hinduism's
myriad forms, and helping, by invoking certain issues, to create
common cause and bridge differences. Thus the Mahasabha is
involved in such enterprises as creating and managing a National
Council of Hindu Priests (NCOHP) to provide certification for
priests that would be in line with standards set by the South African
Qualifications Authority (SAQA) for priests' training. In response
to greater concern about vegetarianism among ordinary Hindus,
the Mahasabha has produced a 'Shudda logo', which is represented
by the lotus, which companies can apply for to include on their
products to indicate that the product is strictly vegetarian. It may,
in this respect, have taken a leaf from the book of Muslim-run
restaurants and food stores that advertise products as 'Halal',

thereby signalling that they are fit for consumption by observant Muslims. The Hindus United 108 Project of the Hindu Mahasabha is aimed at providing social and economic upliftment at a time when many South Africans are experiencing the pangs of economic depression and a breakdown of family and find their communities riddled with a myriad of problems. The Mahasabha has coordinated projects to support the South African Red Cross in relief efforts by providing food hampers and clothing, helping to construct three consulting rooms at the R.K. Kahn Hospital in Chatsworth, donating wheelchairs to the needy, contributing towards the running of a desk for abused women, and other similar initiatives.

While the Mahasabha claims to speak for all Hindus, language and region nevertheless remain crucially determinative in identity formation. Tamil Hindus, Hindi-speaking Hindus and Gujarati-speaking Hindus have in some instances resorted to language or regional affiliation as the basis for ethno-religious identity. The South African Tamil Federation, for example, had suspended its membership in the Mahasabha due to a feeling that the organization was dominated by north Indians who acted as though they were 'superior' to south Indians. But the general assertion of a Tamil identity in South Africa has its own history. Historically, Tamils had organized the Natal Tamil Vedic Society (NTVS) and the Young Men's Vedic Society (YMVS) in the early twentieth century. The South African Tamil Federation (SATF) was established in 1968 to advance 'the Tamil community of South Africa in the social, cultural, educational, political and economic spheres'. The organization has been active in recent years in linking Tamils across their global diaspora. For example, Dr Mickey Chetty, past president of the SATF, is a leading official in the International Movement for Tamil Culture (IMTC), which has its international head office in Canada but also South African headquarters in Lenasia, Gauteng. Among its projects is to produce school textbooks for the study of the Tamil language and culture at school level and this was launched in South Africa in November 2017. The SATF also organized a World Tamil Federation conference in South Africa in 2001 in addition; it has opened Tamil schools and arranged for the training of teachers of Tamil and Hindu priests in Chennai (*The Mercury*, 14 November 2017).

Another feature of Hinduism in the past two decades is the resurgence of large-scale and highly visible public festivals which seems puzzling because such events would appear to go against the agenda of reformist Hindus and others who, until recent decades, sought to appeal to the educated and urban Hindus practice 'modernized' Hinduism. In fact, the most visible form of Hinduism remains temple-centred and ritualistic and is associated with specific deities, such as Shiva, Vishnu and the Goddess (Mariamman, Draupadi, and Kali). Festivals such as the Draupadi firewalking festival, Mariamman 'Porridge' prayer, the Gengaiamman festival, and Kavadi still draw thousands of devotees. The Easter festival historically played a central role in the lives of many devotees. It, too, has witnessed a resurgence, this time at the Shri Mariamman Temple in Mount Edgecombe, an area once populated by thousands of indentured workers and their descendants, but now surrounded by golfing estates and gated villages. Despite opposition from residents, the prayer extends over two weeks and attracts around 1,50,000 people, with a third of them attending on Easter Friday alone. Devotees attend from all over the world, including those coming from as far as Canada, the United Kingdom, and Australia where many Indians have emigrated in recent decades, as well as from various parts of South Africa. Festivals are regularly organized by temples as they are seen as a means to unite communities.

The post-Apartheid period has also witnessed many Hindus and Muslims moving into former white areas, where they have been busy building mosques and temples. From the perspective of temple organizers, temples are essential to meet the requirements of population growth and the needs of devotees, as some practices, like the observance of festivals and ritual prayers, require a priest while the social belonging that comes from temple worship is absent from home worship. Temples and mosques have altered the urban landscape in the face of immense opposition from white residents against these structures, as well as opposition to such practices as Hindus setting off fireworks during the Diwali Festival of Lights. After each Diwali, some whites usually take to social media to criticize these practices, but Hindus have been assertive in laying criminal charges against whites on grounds of racism and

HINDUISM IN SOUTH AFRICA, 1860-2020

have successfully claimed damages and apologies from several critics before the Human Rights Commission. Maushami Chetty, an attorney and professional speaker, who is a consultant on gender mainstreaming and creating a truly South African corporate culture, wrote in 2015,

The days leading up to Diwali are replete with tension between Hindus and animal activists. Watching the interactions escalate, it reflects perhaps a fundamental oversight about what is really going on. South Africa is a stark example of race equals space. Twenty years later, despite the removal of the barriers to living, eating and going to school anywhere, these racial spaces remain. White space explains the experience of a black person when entering a white environment and the increased visibility and whole gamut of preconceptions that this 'intrusion' carries with it. . . . Hindus moving into desegregated neighbourhoods, whether Sandton or Umhlanga, are, consciously or not, perceived as a threat to the status quo of white Christians. . . . Fireworks are obviously a potential health risk, but the reactions on social media each year are telling. The opposition is overwhelmingly white and the interactions, though based on an emotive subject such as animal rights, is racially charged. . . . The reactions to Diwali are also disproportionate to the reactions to New Year or Guy Fawkes Day, when there is no 'other' to rally against. The interactions in formerly white areas often reveal themselves in tweets like 'You are barbaric', or 'Go back to Chatsworth'. This is the crowning moment in the assumption of the moral high ground and the marginalization of values not your own to make the most joyous time in the Hindu calendar into a spiteful bout of online bullying. The opposition to fireworks during Diwali demonstrates all the features of intrusion into white space.

Some concerned Hindus have also objected that huge structures like temples are a drain on the resources of the community which could be better used at a time of great poverty and social deprivation.

South African Hindus have not been immune to the emergence of a more expansive Hindu consciousness since the 1990s in response to the rise of India as a global power and to political Hinduism (Hindutva), which, Lal (2013) argues, aims to 'forge new forms of Hindu identity, endow Hinduism with a purportedly more coherent and monotheistic form, [and] refashion our understanding of the history of Hinduism's engagement with practitioners of other faiths in India'. Hindutva ideology and organizations have been transported to many diasporic communities through organizations such as the Rashtriya Swayamsevak Sangh (RSS), founded in 1925 and with a presence in 150 countries and the Vishwa Hindu Parishad (VHP), founded in 1964. The core belief of the RSS is the idea of a Vedic Golden Age which was destroyed by Muslim and British colonization, and the aim is to transform India into a Hindu state. Internet sites like the *Global Hindu Electronic Network (GHEN)* have been instrumental in forging a global Hindu consciousness. Vinay Lal (2006: 116) has argued that 'the internet . . . is the vehicle for advancing a new conception of Hinduness as a global faith'.

While there are some active members of the RSS and VHP in South Africa, a greater Hindu consciousness is evident, for example, in the assertive manner in which some Hindus defend their faith and the government of Narendra Modi in India and criticize Muslims and Islam in particular, on the whole. However, it would be fair to state that the attraction of these organizations is muted in comparison to other settings, such as the United States, Britain, and Australia. This may in part be due to a conscious effort on the part of the Mahasabha, several of whose leaders have a long history of involvement in non-sectarian sporting, political and academic bodies, to work hard to build bridges across the racial and religious divides in South Africa.

There are signs of change in the embracing approach of the SAHMS as a newly-formed organizations, the Hindu Dharma Association of South Africa (HINDASA) has been more vocal about asserting Hindu identity. A member of the organization, Anand Singh, for example, championed a complaint by a resident in Isipingo Beach, Durban, who tried to get a court to stop a mosque near his home from uttering the *azaan* (call to prayer), arguing that the *azaan* was outdated (*Post*, 9 September 2020); Singh also observed #BlackDay in South Africa for the first time on 22 October 2020, to mark Pakistan's attack on Kashmir in 1947, when he was in conversation with retired army officer Lt. General Ata Hasnain; and he wrote to the Hindvani Radio Station on 24 October 2020 (e-mail in authors' possession) complaining of, amongst other things, the radio using Muslim talk show hosts, playing Islamic songs, and giving too little coverage to the Ramjanmabhoomi Pooja at the Ayodhia temple in August 2020 (where a temple was being built on a land disputed between Hindus and Muslims). According to the e-mail, many Hindus were beginning to feel that 'HINDVANI IS CAPTURED' and unless the radio station fulfilled its mandate of promoting Hindu language, culture and religion, a petition being organized would be 'akin to an obituary'. It is too early to predict how these tendencies will develop among the mass of Hindus.

CONCLUSIONS

This article underscores the fact that Hinduism in South Africa has not been static. It has continued to undergo transformations of all kinds, due in part to the impact of influences from the Indian sub-continent. While the Hinduism practised in South Africa partakes of some of the tendencies encountered in India and in the wider Indian diaspora, South African Hinduism has displayed its own characteristic features. A more exhaustive study of the contours of Hinduism in South Africa, though not possible within the confines of this article, would doubtless yield other insights. One has not, for example, considered the relationship of Hinduism to caste, a contentious subject on which a variety of sentiments continue to be entertained. The celebrated anthropologist M.N. Srinivas gave his opinion in 1956 that 'if and when caste disappears, Hinduism will also disappear' (1956: 495).

Gandhi's principal intellectual adversary in India, the Dalit leader B.R. Ambedkar, was equally certain that caste discrimination was embedded in Hinduism, a religion that he construed as execrable to the core and incapable of being reformed. Now in South Africa, and elsewhere in diasporic settings such as Trinidad and Fiji, the influence of caste is generally held to have been greatly diminished; as John Kelly has written of Fiji's Hindus that to understand them 'one must discuss first of all their egalitarianism. The social life of Fiji Indians is not organised by caste. Many, perhaps most, do not even know "their caste", and "caste" plays little role in marriage and other social calculations' (1988: 41-2). And yet Hinduism flourished, even showing

80 VINAY LAL AND GOOLAM VAHED

signs of prosperity in public spaces when the Indian community was weighed down by political repression or had to contend, as in Trinidad, with African-Creole cultural hegemony.

One could, as well, have raised another set of considerations: to what extent if at all have Hindus in South Africa brought their faith into conversation with African religions? In Trinidad, since the 1970s, some Hindus have been participating in the Orisha cult, or the worship of the Yoruba god Shango (Mahabir & Maharaj 1989). Is something similar at all happening in South Africa? If the reification of Hinduism is taking place, as seems likely, one has to acknowledge also that the faith is opening itself up to other transgressive possibilities. Wherever one appears to find 'fundamentalism', one should also seek out hybrid forms of religion, if not 'syncretism'.

One of the burdens of this article has been to suggest that no form of Hinduism should be regarded as 'authentic'. In the various diasporic settings, such as South Africa, Hinduism should be examined on its own terms, in the very specific social, cultural, political and economic conditions in which it is forged. Understanding how Hinduism is conceptualized and formulated in different settings will allow one to compare, as one have endeavoured to do briefly on more than one occasion, distant diasporic communities with each other, as well as with the 'homeland' and also understand how these communities view each other. As Warrier (2008: 93) points out, this has 'important implications for issues of identity construction in the Hindu diaspora'. While pointing to the various tendencies among Hindus and constant transformation, we should also emphasize that by and large Hindus are integrated into the broader South African society.

REFERENCES

Anderson, Benedict (1983). *Imagined Communities: Reflections on the Origin and Spread of Nationalism.* London: Verso.

Bhana, Surendra (1997). 'Indianness Reconfigured, 1944-1960: The Natal Indian Congress in South Africa', *Comparative Studies of South Asia, Africa and the Middle East, XVII* (2): pp. 100-7.

—— (1997). *Gandhi's Legacy. The Natal Indian Congress, 1894-1994.* Pietermaritzburg: University of Natal Press.

HINDUISM IN SOUTH AFRICA, 1860-2020

—— (1991). *Indentured Indian Emigrants to Natal, 1860-1902. A Study Based on Ships Lists.* New Delhi: Promilla & Co.

Bhana, Surendra and Goolam, Vahed (2005). *The Making of a Social Reformer: Mahatma Gandhi in South Africa, 1893-1914.* Delhi: Manohar.

Bhana, Surendra and Joy Brain (1990). *Setting down Roots: Indian Migrants in South Africa, 1860-1911.* Johannesburg: Witwatersrand University Press.

Bugwandeen, Dowlat L. (1991). *A People on Trial—For Breaching Racism. The Struggle for Land and Housing of the Indian People of Natal: 1940-6.* Durban: Madiba Publications.

Chetty, Maushami (2015). 'Whiteness sours the joys of Diwali', *Mail and Guardian.* Retrieved from https://mg.co.za/article/2015-11-15-whiteness-sours-the-joys-of-diwali. Accessed on 15 November 2015 and 23 March 2019.

Davies, R.J. (1963). 'The Growth of the Durban Metropolitan Area', *South African Geographical Journal, 45*(1): pp. 15-43, December.

Desai, Ashwin and Goolam Vahed (2010). *Monty Naicker. Between Reason and Treason.* Pietermaritzburg: Shuter and Shooter.

—— (2010). *Inside Indian Indenture: A South African Story 1860-1914.* Cape Town: Human Sciences Research Council (HSRC) Press.

Diesel, Alleyn (2003). 'Hinduism in KwaZulu-Natal, South Africa', in Bhikhu Parekh, Gurharpal Singh and Steven Vertovec (eds.), *Culture and Economy in the Indian Diaspora.* London: Routledge: pp. 33-50.

—— (2000). 'Tamil Hindus in KawZulu-Natal (South Africa): History, Identity and the Establishment of Their Place in the New South Africa', Paper presented at the Eighteenth Congress of International Association for the History of Religions (IAHR), Durban, South Africa, 5-12 August.

—— (1998). 'The empowering image of the divine mother: A South African Hindu woman worshipping the goddess', *Journal of Contemporary Religion, 13*(1): pp. 73-90.

Diesel, Alleyn and P. Maxwell (1993). *Hinduism in Natal.* Pietermaritzburg: University of Natal Press.

Durban Housing Survey (1952). *A Study of Housing in a Multi-racial Community.* Durban: University of Natal Press.

Edwards, Iain and Tim Nuttall (1990). 'Seizing the Moment: the January 1949 Riots, Proletarian Populism and the Structures of African Urban Life in Durban during the late 1940s', paper presented at History Workshop on 'Structure and Experience in the Making of Apartheid,' University of Witwatersrand, 6-10 February.

Eickelman, Dale F. (1992). 'Mass Education and the religious imagination in contemporary Arab societies', *American Ethnologist,19*(4): pp. 643-55.

Freund, Bill (1995). *Insiders and Outsiders: The Indian Working Class of Durban, 1910-1990.* Portsmouth, New Hampshire: Heinemann.

Ganesh, Kamala (2010). 'Beyond Historical Origins: Negotiating Tamilness in South Africa', *Journal of Social Science, 25*(1-2-3): pp. 25-37.

Gopalan, Karthi (2014). 'Defending Hinduism or Fostering Division? The Decision to Introduce Hindu Religious Instruction in Indian Schools in South Africa during the 1950s', *Journal of Religion in Africa, 44*(2): pp. 224-50.

Henning, Grenville (1993). *The Indentured Indian in Natal.* New Delhi: Promilla & Co.

Hofmeyr, Jan (1983). 'Homogeneity and South African Hinduism', *Journal of Religion in Africa, 13*(2): pp. 139-49.

Jha, Jagdish C. (1989). 'Hinduism in Trinidad', in Frank Birbalsingh (ed.), *Indenture & Exile: The Indo-Caribbean Experience.* Toronto: Toronto South Asian Review [TSAR]: pp. 225-33.

Jones, Arun W. (2017). *Missionary Christianity and Local Religion: American Evangelism in North India, 1836-1870.* Waco, Texas: Baylor University Press.

Kuppusami, C. (1993). *Tamil Culture in South Africa. Endeavours to Nurture and Promote it among the Tamils.* Durban: Rapid Graphic.

Kelly, John D. (1991). *A Politics of Virtue: Hinduism, Sexuality, and Counter-colonial Discourse in Fiji.* London: The University of Chicago Press.

Kelly, John D. and M. Kaplan (2001). *Represented Communities. Fiji and World Decolonization.* Chicago: University of Chicago Press.

Kulke, Hermann and Dietmar Rothermund (1998). *A History of India* (3rd edn.). London and New York: Routledge.

Lal, Brij (2004). *Bittersweet: An Indo-Fijian Experience.* Canberra: Pandanus Books.

Lal, Vinay (2013). 'When Hinduism meets the Internet', *Lal Salaam: A blog by Vinay Lal.* Accessed 26 January 2013. Retrieved from https://vinaylal. wordpress.com/tag/hindu-holocaust-museum/. [Retrieved on 13 January 2018.]

—— (2010). *Political Hinduism: The Religious Imagination in Public Spheres.* New Delhi: Oxford University Press.

—— (2008). 'Hinduism', in Peter N. Stearns (ed.), *Oxford Encyclopedia of the Modern World.* New York & Oxford: Oxford University Press, 4: pp. 10-16.

—— (2007). *The Other Americans. A Political and Cultural History of South Asians in America.* New Delhi: HarperCollins.

Lal, Vinay and Vahed Goolam (2013). 'Hinduism in South Africa: Caste, Ethnicity, and Invented Traditions, 1860-present', *Journal of Sociology and Social Anthropology*, 4(1-2): pp. 1-15.

Mahabir, Noorkumar and Ashram Maharaj (1989). 'Hindu Elements in the Shango/Orisha Cult of Trinidad', in Frank Birbalsingh (ed.), *Indenture & Exile: The Indo-Caribbean Experience.* Toronto: Toronto South Asian Review: pp. 191-201.

Masuzawa, Tomoko (2005). *The Invention of World Religions: Or, how European Universalism was preserved in the Language of Pluralism.* Chicago: University of Chicago Press.

Mujeeb, Mohammad (1967). *The Indian Muslims.* London: George Allen & Unwin.

Naidoo, Thillayvel (1992). *The Arya Samaj Movement in South Africa.* Delhi: Motilal Banarsidass.

Oberoi, Harjot (1994). *The Construction of Religious Boundaries: Culture, Identity and Diversity in the Sikh Tradition.* Chicago: University of Chicago Press.

Oosthuizen, Gerhardus C. (1975). *Moving to the Waters: Fifty Years of Revival in Bethesda.* Durban: Bethesda Publications.

Pillay, Gerald J. (1997). 'Community Service and Conversion: Christianity among Indian South Africans', in Richard Elphick and Rodney Davenport (eds.), *Christianity in South Africa. A Political, Cultural & Social History.* Cape Town: David Philip: pp. 286-96.

—— (1989). 'Religious Profile', in Arkin, A.J., Magyar, K.P. and Pillay, G.J. (eds.), *The Indian South Africans.* Pinetown: Owen Burgess Publishers: pp. 143-70.

Singh, Kelvin (1988). *Bloodstained Tombs: The Muharram Massacre 1884.* London: Macmillan Caribbean.

Srinivas, Mysore N. (1956). 'A Note on Sanskritization and Westernization', *Far Eastern Quarterly*, 15(4): pp. 481-96.

Swan, Maureen (1985). *Gandhi. The South African Experience.* Johannesburg: Raven Press.

Tinker, Hugh (1974). *A New System of Slavery: The Export of Indian Labour Overseas, 1834-1920.* New York: Oxford University Press.

Vahed, Goolam (2002). 'Constructions of Community and Identity among Indians in Colonial Natal, 1860-1910: The Role of the Muharram Festival', *Journal of African History*, 43(1): pp. 77-93.

Vahed, Goolam and Ashwin Desai (2018). 'Race, Place and Indian Identities in Contemporary South Africa', in Roderick R. Hewitt and Chammah J. Kaunda (eds.), *Who Is an African? Race, Identity, and Destiny in Post-apartheid South Africa*. Maryland: Lexington Books/Fortress Academics: pp. 61-83.

Warrier, Marya (2008). 'Diaspora', in Sushila Mittal and Gene Thursby (eds.), *Studying Hinduism: Key Concepts and Methods*. London: Routledge: p. 89.

CHAPTER 3

Transnational Hindu Movements and the South African Experience after Indenture

KARTHIGASEN GOPALAN

Indentured labourers who began arriving in the then British Colony of Natal from 1860 from various parts of India were predominantly Hindu, and brought with them a myriad traditions, languages, castes and beliefs. International Hindu missionaries who visited Natal at the turn of the twentieth century, worked with local Hindu leaders in an attempt to provide a common ground around which the heterogeneous groups of Hindus could coalesce. These reformist Hindus, saw the heterogeneity of Hindu practices as a potential weakness and believed that this would divide Hindus who needed to coordinate their efforts to ensure the survival of Hinduism in a foreign land. Hindu reformers were concerned at the influence of Christian missionaries in Natal, and felt that the conditions in which indentured Indians lived, combined with an emphasis on ritual-oriented Hinduism would make them more receptive to the influence of missionaries. For these reformers, the uncoordinated rituals that Hindus partook in, portrayed Hinduism in a less favourable light and consequently, Hindu migrants needed to be educated in the fundamental truths of Hinduism, as defined by them.

In 1912, two years after Natal merged with the British Cape Colony and the two Dutch Republics of the Orange Free State and the Transvaal to form the Union of South Africa, Hindu leaders met at the inaugural conference of South African Hindus to discuss the future of Hinduism in the new country. The conference was presided over by Swami Shankaranand, a visiting Vedic missionary from the Punjab whom local Hindu leaders had invited in 1908 to help propagate Hinduism among the masses. The most significant development of the conference was the establishment of the South African Hindu Maha Sabha. The purpose of the Maha Sabha was to establish a unitary Hindu identity and coordinate the affairs of more parochial Hindu institutions. B.D. Lalla, a leader of the Maha Sabha in 1960, recording its history, stated that the Maha Sabha was established when Hindu leaders realized 'that unless they co-ordinated their efforts, there was little hope for the survival of Hinduism which was threatened from all sides (1960: 108).

Throughout the existence of the Maha Sabha, however, some South African Indians criticized the existence of an organization that on the one hand, aimed to unite a very heterogeneous group of Hindus, while at the same time excluded Christian and Muslim Indians. These critics feared sectionalism and were worried that religious tensions that took on political dimensions in India and in a few other parts of the world with large Indian populations, could surface in South Africa. Leaders in the Maha Sabha in South Africa, who were also leaders in secular political organizations in which they worked closely with Christian and Muslim Indians, argued that the Maha Sabha aimed to promote a purely religious identity to safeguard a rich religious heritage and that it would never intervene in political matters.

This article addresses the question why successive leaders of the Maha Sabha saw it as vital to promote a broad 'Hindu identity', one that encompassed various strands of Hinduism, and the debates that this generated with those Hindus who were concerned about the exclusion of Muslims and Christians. Some Hindus were also critical of the body because they did not want to conform to a particular kind of Hinduism promoted by the Maha Sabha. From the forma-tion of Union in 1910, South Africa was a racially stratified country led by a white minority government. In 1948, when many parts of the African continent began agitating for independence from European colonial rule, the white Afrikaner National Party came to power in South Africa and began implementing the policy of apartheid, which aimed to further promote the division of South

TRANSNATIONAL HINDU MOVEMENTS 87

Africans along racial lines. Unlike India and many parts of the diaspora, Indian South Africa were an absolute minority, comprising around 2 per cent of the population. In this climate, the task of keeping unity amongst Indians and working with other racial groups was the primary concern for many of the politically conscious Indians in South Africa.

With the end of Apartheid and the onset of democracy in 1994, there were new pressures facing Hindu leaders. In post-Cold War and post-Apartheid South African society, religious, linguistic and cultural identities seem to be hardening. Globally, this trend has been so noticeable that at the end of the Cold War, when many predicted a 'clash of civilizations' (See Huntington 1993, Waters 1995, Tarock 1993 and O'Hagan 1993). Although this is an extreme viewpoint, to see religion as a cause of global conflict, it is true that people employ boundary markers for various purposes. For Stuart Hall, during times of crises people attempt to hold on to certain characteristics that make them different from others with whom they come into contact (1992, 1). With regard to Hinduism in South Africa, the situation is complex, because although linguistic and secular identities amongst Hindus seem to be hardening, the rate of conversion of Hindus to Christianity is also increasing. Throughout the history of the Maha Sabha, its leaders justified its existence on grounds of preventing conversions to other faiths. However, census figures suggest that conversions of large numbers did not take place during the earlier period but is more prevalent in the contemporary period. Consequently, this article also briefly addresses some of the activities pursued by Hindu leaders in the contemporary period.

DEFINING HINDUISM

One of the difficulties facing an organization such as the Maha Sabha, which strove to create a Hindu identity in South Africa, is the issue of defining Hinduism, especially given the diversity of South African Hindus. The term Hinduism encompasses a number of diverging religious practices originating in the Indian subcontinent. Some authors argue that the term is a British colonial construct

88 KARTHIGASEN GOPALAN

to categorize the wide variety of religious practices that they encountered (see for example Dalmia & Von Stietencron 1995, Frykenberg 1997; and Mishra 2006).

While other scholars challenge this view, even the fiercest critics admit that the complex set of encounters that took place between the British 'Christians' and Indian 'Hindus' during a period lasting little more than a century, was decisive in the way that one has come to understand Hinduism in the contemporary period (Pennington 2005: 6). While careful not to take a particular stance in this debate and acknowledging the existence of religious identity on the subcontinent long before the arrival of the British, what she calls 'fragmented identities', Sharada Sugirtharajah nevertheless argues that 'the notion of a monolithic Hinduism emerged in the colonial era' (2003, xi). The fact that Hinduism is not based on the teachings of a particular prophet, text or set of texts but on a variety of texts, beliefs and traditions that evolved over many centuries in a diverse and multilingual region, highlights the difficulty of defining the term and has led to multiple ways of interpreting Hinduism.

INDENTURED LABOURERS AND HINDU PRACTICES IN SOUTH AFRICA

The difficulty of defining Hinduism relates particularly to the South African situation where around two-thirds of migrants were from South India (Tamil and Telugu speakers) and a third from North India (Uttar Pradesh and Bihar, who spoke Bhojpuri, Hindi and variants). Free migrant Hindus who followed spoke mainly Gujarati. Broadly speaking, these groups (North, South and West Indians) see themselves as different on a number of levels including religious practices, to North Indians believed to be descendants of the Aryans and South Indians of the Dravidians (Rodrigues 2006, 8-16).

C. Kuppusami argues that differences are largely the result of physical hurdles such as the Narmada and Tapti rivers, the Vindhyas and Satpura hills and the dense forests called the Mahakarta, all of which have acted as a barrier separating North India from South India and inhibiting movement between these two regions in past centuries (1993: 10). To a large extent, traditions evolved separately and, today many texts that are seen as synonymous with Hinduism, such as the *Mahabharata, Bhagavad Gita, Ramayana,* and the four *Vedas* are regarded as North Indian by many South Indians who have their own set of religious texts, which includes the *Gnana Bodham, Thirukural, Thevaram* and *Thiruvaimoli* (Kuppusami, 1993: 10). Migrants brought traditions to Natal which were noticeably different.

Apart from the broad differences in religious practices between North and South Indians, Surendra Bhana points out that the two ports that Indian South Africans came from, Madras (South Indian) and Calcutta (North Indian), covered vast and diverse presidencies and Natal's Indians came from numerous villages throughout these regions (1991: 50). The Madras Presidency, for example, covered 141,704 square miles which in 1901 contained a population of approximately 38 million and was divided into 22 districts with 55,000 villages (Bhana 1991: 43-4). Migrants disembarking from the port of Calcutta came mainly from Bihar and the United Provinces of Agra and Oudh, which in 1901 contained approximate populations of 24.5 million and 48 million respectively (Bhana 1991: 46, 48). Bihar was divided into Patna which contained 35 towns and 34,169 villages and Bhagalpur which contained 15 towns and 21,656 villages (Bhana 1991: 48-9). The United Provinces covered a territory of 107,164 square miles and contained nine divisions in 1901, each containing a population of between five and six million (Bhana 1991: 46). Clearly, Natal's Indians came from various locations throughout large and heterogeneous regions bringing with them a variety of traditions, beliefs, and cultural practices.[1]

While there is a paucity of information on the religious practices of indentured migrants in Natal during the formative period, one does know from the little evidence that exists that there was great diversity and an emphasis on ritual-oriented Hinduism (see Brain

[1] See lists of ships containing names and places of origin of each migrant which are available on the Gandhi Luthuli Documentation Centre website http://scnc.ukzn.ac.za/.

90 KARTHIGASEN GOPALAN

1990; Bhana & Vahed 2005: 51-68; Desai & Vahed 2010: 228-48). Migrants sought to recreate their religious life in their new surroundings and practised a form of popular Hinduism. They celebrated a vast array of different festivals and there was no central organization or occasion that represented Hindus as a group.

Ironically, the mostly widely celebrated religious festival amongst Hindus in Natal was Muharram, a Muslim occasion (See Vahed 2002). By the beginning of the twentieth century, this state of affairs increasingly became a concern to a small group of more reform-minded Hindus with their own interpretation of Hinduism. This group consisted of ex-indentured workers who had acquired wealth and status, as well as a small group of free migrants who are referred to as 'passenger' migrants in the literature, comprising predominantly but not exclusively of migrants from Gujarat who arrived of their own volition and at their own expense.[2] Regardless of their wealth and status however, they were 'powerless to have a discursive impact on the "mass of Indians" during the early decades' (Vahed 2002: 90).

One of these free migrants, M.C. Varman, decided that international Hindu missionaries would be more influential and he raised money to bring two Arya Samaj missionaries from India to lecture in Natal. Travelling missionaries belonging to the Arya Samaj missionary movement founded in Bombay in 1875 by the

[2] The term 'passenger Indian' has led to the stereotype of the wealthy Gujarati trader which fails to capture the entirety of this migrant stream. There was a small wealthy elite of Gujarati traders but this stereotype masks important aspects of passenger migration. According to Uma Dhupelia-Mesthrie, 'The term passenger Indian imported into writings about the Cape from the Natal and Transvaal historiography requires redefinition. Its simplified definition leads to a divisive understanding of migration from the Indian subcontinent and contributes to the stereotype of the rich Gujarati. The term needs to embrace workers and in terms of regional origins to include not just those from west India and certainly not just Gujarat but also those from other parts of India . . . [Many] Passenger Indians secured work in . . . in menial positions and some remained in these for more than just an initial phase.' Uma Dhupelia-Mesthrie. 'The Passenger Indian as Worker: Indian Immigrants in Cape Town in the Early Twentieth Century' in *African Studies*, 68: 1(2009), p. 129.

TRANSNATIONAL HINDU MOVEMENTS

Maharishi Dayananda Saraswati (1824-83) to refine Hindu practices, had pivotal influence on Hindu leaders in South Africa (See Singh 1871). Even a cursory glance at the Maha Sabha's history indicates strong tendencies toward this particular approach to Hinduism in spite of the organization's attempts to represent all South African Hindus.

The notion of a homogeneous Hinduism and an organization to unite Hindus to defend it against criticism by creating the idea of a 'glorious era' was promoted by reformers who placed authority on North Indian or Aryan texts and traditions (see Hardy 1990). This applied to Swami Dayananda and other reformers in India who defended Hinduism against western criticism by presupposing homogenizing tendencies within Hinduism (Sugirtharajah 2003: xii). According to Sugirtharajah, the implications for understanding Hinduism extend further than merely 'critiquing totalizing tendencies in Eurocentric as well as nationalistic modes of thinking and practice' in India (2003: xiii). The task of exploring how missionaries and Orientalists used western concepts of religion to create an idea of Hinduism to incorporate various religious practices and how Hindu reformers adopted these modes of thinking in their defence of Hinduism, is a wide field of study.[3] However, for Sugirtharajah, it is vital to look at how Hinduism was (re)constructed in the diaspora where various Hindu leaders remodelled the 'oriental articulations of Hinduism' (2003: xiii). The factors that instigated the formation of reform movements in India were also present in the plantation colonies where indentured labourers had settled. These factors included poverty, the high level of illiteracy, inadequate schools and absence of Hindu institutions.

Swami Dayananda was concerned over what he regarded as inherent weaknesses in Hindu practice, such as the hereditary caste system, idolatry, animal sacrifices, polytheism, child marriage, ancestor worship, unequal gender relations, and the belief that humans could be the incarnations of gods. He argued that Hinduism

---

[3] Edward Said (1978) has influenced scholars to look at the implications of 'post-colonial' theory as it relates to 'Hinduism'. See Peter Van Der Veer (2001) and Pennington (2005).

should be based exclusively on the religious texts known as the four Vedas and sought to eradicate all of the above mentioned practices which, he maintained, had crept into Hinduism through the ages and had distorted its true essence (Naidoo 1992: 15-24). Swami Dayananda was a source of inspiration and an exemplar for many South African Hindus, including members of the Maha Sabha and international Hindu missionaries who visited periodically. However, the fact that Shiva, one of the most widely worshipped deities amongst South Indians, does not feature in the Vedas is an indication that Swami Dayananda's interpretation of Hinduism was not representative of South African Hindus.

Bhai Parmanand, the first Arya Samajist missionary to visit South Africa, was born in the Punjab on 4 November 1876 and was a descendant of a famous Sikh martyr, Bhai Mati Das. Parmanand's father Bhai Tara Chand Mohyal was also an active Arya Samaj missionary and was at one time the president of the Hindu Nationalist movement Akhil Bharatiya Hindu Mahasabha (All India Mahasabha) (Agrawal 2008: 82). While remembered by most Hindu institutions in South Africa as a religious leader, Professor Parmanand was also a nationalist politician and one of the first proponents of a separate state for Hindus and Muslims (ibid.). Regardless of his Hindu nationalist views, there is no evidence of this in South Africa, where he is credited for sowing the seeds for reformation through his lectures as well as the Vedic institutions that he inspired local Hindus to establish (Chotai 1960: 83).

The work of Swami Shankaranand, who made two visits, first arriving in 1908 and finally departing in 1913 and the tensions he created between his supporters and those of Gandhi, has been dealt with some detail and it is not necessary to repeat here (Swan 1985: 16-18, 200-3, 237; Vahed 1997; Desai & Vahed 2010: 237-47; Bhana & Vahed 2005: 57-68). However, it is important to highlight that like Parmanand, he was instrumental in motivating local Hindus to establish reform-oriented Hindu bodies. Shankaranand was also highly instrumental in getting Diwali recognized as the national celebration of Hindus, and at a meeting with local Hindus in April 1912, decided to hold a Hindu conference to establish a national body, the Maha Sabha at the end of May 1912.

TRANSNATIONAL HINDU MOVEMENTS 93

However, when the Swami departed the following year on 31 May 1913, the Maha Sabha became defunct. While the Maha Sabha concerned with an overarching Hindu identity, remained completely inactive during this time, parochial Hindu bodies continued to play an important role in the lives of many. Wherever Indians had settled, voluntary bodies emerged to promote vernacular and religious endeavours amongst groups of Hindus in that locality. The Maha Sabha was revived briefly in 1918 by members of Arya Samaj bodies in Natal, including a South African born travelling Arya Samaj missionary named Bhawani Dayal. The Maha Sabha held only two meetings before becoming defunct again, largely the result of Dayal's departure to India in 1919 to represent South African Indians at an annual convention of the Indian National Congress (Bista 1992, 14).

In 1925, when Arya Samaj bodies across the world celebrated the birth centenary of Swami Dayananda, an umbrella body called the Arya Pratinidhi Sabha (APS) was established with Dayal as its president, to unite all Natal Arya Samaj bodies. However, the passing of the Areas Reservation Bill later in the year meant that many Indian political leaders in South Africa, including Dayal, travelled to India to rally support against this bill. The fact that political leaders also tended to dominate the membership of religious organizations was detrimental to the latter. During December 1926 and January 1927, the Round Table Conference took place in Cape Town between the Indian and South African governments. The conference addressed the question of repatriation and the difficulties faced by returning migrants, which took up the attention of Dayal who wrote a book on the subject.[4] This, combined with the difficulties faced by Indians as a result of the Great Depression, all captured the attention of the Indian political and community leaders of South Africa who also comprised the leadership of bodies such as the Maha Sabha.

During the fiftieth death anniversary of Swami Dayananda in 1933, Dayal was elected president of the APS for the second time

---

[4] For more on the Cape Town Agreement see Mesthrie (1985) and Dayal & Chaturvedi (1951).

94 KARTHIGASEN GOPALAN

and organized a conference where the revival of the Maha Sabha was discussed. During the conference, leaders of the APS discussed reasons for having a national body for Hindus. B.M. Patel stated that 'the primary cause of weakening the community' was the absence of an organization to 'voice the opinions of the Hindu Community as a whole, nor is there a medium of bringing the people together under one banner'.[5] In his presidential address, Dayal implored delegates to 'create a feeling among the Hindus that they are Hindus first and Calcuttyas, Madrasis and Gujaratis, or Sanathanists and Arya Samajists afterwards' (Minutes of the APS 1933 Conference). Without a Maha Sabha, Hindus 'cannot be protected and their interests cannot be safeguarded' (Minutes of the APS 1933 Conference). He appealed to the committee not to miss this unique occasion for the 'formation of a central Hindu organization thus proving [their] love and affection towards Hinduism' (Minutes of the APS 1933 Conference). Dayal's call is interesting because of his strong disapproval of the Maha Sabha in India, which he reiterated in this address. His opposition, he said, was due to that organization's involvement in politics and the tensions that this caused between Hindus and Muslims. Dayal however believed that similar tension was unlikely in South Africa because Hindu and Muslim institutions in South Africa concerned themselves primarily with religious and welfare projects. There was no reason to believe, he said, that a South African Maha Sabha would get involved in politics. He insisted that this 'would not be possible' (Minutes of the APS 1933 Conference).

The conference resulted in the formation of a prospective Maha Sabha which held its first general meeting on 26 December 1933. Representatives from more than thirty institutions attended and unanimously agreed to revive the Maha Sabha. While the likes of Dayal and Patel argued that it was essential to revive the Maha Sabha in order to advance Hinduism, some Indians, such as the editors of the *Indian Opinion* newspaper, viewed this with great misgiving. On 14 May 1934, this newspaper published an article titled 'On

[5] Minutes of the APS 1933 Conference, available at the Gandhi Luthuli Documentation Centre, University of KwaZulu Natal.

TRANSNATIONAL HINDU MOVEMENTS 95

the wrong lines', which stated it was 'averse' to the revival of the Maha Sabha. While acknowledging the 'delicacy' of the matter and warning that the newspaper 'could not dedicate too much space to a religious matter', it nevertheless published a relatively long article on the front page because the 'matter is taking an important turn in the history of Indians in South Africa' and has a 'bearing on the whole Indian Community'. *Indian Opinion* drew comparisons with the Maha Sabha of India to warn against the possible dangers of establishing a similar body in South Africa. The article expressed pride in the fact that South African Indians could hail from the 'motherland' and 'create a little India' and yet, in spite of all the 'evils of caste and communal distinction', they lived as 'Indians first and Indians last' in a 'common brotherhood of men'. The report noted that signs of communalism only became evident during Swami Shankaranand's stay in South Africa (*Indian Opinion*, 14 May 1934).

The report then concluded that while the Swami's lectures on Hinduism were followed with great enthusiasm, on the whole, his activities did not receive unanimous support even from those in whose interests (Hindus) he was purportedly working (*Indian Opinion*, 14 May 1934). This newspaper article, however, needs to be read in the following light. The Maha Sabha in India was in opposition to Gandhi at this time and Swami Shankaran was also Gandhi's adversary during his South African stay. The editor of *Indian Opinion*, Gandhi's son Manilal, was probably opposed to a South African version of the Maha Sabha for similar ideological reasons as his father. Perhaps equally important to this opposition was division in the main Indian political organization in South Africa at the time, the Natal Indian Congress (NIC). The decision by some South Africans to participate in the colonization enquiry scheme which was looking at repatriating South African Indians to other British colonies had split the NIC, with a group led by Albert Christopher breaking away to form the Colonial Born and Settlers India Association (CBSIA) (Bhana 1997: 33-54). Manilal Gandhi was part of this breakaway group, while the majority of those who sought to re-establish the Maha Sabha, including S.R. and V.S.C. Pather, Dayal, and T.M. Naicker remained part of the old NIC which cooperated with the scheme. Bitterness between the two groups was intense and leaders from each camp attacked the other in the newspapers. This may have influenced the *Indian Opinion* to view the revival of the Maha Sabha with suspicion.

The Maha Sabha held its third South African Hindu Conference at the Durban Town Hall on 27 May 1934. The conference attracted delegates from 62 institutions from Natal, the Cape and the Transvaal, which was the highest up to that point. One factor that ensured a large turnout was the presence of the two visiting Hindu missionaries whose countrywide lectures had proved extremely popular. The widely travelled and highly experienced Pandit Mehta Jaimini was invited to South Africa to preside at the conference, while Swami Adhyananda gave the opening address. Despite opposition from some quarters, there was broad support for the conference.

In spite of the enthusiasm shown during the visit of the two missionaries and especially during the conference, the Maha Sabha once again fell into dormancy shortly after the departure of the two missionaries the following year. One possible reason for this was that in South Africa at that time the leaders of religious organizations also led secular political organizations. The 1930s was characterized by political contestations that fractured the political elite and the alignment and realignment of political parties consumed much of the energy of local leaders. The decision of the South African Indian Congress (SAIC) to participate in the colonization scheme resulted in the division of the NIC with the likes of P.R. Pather, S.L. Singh and P.B. Singh amongst those who broke away to form the CBSIA because they rejected the scheme. These individuals were important Hindu leaders and their absence from the Maha Sabha was significant. For example, P.B. Singh, who would become an influential leader in the Maha Sabha, was the CBSIA representative who was sent to India in January 1934 to conduct a study on effects of the repatriation scheme (*Indian Opinion*, 30 March 1934). Those members of the NIC who led the Maha Sabha at this time were preoccupied with political matters. This is hardly surprising and when looking at the Maha Sabha's history it is easy to notice that its leaders were Indian political leaders first, and Hindu religious leaders second.

Subsequently and consequently, the Maha Sabha remained inactive until the arrival of another widely travelled Hindu missionary, Pandit Rishiram in August 1937. He sparked a short-term interest in the activities of the Maha Sabha, as Hindu leaders met to coordinate his lectures. This time however the momentum was maintained. The Maha Sabha faced a few setbacks toward the end of the 1940s, notably a lack of funds. Also crucial was the 1949 Afro-Indian race riots which resulted in 44,738 Indian refugees, which meant that Indian leaders were preoccupied with relief work for months (Vahed 2001: 123).

One consequence was that the fifth Hindu Conference which was originally scheduled for 1949, was postponed. The conference eventually took place from 9 to 11 October 1953 in Durban and attracted 57 affiliated institutions. It dealt with issues such as social services, unity between different Hindu linguistic groups, the advancement of women and religious instruction in primary schools. The conference was characterized by the opening speech given by its secretary S.R. Naidoo, in which he argued that Hinduism was 'under constant attack' in South Africa and that the time had come to implement measures to reverse this trend (*Leader*, 16 October 1953). Given the concern during the 1940s amongst Maha Sabha leaders that Hindus were converting to Christianity in large numbers, this 'constant attack' that S.R. Naidoo referred to was clearly a fear associated with missionaries of other faiths, especially Christianity. The high turnout of affiliated institutions, according to a reporter for the *Leader*, 'animated by a spirit never before evident' and impressed commentators like J.M. Francis who claimed that the conference marked the emergence of 'a rejuvenated and virile organization' (*Leader*, 16 October 1953).

However, other commentators, such as Y.M. Naidoo, were critical that the Maha Sabha was not doing enough for the upliftment of Hindus. As 'the parent organization of the Hindus', Naidoo argued, the organization should 'set a lead to their people'. Naidoo complained that members met only during conferences and national celebrations and that resolutions passed at such meetings were quickly forgotten and rarely implemented. The majority of Hindus in the country, Naidoo added, remained 'ignorant' of their religion

98 KARTHIGASEN GOPALAN

and did 'not know the teachings of Hinduism'. He expressed concern at the large number of Hindus being converted to Christianity, a religion that he specifically identified as 'a challenge to Hinduism' (*Leader*, 16 October 1953).

Naidoo's comments are ironic in the sense that shortly after the conference the Maha Sabha began its most important project to date; approaching the Natal Education Department (NED) to permit Hindu religious instruction at consenting Indian schools throughout the province. This decision became highly contentious and attracted strong criticism from other Indian leaders who feared that it would divide Indian children into 'watertight compartments' and lead to religious sectionalism; it was even referred to by some as 'religious apartheid' (see *Graphic*, 30 January 1955 and 12 March 1955).

Crucial to critics, was the idea of a fragile unity that existed amongst Indians and that had to be preserved especially given the political climate during these years. However, as the Maha Sabha began to explain and reiterate to the public what it meant by 'religious instruction', fears began to subside. In fact, P.R. Pather, who would become the spokesperson of the Maha Sabha's on the matter, opposed the idea when it was addressed at a special conference dedicated exclusively to religious instruction at schools, organized by the Maha Sabha on 23 January 1954 (*Graphic*, 30 January 1955). When it was made clear by proponents of the decision that by religious instruction they meant a general form of Hindu instruction limited to 90 minutes per week taught in English, Pather became a supporter (*Graphic*, 5 March 1955).

It took some time to convince other critics, but their fears revealed the notion that religion could foster division amongst Indians. Some critics were concerned that Hinduism was too diverse and that Hindu instruction would have to be separate for Hindus of different linguistics groups. The fact that the proposed syllabus would be a universal form of Hinduism conducted in English was very important. By the end of March 1955, the NED had agreed to permit this form of instruction at schools that requested it (*Graphic*, 2 April 1955). A Syllabus Committee comprising members of the Maha Sabha and a few Indian teachers was

TRANSNATIONAL HINDU MOVEMENTS

established to draw up the syllabus. Between 17 September 1956 and 28 May 1958, the Syllabus Committee met six times and the draft syllabus was presented to members of the Indian community, including the Natal Indian Teachers Society, for comments and suggestions.[6] The syllabus was finalized in 1958 and by 1959, a number of schools began introducing religious instruction.

THE HINDU PROJECT IN THE CONTEMPORARY PERIOD

One of the key justifications for a body such as the Maha Sabha, was to prevent Hindus converting to other faiths. The fact that the first schools for Indian children in Natal were exclusively Christian mission schools was a special concern and the 'threat' posed by Christian missionaries was repeated whenever Maha Sabha leaders met. Reasons for Hindus converting to other religions is complicated (See Pillay 1994). However, in spite of concerns, statistics reveal that large scale conversions of Hindus to Christianity was not a reality during the formative stages of the Maha Sabha. Between 1921 and 1960, the Hindu population in South Africa increased from 109,163 to 327,783 while the number of Christian Indians increased from 8,716 to 36,620. As a total percentage of the Asiatic population, both groups increased at the expense of a category labelled as 'other' (Oosthuizen 1979: 558). However, in the contemporary period, an increasing number of Hindus are converting. In the 1996 census, Hindus made up 1.4 per cent of South Africa's population. By the time of the 2001 census, that number decreased to 1.22 per cent. A General Household Survey in 2013 indicated that the percentage decreased to one per cent (Schoeman 2017: 2-3).

In spite of the concerns over this trend, Hindu organizations have been ineffective in preventing conversions. In 2018, Ram Maharaj of the South African Hindu Dharma Sabha claimed that

---

[6] Minutes of the South African Hindu Maha Sabha Centenary Conference 1960 available at the Gandhi Luthuli Documentation Centre, University of KwaZulu Natal.

100 KARTHIGASEN GOPALAN

he was going to 'declare war on conversions' which he called 'cancerous'. Working with a Netherlands based organization, the Global Hindu Foundation, his intention was to 'start legal proceedings at the International Court of Human Rights and the UN to seek reparations for the harm which has been 'deliberately inflicted' upon indigenous civilizations in direct contravention of UN resolutions' (*Post*, 9 September 2018).

This prompted the current Maha Sabha president Ashwin Trikamjee to label Maharaj a 'maverick'. Frustrated at the fact that the two organizations are not affiliated, Trikamjee argued that 'despite efforts over the years to unite Hindus, he has steadfastly rebuffed all such attempts and chosen to go his own maverick ways'. Trikamjee added, 'the South African Hindu Maha Sabha has over the years constantly grappled with the challenge of conversions and has followed the path of consolidating Hinduism as opposed to sensationally combating with other religions' (*Post*, 9 September 2018).

The Maha Sabha remains committed in the contemporary period to pursue welfare and religious activities. According to the website of the organization, it has 130 affiliates and 1,500 volunteers. The Maha Sabha has three current projects, Shuddha, to provide a certification for vegetarians to make accurate and informed food choices; the National Council of Hindu Priests to promote standardized practice across South Africa; and Project 108 which has raised money for numerous charitable projects.

CONCLUDING REMARKS

The formation of the Maha Sabha in South Africa in 1912 was significant because it was the first Maha Sabha in the diaspora. This was due entirely to the vision, energy and drive of Swami Shankaranand and the organization faded after his departure. The Maha Sabha in South Africa was different to its counterparts in the diaspora. In British Guyana and Mauritius, the Maha Sabha promoted an orthodox approach to Hinduism (Sanathanism) and provided an alternative to the Arya Samaj (Van Der Veer & Vertovec 1991: 160).

In Guyana, Trinidad and Suriname, Maha Sabhas were also

national organizations dominated by Sanathanists and were, additionally, political organizations 'which represented Hindus to non-Indian communities and government authorities' (Van Der Veer & Vertovec 1991: 161). In Fiji, Arya Samajists formed the Maha Sabha in 1926 and dominated its leadership (Kelly 1991: 5). In 1930, however, a faction was unhappy with the organization's Arya Samaj orientation, broke away (Kelly 1991: 202). The Fiji Maha Sabha remained a political organization that clashed with the Muslim League and Sanathan Dharma (Kelly 1991: 90-1).

The Maha Sabha in South Africa differed from its counterparts in the diaspora in several respects. It was not a political force, it did not create serious tensions between Arya Samajists and followers of the Sanathan Dharma, nor did it create noticeable conflict between Muslims and Hindus. One possible explanation for the difference is that in South Africa Indians constituted an absolute minority, whereas in Fiji and Trinidad they constituted almost half the population and in Mauritius, which lacked an indigenous population, Indians came to constitute an overwhelming majority and were in a position to contest for political control.

South Africa is also different from other colonies that received indentured labour because there were more migrants from South than North India. Both the Arya Samaj and Sanathan Dharma are North Indian movements and had more influence on Hindi-speaking Hindus. South Indian indentured migrants as a percentage of the total indentured population constituted 6.3 per cent in Fiji, 31.9 per cent in Mauritius, and 6.3 per cent in British Guiana (Lal 2006: 46-52). In Natal, South Indians made up 67.9 per cent (Lal 2006: 51). Another difference between South Africa and other diasporic Hindu communities is that whereas there were serious tensions between umbrella 'reformist' and orthodox bodies, it was only in 1941 that a Shri Sanathan Dharma Sabha was established to unite Sanathanists in Natal.

While the Maha Sabha as an organization did not get involved in politics, many of its members did do so in their individual capacities. Bhawani Dayal, a fundamental figure in the history of Hinduism in South Africa in the first half of the twentieth century, publicly criticized the Maha Sabha in India, yet he gave a speech in 1933 as president of the umbrella Arya Samaj body of Natal on the necessity of (re)establishing the Maha Sabha in South Africa. He was confident that the tensions between Muslims and Hindus, so prevalent in India, could not be replicated in South Africa. He argued that a Maha Sabha in South Africa would stick purely to religious, cultural and welfare activities, and not get involved in politics because several political organizations already spoke for Indians. Dayal emphasized the fact that the context in South Africa was radically different to that in India. Dayal wanted to unite Indians, on the one hand, but also unite Hindus specifically. He wanted to unite Indians so that they could resist the discriminatory laws designed to oppress them collectively, and his reason for uniting Hindus was that if they worked together they would be able to preserve their cultural and religious heritage better.

Indians in South Africa constituted a minority and there was little incentive for Hindus to form a political body that excluded Muslims and Christians. The work of Gandhi in promoting 'Indianness' is also important (see Desai & Vahed 2019: 121-45). While many individuals in the Maha Sabha were part of secular political associations, they did not use the Maha Sabha as a platform to voice political differences. Most leaders of the Maha Sabha leaders were involved in a multitude of community organizations. This included secular, political, welfare, sporting and religious bodies. At no time did they use the Maha Sabha to voice political concerns. At the same time the Maha Sabha experienced long periods of inactivity throughout its history and was largely unrepresentative of the majority of Hindus who continued to partake in their religious activities independently of it.

REFERENCES

Agrawal, Lion M.G. (2008). *Freedom Fighters of India*. Delhi: ISHA Books.

Bhana, Surendra (1991). *Indentured Indian Emigrants to Natal, 1860-1902: A Study Based on Ships' Lists*. New Delhi: Promilla & Co.

Bhana, Surendra and Goolam Vahed (2005). *The Making of a Social Reformer: Gandhi in South Africa, 1893-1914*. New Delhi: Manohar.

Bista, Veer D. (1992). 'A Brief Biography', in R. Rambilas (ed.), *Karma Yogi: Swami Bhawani Dayal Sanyasi*. South Africa, Durban: Arya Pratinidhi Sabha: pp. 5-26.

Chetty, Surykanthi (1999). 'The Creation of South African Indian Identity in Relation to Hinduism' (B.A. Hons. dissertation, University of KwaZulu Natal).

Dalmia, Vasudha D. and Heinrich Von Stietencron (eds.) (1995). *Representing Hinduism. The Constructions of Religious Traditions and National Identity*. New Delhi: Sage.

Dayal, Bhawani and B. Chaturvedi (1951). *A Report on the Emigrants Repatriated to India under the Assisted Emigration Scheme from South Africa, an Independent Study*. Published by Bhawani Dayal and B. Chaturvedi.

Desai, Ashwin and G. Vahed (2019). *A History of the Present: Indians in Post-Apartheid South Africa, 1994-2019*. New Delhi: Oxford University Press.

—— (2010). *Inside Indian Indenture: A South African Story, 1860-1914*. Cape Town: Human Sciences Research Council (HSRC) Press.

Frykenberg, Robert (1997). 'The Emergence of Modern "Hinduism" as a Concept and as an Institution: A Reappraisal with Special Reference to South India', in G.D. Sontheimer and H. Kulke (eds.), *Hinduism Reconsidered*. New Delhi: Manohar: pp. 82-110.

Hall, Stuart (1922). 'Introduction: Identity in Question', in S. Hall, Held D. and McGrew T. (eds.), *Modernity and Its Futures*. Cambridge: Polity Press: pp. 274-9.

Hardy, Friedhelm (1995). 'A Radical Reassessment of the Vedic Heritage-The Acaryahrdayam and Its Wider Implications', in Dalmia and Von Stietencron (eds.), *Representing Hinduism: The Construction of Religious Traditions*. New Delhi: Sage: pp. 35-50.

Huntington, Samuel P. (1993). 'The Clash of Civilisations?', *Foreign Affairs*, 72(3): pp. 22-49.

Kelly, John D. (1991). *A Politics of Virtue*. Chicago: University of Chicago Press.

Kuppusami, C. (1993). *Tamil Culture in South Africa*. Durban: Rapid Graphic.

Lal, Brij V. (2006). 'The Indenture System', in Brij V. Lal (ed.), *The Encyclopaedia of the Indian Diaspora*. Singapore: Editions Didier Millet: pp. 46-52.

Lalla, B.D. (1960). 'A review of the work of the South African Hindu Maha Sabha', in R.S. Nowbath, S. Chotai and B.D. Lalla (eds.), *The Hindu Heritage in South Africa*. Durban: The South African Hindu Maha Sabha: pp. 107-11.

Mesthrie, Dhupelia Uma (2002). 'The Passenger Indian as Worker: Indian

Immigrants in Cape Town in the Early Twentieth Century', *African Studies*, 68(1): pp. 111-34.

—— (1985). 'The Cape Town agreement and its effects upon Natal Indian Politics, 1927-34', paper presented at the conference of History of Natal and Zululand, University of Natal, Durban.

Mishra, Pankaj (2006). *Temptations of the West: How to be Modern in India, Pakistan and Beyond.* London: Picador.

Naidoo, Thillayvel (1992). *The Arya Samaj Movement in South Africa.* Delhi: Motilal Banarsidass.

O' Hagan, Jacinta (1995). 'Civilisation Conflict: Looking for a Cultural Enemy', *Third World Quarterly*, 16(1): pp. 5-18.

Oosthuizen, Gerhardus C. (1975). *Pentecostal Penetration into the Indian Community in Metropolitan Durban, South Africa.* Durban, University of Durban-Westville: Human Sciences Research Council.

Pennington, Brian K. (2005). *Was Hinduism Invented?: Britons, Indians, and the Colonial Construction of Religion.* New York: Oxford University Press.

Pillay, Gerald (1994). *Religion at the Limits? Pentecostalism among Indian South Africa.* Pretoria: University of South Africa.

Singh, Bawa C. (1871). *Life and Teachings of Swami Dayananda.* New Delhi: Jan Gyan Prakashan.

Schoeman, Willem J. (2017). 'South African religious demography: The 2013 General Household Survey', *HTS Teologiese Studies/Theological Studies*, 73(2): pp. 1-7.

Sugirtharajah, Sharada (2003). *Imagining Hinduism: A Postcolonial Perspective.* London: Routledge.

Swan, Maureen (1985). *Gandhi: A South African Experience.* Johannesburg: Ravan Press.

Tarock, Adam (1993). 'Civilisation Conflict? Fighting the Enemy under a New Banner', *Third World Quarterly*, 16(1): pp. 5-18.

Vahed, Goolam (2002). 'Constructions of Community and Identity among Indians in Colonial Natal, 1860-1910: The Role of the Muharram Festival', *Journal of African History*, 43(1): pp. 77-93.

—— (1997). 'Swami Shankeranand and the Consolidation of Hinduism in Natal, 1908-1914', *Journal for the Study of Religion*, 10(2): pp. 3-34.

van der Veer, Peter and Vertovec, Steven (1991). 'Brahmanism Abroad: On Caribbean Hinduism as an Ethnic Religion', *Ethnology*, 30(2): pp. 149-66.

CHAPTER 4

Pivotal Developments on Hinduism in Fiji[1]

PRASHNEEL R. GOUNDAR

INTRODUCTION

The total population of Fiji is estimated at around 900,000. According to a census of 2007, 64 per cent of the population was Christians, 28 per cent Hindus and 6 per cent Muslims (Fiji US Embassy, 2017: para. 1). In building and shaping of Fiji, the contributions of Hindus cannot be ignored. They have always taken a step forward in ensuring that their skills, knowledge and experiences are put in best practice for the country. Our forefathers ensured that the practice of Hinduism continued from the very beginning; so, they built temples all around Fiji as well as established schools. Various religious organizations were founded to continue the vision of the people; these included The India Sanmarga Ikya (TISI) Sangam,

[1] The author would like to thank his colleague Ravnil Narayan, a Lecturer in Communications at the Fiji National University for proofreading the manuscript and providing invaluable suggestions. Mr. Narayan also assisted in verifying information related to the Arya Samaj funeral rituals. In addition, the author wishes to acknowledge Nihaal Krishnan Pillay for providing original photographs and advice. A special mention is extended to Dr. Farzana Gounder, Deputy Head of School (Research) at IPU New Zealand Tertiary Institute for offering the author an opportunity to contribute a chapter in this edited volume. The author is extremely grateful to Donal Chand, Sumeet Vishal Pillay and Dikesh Deo for the original photographs. Finally, he is thankful to the two anonymous reviewers for polishing and providing suggestions on improving the manuscript.

Arya Pratinidhi Sabha of Fiji, Fiji Sikh Society, Gujarat Society, and Sanatan Dharam Pratinidhi Sabha. More recently, the International Society for Krishna Consciousness (ISKCON) has gained many followers after having temples in Lautoka, Suva and Sigatoka.

First, the Arya Samaj, was founded in Bombay India in April 1875 by Swami Dayanand Saraswati, was established in Suva, Fiji, on 25 December 1904 by the indentured labourers. They were determined to maintain their faith, culture and traditions, including the strong desire to learn and educate their people, in the face of social hardships of *Girmit*. They started by holding evening classes for adults to learn Hindi. Later they started day programmes for both boys and girls. The efforts of Arya Samaj met with strong opposition from the colonial administration, but it did not deter their action (Arya Pratinidhi Sabha of Fiji, n.d.: para. 2). The Arya Samaj was registered as Arya Pratinidhi Sabha of Fiji in 1918 and soon after that it built its first school Gurukul Primary School in 1918, in Lautoka, to cater for education for all. Now there are several primary and secondary schools operated by the Sabha and institutions of higher learning including the University of Fiji. The headquarters of the Sabha is at No. 1 Ono Street, Samabula, Suva (Arya Pratinidhi Sabha of Fiji, n.d.: para. 1).

Shree Sanatan Dharam Pratinidhi Sabha of Fiji is one of the largest Hindu organizations and includes over 180,000 Hindus in Fiji. The vision of the Sanatan Fiji is to be always a democratic religious, educational, cultural and charitable Hindus organization in Fiji. Its values are to preserve, promote and safeguard the spiritual, social, economic and educational interests of Sanatan Fiji. Many Sanatan schools are operating in Fiji. Their head office is at 1 Kikau Street, Samabula, Suva (Sanatan Dharam Pratinidhi Sabha of Fiji, n.d.: para. 2).

The India Sanmarga Ikya Sangam or TISI Sangam was founded in Fiji in 1926 by Sadhu Kuppuswami, an ex-indentured labourer who inspired South Indians to form an organization to promote their language and culture. It is a very dynamic, religious organization in Fiji playing a very vital role in the social, cultural and educational development of the country as a whole. Sangam operates several primary and secondary schools including a Sangam Institute

PIVOTAL DEVELOPMENTS ON HINDUISM IN FIJI 107

of Technology, and College of Nursing and Health Care Education. The head office of Sangam is at Park Street, Vonovou Lane, Nadi (Sangam Fiji, n.d.: para. 2).

Needless to say, other religious organizations, namely, Christians, Muslims and others, have also concentrated on education and made a considerable contribution to education in Fiji through the many educational institutions started by them.

HIGHLIGHTS ON IMPORTANT *POOJAS* AND FESTIVALS

If someone takes a drive along the Queen's and King's highways in Fiji, they will encounter various temples dedicated to different gods. However, this is the same, even in the most remote places in Fiji. Wherever Hindus have settled in the country, they have built temples and schools (Nandan 2001). For many of them, Tuesday is the day when, in the evenings they either visit temples or gather in small groups called *mandalis* for the recitation of the epic *Ramayana*, after which they sing *bhajans* and *kirtans* in the name of God.

The temples are more vibrant during the Ram Navmi and Sri Krishna Janmashtami. Ram Navmi is a nine-day festival to celebrate the birth of Lord Rama, and Janmashtami is an eight-day festival to commemorate the birth of Lord Sri Krishna. These are very auspicious festivals for Hindus in Fiji.

Even though there are no public holidays designated for these occasions, employees can request a day off from their employers. In primary and high schools, these events are celebrated with many energetic performances from the students, sweets are distributed, and Hindu schools are closed on these days.

TISI Sangam has one of the highest numbers of temples that they fund and operate. The largest temple in the southern hemisphere is in Nadi, Fiji, the Sri Subramaniam Temple. The set-up is very simple, but the sculptures are eye catching, and in a peaceful environment. Visits can be made by arrangement (Sangam Fiji, n.d.: para. 2). They have their annual *taipusam pooja* during which a firewalking ceremony is held. In other temples where firewalking

Figure 4.1: An evening *kirtan* recitation taking place
© Donal Chand, 2020.

is not done, other forms of *poojas* take place. For example, some devotees put small tridents in their body (see Figure 4.2) to seek blessings. Firewalking takes place in the early hours of the morning around 5 a.m. in many temples and for some it is done around 3 p.m. in the afternoons. The fire is lit on a Friday morning with massive logs and a special ceremony is held followed by firewalking on a Sunday. These individuals need to go through various forms of austerities before the tridents, or the firewalking takes place.

The austerities include being vegetarian for at least 21 days, not using foul language, not consuming alcohol or smoking, as well as avoiding sex during this designated period. If they get hurt when performing the firewalking or putting tridents in their body, that implies they did not conduct themselves faithfully during the 21-day period.

The South Indians have other major *poojas* such as the *patraasi pooja* that takes place during September to October. The devotees from the temples go around on the allocated days and perform *pooja* at homes of the residents in that area and collect oil for the lamp that would be lit in the temple.

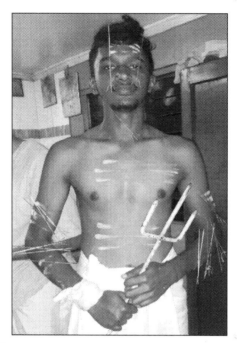

Figure 4.2: A devotee with tridents on his body to
fulfil his vow to the demigod
© Nihaal Pillay, 2020.

For the other Hindu denominations such as the Gujaratis, Navratri, the worship of Goddess Durga for nine days is essential. In the nights, they perform a traditional dance known as *dandiya*.

This particular dance form is performed using sticks specifically designed for it. This is a colourful occasion and one can expect to see people of all ages dressed in unique bright clothing.

Holi is another colourful festival that is celebrated in the month of March every year. Followers of Arya Samaj believe that Holi is celebrated to welcome the arrival of the new crop into the home and has its beginning in India where there are two seasonal crops harvested at the time of Holi and another at the time of Diwali. However, Sanatanis believe the traditional view which embraces the story of Holika and Prahalad. Be that as it may, in Fiji every Hindu celebrates Holi with great joy and happiness.

Figure 4.3: Hindus celebrating Holi with colours
© Dikesh Deo, 2020.

This is generally a festival for the North Indian community, but in recent years, all Hindus take part in it. *Chautaal* is sung during this festival by the various *mandalis*. A night before the festival, a great fire is lit and is recognized as the burning of Holika. On the day of Holi, the people go from house to house singing the *chautaal* with loud music and playing with *rang* (colours).

Along with these festivals, there is also a *pooja* which started in the last decade of Lord Ganesha, the Ganesh Chaturthi. It is celebrated in August/September and marks the birth of Lord Ganesh. This is celebrated primarily in temples and attracts a huge crowd for a week long event. Previously, the statue of the lord was made from plastic or brass, but due to climate change, environment-friendly statues are being made. Usually, it is made from clay as on the last day it needs to be disposed of in the sea. Thus, having an eco-friendly statue would not affect the ocean.

Raksha Bandhan, the bond between a brother and sister, is also a pivotal event for Hindus in Fiji. Each year it is commemorated in August. The sister ties a *rakhi* on the right hand of the brother(s)

Figure 4.4: Singing of *chautaal* during the Holi celebrations
© Dikesh Deo, 2020.

to seek their blessings and protection. Gifts are also exchanged, and sweets are an integral part of this festival.

Finally, the most awaited festival in the Hindu calendar is Diwali or Deepawali. Towards the end of October or early November, the preparations for this festival start. A lot of cleaning takes place at individual houses and the community. Preparation for the celebration begins in advance, especially the preparation of sweets and decorations. A lot of people take time in purchasing lights of various types but must light *diyas* (oil lamps) made from clays. The proper way to light these *diyas* is to use ghee because when ghee burns, it purifies the environment. However, the use of candles is more common these days.

Hindus in Fiji celebrate this festival to mark the triumph of good over evil with the return of Lord Rama from fourteen years of exile. However, Arya Samajis believe that Diwali which has its origins in India is celebrated to mark the harvesting of crops whereas Sanatanis believe that it signifies joy on the return of Lord Rama from exile. Whatever the reason, it is very pleasing to see everyone celebrating together during Diwali. The purpose is to go away from darkness and allow the light to prevail in our lives. Thus, in the nights, the *diyas* and candles are lit followed by fireworks. A special *pooja* of goddess Lakshmi takes place in the evening and it is believed that if there is darkness or if the doors and gates are closed then the goddess will not enter that house. Lakshmi is the goddess responsible for wealth and prosperity, therefore it is considered bad luck if the house is left in darkness.

The most essential characteristics of Holi and Diwali are the socialization of people and removal of all forms of jealousy, hatred and ill feelings. During Holi, the use of colours gives a feeling of togetherness and unity when everyone shares the same colours. On the other hand, the lighting of *diyas* on the darkest night of the year in Diwali gives a beautiful feeling of internal peace and happiness which cannot be achieved in any other way.

Out of all the Hindu festivals, Diwali is accorded a public holiday and celebrated at workplaces as well as schools with much festivities and merry-making. The women of all races in Fiji wear a *sari* or *salwar kameez* during the Diwali week. The men also dress in *kurtas* which is a traditional shirt. The Hindu community invites their friends, families, along with workmates to their homes to share sweets and savouries. It is such a wonderful experience of multiracial harmony!

LANGUAGE DEBATES

Since Fiji's language nature is complex, the Hindu community uses Fiji Hindi to communicate with each other. Standard Hindi language is an essential tool in a proper and more in-depth understanding of Hindu religious texts. The four Vedas—*Rig, Yajur, Saam* and *Atharva*—are written in Sanskrit and are available with translations in standard Hindi. Thus it is imperative to have some knowledge of Sanskrit as well as a good knowledge of Hindi to understand the meanings of the verses. Furthermore, other holy scriptures such as *Ramayana* and *Geeta* which are available in Hindi, also need a good knowledge of this language to appreciate the message in them fully.

However, mother tongues such as Tamil, Gujarati, standard Hindi and others are still practised. The South Indians have been able to maintain their mother tongue specifically for prayers but not for daily communication. The Gujaratis have been most successful from all of the Indian communities in preserving their language as they practise it at home more than others. Mugler (1996: 276) explains that as early as 1910s Indians in Fiji started their own schools, spurred on by the neglect of the colonial government of their children's education, attested by the 1911 census rates for literacy in any language: 86 per cent for Europeans, 52.8 per cent for Fijians and a paltry 9.4 per cent for Indians. By the 1920s, a substantial number of schools had been set up for Indian children in which standard Hindi and other Indian languages such as Urdu, Tamil, Telugu, and later Gujarati were used as languages of instruction (Mugler 1996: 276). As the colonial government gradually took over control of schools from religious organizations, the use of various vernaculars as languages of instruction decreased (Mugler 1996: 276). This changed the language of instructions to English after the first three years of primary school, according to the 1969 Education Commission Report.

A particular debate that has been an ongoing issue is whether Fiji Hindi or standard Hindi should be followed in schools. Fiji Hindi is a mixture of standard Hindi, English and Fijian words. In fact, Fiji Hindi or Hindustani was originally a mixture of North Indian languages and dialects, as developed by the *girmityas*. There are other dialects of Fiji Hindi such as the one spoken by people in Vanua Levu (the second-largest island in Fiji). This debate has brought about heated arguments, and several studies have been conducted that have outlined that both have specific grammar rules. Scholars such as Subramani and Brij Lal have published widely in favour of Fiji Hindi. Subramani's award-winning novel *Dauka Puran* (2001) was written entirely in the Fiji Hindi language.

Academics argue that Fiji Hindi is appropriate to use at home but not in formal functions such as weddings or funerals. When the Hindi Radio Station, Radio Mirchi from the Fiji Broadcasting Corporation (FBC) started using Fiji Hindi during the daily programmes, rage broke out. Despite the criticism FBC received, the radio station continues to use Fiji Hindi in all of its programmes and the majority of the listeners have approved of this. However, Hindu religious organizations have objected to the use of Fiji Hindi on radio, saying that it will destroy the learning of standard Hindi which is vital for the preservation of Hindu religion and culture. Fiji Hindi is used widely as a medium of verbal communication not only among Hindus but also with other faiths such as Christians and Muslim Girmitiya descendants.

Section 31(3) of the Constitution of the Republic of Fiji states: 'Conversational and contemporary Taukei and Fiji Hindi languages shall be taught as compulsory subjects in all primary schools.' Note that Taukei is the language of the indigenous community of Fiji.

While the above is provided for in the Fiji Constitution, not all schools have started teaching conversational Fiji Hindi. No doubt it will take some time to gain ground.

Shanti Dut is the only surviving Standard Hindi newspaper in Fiji that is published weekly. However, there has been a decline in the readership and the future of this newspaper also looks bleak. It does attract a lot of readers for its Diwali issue with a lot of articles on Hinduism, the importance of Diwali, stories associated with the festival as well as an obituary section that features relatives and loved ones who have departed from this world. It also has competitions as well as new recipes for Diwali sweets and savouries.

WEDDING CUSTOMS

The customs of different Indo-Fijian communities are followed in celebrating weddings and according final rites during funerals. Weddings have always been a grand and elaborate affair. The usual for North Indian weddings is the three 'days' events, which is almost the same for the South Indians. The Sikhs, Arya Samajis and Gujarati have their own traditions that they follow. From the very beginning weddings in Fiji among the Hindu society have gained respect from other ethnic groups as well for their unique practices. The food during the wedding is very popular, especially the *aloo baigan* and *puri*. However, traditional wear for the grooms has changed from *dhoti* to a suit, whereas some prefer to wear a

Figure 4.5: Wedding attire of a South Indian bride and bridegroom
© Sumeet Vishal, 2020.

sherwani suit with a turban. These readymade costumes can be purchased easily from the clothing stores. Not much has changed for the brides apart from individuals designing their own attire.

The main differences between Sanatan and Arya Samaj weddings are as follows:

(a) In an Arya Samaj wedding, on the arrival of the wedding procession (*baraat*) of the groom's party at the place of the bride where the marriage is to take place, the bride's father/guardian and his team welcome the groom's party and invites them to take a seat. The bridegroom is escorted to a special seat near the *mandap* to await the arrival of the bride to the *mandap*. In a Sanatan wedding, on the arrival of the *baraat*, the bride's father/guardian and his team welcome the groom's party and the groom proceeds to participate in *dwaar pooja*, followed by *parchhan* and then the groom moves into the Mandap area where the bride arrives to continue the marriage ceremony.

(b) Once in the Mandap, the bride welcomes the groom by garlanding him in an Arya Samaj wedding. In Sanatan wedding both bride and groom garland each other.

(c) In an Arya Samaj marriage, there are only 4 *bhaawars* (walking around the Hawan fire), and both the bride and the groom walk side by side. In Sanatani weddings, there are 7 *bhaawars* whereas the bride leads in the first four rounds, and the groom leads in the remaining three rounds.

(d) In Arya Samaj practices, *sindoordaan* is done openly in front of those present at the wedding ceremony. In a Sanatani wedding, *sindoordaan* is done privately with their heads covered under a sheet of cloth.

(e) In Arya Samaj weddings, there is no *Taag Paat*. In a Sanatani wedding, *Taag Paat* (pink woollen garland) is placed on the bride by the elder brother of the groom who promises to protect her in times of need.

There has been a change in the traditional way of having the legal marriage in the registrar's office and then going out for lunch. Many families now have a grand celebration of the legal marriage at their homes, usually at the bride's place and an engagement party follows this. Some couples have introduced photography as an integral feature during their new journey. They prefer to have a pre-wedding or engagement photo shoot, the wedding day photography and finally post-wedding photography. This concept has been taken from Bollywood. Even though some admire it, it diverts from the Hindu concept of not valuing material elements. Having excessive pride is also a cause for one's downfall. Therefore, this act should not be encouraged.

Religious marriages are still widespread. However, the legality of the marriage has to follow the following system:

(a) The bride and groom can get legally married in the Marriage Registry and then have the traditional marriage ceremony conducted publicly, where families and friends are invited to be witness to the marriage ceremony conducted by a Pundit of their faith.

PIVOTAL DEVELOPMENTS ON HINDUISM IN FIJI 117

(b) The other option is for the bride and the groom to obtain a Special Licence to marry from the Marriage Registry and then be legally married at a traditional wedding ceremony by a Pundit who is a registered marriage officer, and issues a marriage certificate which is then registered at the Marriage Registry.

After the wedding, it is generally a practice that parties take place at the groom's residence with a lot of dancing and drinking, accompanied by meat eating. Over the years, people have adopted the concept of a musical orchestra or a special dancing group that performs on such occasions. This has also become a big business industry as well as a mandatory entertainment medium for the middle class and elite Hindus in Fiji. If one turns to the kind of weddings that are more popular, then it would have to be love marriages over arranged marriages. Within the last three decades, people have moved away from arranged marriages. The youth have been given a lot of freedom to find their own life partners. The majority of couples find each other during their university education or when they commence work. This does not imply that arranged marriages are uncommon. A large number of Fiji Indian diaspora, mainly from Australia, New Zealand, America and Canada, return to Fiji to get married to someone selected by their relatives. The Fijian diaspora still values the upbringing of children in Fiji, the way they have embraced the culture and the importance they give to traditions.

Marriages between North Indians and South Indians were not admired previously, but today they are prevalent. This can be attributed to the concept of love marriage explained earlier in this article. There have been cases of disputes between families because their children chose a life partner from another caste. The conflicts have resulted in complete ignorance of their existence, no talks between families and so on. In some situations, this has been resolved by the birth of the grandchildren and others after long peace talks. More marriages between Hindus and Muslims, Indian and Native Fijians, as well as Indians and other Pacific Islanders, are becoming usual practice too. Acceptance into their family then becomes an issue. Sometimes they are welcomed in Hindu families wholeheartedly, but at times they are subject to discrimination which leads to divorces too.

One thing that does not exist in Fiji is the concept of dowry. Perhaps in other Indian diasporas this practice may still be prevalent; however, in Fiji, it has long disappeared. Parents of the bride do give things happily at the weddings of their daughters, but it is not a compulsory affair. It is more to do with the willingness of parents rather than as a requirement.

FUNERAL CUSTOMS

For Hindus, death is not the end of the journey of 'life', unlike other religions. In Hinduism, the concept of heaven and hell is just a fraction of reality. The eternal abode is where everyone aims to go after the soul departs from the material body. Two kinds of the funeral are held by Hindus in Fiji: either they are cremated, which is in most cases especially with North and South Indians, or some choose to be buried. South Indian funeral ceremonies take more time as they have several *saang-yam* or rituals to perform on that day. Almost everyone uses a coffin instead of a traditional plank made from bamboo to carry the loved ones. These days, Fiji has several funeral directors or companies which operate and cover the needs of the grieving families. Some also provide free services whilst others offer free transportation, from the morgue to the home then to the cemetery, on the purchase of a coffin from their company. South Indians have *dhapla* and *shehnai* that accompany the funeral procession from the house to the cemetery. In the last decade, the central division, that is Suva in Fiji has introduced a modern cremation furnace that is operated by Dignified Cremations Limited.

For the North Indians, a thirteen-day mourning period is observed from the day of the cremation. On the tenth day, the *mundan* or shaving of the head takes place. This is done by immediate male members of the deceased such as the son, husband, father or brother. For the South Indians, there is a period of sixteen days of mourning beginning from the day of the death, unlike the North Indians. *Mundan* takes place on the final day, which is the sixteenth day.

PIVOTAL DEVELOPMENTS ON HINDUISM IN FIJI 119

During the evening the *Bhagavad Gita* is read, and *bhajans* or *kirtans* are also performed.

On the other hand, for the Arya Samajis, the death ritual lasts for three days only. From the day when the deceased is cremated till the last day, Hawan Yajis are performed daily, and Vedic *mantras* are recited from the special prayer book, followed by *bhajans* and discourse on life and death from the Vedas. The Yaj is performed for purification of the environment upon death to bring about peace to the family of the departed soul. Arya Samaj does not have any idols as it does not believe in idol worship. The three-day prayer ceremony brings an end to the ritual, and there is no other activity carried out in respect to the departed soul.

A typical drink during the evening mourning period is *kava*. It is a traditional Fijian drink. Even though it is expensive, as 1 kg would cost close to 150 to 200 Fijian dollars, people believe having *kava* will keep the crowd entertained. Not to put that without the *kava* there will not be any audience, but the reality is that from the very beginning this tradition became a norm and it is expected that the grieving families will provide this drink.

For North Indian families, they have two grand *poojas* after the thirteen days of mourning. One is the *pooja* after six months called *chhamaasi* and the annual one, which is called *saleena*. On the other hand, South Indians have a *pooja* after three months called *teen maina* followed by the yearly *pooja* done a month before the one year death anniversary. The departed cannot be forgotten easily, and their memories live forever, but they say time heals even the deepest of wounds. Hindus in Fiji believe that after the annual *pooja*, the pain gets lighter. Many families have observed that during the one year of mourning, they see the deceased in their dreams continuously. However, after the final *pooja* at the one-year anniversary is over, they rarely come in the dreams or in thoughts as they would have reached the gates of God.

CONFERENCES ON HINDUISM

In the last decades a series of conferences dedicated to Hinduism was started. This particular conference is organized annually by Vishva Hindu Parishad (Fiji) that highlights the achievements by Hindus in Fiji and how they have contributed to the progress of the nation. Apart from this, there are seminars organized mostly by ISKCON that are advertised in the newspapers as well as the social media. Universities also have seminars from time to time on relevant topics but not a full-fledged conference like the one conducted by the VHP, Fiji.

It would be better if all religious organizations in Fiji could have a joint conference with a clear agenda that addresses key issues. If a conference is organized during every quarter of the year, it can serve as a reflective exercise and provide evidence of the progress being made as the year unfolds. Some topics that could be included in the conference could consist of youth engagement, community work, writing and publishing, economic contributions of Hindus and many others.

BOOKS AND PUBLICATIONS ON HINDUISM[2]

Fiji has more printing presses than publishing houses. This could be one of the reason for lack of publications on Hinduism. A few people have tried to publish books on Hinduism, but it has been a challenging pathway for them because of the lack of publishing houses in Fiji. In July 2020, Pacific Studies Press published my third book, *Pursuing Divinity in Paradise* which is a reflection on the teachings of the two Hindu epics *Ramayana* and the *Mahabharata*. For Fiji, the book is undoubtedly a first of its kind as it is aimed at engaging individuals to take the path of *dharma* or righteousness.

According to Minakshi Maharaj, the former Head of School of Language & Literature from the Fiji National University:

It might also be observed that this book may be the first that brings human values from a Hindu perspective to the national discourse in Fiji. I congratulate Prashneel Goundar on his perception and subsequent action, which has translated into this small but valuable book. He has done a great service to the community and to his many students by sharing these noble stories, which help to build

[2] As this article concentrates on Hindus in Fiji, it does not have any data about publications from abroad on Hindus and Hinduism.

Figure 4.6: Head of Language & Literature Department at Fiji National University, Dr Mark Hewson launches academic Prashneel Goundar's *Pursuing Divinity in Paradise*
© Prashneel Goundar, 2020.

character and encourage good decision making. This is a great *gyandaan*, the gift of knowledge, and Prashneel earns much merit for writing such a valuable book at such a young age (Goundar 2020: xiv).

Occasionally, discussions on various topics related to Hinduism can be found in the daily newspapers such as *The Fiji Times* and *Fiji Sun*. The bookshops keep a comprehensive collection of essential texts in stock such as the *Bhagavad Gita*, *Ramayana*, Puranas and the different *chalisas*. Specific books on Sri Krishna can be purchased from ISKCON temples all over Fiji. They have a varied selection of volumes on the teachings of Sri Krishna, how to engage in spiritual life, vegetarian cooking, among many others.

The Sri Ramakrishna Mission based in Nadi also sells books on Hinduism, teachings of Swami Vivekananda, Vedanta philosophy as well as on culture. These books are published by the Sri Ramakrishna Math, Madras, in India and distributed to their centres worldwide. The Mission runs Swami Vivekananda College, a prominent high school in Fiji and books are discussed with the students as well as offered for sale once a year.

POLITICAL PARTICIPATION

Several prominent members from the Hindu organizations have been in the political arena either in the capacity as a Member of Parliament or as a Senator. The National Federation Party (one of the longest serving political parties in Fiji) and TISI have always had a long association. Some of its past presidents were in the NFP until recently when the current president of TISI, during the last general elections in 2018 announced that they would stay apolitical and not participate in politics.

While members of Arya Samaj have participated in politics from early days, recently a member of the Arya Pratinidhi Sabha of Fiji was in the senate as well as Member of Parliament under the Fiji Labour Party, until the 2006 coup. Even the Sanatan Dharam Pratinidhi Sabha had its members contest the past elections. However, they were unsuccessful in securing a seat in the Parliament.

In accordance with the 2013 Constitution of the Republic of Fiji, every citizen of Fiji is a Fijian by common and equal citizenry. Hence there is no representation by race or religion in Parliament. Voting is on the principle of one man one vote and anyone, of whichever faith, who qualifies may stand for election. In the last general elections, some candidates subscribed to Hindu religions, however, no Hindu organization formed a political party.

THE BUSINESS SECTOR

Hindus run a large number of business houses in Fiji. The way they have established their entities constitutes a story of its own which is recorded in their own histories. Also these are internationally acclaimed brands, for example, Tappoos, which is one of the largest suppliers of duty free items and a popular name for tourists.

PIVOTAL DEVELOPMENTS ON HINDUISM IN FIJI 123

It is run by the Tappoo family that has been providing employment in major towns to people from all races. Another famous tourist store in Fiji is run by the Motibhai Group, Prouds Fiji Limited. They have branches in Nadi, Lautoka, Suva and the international airport at Nadi.

Along with them are the Punjas family who have flour and biscuit factories in Lautoka and Suva. They have also diversified in a wide range of products. A similar enterprise is the Flour Mills of Fiji, again owned by a Hindu family. In terms of hardware chain stores, two major groups have earned a powerful name in the country, Vinod Patel Group and R.C. Manubhai Group. Both these hardware chains have stores around the two main islands in Fiji, Viti Levu and Vanua Levu. During natural disasters or turmoil, these companies have provided donations and relief supplies, especially during the devastating cyclone of Winston in 2016.

Apart from these, Hindus have invested a lot in supermarket chains such as R.B. Patel Supermarkets, Shop N Save Supermarkets as well as movie theatres. Previously there were just a few movie theatres owned mostly by Hindus. Damodar Group Cinemas are the only surviving cinema houses in Fiji with state of the art facilities in their theatres in Nadi, Lautoka, Suva and Labasa. These business houses are a testament not only on how to make money but to invest in the economy and provide thousands of ordinary 'citizens' work. Despite the Covid-19 pandemic, they are still engaging in future projects and continue to serve the country.

COVID-19 RELIEF WORKS

The year 2020 will remain memorable for the whole world for one of the biggest reasons in the history of the twenty-first century. The global pandemic Covid-19 has changed the way things are done or lives are lived. It has had a drastic impact on everyone, on their livelihood, especially in the tourism industry for Fiji. This ripple effect has been felt on education, transportation, postal and health services, employment as well as the Gross Domestic Product (GDP) of the nation.

Figure 4.7: A devotee prays at the ISKCON Sigatoka Temple
© Prashneel Goundar, 2020.

According to media reports, the Fijian economy faced a contraction of approximately 20 per cent in 2020, primarily attributed to a sharp decline in tourism, which also had direct repercussions on other sectors of the economy (Xinhua 2020).

To assist the parents and families of the school students, several organizations have come forward. The most significant assistance provided by the Hindu community has been to provide lunch to the students. For example, TISI provides lunch to more than 7,000 students in their schools for three days in a week with an investment of FJD $160,000 in the first eight weeks alone (Hirst-Tuilau 2020). They have been the first to come up with this initiative which has not only been applauded by the country, it has also been replicated by other religious as well as charity organizations. The Sanatan Dharam Pratinidhi Sabha of Fiji has been serving meals to students in 117 schools under their administration, aiding approximately 70,000 students since July this year (Kumar 2020, para. 3).

In their efforts to assist with the Covid-19 pandemic, ISKCON organizes free food distribution on Saturdays in various centres

PIVOTAL DEVELOPMENTS ON HINDUISM IN FIJI   125

spread throughout the country. The food is prepared by the devotees and placed in either the restaurants run by them or in the main towns for collection by individuals.

These are non-governmental organizations who have adopted and embraced the concept of 'service for humanity' that they continue to provide assistance wherever possible, to whoever is in need, irrespective of their race or religion. Some also provide grocery packs for families affected by Covid-19, while others have been offering counselling services as well.

CHALLENGES AND ISSUES TO CONSIDER

In order to maintain the Hindu community in Fiji, there are several key challenges that need to be addressed. Firstly, the biggest challenge for all Hindu organizations is engaging the youth in taking an interest in their activities and preserving the culture. A factor that has impacted the youth is Westernization, which has damaged the connection individuals have with their religion. Whether it comes to dressing style or reading scriptures, there is usually a pessimistic view that the youth demonstrate. The religious texts that are in Hindi can be read only by a minimal percentage of the population under 30 years of age. The reason is that only a handful of 'students' study Hindi in schools and generally parents do not encourage their children to take Hindi as a subject because they claim that studying Hindi will not provide them with employment (Goundar & Prasad 2017: 267). Then, it becomes difficult for them to translate or interpret the scriptures and they prefer English over Hindi.

The Western concepts are taking over the mindset of the youth in terms of their beliefs. For example, marriage is a very sacred bond and in Hinduism there is no concept of dating. This cannot be avoided in the modern era, but it is also important to be faithful in the process. Every second person one meets goes through heartbreak because while they were dating either someone cheated or they had continuous arguments on petty matters. Religion, especially the *Bhagavad Gita* teaches one to have control over temporary and material things as well as objects. This is precisely what the youth are unable to comprehend, and for them, it is easier to end a relationship rather than find possible solutions to join them in marriage. The long-term solution to this problem is to ensure that the boy and girl have similar qualities such as in education, personal characteristics, likes and dislikes, religious belief and so on before they agree to the marriage. Furthermore, the would-be partners must be well informed in advance as to the reason for marriage, namely, while procreation is important, it is equally important to experience the difficulties of married life on this earth so as to encourage them to aim to achieve *moksha*. This will reduce disputes in real life somewhat.

The younger generation has quickly adopted the same Western concept of live-in-relationships or sex before marriage. Even before legal marriage, many couples choose to live together without a Hindu marriage. However, the concept of live-in-relationships or engaging in sex can take place only after marriage and that too for procreation and not pleasure. The union of a man and woman in Hinduism is not for mere pleasure; it is to bring forward children into this world. Therefore, the act of live-in-relationships prior to marriage should be strongly condemned. A point worth noting is how comfortable the different organizations are in discussing such topics in various forums or during religious gatherings. Is the Hindu community willing to see more broken relations and marriages by not articulating on this issue? This needs to be taken up by organizations as well as families to protect the present generation in deviating from principles of Hinduism.

There is a need for people to pay greater attention to their health, especially at a young age. Lifestyle diseases such as diabetes, heart problems and other health issues are common, particularly in the Hindu community. While statistics are not readily available, it is known through observation that many youth of today take intoxicants such as liquor, *kava*, smoking and engage in unnecessary sexual activity, which are all harmful to the body. From media reports, it has also been noted that most of the suicides are committed by Fiji Indians.

Next is the issue of migration. Many people have been migrating to neighbouring countries of Fijis like Australia, New Zealand and Canada as well as America since the first coup in 1987. This has given rise to families encouraging their children to complete their

PIVOTAL DEVELOPMENTS ON HINDUISM IN FIJI 127

higher education in Fiji, then apply to settle abroad. One might see this as no issue; however, a closer look will reveal the long term effect. Those who migrate, leave behind the religious organizations that they belonged to or the places of worship their children were part of. Once they have moved abroad, they enrol their children in institutions in the country of adoption to learn Indian musical instruments, Hindi or classical Indian dances at astronomical fees. Yes, they are maintaining their culture abroad, but in pursuit of a better life, they have left a wound in the citizens who remain here as they get demotivated to continue. How can this issue be tackled? Covid-19 has already shown that Fiji is a safer country compared to many developed countries as it has been able to maintain minimal cases or spread of the virus in the community. Fiji has had 34 cases of Corona Virus to date, with only one death until the end of October 2020. Perhaps this will draw Hindus in Fiji to reconsider moving abroad.

Another factor affecting the Hindu community is social media. It has clearly taken over the lives of people. Nothing is a private affair any more, everything has to be advertised; be it weddings, birthdays even funerals. This, in turn, gives room for egotism and the culture of vanity. They have become so engrossed in uploading photographs and information about themselves that they have forgotten the real purpose of life. They need to go away from vanity and realize the ultimate goal of finding spiritual enlightenment in this temporary life and finally achieving *moksha* or freedom from the cycle of birth and death. Instead of trying to compare themselves with what others are achieving in their lives, there should be an objective to pursue their own talents meaningfully. There is also a new trend in Fiji where those who preach religious teachings during the Hindu *poojas*, do live streaming through video coverage using Facebook. In their pursuit of looking perfect or constantly checking their phone screens for their appearance, they often lose sight of conveying the true message from religious books to the audience.

Further, the issue of alcohol and sexual abuse is increasing daily too. There have been many cases reported of child sexual abuse; this included culprits of up to 80 years and victims who are children as young as 12 months old.

As an example of the gravity of the situation, it was reported in the media that out of the 87 sexual offences by Fiji citizens of all ages, recorded in June 2019, 50 were rape cases (RNZ 2019, para. 2).This is a grave concern for all in Fiji. Hindus need to prepare their children better to ensure that these kinds of social problems do not occur. Alcohol has been reported as a significant contributor to domestic violence and broken families. Leaders need to address this situation and provide necessary guidance and teachings before it escalates even further. Perhaps more community outreach should be planned, and discussion at the temples and schools run by the different Hindu organizations could take charge of this task.

CONCLUDING REMARKS

The legacy left by the Girmitiyas in Fiji continues to this very day by the followers of the Hindu faith. It is the good fortune of scholars along with ordinary citizens that the editors of this volume decided to include a article from Fiji to discuss Hinduism. This article has touched upon some significant developments that have taken place since the arrival of the indentured labourers from India more than 140 years ago. Concerning the Covid-19 pandemic, the write-up has highlighted the kind of work that is being done by the Hindus in Fiji.

The article has also suggested some future directions for the The India Sanmarga Ikya (TISI) Sangam, Arya Pratinidhi Sabha, Fiji Sikh Society, Gujarat Society, Sanatan Dharam Pratinidhi Sabha and the International Society for Krishna Consciousness (ISKCON) to address these with its members. Still, the issues are not limited to them only but also extends to individual families to consider.

Finally, Hindus have a lot to offer outside their communities, whenever an opportunity is extended to them; they should not shy away from being heard. They ought to take the opportunity to voice out the philosophical teachings of Hinduism to the wider audience in the world. That will empower future generations to be bold enough to combat any discrimination and ensure that the legacy lives on forever.

PIVOTAL DEVELOPMENTS ON HINDUISM IN FIJI   129

GLOSSARY

Aloobaigan	potato and eggplant curry famous during Indian weddings in Fiji
Bhagavad Gita	one of the most sacred religious texts for Hindus
Bhajan	a religious song
Chhamaasi	term used for the six month prayers conducted after the death of a loved one in the North Indian families
Chautaal	these are songs sung during the period of *Holi* festival
Dhapla	is a musical instrument, similar to the drum but made from goat skin that can be easily carried in one hand and played using two sticks
Diya	is made from clay soil, is an oil lamp (use *ghee* to light up in preference to oil)
Girmitiyas	are the indentured labourers who went to different parts of the world to serve under the British indenture system
Girmit	this refers to the contract (agreement) signed by the indentured labourers from India
Gyaandaan	gift of knowledge
Havankund	a hollow square receptacle usually made of copper used for lighting fire to perform Hawan Yaj
Hawan Yaj	oblations that are offered in a *havankund* with mantras from Vedas recited during death ceremonies or other occasions
Holi	is the festival that celebrates good triumphs over evil. The story associated with this festival is that of Lord Prahlada. Other reason to celebrate Holi is when the crop is harvested. Celebrated in March.
Janmashtami	is the festival that celebrates the birth of Lord Sri Krishna in August
Kava	traditional Fiji drink, also known as *grog* or *yaqona*

Kirtan	is a religious song that accompanies music with a harmonium, *dhol* and *manjeera.*
Mandali	is a small group of 10 to 20 people who belong to a religious organization
Mantras	verses of prayer from the Vedas
Mundan	shaving of the hair from the head (*mundane sanskar*—ritual of shaving the head)
Patrassipooja	is celebrated by the South Indian community, as prayer to Lord Vishnu, during the month of September for prosperity
Pooja	this is the Hindi term for prayer
Puri	an Indian bread made from flour and fried in oil or ghee
Ram Navmi	is the festival that celebrates the birth of Lord Rama
Saang-yam	these are rituals carried out by South Indians in Fiji during funerals or weddings
Saleena	is the term used to describe the one-year prayer after the death of a loved one in North Indian families
Salwar kameez	traditional Indian wear for males and females, consisting of long shirt and a trousers
Sari	traditional Indian wear for females, consisting of an unstitched drape varying from 15 to 30 feet in length
Shehnai	similar to a trumpet in shape, is an Indian musical instrument (traditionally used at wedding ceremonies)
Sherwani	traditional Indian wear for males. It is a long coat-like garment buttoned to the neck with length usually extending just below the knee
Taipusam	is an annual *pooja* in the South Indian calendar, 2021 date is in January
Teen mahina	term used for the three month prayers conducted after the death of a loved one in the South Indian families

REFERENCES

Arya Samaj (2012). 'Arya Pratinidhi Sabha of Fiji', *Arya Samaj*. Retrieved from http://www.aryasamaj.org.fj/

Fiji US Embassy (2017). *Fiji-International Religious Freedom Report*. United States Department of State: Bureau of Democracy, Human Rights, and Labor. Retrieved from https://fj.usembassy.gov/wp-content/uploads/sites/180/Fiji-Religious-Freedom-Report-2017.pdf

Goundar, Prashneel R. (2020). *Pursuing Divinity in Paradise*. Suva, Fiji: Pacific Studies Press.

Goundar, Prashneel R. and P. Prasad (2017). 'Determinants for the Decline in Hindi Language Students in Fiji National University', *International Journal of Research—Granthaalayah*, 5(8): pp. 267-76. https://doi.org/10.5281/zenodo.890625.

Hirst-Tuilau, Susana (2020). 'TISI Sangam Invests $160,000 in Lunch Packs', *Fiji Sun*, 31 July. Retrieved from https://fijisun.com.fj/2020/07/31/tisi-sangam-invests-160000-in-lunch-packs/

Kumar, Rashika (2020). 'Sanatan Dharam Pratinidhi Sabha to provide meals to students affected by COVID-19 while Arya Pratinidhi Sabha making an assessment', *Fijivillage*, 2 July. Retrieved from: https://www.fijivillage.com/news/Sanatan-Dharm-Pratinidhi-Sabha-to-provide-meals-to-students-affected-by-COVID-19-while-Arya-Pratinidhi-Sabha-making-an-assessment—r8x5f4/

Lal, Brij. V. (1983). *Girmitiyas: the origins of the Fiji Indians*. Canberra: Journal of Pacific History.

Mugler, France and J. Lynch (1996). *Language and Education in the Pacific*. Suva, The University of South Pacific: Institute of Pacific Studies.

Nandan, Satendra P. (2001). *Requiem for a Rainbow: a Fijian Indian Story*. Canberra, Australian Capital Territory: Pacific Indian Publications.

Radio New Zealand Pacific (RNZI) (2019). 'Rape tops sexual offence stats in Fiji', *RNZI*. New Zealand, Wellington, 4 June. Retrieved from https://www.rnz.co.nz/international/pacific-news/391202/rape-tops-sexual-offence-stats-in-fiji.

Sanatan Dharam Pratinidhi Sabha of Fiji. (n.d). 'Brief Background Information', *Sanatan Dharam Pratinidhi Sabha of Fiji*. Retrieved from http://sanatanfiji.com/about-us/brief-background-information/

Sangam Fiji. (n.d). Retrieved from https://sangamfiji.com.fj/contact-us/

Xinhua (2020). 'Fijian economy expected to contract severely in 2020 mainly due to poor tourism activity', *Xinhua Net*, 30 June. Retrieved from http://www.xinhuanet.com/english/2020-06/30/c_139178034.html.

CHAPTER 5

The Impact of the Ārya Samāj on Caribbean Hinduism

FREEK L. BAKKER

INTRODUCTION

In the Caribbean, the Ārya Samāj got a larger adherence than in India itself. In the 1980s the movement counted 40,000 followers in Guyana and 29,274 in Suriname. This meant that Ārya Samājīs amounted to 15 per cent of all Hindus in Guyana and 17 per cent of all Hindus in Suriname (Algoe 2016: 75; Serbin 1979: 152; Vernooij 1994: 61). These percentages are much bigger than the share of the Ārya Samājīs in India, where it is a tiny movement. Therefore it is justified to investigate the reasons of this much larger share of the Aryans—as one will call them shortly—in these Caribbean countries. In Trinidad their number is much smaller, about one thousand perhaps.[1] One of the reasons for this low number may be that in Trinidad many more Hindustanis converted to Christianity at the end of the nineteenth century and the beginning of the twentieth century (Niehof & Niehof 1960: 112). The American scholar Richard Huntington Forbes suggests an additional reason: the many conflicts in Ārya Samājīs circles (Forbes 1985: 350-4).

The present article will offer an overview of the history of the Ārya Samāj in Guyana, Suriname and Trinidad. It will pay special

---

[1] Clear numbers are not available, only two vague indications. Forbes estimates their number in Trinidad at less than eight hundred (Forbes 1985, 11-12), which according to others is too low.

134 FREEK L. BAKKER

attention to the reasons why the movement gained so many adherents in this region. Furthermore, it will heed its special contributions to Caribbean Hinduism thus giving this form of the Hindu religion a special flavour in this area.

THE BEGINNINGS

The Ārya Samāj was an association founded by followers of Swāmī Dayānanda Saraswatī (1824-83) in Mumbai in 1875. In the first decades of its existence it became heavily involved in the struggle for the independence of India. Unlike Mahātmā Gāndhī (1869-1948) the movement did not opt for a non-violent fight, it was prepared to use arms. Consequently, members of the Ārya Samāj were arrested and some of them were banned. Being banned meant that some of them were transferred to London (Yadav & Arya 1988: 18-234). In the meantime, the Ārya Samāj sent travelling preachers with the message of Swāmī Dayānanda to countries where many people of Indian origin had settled. One of those persons was Bhāi Parmānand (1876-1947), who visited South Africa, Guyana and Trinidad. He visited the last two countries in 1910. In Guyana he established the first Hindu school. Parmānand was not the only one, however. There were more, the most important of them being Pandit Hariprasad Sharma, who came in 1914, made much effort for opening Hindu schools and for an improvement of the position of women (Forbes 1985: 20-3, 36). There were, moreover, also Aryans among the contract labourers coming from India (Bakker 1999: 100-1).

The message of the Ārya Samāj was attractive to many contract labourers who had travelled abroad from India. This journey had destabilized the caste system, for the people journeying on one ship had to eat from one pot, which in India was strictly forbidden for Brahmins. A second reason was the big shortage of women of Indian origin in the first decades after the start of the immigration. They comprised no more than one quarter to one-third of the new-comers (De Klerk 1998, vol. 2: 117; Myers 1998: 19; Singh 1995: 53-6). Consequently, the marriage system in which it is prescribed to marry only women of the same caste could not be maintained.

THE IMPACT OF THE ĀRYA SAMĀJ ON CARIBBEAN HINDUISM   135

The Ārya Samāj propagated that one's caste was not determined by the caste of one's father but by one's talents. This meant that someone who was a good businessman belonged to the caste of the *vaiśyas* (merchants) and someone who was interested in religious affairs was a Brahmin (Bakker 1999: 25). This offered new opportunities for non-Brahmins to become pandits (priests)—a position formerly restricted to Brahmins only.

The Ārya Samāj also taught monotheism. They said that the ancient Vedas, the oldest scriptures of Hinduism, learned that all gods were no more than divine forms of the one God and that it was not allowed to have images of these gods. This gave the Ārya Samāj the status of a higher form of religion comparable to Christianity and Islam. The Aryans weren't venerators of idols, on the contrary (Bakker 1999: 24-5). The Caribbean countries were dominated by Christianity at the time so this was also a quality making the Aryan religion attractive to the newcomers.

In the third place the Ārya Samāj promoted a better position for women. Many Hindustani women have great respect for Swāmī Dayānand because of his efforts to improve the position of women by giving widows the opportunity to remarry. The Ārya Samāj modified this teaching so far that the association permitted women to remarry (Jordens 1978: 197). This liberated them from the oppression of their in-laws. In addition, Swāmī Dayānand opened schools for girls (Jordens 1981: 26-7). In this respect he was far ahead of many of his Indian compatriots. The involvement of the Ārya Samāj in the struggle for the independence of India also contributed to its popularity and authority.

One of Swāmī Dayānand's most important motifs for his reformation of Hinduism was to counter the inroads of Muslims and Christians in which they succeeded in converting many Hindus to Christianity or Islam. For this reason, Hinduism had to be cleansed from what was added to it in later centuries. 'Back to the Vedas' was Dayānand's great slogan. Yet his view of the message of the Vedas was modified. Although it is true that the Vedas reject the use of images and that the position of women was better in the time of these scriptures, it can be doubted whether his views on the caste system and on education really tally with what is taught

136 FREEK L. BAKKER

in the Vedas. Nonetheless the Aryan preachers found a fertile soil in the hearts of many immigrants. Their appearance led to heavy debates and even fierce conflicts within the Hindu section of the Hindustani newcomers.

THE FIRST SCHOOLS FOR INDIANS

On 6 January 1868 two Christian missionaries, John and Sarah Morton (1839-1912 and 1843-1915), sent by the Canadian Presbyterian Mission, arrived in Trinidad. That same year they founded a school to educate the children of the East Indians in their own language. In 1878, there were already fifteen of these Presbyterian schools on the island. All of them received financial support from the state. In 1891, the number of these state aided schools had grown to 52 (Myers 1998: 111-17). In 1891, another missionary sent by the Canadian Presbyterian Mission, James Basnett Cropper, opened the first mission school for Hindustani children in Guyana. Here also they received education in their own language. In 1912, the country counted 24 of these schools which were also state aided and had more than a thousand pupils (Schalkwijk 2011: 307). The first schools for East Indian children in Suriname were opened by the Dutch colonial government in 1890 (Gobardhan-Rambocus 2001: 262). It was not before 1905 that the first school for Hindustani children was established by a missionary organization, the Annie School of the Moravian Brethren (Schalkwijk 2001: 21). In 1914, the Surinamese Roman Catholics founded their first school for Hindustani children, a boarding school (Vernooij 2012: 68).

Given this context and the motivation of Swāmī Dayānand it is no surprise that one of the first things Bhāi Parmānand did during his 1910 visit to Guyana was to establish a Hindu school. He had just been in South Africa where Mahātmā Gāndhī had explained to him that his task was not only the founding of Ārya Samāj associations; he should also take responsibility for the education of the Hindustani children in general. The Presbyterian schools in Trinidad had, moreover, much success, which also explicates the relatively large number of East Indian Christians on this island.

ĀRYA SAMĀJ AND THE FIRST HINDU SCHOOL

The first Hindu school of Trinidad was the Vedic Mission School established by the Ārya Samājīs in Chaguanas in 1929 with Pandit Hariprasad Sharma as its headmaster. It ran for two years. The discontent of the East Indian Hindus and Muslims about the treatment of Hinduism on the local Presbyterian school was so big, however, that it was succeeded by a Hindu-Muslim school. Pandit Hariprasad Sharma was also involved in initiating this school. He succeeded in getting the financial support of a rich farmer, Seereeram Maharaj, a Hindu and some rich merchants. Unfortunately, the school had to be closed in 1935. But then the government was prepared to establish a public school where the children of the Hindu and Muslim inhabitants of Chaguanas could be educated without being influenced by Christian teachings.

It is important to notice that Pandit Hariprasad Sharma was an Ārya Samājī as well as Babaji, the headmaster of the Hindu-Muslim school, while Seereeram Maharaj joined the Ārya Samāj in 1934. Maharaj's house was the place where the National Arya Samaj Association was founded in November of that same year (Forbes 1985: 53, 63-5, 89). The Aryans also initiated many other schools with education in Hindi but most of them did not exist longer than one year. Also of importance, is that the Ārya Samājīs accepted everyone, whereas the Sanātanīs, who also established such schools, only accepted the sons of Brahmins (Forbes 1985: 156-8).

In Suriname something similar took place, but much later in the beginning of the 1930s. Arya Dewaker, one of the biggest Surinamese Aryan organizations at the time, opened a Hindu school in Nickerie in 1934, but the school was already closed in 1936 since the government refused to provide financial support (Gobardhan-Rambocus 2001: 257). In Paramaribo they opened a boarding school in cooperation with Bharat Oeday, an association for all East Indians, which also ran a Hindu cemetery. Bharat Oeday wished to establish a public school including the teaching of Hindi as a public school would receive financial support of the government. In the 1920s Bharat Oeday had agitated against the predominance of Christian schools for Hindustani children. Arya Dewaker

138 FREEK L. BAKKER

paid the costs of the accompanying boarding house, which was opened in October 1933 (Bakker 1999: 103-4; Gobardhan-Rambocus 2001: 254-62).

It is clear that the Ārya Samāj was deeply involved in initiating the first Hindu schools in these three Caribbean countries. In Guyana and Suriname their school associations still have a prominent position, although there are nowadays also big Hindu school associations founded by more orthodox Sanātanī Hindus. In Trinidad these Sanātanī Hindus are dominant; the Arya Pratinidhi Sabha of Trinidad manages only nine schools today (Forbes 1985: 242-4; Facebook pages of *The Arya Pratinidhi Sabha of Trinidad* and the *Gandhi Memorial Vedic School*).

ORGANIZATION

Both in Guyana and Trinidad the Ārya Samājīs didn't immediately form separate associations (*samājs*), but they participated in Hindu associations meant for all Hindus in their environment. In Guyana they were involved in the establishment of the Hindu Society in 1922. This society founded a Hindu temple, a school where the teachers taught Hindi, Urdu and English, and a *dharamsala*, where poor people could receive one hot meal a day in Georgetown. The association also had many local branches, in particular in the area of Berbice. After fifteen years, in 1937, these local branches decided to rename the organization to the American Aryan League (Ramdin 2000: 184-6).

It was similar in Trinidad where the Aryans established so-called Hindu Sabhas in the second half of the 1920s. These associations even had an umbrella organization, the Trinidad Hindu Maha Sabha (Forbes 1985: 43). But when Pandit Ayodhyā Prasād arrived in Trinidad on 24 August 1934, the Aryans started founding separate *samājs* and on 11 November 1934 they founded a separate umbrella organization, the Arya Samaj Association in Chaguanas. Remarkably enough, the first assistant secretary was a Creole, Willie Cumberbatch, who had to adopt the name Dharmendra after his appointment. This circumstance, however, shows that the Aryan umbrella organization wished to be open for everyone, including Hindus,

THE IMPACT OF THE ĀRYA SAMĀJ ON CARIBBEAN HINDUISM 139

Muslims and Christians; East Indians as well as Creoles. The organization developed as an association for modern-minded Hindus. In January 1937 its name was altered to Arya Pratinidhi Sabha of Trinidad (Forbes 1985: 78-92, 133-6).

The Surinamese Hindus did not have a period in which they founded common Hindu organizations. As a consequence of this development, probably, Suriname was the first Caribbean country to have an Ārya Samājī national umbrella organization, the Arya Dewaker founded in Paramaribo on 29 September 1929. But earlier, they had already formed a number of local *samājs*, the first one in Duisburg in 1922 and an important one in Nickerie in 1926.

Unfortunately, the Surinamese Aryans got divided and on 13 October 1935 a rival organization was established, the Arya Pratinidhi Sabha Suriname. The Aryans in Suriname remained divided for many years. In 1997 there were four umbrella organizations (Bakker 1999: 100-109), but in the beginning of the twenty-first century Arya Dewaker dominated the Surinamese Aryan scene again. The three other organizations had disappeared.

Unfortunately, the Trinidadian Aryans also got divided. In 1946 the Vedic Dharam Arya Sabha of Trinidad was founded, but this organization did not last long, only three years. In the long term, the Arya Pratinidhi Sabha of Trinidad was the most important Aryan umbrella organization of Trinidad. But since 1968 it had to accept the existence of the rival organization Vedic Mission of Trinidad and Tobago, the result of a split in which a former chairman did not accept the newly chosen person as his successor. The Vedic Mission contained relatively many members from Tamil background (Forbes 1985: 311-14). The biggest problem was that the number of Aryans diminished greatly because of the many conflicts within their ranks. Each conflict led to the formation of a new group of enthusiastic members (Forbes 1985: 346). Up to today there are two national organizations of Aryans in Trinidad, the Arya Pratinidhi Sabha of Trinidad and the Vedic Mission. The Arya Pratinidhi Sabha of Trinidad appears to be the most important one as it manages nine Aryan schools, whereas the Vedic Mission only has a headquarters-building including a temple hall in Chaguanas. It seems that presently there is some cooperation (Websites: Interreligious

140 FREEK L. BAKKER

Organization of Trinidad and Tobago; Facebook pages of the Arya Pratinidhi Sabha of Trinidad and the Vedic Mission of Trinidad and Tobago).

In 1968 the Guyanese Ārya Samājīs altered the name of the American Aryan League into Guyana Arya Pratinidhi Sabha. In 1975 this organization had 40,000 members and 35 branches all over the country (Vedalankar & Somera 1975: 159-60). Due to political twists and turns, the Guyanese Aryans got divided as well. Some leaders of the Guyana Arya Pratinidhi Sabha sided with the then President Forbes Burnham, who was regarded as an anti-Hindustani leader (De Kruijf 2006, 99). Therefore, a group of Aryan leaders spearheaded by Pandit Budhram Mahadeo formed a counter-organization, the Berbice Central Arya Samaj around Pandit. Usharbudh Arya (1933-2015),[2] who subsequently was asked to leave the country; but the Berbice Central Arya Samaj continued. In the late 1970s the organization called for a unification meeting of the Berbice Central Arya Samaj and the Guyana Arya Pratinidhi Sabha resulting in a new organization called the Guyana Central Arya Samaj. This association took over the headquarters of the Guyana Arya Pratinidhi Sabha and currently it is the only national organization of the Ārya Samājīs of Guyana. It has four regional branches, 29 local branches and ten associated branches (Websites Guyana Central Arya Samaj and Wikipedia; Facebook page of the Guyana Central Arya Samaj).[3]

One of the characteristics of the Ārya Samāj is that it is organized in local and often also regional associations with a western demo-cratic structure called *samāj*. Although this structure could give some problems and often led to conflicts and even lawsuits (Forbes 1985: 14-15, 358-66), it also taught the Aryans democracy. This gave them a lead in their contacts and negotiations with the colonial authorities.

---

[2] He is also known under his monastic name: Swami Veda or Swami Veda Bharati. He adopted this name in 1973.

[3] On the *Wikipedia* editing screen, one sees that the sources for the information about the last decades came from members of various boards of the Guyana Central Arya Samaj.

Figure 5.1: Fire-offering in the Arya Dewaker Temple
in Paramaribo, Suriname, June 2018
(Photo: Freek L. Bakker).

NEW ATTENTION TO THE VEDAS

Dayānanda Sarasvatī's focus on a return to the Vedas urged all Hindus including the orthodox Sanātanīs to learn Sanskrit more seriously. Most of them knew Sanskrit in the sense that they were able to chant the mantras used in the ritual ceremonies, but often they were ignorant of the contents of these holy formulae. The Aryans learned also to interpret and translate this ancient language. They paid, moreover, more attention to the contents of these texts, although they certainly also wished to chant them properly. The debates that followed the arrival of the Ārya Samājīs and especially of the Aryan preachers in the Caribbean compelled the Sanātanīs to deepen their knowledge of tradition to withstand the assaults of attackers. Consequently, the knowledge of the Vedas among the Caribbean Hindus increased considerably, which also made the influence of these scriptures bigger than among the orthodox Hindus in India.

142 FREEK L. BAKKER

Dayānanda Sarasvatī had replaced *pūjā* by *havan* or the fire-offering.[4] He claimed that *havan* was the common sacrifice prescribed by the Vedas. Therefore, it had to substitute *pūjā*. *Havan* is a fire-offering in which all kinds of things, such as water, herbal mix, *ghī* (clarified butter) and milk, are thrown in a fire-burning in a square fire-altar. There are no divine images. The deities were supposed to be represented by the consuming fire on the fire-altar. The *pūjā* is a ceremony in which a Hindu venerates the deity by cleaning the environment of its image and placing all kinds of things, such as water, *ghī*, milk, flowers, small pieces of clothes and food before the divine *mūrti* to show his or her devotion and hospitality to the godhead. The presentation of the food is the climax of the ritual. Subsequently the *pūjā* is concluded by closing rituals (Klostermaier 2007: 130; Michaels 2004: 241-5). Since the end of the 1930s the Sanātanīs in the Caribbean increasingly recited Vedic mantras in their rituals and added the *havan*-offering to the *pūjā*-ceremony (Rambaran 1995: 63-4; Singh 1995: 152-63; Younger 2010: 83-4).[5] The *havan* was mostly performed just before the closing rituals of the *pūjā* (De Klerk 1998, vol. 1: 50). Probably they did so to diffuse the pressure of the Ārya Samājīs, who claimed to practice the rituals of the Vedic texts more exactly than their orthodox antipodes. This claim had influence, because the Vedas were also highly esteemed among the Sanātanīs.

THE NEW TEMPLES

The Ārya Samājīs also had a big influence on the appearance and plan of the new purpose-built Hindu temples in the Caribbean, though more in Suriname and Trinidad than in Guyana. Since the 1920s the sanctuaries constructed for individual worship developed to temples for congregational worship. This evolution had started in Guyana already before the Ārya Samājīs obtained an important

[4] Other names for this fire-offering are *agnihotra* and *homa*.

[5] C.J.M. de Klerk suggests that this change had been already made in India (De Klerk 1998, vol. 1: 31, 43-59), but this claim is not supported by other scholars (Michaels 2004: 241-5; Singh 1995: 152-63; Younger 2010: 83-4).

THE IMPACT OF THE ĀRYA SAMĀJ ON CARIBBEAN HINDUISM   143

position within the Hindu population of the country. There the sanctuaries were gradually extended with extensions on all sides of the construction. As a result most Sanātanī temples in Guyana are circular buildings covered with a dome in the centre. The images of the divinities are found mostly at the southern side of the temple hall.

In Trinidad the evolution was different. Because of the debates within the Hindu community concerning religion, politics and other subjects, so-called *koutias* were constructed next to the traditional shrines for individual worship. These *koutias* were rectangular halls with benches appropriate for meetings in which people could listen to speeches and sermons and could discuss the contents of these talks. At the end of the 1950s a new development took place. Now one of the short sides of the *koutia* was left open and the sanctum of the traditional temple was placed towards this open wall. A new type of sanctuary emerged with a dome or *śikhara* at its back, where the *mūrtis* were placed on a raised platform and rows of pews in the room before this elevation. The front of the temple was often adorned with a beautiful facade (Prorok 1990: 90-116; 1991: 82-8).

In Suriname the development went another way. There the Ārya Samājīs started to build their own temples in the 1930s. These were rectangular buildings with a fire-altar on a raised platform at one of the short sides. The rest of the hall was filled with pews where the devotees could sit and attend the *havan*-ceremonies. After these ceremonies, a sermon was given and often some other people gave a lecture (Bakker 1999: 46-9, 101; 2015: 4). All these sanctuaries had three small towers at the front side. When the Sanātanī Hindus planned to build their main house of prayer at the Koningstraat in Paramaribo, they opted for a construction strongly resembling the Ārya Samājī houses of worship of the 1930s. It is a rectangular building with a platform at the eastern smaller side. On this platform, *mūrtis* are placed. On the front side, the edifice has three towers recalling the North Indian *śikharas*.

To say it briefly, the rectangular shape of the Hindu temples in Trinidad and Suriname find its roots in the developments in which the Aryans were predominant. So, the Ārya Samājīs became

144   FREEK L. BAKKER

responsible for various important special features of the Indo-Trinidadian and Indo-Surinamese sanctuaries.[6]

THE STRUGGLE FOR RECOGNITION OF
THE HINDU MARRIAGE

In all three countries the Hindu marriage was not recognized officially. This gave much problems, in particular around the position of the children and the transfer of heritages to these descendants.

In all three countries the Ārya Samājīs were deeply involved in the struggle for the recognition of this marriage by the colonial government. Unfortunately, there is only some information about this fight in Trinidad. It has to be realized that if a Hindu couple opted for a legal marriage on this island, the only option was a Christian marriage. Yet, there were people who opted for this legal marriage as it guaranteed the property rights of the children. But it led to new problems because many women felt themselves less subservient to their husbands after having been married in this way as the Christian marriage, in principle, offered the possibility to divorce. For this reason, the legal marriage threatened the stability of family life (Forbes 1985: 46).

The Aryan Pandit Hariprasad Sharma, who arrived in Trinidad in 1914, made the first change regarding the wedding ceremony. He decided to perform the wedding ceremonies in daytime (Forbes 1985: 22-3). This became common, although there was much resistance from the side of the Sanātanī Hindus (Forbes 1985, 100-1). Later the Ārya Samājīs included in their wedding ceremony an element in which both partners signed a document in which they declared that they had decided voluntarily to marry and with the consent of their parents and other family members. Furthermore, they promised to keep the rules of the Aryan association. Later they also obliged their members to marry only other Aryans. This caused difficulties because of the numerical decline of the Ārya Samājīs in later years (Forbes 1985: 102).

[6] For more detail see Freek L. Bakker (forthcoming), 'New Temples in New Homelands'.

In the 1930s heavy debates about recognition of the Hindu and the Muslim marriage took place in the Legislative Council of Trinidad. In 1935 the colonial government tended to recognize the Muslim marriage. The Hindus were denied this status, because they were unable to come to one single regulation because of the denominational differences among them (Forbes 1985: 73). There was also resistance among a considerable number of Hindus against official recognition of the Hindu marriage as this could include regulations for divorce, which was according to them was forbidden in Hinduism (Forbes 1985: 129).

In May 1946, the Hindu Marriage Bill was accepted by the Legislative Council. In September of the same year, the Arya Pratinidhi Sabha of Trinidad selected the first three pandits who would act as marriage officers. In retrospect it can be concluded that the Aryans made two recommendations to get the Hindu wedding recognized, a transfer of the ceremony to daytime and a signed declaration that the partners in the marriage had taken their decision voluntarily. In this way they adapted their rules to what was common in Christian circles.

In the meantime, the Hindu marriage was also recognized in Suriname. On 14 October 1940, Governor J.C. Kielstra decided to recognize the Hindu marriage beginning from 1 January 1941. It was his own decision for which he was heavily criticized by most members of the colonial legislative council. But their protests were of no avail, as the governor had proclaimed martial law after the occupation of the Netherlands by the Germans in May 1940, which included the abolition of the rights of this body (De Klerk 1998, vol. 2: 188-91; Ramsoedh 1990: 122-31; Verschuuren, 1994: 80-1). Moreover, the chosen members of the council were representatives of the Christian—mostly Protestant—elite of the colony chosen in a system of census suffrage. The Hindustanis, however, accepted Kielstra's decision with great satisfaction (Speckmann 1965: 55).

In Guyana things went differently. In 1891, Hindus and Muslims were offered the opportunity to conclude a legal non-religious marriage. But only a few people made use of this option, merely those who had some big private properties. At the time, however,

146 FREEK L. BAKKER

only few Hindustanis had such possessions (Bisnauth 2000: 96-101).[7] It was not before 1957 that the Guyanese parliament gave the same status to Hindu and Muslim weddings as the Christian weddings. This meant that Hindu priests could be appointed officials to perform the necessary ceremonies according to their own tradition (Algoe 2016: 83; Nath 1970: 147).

POLITICS

Although the political developments in Guyana, Trinidad and Suriname were different, it is possible to draw some mainlines regarding the role of the Ārya Samājīs in the evolution of the Hindustani political parties in these three countries. However, one will focus on Suriname for a more detailed delineation of the developments, as this country provides the most adequate data and information about this subject. After the presentation of what occurred in Suriname, the situation in Guyana and Trinidad will be discussed briefly.

Earlier it was already pointed out that Suriname had a legislative council in the 1930s. Its name was Koloniale Staten and it had thirteen members elected through census suffrage. In 1930 the first East Indian was elected, probably because he was a Roman Catholic. After a reform of this body in 1936, five members of the council were appointed by the governor and ten through census suffrage. Furthermore, its name was altered to Staten van Suriname. Two of the persons appointed by the governor were East Indians, both Sanātanīs, although one of them, Jagesar Persad Kaulesar Sukul (1900-1980), was also one of the founders of Arya Dewaker. So, he was known to have great sympathy for the Ārya Samāj. In other words, already in the first decade, people with some affinity with the Ārya Samāj were involved in the politics of the colony, although

[7] Ruben S. Gowricharn asserts that the religious Hindu and Muslim marriages were recognized in Guyana since 1860 (Gowricharn 2013: 406). Information of Dwarka Nath and the results of Bisnauth's research show that Gowricharn's observation is incorrect (Nath 1970: 145-7).

THE IMPACT OF THE ĀRYA SAMĀJ ON CARIBBEAN HINDUISM   147

it cannot be denied that one East Indian with an orthodox Hindu background and another with a Roman Catholic background also played important roles (Bakker 1999: 231-2). The revolution of the Indonesians, the inhabitants of the largest and most important colony of the Netherlands, persuaded the Dutch government to introduce democracy in Suriname including universal suffrage. In August 1945 the first steps were taken to prepare a constitutional reform of the Kingdom of the Netherlands. The Staten van Suriname appointed a delegation of three persons to attend the conference about this reform to be held in the Netherlands. None of them was of Hindustani or Javanese descent. Therefore, a group of East Indians and Javanese formed the Hindoestaans-Javaanse Centrale Raad (HJCR—Hindustani-Javanese Central Council), which demanded that at least one Hindustani and one Javanese were added. The legislative council added a Chinese and a Hindu East Indian. After strong protests against the absence of a Muslim Javanese in the delegation were lodged with the Ministry of Colonial Affairs in the Netherlands, the Dutch minister hastily added a Javanese Muslim (Dew 1996: 57).

In the meantime, the Sanātanī Hindus founded the Surinaamse Hindoe Partij (SHP—Surinamese Hindu Party) with Jagesar Persad Kaulesar Sukul as its chairman. The party was dominated by Brahmins, including Sukul himself. Shortly later the SHP underscored its elitist attitude by joining those protesting against universal suffrage (Azimullah 1986: 54). So, it is no surprise that Johannes Soekdew Mungra, secretary of the Arya Pratinidhi Sabha Suriname, warned his Hindu compatriots that the SHP had no place for the Ārya Samājīs. This led to the foundation of the Hindoestaans-Javaanse Politieke Partij (HJPP—Hindustani-Javanese Political Party) on 25 February 1947. Shortly afterwards the secretary of the HJCR, Jagernath Lachmon (1916-2001), an Ārya Samājī, was appointed chair of this party. The HJPP advocated universal suffrage.

The Round Table Conference of 1948 decided to implement universal suffrage in Suriname combined with a constituency voting system. This made the Hindustanis realize that they had to unite in order to win as many seats as possible in the new parliament.

Figure 5.2: Two important Caribbean politicians with an originally Aryan background: Jagernath Lachmon (Suriname) and Basdeo Panday (Trinidad) (*Source:* nl.wikipedia.org/wiki/Jagernath Lachmon and https://www.facebook.com/Sangeet1061/photos/basdeo-pandey).

On 16 January 1949 almost all East Indian parties[8] including the Moeslim Partij (Muslim Party) merged into the Verenigde Hindoestaande Partij (VHP—United Hindustani Party), later Vooruitstrevende Hervormings Partij (Progressive Reform Party). Jagernath Lachmon was appointed chair (Azimullah 1986: 32-65; Dew 1996: 72-4) and he would become and remain the political leader of the Surinamese East Indians until his death in 2001. The chairpersons of the Sanātan Dharam Maha Sabha Suriname and of one of the national Aryan umbrella organizations were appointed vice-presidents of the party (Bakker 1999: 95-7).

It is clear that the Ārya Samājīs played a key role in the formation of a political party for Hindustanis. They prevented the orthodox Hindu Brahmins from taking the lead and guaranteed that the

[8] One East Indian party did not join the merger, the Hindoestaanse Oranje Politieke Partij (Hindustani Orange Political Party) (Bakker 1999: 234). Orange refers here both to the sacred colour of Hinduism and the name of the royal family of the Netherlands. Thus, it expressed its loyalty to the mother country, the Netherlands. It never participated in the general elections (Bakker 1999: 234).

THE IMPACT OF THE ĀRYA SAMĀJ ON CARIBBEAN HINDUISM 149

party would defend the interests of all Hindus, not those of the Brahmins only. With the president of one of their national umbrella organizations in the board of the party, the Aryans participated structurally in the VHP, just as the Sanātanīs. They also provided various ministers and once even the prime minister for the cabinets the party engaged in. The religious institutions participating in the VHP were expected to support the party in election times. So, they can be regarded as subsidiaries.

In later times Ārya Samājīs also played a role in other political parties, such as, the Basispartijvoor Vrijheid en Democratie (BVD— Base Party for Freedom and Democracy) which sided with the political party of former dictator Desiré Delano Bouterse in the 1990s (Bakker 1999: 250-1). It is, however, one's impression that currently the Aryans in general tend to oppose Bouterse.

II

Unfortunately, one is unable to go into detail about the role of the Ārya Samāj in Guyanese politics. The Dutch scholar Hans de Kruijf points out that the breaking up of the People's Progressive Party (PPP) led by Cheddi Jagan (1918-97), in 1955, in a section dominated by East Indians and a section dominated by people of African origin, led to a new policy in which the PPP saw the Hindustani civil institutions including the religious ones as its subsidiaries. The People's National Congress (PNC), which originated from the section dominated by the Afro-Guyanese and was led by Forbes Burnham (1923-85), had the same view of the civil institutions dominated by people of African origin (Daly 1976: 302; De Kruijf 2006: 95-7). In this context it is no surprise that the American Aryan League sided with the PPP.

On 7 November 1966, Guyana became independent. Forbes Burnham was elected prime minister and ruled the country (Daly 1976: 307-10). His regime was disputed and therefore he attempted to ease the East Indian civil institutions off from the PPP. In the case of the American Aryan League he was successful. Some prominent board members decided to support Burnham. As we already have seen earlier, this caused opposition and, in the end, a

150 FREEK L. BAKKER

new national Aryan organization was founded, the Guyana Central Arya Samaj, which sided with the PPP again. When the PPP came into power some prominent members of the Guyana Central Arya Samaj were appointed minister. A good example is Satyadeow Sawh (1955-2006) who was president of the Guyana Central Arya Samaj when he was asked to become minister of fisheries, crops and livestock in 2000. In 2001 he became minister of agriculture. Unfortunately, he was murdered in his own house on 22 April 2006 (De Kruyf 2006: 96; website *Guyana Central Arya Samaj*). Since 2015 the PPP is in opposition, but Vishwa D.B. Mahadeo, member of the board of the Berbice Central Arya Samaj, is currently MP for this party [Website *Wikipedia* (English); *Parliament of the Cooperative Republic of Guyana*], which underscores the continuing involvement of the Guyana Central Arya Samaj in the PPP.

III

In 1945 universal suffrage was introduced in Trinidad and the next year the first general elections were held. Efforts to create multi-racial parties failed. Racial equality became the primary issue in the movement for independence in the campaign. The East Indians believed that Afro-Trinidadians were unlikely to vote for Hindustani candidates; therefore they asked for a guaranteed number of seats for East Indians in the legislative council. Only Ranjit Kumar, the president of the East Indian National Congress (EINC), succeeded in winning a seat. He did so by launching a racist campaign in the Hindu temples against the movement for self-government. He was supported by the local branch of the Arya Pratinidhi Sabha of Trinidad in Princes Town. Other branches campaigned for other Hindustani candidates, but they were unsuccessful. Therefore, the Aryans spared their efforts in the campaigns for the next elections of 1950. But then the Sanātanīs were better organized and since then they took the lead in the Hindu community in the person of the Brahmin Bhadase Sagan Maraj (1919-71). In the meantime, Kumar had lost his popularity by divorcing his Hindustani wife and marrying a Creole woman (Forbes 1985: 209-13; Prorok 1990: 205).

THE IMPACT OF THE ĀRYA SAMĀJ ON CARIBBEAN HINDUISM   151

On 22 June 1956, Eric Williams (1911-81) founded the People's National Movement (PNM) on a platform of multi-racialism. He was able to win over East Indian Muslims and Christians who began to feel alienated by the dominant Hindu component of the Indian parties. In his campaign for the 1956 elections he emphasized the strong relationship between the People's Democratic Party (PDP), founded by the political wing of the Sanatan Dharam Maha Sabha, and the Hindu religious organizations to wean the non-Hindu vote from his rivals. The PDP-leaders played into the hands of the PNM by using the temple and Hindu loyalty and faith as the cornerstone of their campaign. They did not realize that they needed the support of the Muslim, Christian and non-Sanātanī Hindustanis to win as many seats as possible. After the elections it turned out that Williams had succeeded even in winning over a number of Ārya Samājīs, some of them being board members of the Arya Pratinidha Sabha of Trinidad. Thus, he won a clear majority of seats. No Hindu was represented in the parliament. This result led to new formation of the PDP: the party merged with the Jamaica-based Democratic Labour Party (DLP) and some other minority parties to become the DLP. In 1958 they succeeded in winning six of the ten seats of the section for Trinidad and Tobago. This victory fortified the power and position of the Sanatan Dharam Maha Sabha (Forbes 1985: 213-14, 261-4; Prorok 1990: 205-8). But later, at least until 1995, the PNM won all elections but one.

More than in Guyana and Suriname, the political party led by the East Indians was under the strong influence of the ortho-dox Hindus. Whereas the Aryans participated in the East Indian dominated parties in Suriname and Guyana, many of them sided with the Afro-Trinidadian-dominated PNM in Trinidad. The United National Congress (UNC) of today can be regarded as the successor of the DLP. Interestingly, its first prime minister, Basdeo Panday, who came into office in 1995, was the son of an Ārya Samājīs and a primary schoolteacher at the Aryan Seereeram Memorial Primary School in Chaguanas and St Clement's Vedic School in Barrack-pore, but as a prime minister he presented himself as mainline Hindu (Forbes 1985: 211; *Hindorama* 1/3 (2000): 28-31; website

152 FREEK L. BAKKER

Aspiring Minds).[9] In other words, although the Aryans first took the lead in Trinidadian politics after the introduction of universal suffrage, their impact is much smaller than in Guyana and Suriname. They were divided because they were found in both the PNM and in the party dominated by the Hindustanis.

In retrospect we can observe that at least in Trinidad and Suriname, the Ārya Samājīs, in the time after the introduction of universal suffrage, were very active in the developments that would ultimately result in the forming of an ethnic Hindustani political party. Unfortunately, one has no data about their activities in this period in Guyana. They took the lead in Trinidad and Suriname. But while in Trinidad they became disappointed by the meagre results of their 1946 campaigns, they got a major role in Suriname in the person of the chairman and leader of the party, Jagernath Lachmon, an Ārya Samājīs, who kept this position till 2001. In Trinidad the Sanātanīs took over in the person of Bhadase Sagan Maraj. The Aryans got divided; part of them sided with the PNM, another part with the Hindustani ethnic party. Therefore, the influence of the Aryans was limited.

Both in Guyana and Suriname, the national umbrella organization of the Ārya Samājīs—or as in Suriname, at least one of them—was integrated in the structure of the ethnic Hindustani party. It functioned as its subsidiary in election times. Furthermore, it provided MPS for the parliament and ministers for the cabinet. Consequently, the impact of the Ārya Samāj was and still is much bigger in these two countries than in Trinidad.

CONCLUSIONS

The Ārya Samāj gained adherence in the first three, perhaps four decades of the twentieth century. Subsequently the number of followers of this movement remained roughly unchanged. In

[9] Both UNC prime ministers did not have a Sanātanī background. Panday came from an Ārya Samājī family and Kamla Bissessar-Persad was baptized when she was twelve years old and regarded herself as a 'Hindu Christian' (Website *Active Voice*). But both came from a Brahmin family Wikipedia (English).

THE IMPACT OF THE ĀRYA SAMĀJ ON CARIBBEAN HINDUISM 153

Trinidad, however, the Ārya Samāj lost support, probably because of the many conflicts within the movement. Trinidad is the only among these three countries where the Ārya Samāj still has two national organizations, whereas Guyana and Suriname have only one today. Notwithstanding that, the Guyanese and Surinamese Aryans also had their conflicts.

The Ārya Samāj focused in the beginning on education, on establishing schools with teaching in Hindi and Hindu religion. In Guyana and Trinidad, they cooperated with other Hindus, in Trinidad in one case even with East Indian Muslims, to achieve the results they wished. In Suriname they did so as well, but the first schools they founded were Aryan schools, which means that religious education was about the teachings of Swāmī Dayānand and the contents of the Aryan tradition. Later the Aryan organizations in Guyana and Trinidad also opened specific Aryan (Vedic) schools. In Guyana and Suriname, the Aryan organizations have a considerable number of schools, in Trinidad nine. Nonetheless it may be concluded that the Aryans played a prominent role in making the East Indians aware of the importance of education in their own language being compatible with the western society, but grounded in their own Hindu religious tradition.

The renewed focus of the Ārya Samājīs on the importance of the contents and the holy formulae of the Vedas led to changes in the Sanātanī *pūjā* ceremony. Because of the teachings of the Aryans many orthodox Hindu *pandits* started to recite Vedic mantras more frequently; furthermore, they added the fire-offering to the *pūjā*. In the struggle for recognition of the Hindu marriage, the Aryans made some accommodations which were followed by many other Hindus. One of them was the habit to hold the religious marriage ceremony no longer in the evening but in the morning.

The debates about religious and political themes made buildings necessary in which the Hindus could discuss these subjects. In Trinidad, rich Hindustanis constructed so-called *koutias* with benches where people could sit and debate. At the end of the 1950s these *koutias* were combined with small shrines housing the images of the deities to form a new type of temple with a platform with images of the divinities under a dome in front of a hall with benches. In

154   FREEK L. BAKKER

Suriname the Aryans also had influence. They had temples with
three towers in the front and also a platform with a fire-altar for
the fire offering in face of a hall with benches. In 1949 the Sanātanīs
took over this model, but placed the statues of their deities on the
platform. The influence of the Ārya Samājīs on the appearance
and plan of the Guyanese temples was very small.

In politics, the role of the Ārya Samājīs was similar to their part
in the establishment of Hindi schools. After the introduction of
elections with universal suffrage, they made the Hindus aware of
the opportunities this renewal offered them. At least in Trinidad
and Suriname they played a key role in the first campaigns. In
Suriname and Guyana their religious umbrella organizations were
integrated in the ethnic Hindustani political parties. They were
regarded as subsidiaries of these parties and they provided MPS
and ministers for the cabinets. Especially in Suriname their influence was considerable, since the East Indian political leader was an
Ārya Samājīs till 2001. In Trinidad the Aryans got divided over
the PNM and the political party dominated by the Hindustanis,
so there their impact was very small.

The rise of the Ārya Samāj in the first decades of the twentieth
century was probably caused by the circumstance that many people
of Hindu background saw them as the Hindus who would be able
to react most adequately at the new situation the Hindu immigrants arrived in in the Caribbean. The Aryans were self-assured,
firmly rooted in their newly formed Vedic tradition and had a vision
of what was necessary to promote the interests of the East Indians,
as well as a well reflected view on the importance of good education
in the pupils' own language and simultaneously based on their own
Hindu heritage. This attitude brought them in the frontline of those
struggling for improvement for all Hindustanis. Therefore, they
were involved in the establishment of Hindi schools, the fight for
the recognition of Hindu marriage and the associations and political
parties labouring for the amelioration of the economic and political
condition of the Hindustanis. Their strong belief in the correctness
of the reforms proposed by Dayānand Saraswatī led to a transformation of the *pūjā*. In later times, however, the Sanātanīs succeeded
in taking the lead again within the Hindustani community, but

THE IMPACT OF THE ĀRYA SAMĀJ ON CARIBBEAN HINDUISM 155

they had to give in with regard to the caste system and in the field of politics. In politics they were compelled to pay attention to the interests of *all* East Indians.

REFERENCES

Algoe, Kirtie (2016). 'Hindu and Muslim Responses to Christian Dominance, Interreligious Relations in Suriname and Guyana 1950-2014' (Doctoral dissertation, Paramaribo, Anton de Kom, University of Suriname).

Arthur, Niehoff and Niehoff Juanita (1960). *East Indians in the West Indies*. Milwaukee: Milwaukee Public Museum.

Azimullah, Evert (1986). *Jagernath Lachmon: Eenpolitiekebiografie [Jagernath Lachmon: A Political Biography]*. Paramaribo: Evert Azimullah.

Bakker, Freek L. (forthcoming). 'New Temples in New Homelands', in M.S. Hassankhan (ed.), *Historical and Contemporary Aspects of Indian Indenture and Migration*. Paramaribo: Series Legacies of Slavery and Indentured Labour, vol. 5.

—— (1999). *Hindoes in eencreoolsewereld: Impressies van het Surinaam-sehindoeïsme [Hindus in a Creole World: Impressions of Surinamese Hinduism]*. Zoetermeer: Meinema.

Choenni, Ramkisoor (1992). *Leven in harmonie: Inzichtenuit de Vedische leer en filosofie [Living in Harmony: Insights from Vedic Teachings and Philosophy]*. Boskoop: Drukkerij Macula.

Dale, Bisnauth A. (2000). *The Settlement of Indians in Guyana 1890-1930*. Leeds: Peepal Tree Press.

Daly, Vere T. (1976). *A Short History of the Guyanese People* (2nd edn.). London: Mac Millan Education.

Dayānanda, Saraswatī (1975). *The Light of Truth: An English Translation of Satyarth Prakash* (tr. from Hindi by C. Bharadwaja). New Delhi: Sarvadeshik Arya Pratinidhi Sabha.

De Klerk, Cornelis J.M. (1998). *Cultus en ritueel van het orthodoxehindoeïsme in Suriname [Cult and Ritual of Orthodox Hinduism in Suriname]* (2nd edn). The Hague: Amrit, vol. 1.

—— (1998). *De immigratie der Hindostanen in Suriname [The Immigration of the Hindustani in Suriname]* (2nd edn). The Hague: Amrit, vol. 2.

Dew, Edward M. (1996). *The Difficult Flowering of Suriname: Ethnicity and Politics in a Plural Society* (2nd edn). Paramaribo: Uitgeversmaats chappij Vaco N.V.

156 FREEK L. BAKKER

Forbes, Richard Huntington (1985). *Arya Samaj in Trinidad: An Historical Study of Hindu Organizational Process in Acculturative Conditions.* Ann Arbor: University Microfilms International.

Gobardhan-Rambocus, Lila (2001). *Onderwijsalssleutel tot maatschappelijkevooruitgang: Eentaal- en onderwijsgeschiedenis van Suriname, 1651-1975 [Education as the Key to Social Progress: A Linguistic and Educational History of Suriname, 1651-1975].* Zutphen: Walburg Pers.

Gowricharn, Ruben S. (2013). 'Ethnogenesis: The Case of the British Indians in the Caribbean', *Comparative Studies in Society and History,* 55(2): pp. 388-418.

—— (2000). *Hindorama.* The Hague: Sampreshan.

Jordens, Joseph T.F. (1981). *Swāmī Shraddhānanda: His Life and Causes.* New Delhi: Oxford University Press.

—— (1978). *Dayānanda Saraswatī: His Life and Ideas.* New Delhi: Oxford University Press.

Klostermaier, Klaus K. (2007). *A Survey of Hinduism* (3rd extended edn). Albany: State University of New York Press.

Kruijf, Johannes G. de. (2006). *Guyana Junction: Globalisation, Localisation, and the Production of East-Indianness.* Utrecht, Universiteit Utrecht: Rozenberg Publishers.

Michaels, Axel (2004). *Hinduism: Past and Present.* Princeton: Princeton University Press.

Myers, Helen (1998). *Music of Hindu Trinidad: Songs from the India Diaspora.* Chicago: The University of Chicago Press.

Nardev, Vedalankar and Somera Manohar (1975). *Arya Samaj and Indians Abroad.* New Delhi: Sarvadeshik Arya Pratinidhi Sabha.

Nath, Dwarka (1970). *A History of Indians in Guyana* (2nd revised edn). Frome and London: Butler & Tanner Ltd.

Prorok, Carolyn V. (1990). *Hindu Temples in Trinidad: A Cultural Geography of Religious Structures and Ethnic Identity.* Ann Arbor: UMI Dissertation Services.

Rambaran, Hari (1995). *Parivartan: Twee geloofslagenonderhindoes in de West door brahmanisering en sanskritisering van het volksgeloof [Parivartan: Two Layers of Faith among Hindus in the West through Brahmanization and Sanskritization of the Folk Beliefs].* Waddinxveen: Hinfor.

Ramdin, Ron (2000). *Arising from Bondage: A History of the Indo-Caribbean People.* New York: New York University Press.

Ramsoedh, Hans K. (1990). *Suriname 1933-1944: Kolonialepolitiek en beleidondergouverneurKielstra [Suriname 1933-1944: Colonial Politics and Policy under Governor Kielstra].* Delft: Eburon.

THE IMPACT OF THE ĀRYA SAMĀJ ON CARIBBEAN HINDUISM 157

Schalkwijk, Jan M.W. (2011). *Ontwikkeling van de zending in het Zuid-Caraïbischgebied: in het bijzonderonder de Hindostanen 1850-1980 [Development of the Mission in the South Caribbean: in particular among the Hindustani 1850-1980]*. The Hague: Amrit.

—— (2001). *Hindoestaansezending 1901-2001 [Hindustani Mission 1901-2001]*. Paramaribo: Theologisch Seminarie der EBGS.

Serbin, Andrés (1979). *Nacionalismo, Etnicidad y Politica en la Republica Cooperativa de Guyana*. Caracas: Bruguera Venezolana.

Singh, Odaipaul (1995). *Hinduism in Guyana: A Study in Traditions of Worship*. Ann Arbor: UMI Dissertation Services.

Speckmann, Johan D. (1965). *Marriage and Kinship among the Indians in Surinam*. Assen: Van Gorcum & Comp. N.V.

Vernooij, Joop G. (2012). *De regenboog is in onshuis: De kleurrijkegeschiedenis van de R.K. kerk in Suriname [The Rainbow is in our House: The Colorful History of the R.K. church in Suriname]*. Zutphen: Walburg Pers.

—— (1994). 'Eenreligieuzekaart van Suriname', *Interactie*, 2: pp. 60-4.

Verschuuren, Stan (1994). *Suriname: Geschiedenis in hoofdlijnen[Suriname: History in Main Points]* (3rd revised edn.). The Hague: SDU Uitgeverij Koninginnegracht.

Yadav, Kripal C. and K.S. Arya (1988). *Arya Samaj and the Freedom Movement, Volume 1: 1875-1915*. New Delhi: Manohar.

Younger, Paul (2010). *New Homelands: Hindu Communities in Mauritius, Guyana, Trinidad, South Africa, Fiji, and East Africa*. Oxford: Oxford University Press.

WEBSITES

Annie, Paul (2010). *Active Voice*, Tuesday 6 July 2010, http://anniepaulactive-voice.blogspot.com/2010/07/lotus-of-trinidad-and-tobago-kamla.html, 4 November 2018.

Aspiring Minds Trinidad and Tobago (n.d.).'Basdeo Panday', *Aspiring Minds Trinidad and Tobago*, Retrieved from https://www.aspiringmindstandt.com/basdeo-panday, accessed on 4 November 2018.

Facebook (n.d.) 'Guyana Central Arya Samaj', *Facebook page*, retrieved from https://www.facebook.com/GuyanaCentralAryaSamaj/ accessed on 22 October 2018.

Facebook (n.d.).'Gandhi Memorial Vedic School', *Facebook page*, retrieved from https://www.facebook.com/pg/gandhimemorialvedicschool/about/?ref=page_internal, accessed on 3 November 2018.

Facebook (n.d.).'The Arya Pratinidhi Sabha of Trinidad', *Facebook page*, https://www.facebook.com/The Arya Pratinidhi Sabha Of Trinidad/ accessed on 3 November 2018.

Facebook (n.d.). 'The Vedic Mission of Trinidad and Tobago', *Facebook page*, retrieved from https://www.facebook.com/thevedicmissionoftnt/ accessed on 3 November 2018.

Interreligious Organization of Trinidad and Tobago, retrieved from http://www.iro.co.tt/portfolio-2-columns/ accessed on 3 November 2018.

Parliament of the Cooperative Republic of Guyana. Retrieved from http://parliament.gov.gy/about-parliament/parliamentarian/dr-vindhya-vasini-persaud/ accessed on 2 November 2018.

The Arya Samaj (n.d.). 'Guyana Central Arya Samaj'. Retrieved from http://www.thearyasamaj.org/Guyana, accessed on 21 October 2018.

Wikipedia (English). Retrieved on https://en.wikipedia.org/wiki/Main_ Page, accessed on 22 October 2018.

CHAPTER 6

'They Came to Mauritian Shores':[1] The History and Symbolism of Ram Leela and *Ramayana* in Mauritius (1870-1950)

SATYENDRA PEERTHUM

THE HISTORIC IMPORTANCE OF THE *RAMAYANA* TRADITION AND RAM LEELA IN MAURITIUS

In early November 1883, in a dispatch to Governor Sir John Pope Hennessy, John F. Trotter, the Protector of Immigrants, reported that more than one week earlier, almost all of the 151 Indian indentured workers and some Indo-Mauritians on Deep River Sugar Estate went on strike in the district of Flacq. The main reason behind this was that Jean-Francois Rouillard, the estate owner, did not allow them to take a day off in order to celebrate Deepavali or the festival of lights which is associated with the glorious return of Lord Ram to Ayodhya. The estate owner refused because it was the start of the sugar harvest season and would affect sugar production on his estate. The following day, Dharamsingh, the Chief Sirdar of Deep River, along with a delegation of 22 labourers, showed up at the office of the Protector of Immigrants and filed a complaint against their employer.

After a mediation by the Protector Trotter, Rouillard allowed his workers to take their day off, if they agreed to work for a

---

[1] The title was inspired and obtained from Satyendra Peerthum, *They Came to Mauritian Shores: The Life-Stories and History of the Indentured Labourers in Mauritius (1826-1937)* (AGTF, Mauritius, 2017).

whole day the following Sunday (MNA/PB 28, Protector Trotter to Governor Pope Hennessy, 4 November 1883). Immigrant Dharamsingh also played a key role in negotiating this deal. He was a Brahmin Hindu and a literate skilled worker from Bihar and, for many years, the leader of the contract workers on Deep River. Ever since the early 1870s, Dharamsingh promoted the holding of the Ram Leela or 'Ram's Play' in the local estate camp and in observing important Hindu religious days such as Deepavali and Mahashivaratree.[2]

Between 1883 and until the end of indenture in 1910, three successive Protectors of Immigrants reported at least another 13 complaints and incidents where Hindu, Muslim, and Christian Indian workers and Indo-Mauritians under contract, on and off the sugar estates, in the emerging villages and in Port Louis, refused to work during the harvest season because of their need to observe the sacred days of their religions (MNA/PB 30, 1883-5 to PB 54 for 1909-11, Letters and Reports of the Protector of Immigrants to other Government Departments). It is from the letters and petitions that some of the Indian immigrants either signed complaints which were written by themselves or on their behalf, and the actions they took as active agents in order to exercise greater control on their lives, that one can recover their voices from the edge of the archival records and history (Stoler 2009: 19-53; Rolph-Trouillot 1995: 1-31).

In addition, between the early 1860s and the early 1880s, collective group actions such as group protests and strikes took place frequently on the sugar estates, in Port Louis, and emerging villages, such as the one organized by Dharamsingh and most of the Deep River workers. At the same time, the reports and letters from the Stipendiary Magistrates indicate, to a certain extent, the genesis of group and community formation and action and a sense of

---

[2] Interview with the Late Mr. Sanjay Dharamsingh, 85 years old and great grandson of Immigrant Dharamsingh, conducted on 22 December 2013; The Dharamsingh Family Papers; Mahatma Gandhi Institute Indian Immigration Archives (MGIIIA), PE 1, Ship Arrival Register for 1826 to 1842.

'THEY CAME TO MAURITIAN SHORES' 161

collective consciousness and solidarity among the indentured workers (MNA/RA 1561 for 1860 to RA 2562 for 1880, Letters and Reports of the Stipendiary Magistrates to the Governor).

During the second half of the 1960s, the late Dr Burton Benedict, famous American anthropologist, indicated, that during last years and decades of the Age of Indenture, on the sugar estates and in the emerging villages, was the period when the Old Indian Immigrants, the new indentured immigrants, and the Indo-Mauritians were going through the process of community formation. During this period, they were purchasing, selling and leasing land, leaving the sugar estates, became skilled and semi-skilled workers and entrepreneurs, established hamlets and villages and also achieving some measure of social and economic mobility by thousands of individuals. As a result, they were reasserting their religious lives and cultural activities which gradually led to the emergence of several small Hindu religious groups such as the Arya Samajis, Sanathanists, Pauranics, and Brahmo Samajis (Benedict 1967: 22-31; Peerthum 2017: 54-6).

More than a century later, in January 2013, His Excellency Kailash Purryag, the former President of the Republic of Mauritius, made an emotional and historic trip to his ancestral village in Bihar, India. On that special occasion, some of the talented villager artists gave a vibrant and popular rendition of Ram Leela or the popular version of the story of Ram which served as a symbolic reminder to the former Mauritian President that one of their lost sons had returned home to Bihar where the kingdom of Lord Ram once existed. Ram Leela or 'Ram's Play' (emanating also from the *Ramacharitmanas*), a popular performance of the *Ramayana* epic in a series of scenes that include songs, narrations, recitals and dialogues aimed at the common people.

This fact is important when looking at Mauritian history and the history of the Aapravasi Ghat World Heritage Site or the Immigration Depot and of the Indian indentured labourers. After all, the Aapravasi Ghat was inscribed under UNESCO World Heritage Committee's *criterion vi* which deals with the intangible heritage of a particular people, place and country (Peerthum 2018:

162 SATYENDRA PEERTHUM

1-2; AGTF 2006: 1-10). Ram Leela is a key example of this intangible heritage and it is important to remember that in December 2005, the former Director-General of UNESCO, Koïchiro Matsuura, proclaimed 43 new Masterpieces of the Oral and Intangible Heritages of Humanity, including traditional Indian performances of the *Ramayana*, the Ram Leela (http://ich.unesco.org/en/RL/ramlila; http://www.aapravasighat.org).

Recently, Pandit Rajendra Arun, the Chairman of the Ramayana Center explained in Mauritius,

ever since the late nineteenth century, the popular enactment of the Ram Leela has been a constant source of inspiration and strength to the Indian Diaspora, in particular amidst Indians who were lured away to the colonies, such as in Mauritius, in the nineteenth century to work in the sugar cane field. It allowed them not only to face the harsh conditions but also to keep their culture alive. This *Ramayana* consciousness continues to this day among Mauritian Hindus (Keynote speech of Pandit Arun on 18 August 2016 at the GOPIO International Conference in Mauritius).

Pandit Arun, a naturalized Mauritian citizen, originally from India, described the impact accurately which this '*Ramayana* consciousness' has had among Hindu Indo-Mauritians. After all, for more than a century and a half, it has survived and prospered through the public enactments of the Ram Leela. Ever since they arrived in Mauritius between the late 1820s and 1860s, many of the Indian immigrants brought with them knowledge of their sacred texts such as the Vedas, the Upanishads, the *Bhagavad Gita*, Ram Leela, and even copies of the *Ramayana* (Arun 2016).

This fact is clearly illustrated today, around half a dozen authentic copies of the *Ramayana* dating from the late nineteenth century and written in the Kaithi and Devanagari scripts of northern India are preserved in Mauritius. A copy in the Kaithi script exists in the Beekrumsing Ramlallah Interpretation Centre at the Aapravasi Ghat World Heritage site and the Mahatma Gandhi Institute Folk Museum. At least four known copies also exist among Indo-Mauritian families who are descendants of Indian indentured workers such as the Gopal and Peerthum families.

THE PIONEERING WORK OF SIRDAR RAMDHUNY NUNDALL, IMMIGRANTS SERVANIN AND RUNGASSAMY

Between the 1830s and 1840s, there were hundreds of immigrants who came from Bihar, Uttar Pradesh, Tamil Nadu, Kerala and other parts of India who were literate and semi-literate. Many among them are known as the 'early pioneer Indian indentured workers' who by the mid-nineteenth century, after terminating estate labour had achieved some measure of social and economic mobility and obtained some rudimentary education as well (Peerthum 2018: 1-5).

Old Immigrant entrepreneurs as sirdars, job contractors, overseers, head of workshops, skilled artisans and moneylenders, who wielded a lot of power, had access to financial resources, and regularly obtained favours from the plantation and the colonial elite. Marina Carter and Crispin Bates called these the *avenues of socio-economic mobility*. Between the 1830s and 1870s, for the New and old immigrants apart from the planters, employers and estate managers, these old immigrant entrepreneurs became their points of reference, as they provided help to their fellow immigrants during the best and worst of times, and acted as *intermediaries* with the plantation owners/employers.

Old immigrant entrepreneurs in their roles as sirdars, overseers, job contractors, skilled artisans, servants/domestics, head of workshops, merchants, gardeners, traders, shopkeepers and moneylenders developed a *chain of personal relationships* with the other old and new immigrants, and even with some of the remaining ex-apprentices. Essentially, it was a patron-client relationship—social and economic as well as paternalistic in nature, which created a certain amount of dependency.

Between the 1830s and the 1870s and afterwards, this formed part of the complex and long-term networks of social and economic relations which the old immigrant entrepreneurs had created and maintained. Bates and Carter observe that this 'sirdari and contractor elite was a form of semi-autonomous subaltern careering' dominated by the old immigrant entrepreneurs which emerged from within the indentured labour community. This clear example of indentured and ex-indentured immigrant agency enabled them to secure their niche in colonial society, especially on the sugar estates and their survival in the plantation hierarchy during the mid- and late nineteenth century and afterwards, as they tried to exercise some control on their lives and economic activities (Bates & Carter 2017: 462-7/473-4/480-4; Carter 2002: 93-6).

During this period, as Carter accurately noted in her brilliantly written article 'Subaltern Success Stories: Socio-Economic Mobility in the Indian Labour Diaspora—Some Mauritian Case-Studies' that:

the first generation of Indian immigrants established themselves in positions of authority on the plantations of authority on the plantations, and as wealthy land-owners and religious and cultural patrons in the Indian villages which grew (Carter 2002: 96).

It was through the actions, the funds, the decisions and the organizational capacities of these successful early Indian immigrants who played a key role between the 1870s and 1890s, that Ram Leela was being enacted on some of the sugar estates, hamlets and villages such as in Grand Port, Flacq and Riviere du Rempart and also in other rural districts. How does one know this? Essentially through fragments of archival documents from the National Archives of Mauritius, Mahatma Gandhi Archives and the National Library of Mauritius, a study of the life stories and experiences of some of these outstanding and forgotten Indian indentured workers and the family stories/oral family narratives and their private family documents which bring to light the contributions of some of these important immigrants (Peerthum 2018: 1-20).

This scholarly approach, such as a focus on the subaltern experiences or *subaltern lives*, life stories and agency of these Indian workers who eventually became *settlers* in their own right in a complex, racist and highly stratified colonial society, has been suggested in some of recent publications on colonial India, *The British Colonial World* and *The Indian Ocean World* by Clare Anderson and David Arnold (Anderson 2012: 1-22; Arnold & Blackburn 2004: 1-23; Chaturvedi 2012: 1-20).

At the same time, it allows one to take up the challenge which was put forward several years ago by Frederick Cooper and Ann Laura Stoler, two American social historians, to a *rethinking of a research agenda* by historians and scholars when looking at social history in modern European specifically British colonies and its relation with the Mother Country during the nineteenth century and afterwards (Stoler & Cooper 1997: 1-5, 35-40). This type of academic analysis allows one to gain a better insight into how intangible traditions and knowledge were transmitted and preserved among the Indian indentured and ex-indentured workers and their descendants as they chose Mauritius as their new home while still remembering and longing for their ancestral homeland.

Between the mid-nineteenth and mid-twentieth centuries, in all the eight rural districts, there were important old Indian immigrants who showed clearly that one man can make a difference in this transmission of cultural heritage and traditions from the Indian immigrants to the first, second and third generations of Indo-Mauritians. It is essentially oral traditions which serve as the vehicle for this transmission, perpetuation and preservation of these important aspects of their intangible cultural heritage including their Hindu religious practice.

Between the 1890s and 1910s, Sirdar Ramdhuny Nundall, the son of Immigrant Nunlall (a Bengali who arrived in Mauritius in 1849), and my great grandfather, established a *baithka* (or places of learning for the Indian immigrant children in particular) on the estate camp of Labourdonnais Sugar Estate. It was one of the first places in Riviere du Rempart district, the *Ramayana* was being read on a weekly basis and the Ram Leela was enacted four times per year by children of the Indian immigrants. Sirdar Nundall helped to establish the tradition of the *Ramayana* such as Ram Leela and even reading of the *Ramayana* by Hindu priests and literate Hindus in Labour donnais estate camp (Interviews with Dr Satyendra Peerthum conducted in 2010 & 2016; The Peerthum Family Papers).

During the mid-nineteenth century, especially among the majority of the non-literate immigrants, Ram Leela was one of the important forms of entertainment. Between the 1870s and 1890s, in Grand Port district, immigrant Rungassamy from Tamil Nadu

Figure 6.1: Immigrant Servanin was photographed at the age of 75 at the Immigration Depot or Aapravasi Ghat in 1883 (MGIIIA/PG 28, Immigrant Photo Registers for 1882-3).

and immigrant Servanin of Kerala, two job contractors and small planters encouraged their fellow countrymen to uphold and observe their religion and traditions.[3] They arrived in Mauritius in 1839 and 1836 respectively under 5-year contracts as labourers and were registered at the Police Headquarters in Port Louis.[4]

These two immigrants established different *baithaks* on the sugar estates of Union Vale, St. Hubert and Beau Vallon and brought pundits to encourage the reading of the *Ramayana*. Over a period of more than 30 years, they encouraged the children of the immigrants and Indo-Mauritian boys to hold the Ram Leela twice per year. They were two former indentured immigrants who pioneered

---

[3] Peerthum 2018: 1-2/14-15; Interview with Mr. Kartikeya Servanin, 90 years old and the great great grandson of Immigrant Servanin, conducted on 30 November 2015; The Servanin Family Papers; Interview with Mr. Naga Rungassamy, 83 years old and the great grandson of Immigrant Rungassamy, conducted on 15 October 2014; The Rungassamy Family Papers.

[4] MGIIIA, PE 2, Ship Arrival Register for 1835 to 1839; MNA, RC 31, 1844 to 1846, Letters and Petitions from Individuals to the Governor and Colonial Secretary.

Figure 6.2: Immigrant Rungassamy was photographed at the age of 70 in 1881 at the Immigration Depot (MGIIIA/PG 27, Immigrant Photo Registers for 1881-2).

the tradition of reading the *Ramayana* and the Ram Leela in Grand Port or the south of Mauritius.[5]

THE MAJOR CONTRIBUTIONS OF IMMIGRANTS DHARAMSINGH, CALLEE, VIRAMEN TO RAM LEELA

What about the other parts or districts of Mauritius? Between the late 1820s and the 1840s, there were hundreds of immigrants who came from Bihar, Uttar Pradesh, Tamil Nadu, Telugu districts, present-day Maharashtra, Kerala and other parts of India who were semi-literate with several among them even fully literate. After all, in part of the Miscellaneous Letters and Petitions Collection of the RA Series (23 volumes) of the Mauritius National Archives, for the

---

[5] Interview with Mr. Kartikeya Servanin, 90 years old and the great great grandson of Immigrant Servanin, conducted on 30 November 2015; The Servanin Family Papers; Interview with Mr. Naga Rungassamy, 83 years old and the great grandson of Immigrant Rungassamy, conducted on 15 October 2014; The Rungassamy Family Papers.

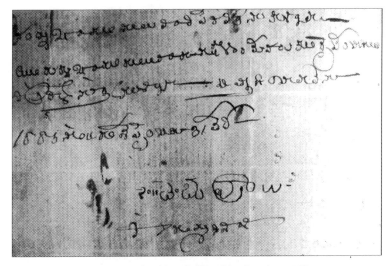

Figure 6.3: A Letter written and signed by Immigrant Rungassamy, Job Contractor, to Henri La Hausse, owner of Beau Vallon Sugar Estate, requesting that the Indian Indentured Workers be allowed to observe Deepavali in 1875 (*Source:* The Rungassamy Family Collection).

period between 1841 and 1859, there are an estimated 151 petitions and letters that were signed and even around 22 petitions and letters that were partly or written entirely by Indian Old Immigrants in their native languages and scripts (MNA, RA 676 for 1841 to RA 1530 for 1859, Miscellaneous Letters and Petitions).

In addition, according to 36 oral interviews which I carried out between 2010 and 2018 with elderly descendants of Indian indentured workers (who had completed their genealogies and were well versed in their family histories), it was apparent that many of their ancestors were semi-literate immigrants, and several among them were fully literate.

Further, the interviewees also informed this writer that many among their ancestors were very knowledgeable in the Hindu scriptures and texts. According to the oral traditions of their families, their forebears narrated stories from the *Ramayana* and encouraged the enactment of the Ram Leela and also the Ram Katha or popular

Figure 6.4: Immigrant Dharamsingh was photographed in 1874 at the age of 60 at the Immigration Depot (*Source:* PG 9, Immigrant Photo Registers for 1873-5).

oral recitals of that Indian epic.[6] An immigrant ancestor such as Dharamsingh, a Brahmin from Bihar, who was a sirdar, was literate and arrived in Mauritius in 1835.[7]

Between the 1870s and 1880s, he established several *baithaks* in southern Flacq district at the sugar estates of Deep River, Beau Champs, and La Louise. Over a period of more than 20 years, he funded schools for Indian children and encouraged the enactment of Ram Leela. It becomes evident that since the mid-nineteenth

---

[6] The 36 aforementioned oral interviews were carried out for the Aapravasi Ghat Trust Fund, the Truth and Justice Commission, and for this personal research and genealogy between January 2010 and December 2018. At the time of writing (October 2020), only 21 out of 36 interviewees are still alive. More than 36 family paper collections were also consulted during the same period to supplement and cross-check the oral accounts.

[7] MGIIIA, PE 4, Ship Arrival Register for 1835 to 1842; PF 2, Indenture Contracts for 1835 to 1842; MNA, RC 26, Letters and Petitions from Individuals to the Governor and Colonial Secretary for 1838 to 1841.

Figure 6.5: Immigrant Callee was photographed in 1886 at the age of 85 at the Immigration Depot (MGIIIA/PG 32, Immigrant Photo Registers for 1885-6).

century, the seeds of *Ramayana* consciousness and the tradition of Ram Leela had already been sown and gradually established in rural Mauritius (Interview with the Late Mr. Sanjay Dharamsingh conducted in 2013; The Dharamsingh Family Papers).

During the second half of the nineteenth century, Flacq was not the only Mauritian district where the performance of the Ram Leela was encouraged. Immigrant Callee, a skilled worker from Orissa, arrived in Mauritius in 1837. Between 1870 and 1890, he was active in the district of Savanne in the estate camps of Bel Ombre, Chamouny and near the village of Souillac.[8] During the period of more than 30 years, he encouraged the performance of Ram Leela in some of the estate camps and newly established Indo-Mauritian villages (Interview with the Late Mr. Virendra Callee conducted in 2014; The Callee Family Papers). Immigrant Viramen or Veeramen

---

[8] MGIIIA, PE 2, Ship Arrival Register for 1835 to 1839; MNA, RC 29, Letters and Petitions from Individuals to the Governor and Colonial Secretary for 1843; Interview with the Late Mr. Virendra Callee conducted in 2014; The Callee Family Papers.

Figure 6.6: Immigrant Viramen was photographed in 1876 at the age of 82 at the Immigration Depot (MGIIIA/PG 11, Immigrant Photo Registers for 1876-7).

arrived in Mauritius in 1838 at the age of 45 as a sirdar from Madras, India. He was classified as a 'Malabar' who was from the district of Madurai in the Madras Presidency (MGIIIA, PE 4, Ship Arrival Register for 1835 to 1842; PF 2, Indenture Contracts for 1835 to 1842). Viramen was semi-literate when he arrived in Mauritius and worked as a sirdar for ten years and then became a job contractor for Trianon Sugar Estate.

Between the 1870s and 1880s, he encouraged the immigrants of Trianon and those in nearby settlements such as Moka and Saint Pierre villages, to observe their religion and cultural traditions such as Ram Leela and storytelling. During the same period, he became a small sugar cane planter and set aside some land close to Trianon where he built a *baithak* for some of his fellow ex-Indian indentured workers. He died in 1885 at the age of 92 (Interview with the Late Mr. Mootoo Viramen conducted in 2013; The Viramen Family Papers).

It should be possible in Mauritius to discover through oral traditions and family genealogies, how immigrants such as Dharamsingh, Callee and Viramen were able to promote Ram Leela and *Ramayana* consciousness among their fellow indentured workers,

172   SATYENDRA PEERTHUM

their children and grandchildren at the grassroots level in different
districts of the island.[9]

RAM LEELA AND THE READING OF THE *RAMAYANA*
AS PART OF VILLAGE/ESTATE CAMP CULTURE
IN THE TWENTIETH CENTURY

Between the 1870s and the early 1900s, the enactment of Ram
Leela gradually became an integral part of the popular entertainment and culture of the Indian workers and Indo-Mauritians and
their descendants in the estate camps and villages on the island. It
formed a key component of the cultural landscape of the Indo-
Mauritians in all of the island's rural districts along with *Divali*,
Mahashivaratree, pilgrimage to Grand Bassin.[10] The Late Balram
Narsimooloo of the village of Cottage (the village where my family
comes from), in the north of Mauritius in Pamplemousses district,
was a sirdar on Labourdonnais and Forbach Sugar Estates and he
reiterates these facts. He was the grandson of a Telugu indentured
labourer who arrived in Mauritius in 1885 and a good friend of
my great grandfather and grandfather.

In 2010, in a two-hour interview, he explained the importance
of Ram Leela for the villagers of Cottage and other villages in the
north of the island such L'Esperance Trebuchet, Poudre d'Or Village and Hamlet including Forbach Estate Camp. He explained
that between the 1920s and the 1950s, it was one of their rare
forms of entertainment which was sanctioned by the local village
council or panchayat and verses from the *Ramayana* were recited
in the local *baithak* (Interview with the Late Mr. Mootoo Viramen
in 2010; Interviews with Dr. Satyendra Peerthum conducted on
10 November 2010 and 13 November 2016).

---

[9] Refer to the aforementioned oral interviews which were carried out for the
Aapravasi Ghat Trust Fund, the Truth and Justice Commission, and for my
persona research and genealogy between January 2010 and December 2018.

[10] Peerthum 2018, 1-20; The 36 oral interviews conducted between 2010
and 2018 with the elderly descendants of Indian indentured workers also
indicated the same thing.

'THEY CAME TO MAURITIAN SHORES' 173

Between the early 1900s and 1950s, great historical figures such as Manilall Doctor, Swami Satantranand, Dr. Bharatwaj, Pandit Kistoe, Pandit Sahadeo, Pandit Bissoondoyal, Pandit Ramnarain and Sookdeo Bissoondoyal encouraged Hindu Indo-Mauritians to become educated, read the *Ramayana*, and hold the Ram Leela regularly on the sugar estates and in the villages. Between the 1920s and 1950s, hundreds of Hindi schools were established all over the island, in the villages and some estate camps, by the Hindu Sanatanists, Pauranics, and Arya Samajis. At the same time, the Jan Adolan Movement, or the People's Movement, a Hindu revival social movement, led by Professor Basdeo Bissoondoyal, also played a key role in the setting up of these schools. In their curriculum, they also included the teaching of Hinduism, reading of the *Ramayana* and enactment of the Ram Leela. During the 1940s and 1950s, these facts were duly noted and praised by K. Hazareesingh, ex-Director of the MGI.[11]

Between the 1930s and 1950s, Chubylall Mathur was a Hindi teacher and one of the well-known organizers of Ram Leela in Riviere du Rempart district. He held thousands of performances throughout that particular district over a period of more than the quarter of a century. It was thanks to the efforts of such visionary Hindu leaders and teachers between the 1920s and the 1960s, that this '*Ramayana* consciousness' has been nurtured through the reading and chanting of the *Ramayana*, and the enactment of Ram Leela has become an integral part of the intangible heritage of the Hindu Indo-Mauritian community.[12]

During the mid-twentieth century, Ram Leela performance became very common in the Mauritian villages and estate camps. It

[11] Interview with the Late Uttam Bissoondoyal, Former Director of the MGI and son of Sookdeo Bissoondoyal and nephew Basdeo Bissoondoyal, on 3 February 2011; 'The Bissoondoyal Family Papers'; Peerthum 2018, 18-20; The 36 oral interviews conducted between 2010 and 2018 with the elderly descendants of Indian indentured workers indicated the same thing.

[12] Interview with Vijay Mathur, 76-year old and the son of Chubylall Mathur, conducted on 3 May 2014; 'The Mathur Family Collection'; Interviews with Dr Satteeanund Peerthum, conducted on 10 November 2010 and 13 November 2016; Peerthum 2018: 18-20.

was carried out at least once per year in many of the major villages and estate camps and they also had *baithaks* where children were told stories of the *Ramayana* and encouraged to read the famous Indian epic. In villages such as Cottage and Morcellement Sainte Andre, the panchayats and village leaders and elders such as Viren Mootoo Carpen, a sirdar and great grandson of Mootoo Carpen, a Telugu immigrant who arrived in Mauritius in 1836, actively encouraged the enactment of the Ram Leela during the 1940s and 1950s. Therefore, the panchayats, the *baithaks*, the recitation of the *Ramayana* and the enactment of the Ram Leela helped to consolidate the *Ramayana* consciousness and Hinduism and Hindu traditions in Mauritius.[13]

Between the 1940s and 1960s for more than 30 years, Pandit Bissoondoyal and the Jan Andolan established hundreds of schools and *baithaks* through the island including in Port Louis. They encouraged the enactment of the Ram Leela, *Ramayana* and the *Gita*. The enactment of the Ram Leela contributed to the cultural revival of Hinduism and Hindu traditions during the mid-twentieth century and cultural liberation of the Indo-Mauritian masses. It allowed the Hindus of Mauritius to reappropriate their culture and traditions and revalorize their history. In December 1943, a reenactment of the Ram Leela was carried out after the Mahayag at Pouce Street in Port Louis with the blessings of the Jan Andolan (Interview with the Late Uttam Bissoondoyal conducted in 2011; 'The Bissoondoyal Family Papers'; Bissoondoyal 1991: 1-5/101-3).

CONCLUSION

The tradition of the enactment of Ram Leela and the oral tradition of narrating stories from the *Ramayana* have existed in Mauritius for close to two centuries. It forms a pillar of Indo-Mauritian popular

[13] Interview with Sandiren Mootoo Carpen, 51-year old and great grandson of Viren Mootoo Carpen, conducted on 10 December 2014; 'The Mootoo Carpen Family Papers'; Peerthum 2018, 18-20; The 36 oral interviews conducted between 2010 and 2018 with the elderly descendants of Indian indentured workers indicated the same thing.

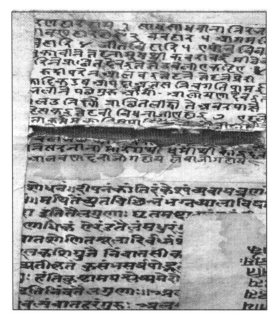

Figure 6.7: An extract from a *Ramayana* text in the Kaithi script from northern India which was brought by immigrant Gopal Ram in 1871 (The Gopal Ram Family Collection).

culture and intangible values which the Hindu indentured labourers brought with them and established in the Mauritian estate camps and villages during the mid-nineteenth century and later, which were first encouraged by the Indian immigrants themselves and consolidated by their descendants. This helped to perpetuate the Ramayana consciousness in Mauritius.[14]

It was a long and complex process which allowed them to consolidate and expand their religion and cultural traditions. The

---

[14] Interview with the Late Uttam Bissoondoyal on 3 February 2011; 'The Bissoondoyal Family Papers'; Peerthum 2018, 1-20; The 36 oral interviews conducted between 2010 and 2018 with the elderly descendants of Indian indentured workers indicated the same thing.

176 SATYENDRA PEERTHUM

perennial values from the *Ramayana* and the Ram Leela of Ram as the ideal husband, Sita as the perfect wife, Lakshman as the forever loyal brother and Ram's Ayodhya or Ram Raj as the Golden Age of truth and justice in ancient India is still admired and emulated in Mauritius and India as well.

These values form an integral part of the values of our society today and for decades to come and contribute to the entrenchment of the *Ramayana* consciousness such as the Ram Leela and the Ram Katha and its popularity in early twenty-first century Mauritius. This can clearly be seen ever since 2001, with the enactment of the Ramayana Centre Act and with the establishment of the Ramayana Centre itself at Rose-Belle, a village in the southeast of Mauritius.

Finally over the past forty years, Mauritian historians, scholars and academics have been striving to write the history of the Indian indentured workers and their descendants. For many years, they have researched, recorded, and analysed information from the archival records, family collections, and oral family histories in order to recover the subaltern voices of the Indian immigrants who came to Mauritian shores (Peerthum 2018: 19-20; Interview with Dr Satyendra Peerthum conducted in 2016).

REFERENCES

ARCHIVAL SOURCES

I. MAHATMA GANDHI INSTITUTE INDIAN IMMIGRATION ARCHIVES

PC Series, Immigrant Certificates.
PE Series, Immigrant Ship Arrival Registers.
PG Series, Immigrant Photo Registers.

II. MAURITIUS NATIONAL ARCHIVES

PB Series, Letters and Reports of the Protector of Immigrants to other Government Departments.
RA Series, Letters and Reports from the Stipendiary Magistrates to the Governor and Colonial Secretary.

'THEY CAME TO MAURITIAN SHORES' 177

RA Series, Miscellaneous Letters and Petitions from Individuals.
RC Series, Letters and Petitions.

III. Secondary Sources

Aapravasi Ghat Trust Fund (AGTF) (2006). The AGTF Nomination Dossier submitted to UNESCO in 2005 and revised in 2006. Mauritius: AGTF.

Anderson, Clare (2012). *Subaltern Lives: Biographies of Colonialism in the Indian Ocean World, 1790-1920.* United Kingdom: Cambridge University Press.

Arnold, David and Stuart Blackburn (2004). *Telling Lives in India: Biography, Autobiography and Life History.* Bloomington: Indiana University Press.

Bates, Crispin and Marina Carter (2017). 'Sirdars as Intermediaries in Nineteenth-Century Indian Ocean Indentured Labour Migration', *Modern Asian Studies, 51*(2): pp. 462-84.

Bissoondoyal, Uttam (1991). *Promises to Keep.* Mauritius: MGI Press.

Burton, Benedict (1967). 'Caste in Mauritius', in Barton M. Schwartz (ed.), *Caste in Overseas Indian Communities.* San Francisco, California: Chandler Publishing Company: pp. 21-42.

Carter, Marina (2002). 'Subaltern Success Stories: Socio-Economic Mobility in the Indian Labour Diaspora—Some Mauritian Case Studies', *Internationales Asienforum, 33*(1-2): pp. 91-100.

Peerthum, Satyendra (2018). 'The Tradition of the Ram Leela and Ramayana (Ram Katha) in Mauritius during the Age of Indenture between 1870 and 1910', Conference Paper presented at the International Indentured Labour Conference in Reunion Island, August.

—— (2017). *They Came to Mauritian Shores: The Life-Stories and History of the Indentured Labourers in Mauritius (1826-1937).* Mauritius: Aapravasi Ghat Trust Fund.

Stoler, Ann Laura (2009). *Along the Archival Grain: Epistemic Anxieties and Colonial Common Sense.* New Jersey: Princeton University Press.

Stoler, Ann Laura and Frederick Cooper (1997). 'Between Metropole and Colony: Rethinking a Research Agenda', in Frederick Cooper and Ann Laura Stoler (eds), *Tensions of Empire: Colonial Cultures in a Bourgeois World.* Berkeley: University of California Press: pp. 1-56.

Tosh, John (2010). 'Memory and the Spoken Word', in John Tosh (ed.), *The Pursuit of History* (5th edn.). London: Routledge: pp. 303-29.

Trouillot, Michel-Rolph (1995). *Silencing the Past: Power and the Production of History.* Boston: Beacon Press Books.

IV. Other Sources

A. *Family Collections*

1. The Bissoondoyal Family Papers consulted on 3 February 2011.
2. The Callee Family Papers consulted on 2 February 2014.
3. The Dharamsingh Family Papers consulted on 22 December 2013.
4. The Mathur Family Collection consulted on 3 May 2014.
5. The Mootoo Carpen Family Papers consulted on 10 December 2014.
6. The Peerthum Family Papers consulted on 10 November 2010/ 13 November 2016.
7. The Ram Gopal Family Collection consulted on 15 May 2015.
8. The Rungassamy Family Papers consulted on 15 October 2014.
9. The Servanin Family Papers consulted on 30 November 2015.

B. *Oral Interviews/Oral Sources*

1. The keynote speech of Pandit Arun on 18 August 2016 at the GOPIO International Conference on Indentured Labour and the Global Indian Diaspora at the Ramayan Centre in Rose-Belle.
2. Between January 2010 and December 2018 or over a period of 9 years, a total of 36 oral interviews were carried for the Aapravasi Ghat Trust Fund, the Truth and Justice Commission, for my personal research and genealogy.
3. Interview with the Late Uttam Bissoondoyal, former Director of the MGI, on 3 February 2011.
4. Interview with the Late Virendra Callee, 80 years old and great great grandson of Immigrant Callee, conducted on 2 February 2014.
5. Interview with the Late Sanjay Dharamsingh, 85 years old and great great grandson of Immigrant Dharamsingh, conducted on 22 December 2013.
6. Interview with Vijay Mathur, 76 years old and the son of Chubylall Mathur, conducted on 3 May 2014.
7. Interview with Sandiren Mootoo Carpen, 51 years old and great grandson of Viren Mootoo Carpen, conducted on 10 December 2014.
8. Interviews with Dr. Satteeanund Peerthum, Senior Historian, Ex-Minister, Ambassador, Teacher and Journalist, 78 years old and the great grandson of Sirdar Ramdhuny Nundlall, conducted on 10 November 2010 and 13 November 2016.
9. Interview with Naga Rungassamy, 83 years old and the great grandson of Immigrant Rungassamy, conducted on 15 October 2014.

10. Interview with Kartikeya Servanin, 90 years old and the great great grandson of Immigrant Servanin, conducted on 30 November 2015.

C. *Websites*

1. UNESCO. 'Ramlila, the traditional performance of the Ramayana', *Representative List of the Intangible Cultural Heritage of Humanity.* Retrieved from http://ich.unesco.org/en/RL/ramlila-the-traditional-performance-of-the-ramayana-00110. Accessed on 20 December 2015.
2. http://www.aapravasighat.org. Accessed on 17 January 2016.

CHAPTER 7

'Beyond *Vanvaas*: Hinduism in Trinidad'

SHERRY-ANN SINGH

INTRODUCTION

Between 1845 and 1917, the British colony of Trinidad drew extensively on Indian indentured labour to fill the gap left by the abolition of African slavery in 1838. During this period, a total of 143,939 Indians migrated to Trinidad (Brereton 1981: 103), approximately 88 per cent of whom practised various facets of Hinduism. Because Indian indentured immigration encompassed a wide sweep of the Indian subcontinent, there was a remarkable degree of social, religious and cultural diversity within the immigrant population in Trinidad. This social and geographical diversity also underscored a 'jumbled medley of beliefs, doctrines, rites, experiences, relationships, restrictions, polities, economies and orientations regarding matters supernatural and spiritual' (Vertovec 1992: 106). Specific regions in India yielded particular religious traditions which, were inevitably, transported—albeit often in highly attenuated forms— to the Trinidad context with the indentured immigrants. The Bengal, Bihar and Orissa regions were dominated by Shaktism (ecstatic type worship of the Mother Goddess) and, to a lesser extent, by Vaishnavism (worship of the various forms of the God Vishnu). Eastern and Western Uttar Pradesh were also primarily Vaisnavite and permeated by the Bhakti tradition. Yet, some of these regions were also strongholds of Shaivism (worship of the God Shiva) (Vertovec 1992: 106).

Regions in the south of India also provided a high concentration of Shakti traditions. Compounding this religious mélange was the presence of a number of socio-religious subgroupings specific to the different religious traditions. In his 1893 *Note On Emigration*, Surgeon Major W.D. Comins identified the presence of sects such as the *Ramanund Phunt*,[1] the *Kabeer Phunt*, the *Oughur Phunt*, and the *Sewnarain Phunt*.[2] The diversity among these four groups was very evident. Much of this diversity was situated in the presence of elements of both the Great and Little Traditions of Hinduism[3] in Trinidad. However, by the beginning of the twentieth century most of these smaller traditions were being subsumed by the drive for a standardized form of Hinduism.

Despite the trying conditions experienced under the indenture system,[4] about four of every five Indian immigrants opted to make Trinidad their permanent home (Vertovec 1992: 73). The three decades after the end of Indian indenture were a crucial turning point in the development of Trinidad Hinduism. By the 1920s, factors such as the acceptance of Trinidad as their homeland by those immigrants who had opted to remain in the colony, the leavening out of the male-female ratio and the age imbalance, and the noticeable increase in the birth rate of Indians saw the Indian population emerging as a 'whole' population (Haraksingh 1988: 117) which would, in turn, facilitate the establishment of the community. By 1921, Indians comprised 33 per cent of the entire population, with a rise to 35 per cent in 1946.[5] Interestingly,

---

[1] The term *phunt* is a corruption of Hindi *panth* which refers to a religious sect or group.

[2] I.O.R. Official Series V/27/820/10: Note On Emigration From India To Trinidad by Surgeon Major W.D. Comins (Calcutta: Bengal Secretariat Press, 1893).

[3] In Hinduism, the Little Tradition refers to those aspects which have evolved independently of the Great Tradition. These are usually embedded in orality, and are geographically localized and linguistically restrictive. The Great Tradition refers to the essentially Sanskritic/Brahminic strand of Hinduism which is embedded in the Vedas and other Sanskrit literature.

[4] A detailed description and analysis of the system of indenture can be found in K.O. Laurence, 1994.

[5] Colony of Trinidad and Tobago Census Album, 1948.

'BEYOND *VANVAAS*: HINDUISM IN TRINIDAD'   183

enough, the figure for Hindus showed a gradual decline during these years. In 1921, Hindus comprised 72.7 per cent of the Indian population; in 1931, 67 per cent; and in 1946, 64.5 per cent (Ramesar 1994). However, by 1938, J.D. Tyson, reporting on the conditions of Indians in Trinidad, was of the opinion that 'the Hindu community on the island . . . has undoubtedly been "quickened" in its Hinduism during the last few years' since many elements of sustained Hindu worship and practice had increased in terms of both visibility, and frequency and scale of practice (J.D. Tyson Report, 27).

The relocating of Hinduism from India to Trinidad necessitated attempts at community and religious reconstruction. Elements of religion were variously truncated, modified, diluted, intensified or excised. Thus, reconstitution and telescoping, rather than transplanting, were two of the dominant processes that could be observed. Subsequently this yielded a form of Hinduism in which some of the more visible and tangible elements were notably modified; in accordance with local conditions, demands and requirements. At the same time, however, the Hinduism which emerged was unarguably rooted in the broad philosophy and in the general tenets of many of the strands of Hinduism practised in India.

The period 1945-90 was characterized by tremendous economic and political change which, in turn, served to shape the extent and nature of Hindu religious transformation in Trinidad. Within this context, the Hindu community proceeded with its efforts at transforming and establishing itself in terms of both its internal operations and its relation with the national community. This entailed substantial navigation, assimilation, excision and accretion, often seasoned with a diametric pull between the community's intrinsically Hindu systems and values and the sometimes dissonant systems and values of the wider Trinidad society. The crux of the challenge of Hindu socio-religious development during this period resided in the establishment of a balance between retaining the essence of Hinduness in the more private settings, while simultaneously yielding to the often contradictory requirements of integration into the wider Trinidad society. This article seeks to explore how fundamental processes in the formation of diaspora communities have worked

184 SHERRY-ANN SINGH

to create what can be referred to as 'Trinidad Hinduism', which carries with it elements of both its Indian origin and its Trinidadian location. The article focuses on the period between the termination of the system of Indian indenture and the turn of the century since, no longer fettered by the system of Indian indenture, Hinduism was able to develop, evolveand flourish in the local Trinidad context; a process that was marked by substantial degrees of adjustment, assimilation, recreation and substitution.

NEGOTIATING PRACTICE

The slow yet increasingly observable move towards the notion of a 'Trinidad Hinduism' was evident from as early as the 1920s.[6] This idea of 'Trinidad Hinduism' can be best defined as the synthesis and retention of the fundamental tenets, beliefs and rituals of the various strands of Hinduism brought from India and reconstructed by the indentured immigrants within and in consonance with a specifically Trinidadian context. The inevitable adoption, omission or altering of certain dimensions essentially mirrored the conscious or unconscious movement towards a 'Trinidad idea of religion'; that is to say, what Hinduism could or should constitute in Trinidad.

The 1920s came to incorporate what was popularly referred to by the Indian middle class in Trinidad as the 'Indian Renaissance', and saw the local move to reinterpret and present Hinduism (Sanskritic ideology) as more of a universal religion, whose principles and practices could apply to and, in some aspects, parallel those of the wider society. Locally, this concept was evident in the gradual emergence of a highly simplified and uniform culture, one that tended to incorporate all the varying strands of Hinduism present in Trinidad. Standardization of the many strands of Hinduism brought from India to Trinidad was a key operative in this process. Thus, vegetarianism, practised by the priestly caste, was upheld as the ideal; for its health benefits and as a signifier of greater ritual

---

[6] Some interviewees, mainly those in leadership positions, are still quite reluctant to accept the idea of a 'Trinidad Hinduism', due primarily to political purposes, or the desire to maintain 'purity and exclusivity'.

'BEYOND *VANVAAS*: HINDUISM IN TRINIDAD' 185

purity, and higher religious and social merit. While Hinduism could never fit into the Western definition of monotheism, there was increasing emphasis on the principle of one god with multiple forms and names.[7]

Several aspects of Hinduism, usually originating in the Little (folk) Tradition in India, were rejected by some of those who aspired for higher status. Practices such as animal sacrifices, the fire pass ritual, and the worship of deities connected to these events were toned down, modified or dropped altogether and denounced both publicly and privately. In an attempt to emulate the ritually higher Sanskritic practices, the common practices by the *Madrassis* (and non-Madrassis) of smoking *ganja* (marijuana), consuming alcohol during and after certain ritual readings, and even consuming meat on *Divali* day were also abjured.[8] The increased emphasis placed on socio-economic advancement during the 1970s, along with the religious languor of the period, led to a further de-emphasis of those religious practices and observances that could possibly add to the still widely held perception of Hindus as a superstitious or idolatrous group. However, despite the decline in such practices on the individual level, there emerged, during the 1970s oil boom, a number of 'modern Kali temples' (Guinee 1970, 4) in Trinidad, several of which performed animal sacrifices. Through the 1990s, Hindus and non-Hindus of various socio-economic and professional brackets were visiting these temples in hope of relief from physical ailments, reprieve from an inexplicable period of 'bad luck', or to deflect 'strange happenings' which seemed to extend beyond the realm of the scientific and the logical.

Temple-based collective worship became more noticeable in Trinidad from the 1930s due to remarkable growth in the construction of temples. The rise of temple-based worship at this time was also observed in Guyana (Bisnauth 2000, 142). The durability of the construction material being used (stone, clay, bricks, wood),

---

[7] Crystallized towards the end of *Rig Veda Samhitas*, and fully developed between the *Samhitas* and Brahmins.

[8] This was confirmed by oral interviews conducted during the period 2000-2004.

the addition of the *kuthiya* (a hall extending away from the traditional temples) alongside the traditional temples and the temple's increasing use for the purposes of preaching and politicking provided additional indicators of changes in Hindu society. According to Carolyn Prorok, 'changes in temple form reveal changes specifically associated with the Hindu population . . . changes which indicate processes of Sanskritization and Westernization' (1988: 74-5). Temples also served as the village community centre where *panchayats*, village council meetings, lectures, discussions, Hindi language and music classes were held. Until the 1960s, the observance of almost all religious festivals and events were conducted in the home. The temple functioned primarily as 'the formal house of the Gods'. The economic boom of the 1970s led to the rise of family or communally organized religious *jags/yagnas* (a series of religious rites and ceremonial readings) and *pujas* (Hindu prayer ritual) at temples, and the revitalization of Hinduism saw an increasing number of festivals and religious occasions being communally observed in that setting; temples had become the formal 'Hindu house of worship'. During the 1980s, a number of temples became the venue for free medical clinics, run mainly by Hindu doctors and nurses (Preetam 2000).

The introduction of Hindi films in Trinidad in the year 1935 contributed notably to the process of religious reconstruction. Through this medium, individuals began aspiring to what was being projected as Hindu culture in terms of dress, names, music, dance, language (standard Hindi), song, and even some rites and rituals. Hindi films also reinforced the standards of Hindu family relations, social interaction and important life-cycle rituals such as marriage ceremonies and death rites. In this respect, what the advent of Hindi films in Trinidad did was to establish within the Hindu community a sense of affirmation and rejuvenation of both Hinduism and Indian culture by providing a more tangible though tempered form of the culture and lifestyle which the community had constantly striven to emulate since the days of indenture. Many of these films depicted stories from the religious texts and of the gods, thereby deepening aspirations for the sanskritic culture exalted in these films.

'BEYOND *VANVAAS*: HINDUISM IN TRINIDAD' 187

The inclusion of non-Hindu elements and observances, was an inevitable consequence of the location of Hinduism in the Caribbean, and more specifically, in Trinidad. During the period of Indian indenture, the La Divina Pastora deity was adopted into the Hindu pantheon as *Sipari Mai* (Mother of Siparia). This was facilitated through the Goddess-worship aspect of Hinduism and the prominence placed on spiritual-curative aids. Since then, Hindus continued to journey to Siparia to make offerings to the statue, which was quite similar in appearance to some *murtis* (images) of female Hindu deities. The deity was worshipped in the church in a recognizably Hindu manner. The primary purpose of visits to *Sipari Mai* was to secure relief from illnesses, and to pray for the offspring. Many Hindus often conducted the first ritual shaving of a child's hair at that location and symbolically offered the shaved hair to *Sipari Mai*. The inclusion of La Divina Pastora into the Hindu pantheon also instigated the observance of Good Friday as an auspicious day. All Saints Day was also incorporated into the rituals pertaining to the dead. On that day, many Hindus cleaned the graves of their dead, decorated them with flowers, and lit candles on the graves. It was also not uncommon to see images of Jesus and Mary placed alongside the Hindu images at family and even communal altars. All of the rituals performed to the Hindu images were also accorded to the non-Hindu images.[9]

CASTE

Any examination of Hinduism in Trinidad demands some insight into the dynamics of caste. Much work has been done on the caste system within the diaspora and it has been established that, rather than a full-blown transplantation, there was more of an attenuation and reworking of the traditional system, resulting in, among many other modifications, the almost total dissolution of the concerns, restrictions and boundaries of the numerous *jatis* or subgroups and emphasis on the basic and very diluted gradation of the four

[9] Information confirmed by participant observation and interviews conducted.

188   SHERRY-ANN SINGH

main *varnas* (caste groupings).[10] Thus, rather than a fixed 'caste system', what emerged by the end of the nineteenth century can more aptly be described as a very modified and fluid ideology or sentiment of caste, becoming, through the decades, even more diluted and modified by constant interaction with divergent systems, lifestyles, values and beliefs. Among the studies conducted in different Indian communities in Trinidad during the 1950s and 1960s, Arthur Niehoff concluded that caste was 'functionally a matter of little concern' among Hindus of the Oropuche Lagoon area (Niehoff 1967: 162). However, it is clear that there were two principal areas wherein caste considerations were visible and persistently dominant until the 1970s; these were priesthood and marriage.

By the 1940s, it was generally preferred that ritual specialists (pundits) should be of Brahmin stock. The following captures the most common rationale of such an attitude:

I would prefer a Brahmin pundit because he is from a high nation [caste]. They come from a home where they are religious. They don't mix with all different kinds of people. They are a high nation. It is better to have a godfather [spiritual preceptor] or pundit like that (Ramdass 2002).

During the 1950s and 1960s, however, an increase in the influx of swamis and other religious figures from India generated a more active counteraction of Brahmin aspirations at monopolizing rituals 'by a group of largely non-Brahmin pundits who were refused official recognition as Hindu priests by the major Hindu socio-religious group, the Sanatan Dharma Maha Sabha (SDMS). This was possibly the most visible challenge to Brahmin religious supremacy. By the 1980s, an increasing number of individuals began to express the view that pundits 'don't have to be Brahmins'. As one person said: 'I would not mind a non-Brahmin pundit doing my *puja*. He must be a learned person with good character, who can guide by example and precept' (Bissoon 2002). However, despite the proliferating support for a non-Brahmin priesthood,

[10] The works of Colin Clarke, Morton Klass, Arthur and Juanita Niehoff and Barton Schwartz provide detailed examinations of caste in Trinidad.

'BEYOND *VANVAAS*: HINDUISM IN TRINIDAD' 189

the preference for Brahmin ritual specialists was still the norm, even by the 1990s. This echoed the deep-seated affinity for tradition and custom, and a wariness of deviating from the 'correct way' with regard to religious matters.

RAMAYANA

A defining marker of Trinidad Hinduism, since the earliest days of Indian indenture, is the most prominently subscribed to Hindu religious text in Trinidad and Tobago, the *Ramayana*, and more specifically, the popular version of the text brought by the indentured labourers, the *Ramcharitmanas*. V.S. Naipaul described the *Ramayana* as something that 'lived among us' and as 'something I had already known' (Naipaul 2000: 12). So pervasive is this version that many refer to the author as the 'Father of Caribbean Hinduism'. During the indenture period, the vast majority of the indentured immigrants originated from the Uttar Pradesh and Bihar regions (Brereton 1989: 103) which was by then deeply immersed in the *Ramayana* ethos. This can account for the *Ramcharitmanas* quickly becoming a religious, social, cultural and emotional anchor for the early indentured labourers.

The specifically diasporic appeal of the *Ramcharitmanas* was based on a number of factors. Its focus on the Bhakti (devotional) tradition served as a link to the emotional and cultural ethos of the motherland. Its treatment of the themes of exile and return provided immense solace and emotional support—'a balm for troubled minds'—(Bahadur 1976: 11) to the immigrants who considered their indenture as a type of exile. The uncomplicated nature of the story, along with a clearly established dichotomy between good and evil rendered it an appropriate authority in the attempts of the Trinidad Hindu community at reconstruction and reconsolidation. The focus of *Ramcharitmanas* on interpersonal relationships provided both positive and negative models for the reconstruction of both family and community networks.

However, since the very earliest days of Indian indenture in Trinidad, the *Ramayana* has expanded beyond the boundaries of the textual into a larger *Ramayana* tradition which encompasses a multitude of dimensions spun out of the textual, all of which simultaneously yield to and reflect transformation in society. Such dimensions include locally produced commentaries; street and theatre dramas; versions of the *Ramayana* aimed at children, including abridged prose narratives and comic books; dance dramas and other performances; paintings, sculptures, handiwork, poems, stories, songs, musical forms and local recordings of verses from the *Ramayana*. While the basic storyline and the characters are the same, the symbiotic relationship between the society and the *Ramayana* tradition generated changes in interpretation, thematic emphasis, focus, style and modes of presentation. Yet, it still managed to retain its tenets, themes and status as a religious and social doctrine. According to Romila Thapar: variants [of the *Ramayana*] point to the richness of a narrative which has been appropriated by a vast number of people in diverse ways. . . . Investigating these would involve investigating authorship, audience, location and purpose (Thapar 2001: vii).

In other words, since this *Ramayana* tradition would have been conditioned by the Hindu experience in Trinidad, an examination of the former would, in effect, divulge related dimensions of the latter. This inevitably bears upon the idea of the *Ramayana* as a mirror and metaphor of society and socio-religious change among Hindus in Trinidad.

The most popular and long-standing dimension of the *Ramayana* tradition in Trinidad is undoubtedly the Ram Leela (depiction of the Rama story in dramatic form), the first performance of which was staged in 1888 in Dow Village, California, in Central Trinidad. Public notices of later productions began to appear as early as 1898 in the *Koh-i-Noor Gazette*. Indeed, the dramatic form of the Ram Leela served as a very effective means of incorporating uniquely Trinidadian issues and elements into the *Ramayana* tradition. The most popular motif for this has been the depiction of the villain of the epic, Ravan. Whether it was the white colonial oppressors, other political elements, the negative impact of Western elements, or any other more palpable threatening agents such as drugs, violence or criminal activity, the effigy of the evil Ravan constantly reflected the concerns of the Indo-Trinidadian society. During the

'BEYOND *VANVAAS*: HINDUISM IN TRINIDAD' 191

period of indenture, effigies of Ravan were often dressed to represent colonial authority; burning of the effigy signified the Indian discontent with the former. From the 1950s, the essentially 'non-Indian-friendly' policies of the ruling People's National Movement generated presentations of the Ravan figure wearing dark sunglasses and hearing aid similar to those worn by Dr. Eric Williams. Historian Clem Seecharan confirmed in his study, *The Development of the East Indian Community in British Guiana, 1920-1950*, that this was also the case in British Guyana where stories from the *Ramayana* greatly influenced Hindu perceptions of the new environment, and where President Burnham acquired the title of Ravan on account of his overtly anti-Indian policies. The working of contemporary issues into the oral commentary that accompanied the performance further supplemented the 'local flavour' of the tradition. Social, religious and political leaders all made use of this motif to drive home their arguments effectively. While not the norm, by the beginning of the twenty-first century it was not uncommon to find individuals of African descent being included as actors in some Ram Leela productions.

Derek Walcott referred to the Ram Leela performance in the village of Felicity in Trinidad as both a metaphor of history and a vital aspect of the Indian attempt at community reconstruction within the diasporic context (Walcott 1993). He asserted that 'the performance was like a dialect, a branch of its original language, an abridgement of it, but not a distortion or even a reduction of its epic scale' (Walcott 1993: 6).

NEGOTIATING LANDSCAPE

In its long history, Hinduism has constantly acquired new elements and trends which often embody its development in a specific context. According to J.L. Brockington, such innovations are:

. . . not the enemy of tradition but that by which it [Hinduism] maintains its relevance. Hinduism does not reject the old in favor of the new but blends the two, expressing new dilemmas in traditional language and accommodating fresh insights to established viewpoints (Brockington 1981: 209).

192 SHERRY-ANN SINGH

Similarly, in Trinidad, attitudes, trends and practices have emerged which all reflect, in varying degrees, the experience and evolution of what can be termed Trinidad Hinduism. Before the 1970s this was primarily on account of the innate Hindu tendency to sanctify almost anything associated with religion. For example, the *lota* and *thali* used in pujas, though essentially just brass vessels and performing the practical function of vessels in *pujas*, were, in Trinidad, treated as 'religious' items to be used exclusively for religious purposes. There would be a similar reluctance to use the *sohari* leaf (upon which food at Hindu socio-religious events is served) when consuming any kind of meat. This sanctifying tendency was most evident in the consecration of sites where rocks were claimed to have emitted blood or milk, most popular of which was the Patiram Trace Mandir in Penal in the late nineteenth century (Seeloch 2002). The incorporation of the Christian figure of La Divina Pastora into the Hindu pantheon as an aspect of the Mother Goddess was another prominent example of this tendency. Both subsequently provided the earliest Hindu pilgrimage sites in Trinidad (Comins 1893: 36).

According to Surendranath Capildeo, even the famous 'Lion House', also popularly referred to as 'the Hanuman House', was treated as a '. . . pilgrimage for people to come from the deep south, all the way into Chaguanas, and to sit at the feet there . . . to talk . . .' (Siewah 1994: 256). This pilgrimaging tendency was evident in yet another practice initiated during the late nineteenth century— visiting the most prominent Hindu temple during that time, the Green Street Hindu Temple in Tunapuna, especially for the observance of *Shiv Ratri* (POSG, 1920). From the 1950s, the Temple in the Sea in Waterloo would also become a very popular pilgrimage site. Brockington explained the Hindu preoccupation with pilgrimages as:

. . . a popular way to remove sins and accumulate merit; the merit acquired in visiting them was commonly reckoned in terms of the performance of so many Vedic rituals, but unlike the sacrifices that they thereby replace, the sacred sites were open to all (Brockington 2002: 196).

He added that in as much as many pilgrimage sites are associated with water and its purifying function, they invoke the universal

Hindu concern with purity and pollution, the latter of which is held to be washed away by bathing in such places (Brockington, 198). This can account partially for the rise in the observance of *Kartik Nahaan* (ritual bath during the eighth lunar month of the Hindu calendar), and the post-1990 consecration of many local rivers and beaches as Hindu pilgrimage sites. Ultimately, however, the establishment of pilgrimage sites throughout Trinidad can be interpreted as a direct pronouncement of Hinduism claiming Trinidad's landscape—both physically and ideologically.

After the 1970s, however, the appearance of such pilgrimage sites and new observances could be classified as more contrived, deliberate phenomena, almost always the work of some socioreligious organization. Notwithstanding the possible motives of reworking Hinduism to more tangibly situate it in the Trinidad context and to generate contemporary appeal, such developments had a mobilizing, revitalizing and cohesive effect on both the Hindu community as a whole and within the various socio-religious sects. The initiation of the *Divali Nagar* in 1986 served both as a new age annual pilgrimage of sorts and provided the context for the promotion of Hinduism as situated within Trinidad, rather than solely in relation to its Indian origin. The advent of the first 'national' *pradakshina* (ritual circumambulation of Trinidad) in 1987 also served the latter purpose by declaring Trinidad '. . . a *janmabhoomi* or a sacred motherland. . . .' (*Express* 1996). Similar claiming of space was evident in the increasing number of large-scale 'national' *pujas* conducted 'for the welfare of the country'. In fact, in one such event, the ritual altar was shaped like a map of Trinidad.

Two major school-based programmes also assisted in situating elements of Trinidad Hinduism within more securely the larger society: the Secondary Schools' *Sanskritic Sangam* (Secondary School's Cultural Meeting) in 1979 and the *Baal Vikaas* Festival in 1986. These annual programmes were structured along the lines of interschool competitions in several categories and aimed at both SDMS and non-SDMS schools. Both these competitions entailed the study of selected Hindu religious texts, Hindi, the performing arts, essay writing and public speaking (Baal Vikaas Festival

194   SHERRY-ANN SINGH

Syllabus 2003: 1). Through the years, non-Hindu participation in almost all categories of the competitions has notably increased.

The growing appetite for transporting elements of Hindu religion and culture out of the communal and into the national sphere heightened considerably during the 1960s. This was most evident in the struggle for the declaration of the Hindu festival of *Divali* as a national holiday. According to a newspaper article titled 'Hindus Ready To March For Their Own Holiday', the Member for Caroni South, Surendranath Capildeo, received a petition from the Dow Village Hindu Youth Organization to press for the granting '. . . of at least one public holiday in honour of the second largest religious group in the country' (*TG*, 8 January 1966). If not, they would be prepared to hold marches and public meetings throughout Trinidad to agitate for the holiday. Their efforts proved successful when *Divali* day was declared a public holiday in 1966.

Religious observances also transcended individual and communal boundaries to acquire a more structured, large-scale format. In 1964, all SDMS schools were closed in observance of both *Divali* and *Kartik Nahaan* (*SG*, 1 November 1964) and a '*Divali* Show' was held at the Naparima Bowl in San Fernando (*TG*, 3 November 1964). By 1965, large-scale celebrations in areas such as Caroni, St. James, El Dorado, Warrenville, Aranjuez and the University of the West Indies stimulated the press to comment that for 'the first time Trinidadians were nationally aware of *Divali*, the Hindu Festival of Lights' (*EN*, 14 November 1966). This trend would intensify through the 1990s. A most notable aspect was the advent of *Divali Nagar* in 1986. It provided the opportunity for individuals to enjoy various facets of Indian culture (the art forms, food, and dress) in one place. Its location outside the boundaries of any particular village or community augmented its appeal as a national rather than a communal event, and its location along one of the major highways in the country made it very accessible.

The *Phagwa* festival was another area that reflected transformation in Trinidad Hinduism. Until the 1970s, alcohol, *bhang* (hemp, either smoked or consumed as a drink) and *ganja* were readily consumed during *Phagwa* festivities by both singers and the other male celebrants, as was the custom in India. The earliest attempts at weeding out intoxicants from this festival proved extremely difficult. In fact, the first public *Phagwa* celebration at Aranjuez Savannah in 1968 was marred by alcohol related misdemeanors. Substantial success in this undertaking was achieved only during the 1980s in the context of rejuvenated efforts at purging Hinduism of elements that threatened to stigmatize both the religion and its adherents within the larger Trinidad framework.

In 1990, the Hindu Prachar Kendra inaugurated what was to become its annual Kendra Phagwa Festival. In the subsequent decade this event evolved into one of the most visible and controversial forums for the ventilation of issues affecting the Hindu community and for further locating Trinidad Hinduism within the larger multicultural framework. Staged during the annual *Phagwa* festivities, it entailed the singing of social commentary songs or *pitchkaarees* (in various combinations of Hindi, Bhojpuri and English) which sometimes sought to refute calypsoes that were deemed offensive to Hindus and Hinduism, to highlight social ills and to air grievances within the Hindu community. In its uniqueness to Trinidad, the *pitchkaaree* form is a definite marker of the evolution of what can be termed as 'Trinidad Hinduism'.

NEGOTIATING IDEOLOGY

In multicultural societies, conflict among different religious denominations or with elements of the secular sphere is, for the most part, inevitable. The pervasive nature of Hinduism, together with its lack of any categorical definition between the sacred and secular renders making it more prone to such religio-ideological conflicts than the other Semitic religions with relatively clearcut distinctions between the sacred and the secular. The perception widely held by the Christian population until as late as the 1980s, of Hinduism was that a subordinate religion rooted in superstition and idolatry; and as being essentially heathen, also accentuated such conflicts substantially.

The Hindu community's extended and intricate contact with Christian elements has impacted significantly on almost all aspects of life. There was a widespread perception of the *Ramayana* and

196 SHERRY-ANN SINGH

sometimes, the *Bhagvadgita* (held both by Hindus and non-Hindus) as being the 'Hindu Bible' from as early as the 1930s and possibly even before. That Trinidad Hindus themselves promoted such an analogy echoed several religious trends within the community. There is the debatable idea that Hindus in Trinidad might have been, subliminally, 'Christianized' in terms of both their systems and values. Lending credence to this notion were the Hindu observance of 'Sunday services', the relegating of Hindu weddings and other religious observances to the weekend in order to conform to an essentially Christian oriented calendar and the perception of the *Dharmachaarya*[11] as the 'Hindu Archbishop', all of which echoed Christian systems and principles. Such infiltration of Christian ideas could be seen as a response to the criticism heaped unto Hindu social and religious beliefs and practices by non-Hindu members of the larger population. In his examination of Hinduism in Fiji, John Kelly identified two possible additional effects of this influence of Christianity on Hinduism. First, the dialogic influence of the Christian missions and schools had a notable impact on the institutions of the Arya Samaj movement, which eventually filtered into the larger Hindu community. Second, it was also quite possible that the structural pressure generated by the Christian Holy Book led to the Hindu need to somehow formally establish a 'Holy Book of truth and punishment powers' (Kelly 2001: 329-51). Both these factors were also evident in Trinidad Hinduism during the 1930s and the 1940s. The close association in Trinidad between Presbyterianism and Indians also accounted for the inevitability of such pressures and influences.

CREMATION

The issue of cremation was, between 1950 and 1980, a major preoccupation of the Hindu community, with the crux of the matter lying essentially in the conflict between the Hindu and Western methods of disposal of the dead and the associated ideological differences. The Hindu population's growing awareness

[11] Literally, a preceptor or instructor on the Hindu notion of *dharma* (one's duty, righteousness and proper conduct).

'BEYOND *VANVAAS*: HINDUISM IN TRINIDAD' 197

of and discontent with not being able to perform the last rites of their loved ones in accordance with Hindu religious prescriptions, deemed crucial to the transmigration of the soul, was the most powerful impetus in this issue. Failure to perform these death rituals was more than just a contravention of religious prescription; it carried with it deep-seated moral, emotional and social ramifications. These concerns, however, were met with indifference, ignorance and opposition at the administrative and official levels. In 1953, the Minister of Agriculture and Lands the Hon. V. Bryan declared that Government was prepared to '. . . agree to cremation of the dead in accordance with accepted modern methods and in suitable crematoria' (Hansard, 8 May 1953). This decision was in spite of the administration's knowledge of the requirements of the Hindu community (Hansard, 8 May 1953).

The Government proceeded to refute the requirements of Hindus with the argument that such a method would ' . . . offend the sensibilities of the majority of the population and [that] there was also the danger of pollution of rivers by casting the remains in them' (Hansard, 8 May 1953). The complicated nature of the forms (especially for those unable to read and write English) and the procedure for acquiring the relevant permission to cremate were major points of contention (Hansard, 22 October 1965). So disenchanted were some Hindus with the numerous fruitless committees looking into the matter that they eventually took it upon themselves to start '. . . setting up areas like the Caroni Savannah Extension Road, and the Caroni Bank, on the Highway' to cremate their dead (Cremation Ordinance 1953: 136). The fact that they were essentially breaking the law in a very public manner and were risking punishment demonstrated just how strongly they felt. Such illegal cremations continued at several sites until the 1980s under the most deplorable physical conditions. There was not even a permanent base upon which the pyre could rest (Hansard, 23 May 1969). The issue was resolved, only after much debate, with the passing of the Cremation Amendment Act of 1976. The procedure was simplified into four basic steps and open air cremations and the disposal of the ashes of the dead into a river were permitted (Hansard, 30 April 1976).

198 SHERRY-ANN SINGH

MARRIAGE

The institution of marriage emerged on a national level as possibly the most contentious of Hindu issues in the form of the Marriage Bill. This issue was taken up from as early as 1923, at the seventh meeting of the ordinary session of the Legislative Council (*POSG*, 5 May 1923), but was resolved (somewhat) two decades later in 1945. The problem was deeply ensconced in the conflict of religions, ideologies and cultures and the inability of the various Hindu groups to appoint marriage officers jointly. The registration of marriages, a civil ceremony, was far removed from the sacred nature of the Hindu ceremony and rituals. As far as the Hindu community was concerned, once their ceremony had been performed, and hence, sanctioned by their gods, no further validation was needed.[12] Many aspects of the ceremony were being undermined by the conditions of the proposed Marriage Bill. Connected to the issue of the legalization of Hindu marriages, was the 'illegitimacy' of persons born of such unions. Within the boundaries of the Hindu community, neither was viewed as an issue since their traditional marriage ceremony was all the validation needed for both the union and offspring. However, the need to ensure inheritance rights was a key push factor in that direction, since, in addition to lengthy and expensive court procedures, there were many cases of property being escheated to the state upon the death of the owner. The Hon. T.M. Kelshall voiced this concern:

Is Government aware that (a) children born out of Hindu or Muslim wedlock are branded as 'illegitimates' in the Colony, thereby leaving the stigma of immorality on their parents and (b) that they are dispossessed of their rights of inheritance of their parent's estate? (Hansard 1941: 117)

CARNIVAL

The annual Carnival revelry in Trinidad had, until the 1980s, been viewed as morally and ideologically in opposition with the tenets

---

[12] The marriage issue was not only a problem for the Hindus, but also for the Muslim indentured labourers and their descendants. This was also the case with the attitude of Indians regarding the carnival. In this article the author is dealing however only with the Hindus.

'BEYOND *VANVAAS*: HINDUISM IN TRINIDAD' 199

of Hinduism (as practised in Trinidad), and Hindu participation in Carnival was therefore more of the exception than the norm. The major points of contention resided in the free interaction of semi-nude male and female bodies, and the sexually provocative public dancing and behaviour. Calypsoes which ridiculed Hindu beliefs and practices and the almost annual coinciding of the Carnival with the Hindu religious observance of *Shiv Ratri* (night dedicated to the worship of the god Shiva) also intensified the dissension. Against this backdrop emerged vigorous objections to the use of aspects of Hinduism, especially its Gods and Goddesses, in calypsoes and Carnival bands. Given the extremely low level of participation by Hindus in Carnival activities, it can be argued that the inclusion of Hindu religious elements into the portrayals was almost solely the 'creative' initiatives of non-Hindu artistes such as band leaders and costume designers.

In 1965, the attempt to portray both Hindu deities and practices in two Carnival bands, namely 'Gods And Worshippers Of India' (*EN*, 9 February 1965) and 'Vishnu's Kingdom' (*EN*, 8 February 1965) evoked intense objection from Hindus. In addition to individual protests, the issue was taken to Parliament in 1965, where the Member for Caroni South, Surendranath Capildeo claimed that three delegations of Hindus aired their grievances over the Carnival band which proposed '. . . to portray the Great Hindu God, Hanuman, the coronation of Ram Chandra, the Hindu God, and an authentic portrayal of the unblemished love between Lord Krishna and his wife Radha' (Hansard, 5 February 1965). Seemingly insensitive and sensationalizing newspaper headlines such as 'Two Days When Ancient India will come to Trinidad' (*DM*, 4 February 1965), and the justification of '. . . playing history, not religion' (*EN*, 8 February 1965), by one of the bandleaders just added to Hindu indignation. The leader of the *SDMS* subsequently formally asked the bandleader to shelve the band (*EN*, 9 February 1965), a move which proved successful, but only after much vacillation on the part of the bandleader.

Calypsoes were also a constant source of aggravation. This was due to their projection of Indians as clannish, racist, backward and miserly. The persistent ridicule of what was perceived as the rather clumsy adoption of Western mannerisms and style by Indians and their use of language served to further alienate the Indian community both from the art form and its context. Some Hindus were deeply offended by the inclusion of the Hindu ritual incantation *Om Shanti Om* in a calypso sung by Ras Shorty I.

In addition to these sustained carnival-related conflicts, several isolated issues propelled the journey to locate Hinduism further within its Trinidadian framework. During the general elections of 1986, the absence of the *Bhagvadgita* and the *Quran* for oath-taking at polling stations was interpreted as a '... gross insult to Hindus and Muslims' (*Sandesh*, 23 January 1987). The absence of any Hindu religious texts at the official residence of the President of the Republic, where the formal swearing-in of the new Government in 1986 was taking place, added injury to this insult: it resulted in a mad rush to find a text when a Hindu minister refused to take his oath until one was provided.

CONCLUSION

It is evident that, beyond the *vanvaas* of indentureship, Hinduism in Trinidad has been engaged in a continuous process of localization on several levels; one that entailed, simultaneously, change and continuity. The nature and degree of the change evinced both the propensity for adjustment of Hinduism and the inevitability of such change within the context of a multicultural society. Transformations in structures and attitudes at the communal level also succumbing to the impact of western, secular and non-Hindu influences indicated the collective or, one can suggest, the 'official' acknowledgement by Hindus of the need to at least consider the prescriptions of the larger Trinidad society. In order for Hindu religious and social practice and belief to obtain within the larger Trinidad society, the need for omissions and accretions was recognized. However, the simultaneous retention of the most fundamental concepts, systems and values, though often in varyingly mutated forms, exemplifies the tendency of diasporic communities to cling to their reconstructions, since they seem to provide the major source of identity and stability in an otherwise often ambiguous and tenuous situation. In the Trinidad context, this diametric pull between change and continuity is situated largely in the tension between 'being Hindu' while belonging to a national community. What occurred was the drive to establish itself as a 'community within a nation', a process which can be safely described as multi-layered, arduous, oftentimes misinterpreted or disregarded and by no means uniform. The success of this venture resided in the ability to strike a balance between 'being and belonging', that is to say, being Hindu but also belonging to the Trinidad society. Invariably, these selfsame 'localizing' processes were transfigured into 'globalizing' processes when Trinidad Hinduism was taken to and had to carve a space for itself within the 'double diasporic' condition evoked by the migration and settlement of Trinidad Hindus in Canada and the United States.

REFERENCES

OFFICIAL RECORDS

I.O.R. Public and Judicial Department Records L/PJ/8/338: Royal Commission on the West Indies, Deputation of J.D. Tyson to the West Indies; Tyson's Report on the Condition of Indians in Jamaica, British Guiana and Trinidad; Labour Conditions in the West Indies (1938-43).
I.O.R. Official Series V/27/820/10: Note On Emigration From India To Trinidad by Surgeon Major W.D. Comins. Calcutta: Bengal Secretariat Press, 1893.
Colony of Trinidad and Tobago Census Album, 1948.
Baal Vikaas Festival Syllabus (St. Augustine: Sanatan Dharma Maha Sabha Incorporated), 2003.
Hansard 8 May 1953.
Hansard 22 October 1965.
Cremation Ordinance 1953, 136.
Hansard 23 May 1969.
Hansard 30 April 1976.
Hansard 1941, 117.
Hansard 5 February 1965

NEWSPAPERS

Daily Mirror (*DM*), 4 February 1965.
Evening News (*EN*), 8 February 1965.

202 SHERRY-ANN SINGH

Evening News (EN), 9 February 1965.
Evening News (EN), 14 November 1966.
Express, 23 August 1996.
Port-of-Spain Gazette (POSG), 18 February 1920.
Port-of-Spain Gazette (POSG), 5 May 1923.
Sandesh 23 January 1987.
Sunday Guardian (SG), 1 November 1964.
The Indian Koh-I-Noor Gazette (KG), 1898.
Trinidad Guardian (TG), 3 November 1964.
Trinidad Guardian (TG), 8 January 1966.

ORAL INTERVIEWS

Bissoon, Jaggernath. Personal interview. 5 June 2002.
Preetam, Harry. Personal interview. 4 November 2000.
Ramdass, Joyce. Personal interview. 7 July 2002.
Seeloch, Rampersad. Personal interview. 6 June 2002.

SECONDARY SOURCES

Bahadur, Krishna P. (1976). *Ramcharitmanas: A Study in Perspective*. Delhi: Ess Ess Publications.
Bisnauth, Dale (2000). *The Settlement of Indians in Guyana, 1890-1930*. England: Peepal Tree Press.
Brereton, Bridget (1981). *A History of Modern Trinidad, 1783-1962*. New Hampshire: Heinemann International.
Brockington, John L. (2002). *The Sacred Thread: A Short History of Hinduism*. New Delhi: Oxford University Press.
Guinee, William (1970). 'Ritual and Devotion in a Trinidadian Kali Temple' (M.A. dissertation, Indiana University).
Haraksingh, Kusha (1988). 'Structure, Process and Indian Culture in Trinidad', *Immigrants & Minorities*, 7(1): pp. 113-22.
Kelly, John (2001). 'Fiji's Fifth Veda: Exile, Sanatan Dharm, and Counter Colonial Initiatives in Diaspora', in Paula Richman (ed.), *Questioning Ramayanas: A South Asian Tradition*. Berkeley: University of California Press: pp. 329-52.
Laurence, Keith O. (1994). *A Question of Labour: Indentured Immigration into Trinidad and British Guiana, 1875-1917*. Jamaica: Ian Randle Publishers.
Niehoff, Arthur (1967). 'The Function of Caste among the Indians of the Oropuche Lagoon, Trinidad', in B.M. Schwartz (ed.), *Caste in Overseas*

'BEYOND *VANVAAS*: HINDUISM IN TRINIDAD'   203

Indian Communities. San Francisco: Chandler Publishing Company: pp. 149-63.

Naipaul, Vidiadhar S. (2000). *Reading and Writing: A Personal Account.* New York: New York Review Books.

Prorok, Carolyn V. (1988). 'Hindu Temples in Trinidad: A Cultural Geography of Religious Structures and Ethnic Identity' (Ph.D. dissertation, University of Pittsburgh).

Ramesar, Marianne (1994). *Survivors of another Crossing: A History of East Indians in Trinidad, 1880-1946.* St. Augustine: University of the West Indies School of Continuing Studies.

Siewah, Samaroo (1994). *The Lotus and the Dagger. The Capildeo Speeches (1957-94).* Trinidad: Chakra Publishing House.

Thapar, Romila (2001). 'Foreword', in Paula Richman (ed.), *Questioning Ramayanas: A South Asian Tradition.* Berkeley: University of California Press.

Vertovec, Steven (1992). *Hindu Trinidad: Religion, Ethnicity and Socio-Economic Change.* London: Macmillan Education Ltd.

Walcott, Derak (1993). *The Antilles. Fragments of Epic Memory: The Nobel Lecture.* New York: Farrar, Straus and Giroux.

PART II

ISLAM AND MUSLIMS IN THE *GIRMIT* DIASPORA

CHAPTER 8

The *Ummah* in the Caribbean: African and Asian Origins of Caribbean Islam

BRINSLEY SAMAROO

ISLAMIC FAITH

One of the significant forces of influence in the modern world is Islamic beliefs and practices. There are approximately 1.6 billion Muslims in some 40 countries covering most of the globe from Morocco to Indonesia towards the East and in the reverse direction from West Africa to North America and the Caribbean. The vast majority of those who came to the Caribbean during slavery and indentureship were Sunnis with a sprinkling of Shias and Ahmadiyyas, deriving from the Indian subcontinent. These three groups are of particular relevance to Caribbean Islam.

The Shias and Sunnis date back to the early foundations of Islam. After the death of the Prophet in 632, there was a protracted struggle for the Caliphate waged by two major factions. Some believed that the honour should go to the descendants of the Prophet, beginning with his son-in-law and cousin Ali, who had a divine right to the headship. They came to be known as the Shias (Party of Ali). On the other side were those who believed that the Caliphate should be decided through consensus and was not a hereditary privilege (see Hazleton 2009). These were the Sunnis who were in a clear majority.

Around 90 per cent of Muslims today are Sunnis and this is roughly the proportion of those Muslims who came to the Caribbean. The Ahmadiyyas are the followers of Mirza Ghulam Ahmad (1835-

1908), from the Punjab region in South Asia, who created a synthetic religion combining elements of Islam, Christianity and Hinduism. Amongst his claims was that he was the *Mahdi*, the guided one, who had come to renew righteousness among Muslims. After his death, the Ahmadis broke into two factions, the Qadianis and the Lahoris, the former being from Ahmad's hometown and the latter being those who had settled in Lahore. There were small groups of Ahmadis in northern India, the primary recruiting centre for indentured labourers, and members of both sects came to the Caribbean (see Khan 2015).

In order to explain this continuous growth of Islam from the seventh century to the present, we must pause briefly to examine the attraction of the faith through the ages. Islam offers a one-package formula for the guidance of its followers which does not involve the complications which are inherent in Christian theology. Whereas Christianity generally requires a separation between religion and politics, Islam offers a totality in which the secular and religious are inseparably united. The Christian theologian St. Augustine draws a line between these spheres in the doctrine of the two swords namely, the religious and the secular. This follows the dictate of Jesus who advised his followers to give unto Caesar what was his due and to God what was due to the divine. In Islam, all aspects of human existence are interwoven into a comprehensive skein guided by Five Pillars, namely, Shahadah (belief in one God), Salah (daily prayers), Saum (fasting), Zakah (charity) and Hajj (pilgrimage). The religion offers a series of philosophical principles which appeal to mankind's spiritual needs in a system that is all-embracing, making no separation between the secular and the religious as in the case with Christianity. The *Qur'an* and the Hadith, which are edicts from the sayings of the Prophet are manuals for the conduct of human affairs. The religion is particularly appealing to oppressed and marginalized people since it recognizes no class or caste hierarchy as it brings together people of all races under a common umbrella. The Hajj pilgrimage provides a remarkable opportunity for the gathering of millions at the sacred places of Mecca and Medina where lifelong friendships are created, and a strong sense of identity is fostered.

THE *UMMAH* IN THE CARIBBEAN   209

Another attribute of Islam is its emphasis on education and the acquisition of knowledge for personal and social development. Both the *Qur'an* and the Hadith are full of injunctions which praise those who acquire knowledge. This continuous advocacy of the spread of knowledge has been, from the seventh century, a major selling point for Islam. In the very first Surah, the angel Gabriel instructs the messenger to 'Read in the name of the lord who created thee. Read and thy lord is most honourable who taught thee to write with the pen' (*Qur'an* 96: 1-5). Later on, the Book tells us that 'whoever is given knowledge is given abundant wealth' (12: 269) and 'Those who truly fear god, among his servants who have knowledge' (35: 28). Propelled by these ideologies Islam, as a forceful and dynamic faith reached Syria in 635, Iraq in 637, Palestine in 640 and the Persian Empire by 650. By the eighth century, Islam had gained a dominant foothold in the Iberian Peninsula. Against heavy odds there was the proverbial urge to spread Islam.

IBERIAN ISLAM

Spain faced an unending colonial dilemma. It continued suppressing the Islamic threat in Europe against which it had fought the centuries-old Reconquista, as it sought to establish hegemony in the American hemisphere. Spain had to find a labour supply to replace the decimated Amerindian population, and Las Casas recommended, in 1516, the substitution of African slaves for Amerindians. Both Las Casas and the Conquistadores seemed unaware of the strength of Islam among West African kingdoms and a large number of Muslims—at least 10 per cent—who came as slaves (Gomez 2005: 14). Spain made constant efforts to stem the arrival of Muslims in its New World possessions. Before and during slavery, the faith was carried from Arabia by traders, missionaries and teachers to Sudanic kingdoms such as Ghana, Kanem, Songhay, Hausaland and Dogomba. Here, Islam was organized among the Mandinka, Fulah, Susu, Ashanti, and Hausa who became part of the Dar-ul-Islam (the abode of submission) long before Christianity reached those areas. By the fourteenth century, Borno, Kano, and Timbuktu

210 BRINSLEY SAMAROO

had become centres of Islamic learning of the *Qur'an*, Hadith and Sharia. These institutions were havens of linguistic studies, history, mathematics and astronomy equally (see Spencer 1962). The University of Sankore in Timbuktu housed a cosmopolitan community of scholars under the leadership of the Qadi (religious judge). African rulers employed many of the graduates as administrators and as teachers who would 'civilize' their subjects (July 1974: 71).

As one has seen, there was also the flow of the religion to the East, across Central Asia to India and Indonesia. From the splendour of Mughal India, Islam was carried to the Caribbean by indentured labourers, while from Java, a different brand of Islam was taken to Suriname by indentured and free labourers. This combination of Iberian Muslims and African followers of Islam proved to be a constant thorn in the flesh for Spanish rulers well into the nineteenth century. In 1501, Spain decreed that Jews, Moors, heretics and 'new Christians' were not to enter the Americas but by 1510, blacks and Ladinos were almost twice as numerous as Europeans in Hispaniola (Gomez 2005: 14). In 1530, Charles V continued this impossible mission when he banned 'Barbary Slaves of the caste of Moors, Jews or Mulattoes' from entering the Americas (Gomez 2005, 18). In 1543, the Holy Roman Emperor ordered the expulsion of all Muslim descendants after hearing complaints that these people were spreading 'bad manners' to the first peoples (Winters 1978: 41). By this time, there were substantial Muslim groups in Mexico, Puerto Rico and in the Southern Caribbean settlements. Muslim slaves in continental North America carried similar attitudes to non-Muslims. In Calvert County, Maryland and in Trinidad, Jamaica and Bahia, these groups refused to mix with other slaves because they considered these 'Others' beneath their rank and former dignity (Gomez 2005: 177).

ISLAM IN THE NON-HISPANIC COLONIES

In Jamaica, where the (pre-British) Spanish administration was weak, two Maroons were incorporated to high office, one as governor and the other as lieutenant-general. Both had Islamic names (Afroz 2012: 183). After the British conquest in 1655, Islamic influence

THE *UMMAH* IN THE CARIBBEAN 211

diminished in the face of determined efforts by the State and the plantocracy to wipe out all 'heathen' influences. Today, a few Islamic words and greetings remain in the Maroon vocabulary.

After the British conquest of Jamaica, batches of enslaved Africans were purchased by British planters who actively promoted the suppression of African beliefs and their replacement by Christian doctrines, which were alien to the African mind. Even so, there is clear evidence of the Islamic presence there. Dr. Robert Madden, a special magistrate, sent to supervise the operation of the Emancipation Act, regularly met black Muslims about whom he wrote (Afroz 2012: 220). Abu Bakkar al Siddiqui was born in Timbuktu around 1790. He was the son of the class of Ullema (men of learning) and had been educated in the academies of Bouna and Jenne, after which he was kidnapped sometime around 1805 and sold in Jamaica. He was a Hafiz (one who had memorized the *Qur'an*), but in Jamaica, he was christened Edward Donnelan. Despite this conversion, he never abandoned Islam after three decades of enslavement. In 1834, he was freed and brought to England, where he joined an expedition to North Africa. Upon returning to his ancestral place, he was received with great pomp, a tribute to his high ancestry. Another Muslim slave, Mohammed Kaaba, now Robert Tuffit, had studied Sharia at Timbuktu. He was sold to slave traders in 1777 and spent five decades as a slave, never forgetting his Islamic roots (Afroz 2012: 256).

Bryan Edwards, the planter historian, noted the presence on his estate of an old faithful Mandinka servant who had been circumcised and had never forgotten his morning and evening prayers (salah) and observed Friday as a day of fasting. Dr Madden wrote of the 'irrepressible fervour' of Benjamin Cockrane, the son of a Muslim chieftain, among the Mandingoes and a group of his compatriots. This group would have inflicted the whole of the *Qur'an* on him had he not chastised them for pretending to be 'that which they were not'. Madden was told that there were hundreds of Muslims in Jamaica. Despite the suppression, Dr. Afroz found vestiges of Islamic practice among post-slavery Africans. These included strict cleanliness of their places of prayer (Masjid) and the practice of *wudhu* (ritual cleaning) before prayer. Today, most

Jamaican Muslims are of African descent and are members of the Jamaica Interfaith Organization in a nation that facilitates freedom of worship (Afroz 2012: 256).

In Trinidad, as in Jamaica, there is clear evidence of the Islamic African presence. During the final years of slavery, black Muslims made efforts to be released from bondage and for repatriation to West Africa. An English captain stationed in Trinidad during the last years of slavery, expressed his disgust at the cruelty of the island's slave owners. He also gave an account of the life of an elderly slave, the Imam Slamank, who had been christened Adam in Trinidad. Born around 1768, Slamank was trained as an imam but was captured and sold into slavery in 1803 and was penned at the Marli estate, just outside the capital city. For some three decades, he was forced to work on the cane field, and when, in his old age, he complained against the hard work, he was imprisoned by his proprietress. Now crippled and in jail, he petitioned the governor to be released and freed, giving the assurance that he would not seek compensation since he would be looked after by the Mandingo community (Hodgson 1838: 368).

The leader of that community was Jonas Mohammed Bath, who claimed that he was a sultan in the Gambia. He was well versed in the *Qur'an*, dressed as an Imam and was regarded as the patriarch of the Mandingoes. Bath and his compatriots had survived the rigours of slavery but were not culturally de-humanized. 'They were active, confident and successful' (Campbell 1974). They wanted to be repatriated to Africa and petitioned the Colonial Office in January 1838, asking the State to organize this. They claimed they were afraid to venture into the open sea lest they be captured and sold into slavery. They now wanted a British armed vessel as the agency for transport across the Atlantic (British National Archives CO 295/12).

The British ignored this request. Despite this refusal, there was one Muslim who refused to be deterred. Mohammedu Sisei, an Islamic scholar from the Gambia, was captured and sold to a French slaver in 1810. However, that cargo was seized by the British, who had banned salve trading in 1806. Sisei was first sent to Antigua, where he was enlisted in the British West India Regiment, christened

THE *UMMAH* IN THE CARIBBEAN   213

Felix Ditt. In 1816 he was sent to Trinidad, where he joined the group led by Bath. After the British refusal to repatriate the Mandingoes, Sisei borrowed money from fellow Muslims and paid passages for himself, his wife and child to London. There he came under the protection of the Royal Geographical Society, which took him back to the Gambia (Campbell 1974: 38-9).

The largest group of black Muslims to arrive in Trinidad was the army of some 744 former soldiers and their families who were refugees from the Anglo-American War of 1812 and disbanded soldiers from the British West India Regiment after the Napoleonic War, which ended in 1815. Whereas other West Indian colonies were unwilling to accept free people in a slave society. Trinidad received these immigrants and settled them in the Hondo River Valley in Valencia, North East Trinidad, between 1819 and 1825. The settlement was organized in military style under a former sergeant, the Imam Abu Bakkar (Reid & Gilmore 2014: 186).

Under his leadership, the group produced yams, plantain, rice, ginger, corn and cocoa, selling their produce in Sangre Grande and Arima. However, the persistent Anglicans soon became a thorn in their flesh. Revd Hamilton, the pastor for the region, complained bitterly against these 'Mohammedans' who had come under the influence of 'so-called Mandingo priests' by whom they were instructed. Hamilton was eager to have a bridge constructed over the Quare' River, which separated the settlement from the wider Christian community. Such a bridge, he claimed, would enable him to reach and convert these 'heathens'. Gradually, State support was cut off. Many former soldiers were employed as policemen, who accompanied stipendiary magistrates after emancipation, and inducements were offered to those who converted. Even the elderly sergeant Abu Bakkar became a landowner under the name of John Brooks (Reid & Gilmore 2014: 187).

After the closure of the Hondo River by the 1840s, many of its members relocated to form secret Jamaats in Port of Spain and Central Trinidad. Some went to the south, where the community of Mandingo Road still carries that name. Also, a new word, 'Mandinga', was added to the local vocabulary in the same way that 'Fulahman' referred to Muslims in Guyana.

214 BRINSLEY SAMAROO

A contemporary researcher on African survivals in Tobago has found ample evidence of Islamic practice among the descendants of enslaved Hausa, Yoruba and Mandingo. One group of Muslims, who migrated from Tobago to Trinidad, remembered their Islamic heritage:

Tobago, Tobago
Tobago Ali's home
A man who is generous, as I said.
Tobago Ali's home (Warner-Lewis 2015: 109).

This is one of many Islamic chants recorded by Warner-Lewis, who also recalls the veiled headdress worn by Indian and Mandingo women, the blending of Islamic and Yoruba rituals, and the Islamic memories of African Trinidad elders (Warner-Lewis 2015: 24, 67, 113, 116).

The African Islamic presence in Suriname and Guyana has also been established. As in the rest of the region, Muslims waged constant jihad against slavery. European slave owners, for their part, were always aware of the paucity of their members vis-à-vis the slaves. This caused them to stamp out any hint of insurrection with exemplary harshness. In 1807, for example, a plan for an uprising in Essequibo was betrayed by a slave girl. In the enquiry which followed, a letter, written in Arabic, which allegedly gave directions to the plotters, was discovered. Although the court had no facility for translating the letter, the panic caused by the incident led to the execution of nine supposed plotters. Later, a list of recaptured runaways in Suriname gave Muslim names such as Bacchus, Mohammed, Moussa, Sabah, Feekea and Russanah (Chikrie & Khanam 2016: 109-10).

Slave registers have names like Assat, Madar, Akhrum and Assiya, many of which are derived from the maroon 'Bush Negro' society, which waged constant warfare against the Dutch. Maroons, such a Samsam and Arabi, are among those who signed a peace treaty with the Dutch in 1760 and a missionary narrative tells of a slave, who translated the *Qur'an* into Sranan and of others, who held a low view of Christianity (Hassankhan 2016: 189-90). In 1830 a law was passed in Suriname which decreed that no negress was to

THE *UMMAH* IN THE CARIBBEAN 215

wear clothes above the waist. They could wear a petticoat from the waist to the knee. This was very depressing for all slaves but particularly to Muslims, whose code required covering of the body. Religious observances were particularly difficult for Africans in the continental South American colonies, where slave locations were far apart, extending over distant locations. Those who wished to follow the tenets of Islam were forced to do so secretly and partially, in small pockets, become Christians ostensibly or live a life as the other, alienated from the self.

In the post-slavery period, when there was an influx of Indians and Javanese, there was greater solidarity and better communications. This enabled closer observance of non-Christian religions in the region. Under the new Asian umbrella, there was room for the revival of Islamic *dawah* encouraged by North American Islamic practices. Such practice was transferred through frequent visits by black Muslims from North America and by returning Muslims who had sojourned there. Aliyah Khan, in her recent comprehensive publication on Caribbean Islam, highlights the career of one such returnee (Khan 2020: 134-71).

INDIAN AND JAVANESE ISLAM

In 1898 Munshi Rahaman Khan, an outstanding Indo-Surinamese teacher, arrived as an indentured labourer in Suriname.

We travelled a great deal and saw sea and storms. With Allah's blessings, we reached safely by ship. Everyone thanked God (Khuda) and felt happy when we reached the depot (In Paramaribo). Having been three months at sea had made a village out of the ship called *Avon*. Today we put our feet on earth with God's blessings (Sinah-Kerkhoff, Ellen Bal & Deo Singh 2005).

The demand for new source of labour in the circum-Caribbean region after Emancipation added to the already cosmopolitan character of the society, populated as it was by First Peoples, Spanish, French, Dutch, English, African and mixtures of all these. From 1838 to 1917, about half a million indentured Indians or *girmityas* (agreement signers) were transported to the British, French and Dutch colonies, among whom were about 14 per cent Muslims.

After Emancipation in the Dutch colonies in 1863, some 32,000 Javanese were imported into Suriname, 85 per cent of whom were Muslims. These substantial numbers of Muslims proved to be a barrier to the Christian missionaries bent on cleansing the region of 'heathen' influence. The majority of those who came from India were Hindus who, in the Caribbean, joined hands with the Muslims in resisting Christian conversion as they had been doing in India since the early nineteenth century. Among the Muslims who came were Imams and Moulvis, who had studied, like their African counterparts, in centres of learning in Lucknow, Shahabad, Azamgarh, Faizabad and Agra. These migrants brought features of Mughal India to this region (Afroz 2000).

In the villages from which most of the indentured came, Hindus and Muslims lived in relative harmony, away from the turmoil of the large cities where communal rivalries were encouraged and facilitated by the British through their policy of divide and rule, particularly after the great mutiny of 1857. There was intercommunal harmony which was largely brought to the Caribbean. Among the Muslim groups which came to the Caribbean were *julahas* (weavers), *fakirs* (wandering holy men), Mughals (descendants of former rulers) and Pathans (Afghans who had settled in India) (Sinah-Kerkhoff, Ellen Bal & Deo Singh 2005: xviii).

A number of Muslims, particularly Pathans, had joined the Hindus in the 1857 Revolt, and these were now hunted down, to be hanged or banished to the bleak Andaman & Nicobar Islands, deep in the Indian Ocean (Samaroo 2012: 71). Muslims came in small numbers to the Caribbean before 1857, but there was a marked increase after 1857 as they had fled British revenge. The first ships to bring Indians to Guyanese plantations in 1838, the *Hesperus* and *Whitby*, had Muslims such as Kyut Ali, Ally Buckus, Sheebah, Jeewan Khan and his wife, Bharrup. The first ship to bring them to Trinidad in May 1845 was the *Fath-al-Razak* (Victory to Allah as provider), owned by the Bombay merchant Ibrahim bin Yoosuf. Among the passengers were Omrudee, Furred, Faize, Madar, Buxo, Bahdur and Faizan (Kirpalani 1945: Frontispiece). When the *Lalla Rookh* arrived in Suriname in 1873, there were 37 Muslims aboard.

THE *UMMAH* IN THE CARIBBEAN 217

Of particular interest to the study of the *Ummah* in the Caribbean has been the significant role played by the Pathans. As an established community of Afghanistan, they guarded the northern boundaries of the Mughal Empire with which they were close allies. They have never been subdued by invading forces and today continue to resist domination as the Americans are finding. From the northern hills, they descended into the Indo-Gangetic Plains, taking with them their bravery and abhorrence of injustice. Raymond Chikrie has amply demonstrated the role of Guyanese and Surinamese Afghans in resistance movements (Chikrie 2002).

Mazar Khan, for example, was among those who were exiled by the British, for his anti-British activities in India during the post-1857 period. In 1883 he was transported to Guyana, where he continued the struggle for justice on the Caledonian plantation, Essequibo. In the Rose Hall uprising of 1913, a determined struggle against indentureship, there are typical Pathan names such as Moula Bux, Jahangir Khan, Dildar Khan and others. The Queen's masjid in Georgetown was built by Pathans led by Gool Mohammed Khan and other.

The most outstanding Pathan teacher in Suriname was Munshi Rahman Khan (1874-1972), about whom much has been written. He arrived in Suriname in 1898 as an indentured labourer on 'Plantation Lust and Rust' and moved upwards for the rest of his life. His importance lies in the fact that he came as an educated person, fulfilled his indentureship and became a writer of prose and poetry, a teacher (munshi) to Hindu and Muslim clerics, court interpreter and Indian congregational leader in Suriname. He epitomized the all inclusive nature of Indian religions wherein there was no separation between the secular and religious spheres of life. As a historian, he chronicled the history of India, the indentureship system and stressed the need for diasporic Indians to maintain the culture. To him, the *Ramayan* and *Qur'an* were essential in maintaining the culture. He took time to translate these texts into the languages spoken by the *girmityas* as a means of building confidence in a strange land. Fortunately, he has bequeathed posterity in four volumes of his life and work (Sinah-Kerkhoff, Ellen Bal & Deo Singh 2005).

218 BRINSLEY SAMAROO

THE JAVANESE IN SURINAME

The Javanese were the last of the Asian labourers to come to the Caribbean after the late Emancipation of slaves in Dutch colonies in 1863. This migration of the Javanese lasted from 1890 until 1939. About 85 per cent of the 32,000 Javanese who arrived were Muslim. However, from 1890 to the present, there has been considerable controversy between those who wish to maintain the imported Islam and the reformists keen to 'cleanse' the faith of supposedly non-Islamic practices and return it to Islam of the *Qur'an* and the Hadith. The traditionalists (abangan) brought an Islam which was an amalgam of pre-Islamic Indonesian religion with the Buddhist influences and weak Islamic content. The reformists (santri), for their part, believe that the non-Islamic accretions would be excised and that the original tenets should be strictly observed. In Suriname, the reformers faced another problem, namely the mixing with Indian Muslims whose practices were influenced by the Hindu tradition from which they emerged. One point of contention, for example, was the direction in which Muslims should prostrate themselves when offering prayer. The traditionalists believed that they should face westwards, which they did in Java, as that was the direction of Mecca. Now that they were in the west, the reformers argued they should face the northeast, which is in the direction towards Mecca (Soeropawiro 2016: 234-6).

Associations have been formed representing the divergent views and the differences were even carried to the Netherlands after 1975, when Surinamese independence caused a mass migration to the former colonial power. These divergent views have not weakened the fabric of Surinamese Islam since all groups cooperate in civil and political matters concerning the total interest. Their joint agitation, for example, led to the State's formal recognition of Islam as a valid Surinamese religion in 1940, when Muslim marriages were legally accepted. In the rapid Arabization of Islam, the reformists appear to have the upper hand, and, over a period of time, it appears, will continue to make inroads and dominate the scene (Soeropawiro 2016: 237-41).

THE *UMMAH* IN THE CARIBBEAN

TWENTIETH CENTURY INITIATIVES

The end of indentureship in 1920 witnessed a strong revival of Islamic activity in the Southern Caribbean. As many thousands of Hindus and Muslims were released from bondage, there was an efflorescence of activity characterized by visits of Hindu and Muslim missionaries and scholars from India, the construction of additional mosques and mandirs for worship and education without any State assistance, and the joining of Hindu, Muslim and Christian leadership, which agitated for better conditions. They wanted better working and housing conditions on the sugar estates, improved health facilities, State assistance to non-Christian schools, the legalization of Hindu and Muslim marriages and representation in colonial legislatures. Whilst they remained part of these Pan-Indian organizations, Hindus and Muslims formed their own associations, which increased after the First World War (1914-18) (Kassim 2016: 140-7).

In 1895, the Queenstown Jama Masjid (JMQ) was founded in British Guiana by Gool Mohammed, a Pathan moulvi, who had completed his indentureship (A. Hamid 2007: 3). Today, this masjid serves as a focal point for Muslim identity. In 1926, the Young Men's Muslim Literary Society was created, and in 1949, the United Sad'r Islamic Anjuman was started. In similar manner, Trinidad Muslims moved to form kindred groups such as the Islamic Guardian Association (1898) and the Tackvee Yatul Islamic Association (Society for the Strength of Islam) in 1926. In 1935 the Anjuman Sunnat al Jamaat Association (ASJA) was incorporated and in 1938, the Tabligh-ul-Islam followed. In 1947, the Trinidad Muslim League was formed (Kassim 2016: 140-7) .

From the early twentieth century onwards, there was close interaction between Trinidad and Guyana as jamaats in the two colonies maintained regular contact. This mutuality led to two crucial initiatives led by Trini/Guyana Islamic leadership. On the partition of India in 1947, the majority of Caribbean Muslims affiliated themselves with Pakistan, considered as the Islamic 'homeland'. Shortly after 1947, British Caribbean Muslims petitioned the Colonial Office requesting separate representation in colonial legislatures.

When this was refused, the petitioners sought the assistance of Pakistan's High Commissioner, Abul Hasan Isphahani, who sought to intercede with the Colonial Office from his London office. The Colonial office was very clear on the matter. 'Caribbean Muslims had to throw in their lot with the territory in which they have settled and play their part locally in evolving political institutions' (British National Archives CO 1031/899).

The Colonial Office was annoyed that Caribbean Muslims were also appealing to Pakistan's ambassador to Washington to plead on their behalf. This attitude, the Office indicated, 'should clearly be discouraged'. By the end of 1952, this debate, so far as the Colonial Office was concerned, was over. However, the matter was far from finished for a group of young Muslims in Trinidad and Guyana. This time, the inspiration was the Egyptian Revolution of 1952, which ousted the British-backed Muhammad Ali dynasty and replaced it with a military regime led by Colonel Gamal Abdel Nasser. In June 1953, King Faruq was deposed, and Egypt was declared a republic. One of Nasser's trusted lieutenants was Col. Anwar Sadat, who would later become President of the Republic.

Muslims in the Caribbean were closely following these events. A Muslim Committee of the West Indies was created under the leadership of Wahid Ali (1928-2008), then a young Trinidadian pharmacist with extensive international connections. In September 1954, Ali passed through Cairo after he had attended a conference of Muslim youths in Pakistan. Ali discussed the absence of Muslim representation in Caribbean legislatures with Sadat, then a Minister of State in the Egyptian government and chair of the newly created Islamic Conference. Sadat endorsed Ali's request for separate Muslim representation and recommended it to the British ambassador in Cairo. The ambassador advised London that serious attention should be paid to this matter because of the importance of Egypt in British foreign policy. The Colonial Office, however, declined this request. It held on to the view that colonial legislatures 'should not be nominated to represent interests but should be appointed to serve the broad and best interests of the colony as a whole' (British National Archives CO 1031/1297).

This negative Colonial Office response was sent to Cairo and

THE *UMMAH* IN THE CARIBBEAN 221

Port of Spain, and there the matter ended. In fact, two of the key leaders, Wahid Ali and Rahaman Gajraj (of Guyana), joined the more prominent national movement and rose to high office. Wahid Ali went on to qualify as a medical doctor and later became President of Trinidad and Tobago Senate from 1971 to 1987. Gajraj was nominated to the Guyanese legislature, where he served from 1951 to 1961, later becoming Speaker of the House. From this time, the demand for separate representation died as Muslims joined the major political parties in the region.

THE STATE OF THE *UMMAH* IN CONTEMPORARY CARIBBEAN

In a world of globalized conflict, the *Ummah* in the Caribbean has had its share of challenges. Among these is the division of the faith into ethnic/racial moulds, that is, the separation between Asian-Caribbean and African-Caribbean Muslims. A significant reason for this was the European strategy of divide and rule among the colonial subjects so that they could hold the dominant hand. Muslims in the Caribbean, as members of two major ethnic groups, were socialized into this separatist pattern. There were brief moments of solidarity to achieve particular goals, but the separation has persisted. Neither Indian nor African Muslims constitute homogenous groupings. The arrival of reformist tendencies, the rise of neo-Sufi movements, social media and the availability of global Islamic preachers online creates fissures among Muslims beyond race and ethnicity. Another cause of much debate has been India's recent efforts to redress the perceived historical wrongs under Mughal domination during the pre-modern era. This desire to ensure a Hindutva hegemony under the government of Narendra Modi has stimulated considerable debate in the Caribbean region as in the rest of the international community due to the rise of Hindu consciousness and greater tension amongst Hindus and Muslims.

BRINSLEY SAMAROO

REFERENCES

Afroz, Sultana (2003). 'Invisible yet Invincible: The Muslim *Ummah* in Jamaica', *Journal of Muslim Minority Affairs*, 23(1): April, pp. 211-22.

—— (2000). 'The Moghul Islamic Diasporas: The Institutionalization of Islam in Jamaica', *Journal of Muslim Minority Affairs*, 20(2): pp. 271-89.

British National Archives: CO 1031-899, CO 1031-1297 and CO 295/12.

Campbell, Carl (1974). 'Jonas Mohammed Bath and the Free Mandingos in Trinidad: The Question of Their Repatriation to Africa 1831-1838', *Pan African Journal*, 7(2): pp. 129-52.

—— (1971). 'Mohammedu Sisei of Gambia and Trinidad', *African Studies Association of the West Indies Bulletin*, 7: pp. 29-38.

Chickrie, Raymond (2002). 'The Afghan Muslims of Guyana and Suriname', *Journal of Muslim Minority Affairs*, 22(2): pp. 381-99.

Chickrie, Raymond and B. Khanan (2016). 'Hinduism and Muslims in Guyana', in Maurits S. Hassankhan, Goolam Vahed and Lomarsh Roopnarine (eds.), *Indentured Muslims in the Diaspora*. New Delhi: Manohar: pp. 109-40.

Gomez, Michael (2005). *Black Crescent: The Experiences and Legacy of African Muslims in the Americas*. New York: Cambridge University Press.

Hamid, Ahmad (2007). *Muslims in Guyana*. Transcript.

Hassankhan, Maurits (2016). 'Islam and Indian Muslims in Suriname. A Struggle for Survival', in Maurits S. Hassankhan, Goolam Vahed and Lomarsh Roopnarine (eds.), *Indentured Muslims in the Diaspora*. New Delhi: Manohar: pp. 181-228.

Hazleton, Lesley (2009). *After the Prophet: The Epic Story of the Shia-Sunni Split in Islam*. New York: Anchor.

Hodgson, Studholme (1838). *Truths from the West Indies: Including a Sketch of Madeira in 1833*. London: William Ball, Paternoster Row.

July, Robert W. (1974). *A History of the African People*. New York: Charles Scribner & Sons.

Khan, Adil Hussain (2015). *From Sufism to Ahmadiyya: A Muslim Minority Movement in South Asia*. Bloomington: Indiana University Press.

Kassim, Halima Sa'adia (2016). 'Identity and Acculturation of Trinidad Muslims', in Maurits S. Hassankhan, Goolam Vahed and Lomarsh Roopnarine (eds.), *Indentured Muslims in the Diaspora*. New Delhi: Manohar: pp. 141-80.

Khan, Aliyah (2020). *Far from Mecca: Globalising the Muslim Caribbean*. New Brunswick, New Jersey: Rutgers University Press.

Kirpalani, Murli J. et al. (1945). *Indian Centenary Review*. Trinidad, Port of Spain: Guardian Printery.

THE *UMMAH* IN THE CARIBBEAN 223

Rahman Khan, Munshi (2005). *An Autobiography of an Indian Indentured Labourer*. New Delhi: Shipra.

Reid, Basil and G. Gilmore (eds.), (2014). *Encyclopedia of Caribbean Archaeology*. Gainesville, Florida: University Press of Florida.

Samaroo, Brinsley (2016). 'The Caribbean consequences of the Indian revolt of 1857', in R.L. Hangloo (ed.), *Indian Diaspora in the Caribbean: History, Culture and Identity*. New Delhi: Primus: pp. 71-93.

Sinah-Kerkhoff, K., E.W. Bal, and A. Deo Singh (eds.) (2005). *Autobiography of an Indian indentured labourer: Munshi Rahman Khan (1874-1972)*. Delhi: Shipra.

Soeropawiro, Stanley (2016). 'The development of Islam amongst the Javanese in Suriname', in Maurits S. Hassankhan, Goolam Vahed and Lomarsh Roopnarine (eds.), *Indentured Muslims in the Diaspora*. New Delhi: Manohar: pp. 229-74.

Spencer, Trimingham (1962). *History of Islam in West Africa*. New York: Oxford University Press.

Warner-Lewis, Maureen (2015). *Guinea's other Suns*. Jamaica: The University of the West Indies Press.

Winters, Clyde Ahmad (1978).'Muslims in pluralistic societies the case of the West Indies', *Al Itihad*, July, pp. 41-2.

CHAPTER 9

From Indentured Labourers to Permanent Settlers: Muslims in Fiji

JAN A. ALI

INTRODUCTION

Fiji is a small island republic situated in the south-west of the Pacific Ocean, an archipelago with 322 islands out of which 106 are inhabited. It has two main islands—Viti Levu and Vanua Levu. Viti Levu is the largest island among the group of islands with an area of 10,388 sq. km and accommodates approximately 70 per cent of Fiji's population. Fiji is approximately 2,797 km north-east of Sydney, Australia and 1,848 km north of Auckland, New Zealand.

Suva, the capital and the largest city, is located in south-east of Viti Levu. Lautoka is the second largest city which lies on the western side of Viti Levu and 24 km south of the Nadi International Airport. The second largest island, Vanua Levu, has an area of 5,538 sq. km and north-west of the island is Labasa, its largest and main town. To the south-east of Vanua Levu lies Savusavu, a relatively smaller town, but a popular local and international tourist destination.

The British colonized the islands in 1874. The Colony of Fiji was a British crown colony which Britain ruled from 10 October 1874 to 10 October 1970 when Fiji became independent. Following a series of *coup d'état* in 1987, Fiji was declared a republic.

Fiji is a multicultural society. Its current population is 926,276 with the Taukei (the Indigenous settlers of Fiji) making up about

56.8 per cent of the total Fijian population, followed by Indo-Fijians (37.5 per cent), Rotumans (1.2 per cent), and others (Europeans, part Europeans, other Pacific Islanders, and Chinese) 4.5 per cent (Fiji Demographics Profile, 2019). In regard to religion, Christianity is the main religion of the nation, followed by Hinduism and then Islam (Lal 2016). In terms of the breakdown of religious demography Christians from various Christian denominations most of whom are indigenous Fijians constitute 64.5 per cent of the total population followed by Hindus making up 27.9 per cent, Muslims 6.3 per cent, Sikhs 0.3 per cent, identified as 'other' 0.3 per cent, and 'no faith' identified as 0.8 per cent (Fiji Demographics Profile, 2019).

Within this very broad range of religious and ethnic groupings, Muslims constitute a minority group. Muslims in Fiji came between 1879 and 1916 as part of a larger contingent of Indian indentured labourers brought in to work on the sugarcane fields during the British colonial rule. Under the harshness and inhumanity of the indentured labour system, religious rituals and practices of Muslims were hugely compromised and remained a strictly private affair. Islam had no public appearance at all but Muslims nonetheless held on firmly to their religion through engaging in religious practices to varying degrees through personal religious conviction. Then, as indenture came to an end in 1920 and numbers of Muslim increased, both through indenture first then birth and migration, Muslims become more organized and resourceful.

Over the years Muslims have established their own identity in the Islands and have made substantial investment in religion through the establishment of mosques and *markazes* (Islamic centres), education through establishing primary and secondary schools and *madrasas* (singular—a religious college for Islamic instruction), and civil society organizations spread throughout Fiji. Mosques and *markazes* serve dual purposes of religious and social activities for Muslims and are regularly used for Friday *juma* (congregational prayer), breaking fast and *tarawih* (additional ritual prayer) during the holy month of Ramadan, marriage functions, and celebration of other religious events.

A vast majority of Muslims in Fiji are Sunni (Sunnis stress the

FROM INDENTURED LABOURERS TO PERMANENT SETTLERS   227

primacy of sunnah—the Prophet Muhammad's sayings and deeds), most of whom are followers of the Hanafi school of jurisprudence followed by a handful of obscure Shafi'i school of jurisprudence, Ahmadis, who are considered by the majority Muslims globally to be a heterodox group, are in the minority among Fijian Muslims. Within the Sunni group, there are various subsects or out-groups such as Ahl-i-Hadith (an offshoot of the Wahhabi movement), Miladis (a part of Indian Barelvis who follow the Maturidi school of Islamic theology), and the Tablighis (members of the Tabligh Jama'at who subscribe to Deobandism—an Indo-Pakistani reformist ulema movement centred in the Dar al-Ulum of Deoband, India).

This article explores the evolution and development of Muslim community in Fiji. It examines the emergence of the Muslim community in Fiji as a product of the broader processes of geographical and social mobility produced by the international labour market and social and economic growth through personal initiatives sought by Muslims in pursuit of a better existence. In other words, Muslims arrived in Fiji not as permanent settlers but temporary workers seeking opportunity for wealth creation and then returning 'home' to recommence a prosperous and fulfilling existence. Life for Muslims, however, did not turn out the way it was imagined and many of them ended up staying back in Fiji. Muslims became permanent settlers from indentured labourers in Fiji.

THE INDENTURED SYSTEM

In the nineteenth century, the British adopted the indenture system to facilitate the movement of people between the colonies, resulting in a global phenomenon. The indenture system was in many respects a reformed version or a disguised form of slavery involving mass movement of contract workers. Mauritius was the first country to receive indentured labourers from British India in 1829 and after its success in Mauritius, the British started using it more widely. It has been suggested that approximately 1,194,957 Indian indentured labourers in total were mobilized to 14 British colonies during the indenture period (Ali-Chand et al. 2016).

The prospective indentured labourer and his or her recruitment

228   JAN A. ALI

agent were required to appear before a government official with a written statement of the terms of the contract. The length of service was to be five years extended to another five years upon request by the labourer. The indentured labourer was to be paid an agreed wage and was to be returned at the end of the service to the port of departure.

The indenture system carried with it a harsh state organizational structure with rigid rules and imposed policies. The life of indentured labourers was very tough. Apart from one day off, the labourers worked long hours for the rest of the week. The day would commence with early morning (3 a.m. or 4 a.m.) roll-call, simple breakfast, and then often long walk to the sugarcane plantations. Punctuality breach was unacceptable and severely punished. There were beatings of the labourers for simple errors or rule breach and many times simply for being seen to be working slowly. Women were beaten, abused, and even raped.

Indentured labourers were first introduced to Fiji in 1879 from India to work in the sugarcane fields. The Agreement of Indenture, which famously became known as the *Girmit* among the indentured labourers, seemed a harmless open contract between two parties but deep below the surface it was a new form of enslavement (Lal 1998).

On 14 May 1879 the first Indian indentured labourers arrived in Fiji on the *Leonidas* ship to serve for five years with a possibility of a renewal for another five years with mutual agreement between the labourer and plantation administrator. After ten years of service the labourers were entitled to a free repatriation. From 1879 to 1916, 42 ships made 87 voyages carrying Indian indentured labourers from India to Fiji. The recorded age range of the indentured labourers was from 11 years to 30 years, it has been suggested that some lied about their age in order to meet the recruitment criteria (Ali 1979). From early 1900s free Indian migrants also started arriving in Fiji as a mixture of traders, missionaries, and teachers (Ali 1977). Although the indenture system was abolished in 1916, in Fiji it actually ended in 1920 because there were still labourers under contract who had to complete their term. At the end of the indenture system, more than half, 39,261 (64.8 per cent) of

FROM INDENTURED LABOURERS TO PERMANENT SETTLERS   229

labourers were repatriated including the children born during indenture (Ali-Chand et al. 2016). The remainder opted to stay back permanently in Fiji as free citizens of the British Empire upon completing thirteen years of service (Ali 1976).

MUSLIMS AS INDENTURED LABOURERS

Muslims first arrived in Fiji as part of a mixed Muslim-Hindu contingent of 60,553 indentured labourers to work the sugarcane fields during British global colonial reign from the colonial Indian subcontinent in 1879. The transportation of indentured labourers which spanned from 1879 to 1916 saw 7,635 Muslims (5,098 males and 2,537 females) or 12.61 per cent of the total indentured labour population entering Fiji (Ali 1981, 174) principally from North India and to a lesser extent from South India mainly from Madras Presidency controlled by the British and the princely states of Mysore, Travencore, Hyderabad, and Cochin (Ali 1980; Brennan et al. 1992). Muslim indentured labourers were a group of relatively young individuals with only a handful of them over the age of 35 years (Brennan et al. 1992). Brennan et al. note that:

. . . the largest proportion of Muslims came from modern Kerala, that is, the west coast districts of Malabar and South Canara, and princely states of Travancore and Cochin. Following them there were contingents from the Tamilnad and Andhra regions of the Madras Presidency, and a substantial number from Hyderabad state (1992: 402).

Like indentured labourers in general, Muslim indentured labourers arrived in Fiji as temporary contract workers to profit from the sale of their labour in an attempt to improve their material conditions back home upon their return. The aim was to return home to India after some time with the acquired wealth to resume a more materially satisfactory and prosperous life.

Two sets of factors were involved in prompting Muslims to leave their ancestral abode temporarily. One set of factors often described in the academic literature as 'push' factors were, in the main, economic and socio-political in nature. These were a response to conditions at home such as overpopulation, increased economic

230   JAN A. ALI

hardship, poor harvest, high unemployment, poor pay, famine, social inequality, community hostility, legal and family problems, and general insecurity in India. Sandhu states:

> . . . vast majority [of Indians] led a hand-to-mouth existence in a chronic state of semi-starvation, or to use a Gandhian hyperbole, in 'perpetual fast'. Life for them was not so much a question of the degree of discomfiture but more a ceaseless struggle just to hang on to the very breath of life (1969: 41).

The other set of factors were what is known in the academic circle as 'pull' factors and they were the promise of a newly discovered land—a Fijian paradise with the land of opportunity and plenty, good and regular pay, free accommodation, and a free repatriation. Ali summarizes this as follows:

> It was the push of insecurity in India created by depressing social and economic conditions that led Indians to want to migrate from their homes, and the economic needs of the British Empire provided the necessary enticement to move to the colonies. The pull of Fiji was the result of the glorious picture painted by the recruiter's agent, the *arkathi* (italic in original) (1979: 3).

Indenture failed to deliver on its promises and Muslims were aghast. It proved to be a shadow of slavery and many indentured Muslims found that they had exchanged one form of poverty and servitude for another and there were some who experienced only death and disease in the new life. When balanced between benefit and hardship Muslims found that they had exchanged a society and a living community although with some inherent quandaries for a totally lifeless system bereft of humanity and compassion and pregnant with exploitation and abuse for no other purposes than for capitalists and imperialists to make material gain from it (Tinker 1974: 60). Muslims found practising their faith extremely difficult not only because the colonial authorities paid no attention to or offered provision for religious needs such as religious marriage and *halal* (permissible) food but the prevailing working conditions were simply appalling, working hours were exceptionally long, and dietary intake was clearly inadequate all of which collectively '. . . contributed towards a harsh existence for labourers' (Ali 1980:

FROM INDENTURED LABOURERS TO PERMANENT SETTLERS 231

107). In addition to this the hierarchical structure of the indentured system in which the British was the owner of the plantation enterprise assisted by his or her white manager and who in turn was supported by the Indian *sardar* (foreman) ensured that the labourers were kept disciplined and absolutely subservient. This meant that the labourers were left without recourse, and any questioning of the authorities regarding their requirement to work under extreme conditions and live an unforgiving life was tantamount to disobedience, carrying a severe penalty, including physical punishment. Indentured labourers discovered quickly that indenture was an imbalanced contract favouring the employer and life under it was unequivocally traumatic. They were indiscriminately housed in what was called the coolie 'lines' that lacked even the basic sanitation facilities. The general shortage of women also exacerbated the social problems in the Indian population as males competed for scarce Indian women which was the result of Fiji regulations that restricted the recruitment to 40 women for every 100 men (Ali 1980: 107). Ramesh elaborates on the situation saying that 'While the colonial regime in Fiji recruited physically fit men, they deliberately neglected the number of women in each intake, thereby creating competition for sexual partners on the sugar plantations in Fiji, resulting in high rates of suicide and murder' (2017: 71). Life was very seriously demoralized due to the conditions under which indentured labourers lived and murders and suicides were widespread. Ali notes, '*Girmit* proved to be *narak* or hell: there was illness, murder and suicide, over-tasking, bullying and beating of labourers. Personal privacy and normal family life proved difficult to maintain in the environment of the coolie lines (italics in original)' (1981: 22).

Indentured labourers were discouraged from permanent settlement through the imposition of a special tax on free Indian residents and therefore, repatriation was an option some opted for returning to India using their own funds after completing their five-year contract, however, despite this a vast majority of them chose to make Fiji their new home especially when the indenture system was abolished in Fiji in 1920. Yet, life was not easy and many Muslims struggled to balance between work demands and fulfilling religious obligations with the latter receiving reduced

232   JAN A. ALI

priority. Living conditions were really tough and so they needed all the support they could garner and in the process were compelled to forge a bond with Hindus for mutual protection and assistance. Under such conditions survival took precedence over religious rituals and practices but Muslim faith in a single God and many teachings of Islam remained etched in the Muslim psyche. The hierarchical and diverse social order that existed in India was profoundly transformed in the context of the indenture system. Voyaging on the ocean waters for days on end, eating and sleeping with members of different castes and religions, the absence of suitable spouses, and the dissolution of the rigid hierarchies and occupational structure of Indian caste system rendered the indentured community homogeneous and largely egalitarian. Prasad remarks that:

> During the indenture period, these differences were irrelevant, due to the shared experience of living through *narak*, or hell, as the labourers referred to it. This provided them with a shared identity based on the suffering they endured, and was further strengthened by the concept of the *jahazibhai* ('ship brothers'). . . . Their relationships were based upon common experience, and cut across religious, regional and caste differences, with groups co-existing and sharing in one another's culture and religious functions (italics in original) (2007: 317-18).

For both Muslims and Hindus, survival become a priority in the indentured system requiring them to consistently assist each other and set aside all social and religious differences. Ali remarks:

> Under such rigorous circumstances the laborers developed a sense of brotherhood which discouraged unnecessary squabbles (except over women); there was little scope for religious [and social] bickering. In fact, when religious intolerance and strife appeared this did not originate in the plantation of indentured labourers, but rather amongst those who had completed their contract and became 'free' (1980: 108).

Categories of difference based on culture, ritual, race and maintenance of boundaries founded on the distinction of religions, features that distinguished Indians from one another and operated as a means of defining boundaries were simply eradicated. Muslims and Hindus had no choice to operate in isolation from one another

FROM INDENTURED LABOURERS TO PERMANENT SETTLERS **233**

because all their usual and familiar support systems characteristic of 'home living' were taken away from them. The new cultural and socio-economic problems they underwent in a strange land could not really be countered but experienced with those with whom they shared some commonality. Such camaraderie remained beyond the indenture period and Muslims and Hindus became an integrated community in Fiji.

INITIAL MUSLIM-HINDU COOPERATION AND CO-EXISTENCE

Muslim cooperation with Hindus in the indenture system was absolutely necessary as their very survival depended on it. Not only with Hindus but Muslims had to work together among themselves and ignore any internal divisions they had based on theology and sectarian teachings. In the process, closeness and co-dependence particularly during the indenture period dissolved all religious (Muslims and Hindus) and Muslim denominational variations (Ali 1979; Miller 2008). The shortage of women also played a critical role in bringing particularly Muslims and Hindus together through numerous mixed marriages and further contributed to a strong sense of cooperation and reciprocal forbearance amongst the indentured labourers ultimately producing a diminished sense of religious identity.

Occasionally there were a few minor disputes either over women or religious values but overall there was a strong sense of brotherhood among the Indian indentured labourers (Ali 1980). Muslims from various denominational and theological persuasions and Hindus lived congenially during and beyond the indenture system. They visited each other's homes, shared meals, took part in each other's religious rituals and practices such as in the recitals of holy books, and celebrated each other's religious festivals—Muslim Eid and Hindu Diwali. Muslims and Hindus stood in solidarity in times of need such as during ousting and punishing by oppressive Indian *sardars* and white overseers (Ali 1979) and the industrial strikes of 1920 and 1921 (Ali 1980). Such was the nature of the bond between the two groups that one of the early mosques in Fiji

234 JAN A. ALI

built at Nausori before the end of the indenture system was funded in large part by Hindus (Gillion 1962: 149).

When the indenture system ended, the issue of Indians human rights and freedom came to the fore and Muslims and Hindus collectively demanded their political rights and equal status in the Fijian social structure. Muslims and Hindus, would therefore, collaborate in this endeavour and seek political representation in the Legislative Council for Indians as one people. This was clearly demonstrated in Fijian colonial politics when Muslims cooperated with Hindus in lobbying for separate Indian representation in the colonial legislature rather than seeking separate Muslim represent-ation and autonomy from the colonial powers. Ali notes:

> . . . more significantly when the Governor appointed a Commission in August 1920 to take public evidence to recommend the method of enfranchising Indians, there was no call from Muslims for separate representation. . . . With the colonial regime prepared to grant Indians only two elected members to the Fiji Legislative Council, . . . the reserving of one of these seats for Muslims . . . would have sown the seeds of complaint and dissatisfaction among the overwhelming majority. Since politics based on religious allegiance was absent . . . there was no point in introducing it. In this case the Muslims themselves did not request it. Obviously they felt no threat (1980: 110).

However, Muslim-Hindu cooperation and cordiality did not last too long after the end of the indenture system in 1920. The dis-cordiality slowly began to simmer and became visible as the religious peace between Muslims and Hindus in Fiji began to erode. This was a reflection of local situation as well as what was developing in Indian politics in the subcontinent at the time.

In the 1930s, relations between Muslim-Hindu began to show real signs of fracture as the militant Hindu sect of Arya Samaji in Fiji, not the Hindus as a whole, began engaging in an extensive importation of missionaries and school teachers from India to promote Hinduism and developing suppressive attitude towards Muslims (Prasad 2007). Arya Samaj formed the Sangathan Movement in Fiji and began the onslaught on Muslims through a string of social and commercial boycotts, which almost crippled the Muslim petite bourgeoisie and intensified the conversion of

FROM INDENTURED LABOURERS TO PERMANENT SETTLERS   235

Muslims to Hinduism. The Muslims countered this with intense proselytization by inviting *ulemah* (Muslim scholars) from India and subsequently also from Pakistan after the Indian partition. Politically, there was a shift from calling for collective Indian representation in the colonial legislature to a separate ethnic Indian Muslim representation. The push for a separate Muslim identity within the larger structure of Fijian society was reinforced by the experiences in India, which ultimately led to the partition of India and the creation of Pakistan as a Muslim state in 1947.

Now that the indentured system was terminated, Muslims felt a greater sense of freedom and the custodians of Islamic faith in Fiji—the likes of Mullah Mirza Khan who paid his own way from India to arrive in Fiji in 1898 and Mullah Nasrullah Shah—increased their *da'wah* (preaching) efforts. Theirs and other self-styled *maulvis'* (Muslim teachers) call for conformity to Islamic rituals and practices began to be heard by ordinary Muslims and many started to pay serious attention to the requirements of prayer, dress code, dietary rules, and other aspects of worship. Soon Islamic faith became an important marker of identity.

MUSLIM COMMUNITY BUILDING AND THE EMERGENCE OF MUSLIM ORGANIZATIONS AND SUBGROUPS

Although indenture was harsh, even horrendous and many profound social and religious adjustments and sacrifices had to be made, Muslims never lost faith. Despite being overworked, women sexually abused, and the persistence of violent British rule of law, Muslims held on firmly to Islam. Not just that but Muslims even transmitted whatever Islam they knew to their Fijian-born children with women playing a gallant and pivotal role in the process. Muslims were able to achieve all these and survive the outrageous sufferings and injustices of indenture because of their Islamic faith. All these and the impetus provided by *mullahs* (Muslim educated in Islamic theology and Islamic law) and *maulvis* in a new found 'free' environment began to pave the way for Islamic faith renewal and refinement of Muslim identity.

236   JAN A. ALI

By 1908 there were approximately 4,000 Muslims in Fiji principally from the United Provinces, Bengal and Punjab, approximately a third of whom were indentured labourers and the remainder were free individuals (Ali 1971: 58). Almost all of them were Sunni Muslims and the majority were subscribers to the Hanafi School of jurisprudence. Muslims were still a minority group and due to their minority status, particularly educated individuals, quickly realized the vulnerability of ordinary Muslims to convert to Hinduism and Christianity. Fearing that their community would be targeted by Hindu preachers and Christian missionaries, they organized themselves as a group and embarked on preaching missions working on religious rituals and practices of ordinary Muslims namely daily prayers and dietary rules and on those who had converted from Islam to Hinduism and Christianity. The *da'wah* missions were particularly challenging as Muslims were widely dispersed across Fiji who were either living in hard-to-get places or working in small groups on different estates. Nevertheless, preachers continued their mission providing Muslims religious guidance, telling them stories about past prophets and other Qur'anic narratives related to early Islamic events such as battles between Muslims and their opponents, and imparting various prophetic traditions. Burton notes that learned Muslims distributed written materials on Islam and Prophet Muhammad widely to ordinary Muslims in Fiji and the Muslim communities received regular funding from India as well as Muslim clerics who travelled to Fiji to teach Muslims free about their faith and the prophet of Islam (Burton 1909). As early as 1884, educated Muslims versed sufficiently in Islamic theology and law who opted to remain in Fiji after completing their indenture took the leading role in guiding their communities including leading and organizing prayers and issuing advice on personal and family matters (Ali 1980). A preacher known as Buddha Khan is a good example of individual effort directed towards Muslim spiritual growth. He was committed particularly to *da'wah* who started his mission in 1887, drafted an Islamic Code of Conduct covering fundamentals of Islam, and travelled on foot to distant places within Fiji to impart his knowledge and message (Ali-Chand et al. 2016).

Apart from these clerics, the Muslim community still lacked

FROM INDENTURED LABOURERS TO PERMANENT SETTLERS **237**

competent leaders and there were no mosques at this point in time. The fear of loss of identity amongst Muslims continued to be strong and therefore, the push for more clerics and the establishment of Islamic institutions such as mosques was ongoing. The need for religious centres was recognized as early as 1898 for serving as places of worship and centres for the teaching of Urdu as an essential symbol of Muslim identity and Arabic as the language of Islam in Fiji (1980). Then, in 'about 1900 a mosque was built at Navua by public subscription on land bestowed by the Fiji Sugar Company, with the Mullah [Mirza Khan] in-charge at first; shortly afterwards another small mosque and school were erected at Nausori on land leased from the C.S.R. company' (Gillion 1962: 149). Subsequently, mosques were built in Labasa (1902) and Samabula (1914) and later in other places where Muslims lived in considerable numbers (Ali 1980). In 1900s several *markazes* (an Arabic term meaning 'centres') sprung up and in 1924, Muslims purchased a property in Toorak, Suva on which the current Toorak Jame Masjid is located, and several years later in the mid-1930s, the Vunimono Islamic School in Nausori was established by a couple—Mohammed Abdullah and Hameeda Abdullah, who were followers of Ahmadism (Ali-Chand et al. 2016).The mosques were simple structures built out of corrugated iron and weathered boards and became the most visible and prominent markers of existence of Islam and Muslim identity in Fiji. Following this, as early as 1915, Muslims started to establish their own organizations and the institutionalization of Islam ensued (Ali 2003). Muslim associations such as the Anjuman-i-Hidayat-ul-Islam (Muslim Teaching Society established in Nausori in 1915), Anjuman Ishait El Islam (Muslim Place of Gathering founded in Lautoka in 1916), and Anjuman-e-Islam (Organization of Islam formed in Suva in 1919) were established within Muslim communities (Ali 1980: 110).

THE ESTABLISHMENT OF FIJI MUSLIM LEAGUE

To bring together, organize, and look after the affairs of Muslim communities and their separate organizations, the Fiji Muslim League as an umbrella body was established in 1926 and headquartered

238   JAN A. ALI

in Suva (Ahmed 1980). It was a succedent of Anjuman-e-Islam (1919) with the following fundamental objectives:

(a) to disseminate the moral ideals and teachings of Islam;
(b) to unite the Muslims and promote social intercourse between them;
(c) To render religious and secular service to the Muslims;
(d) to promote and arrange for the learning of Islamic literature by Muslim children;
(e) to endeavour to eradicate the use of intoxicants and narcotics such as alcohol, opium and other obnoxious drugs by the Muslims; and
(f) to bring about a close tie and better understanding between the Government and its subjects (Ali 1980: 114).

The Fiji Muslim League executive consisted of the president, vice-president, treasurer, secretary and assistant secretary and they came from all walks of life ranging from white collar workers to self-employed entrepreneurs and businessmen, several of whom were Fiji born (Hussain 2018). The members of the executive were unpaid volunteer workers who were elected by their peers through the democratic voting process. The process has survived to the present times, however, its purported democratic procedure is often questioned by broader membership of the League and by the general Muslim community in Fiji. Allegations of mismanagement, nepotism, corruption and the executive's level of Islamic knowledge and commitment are some of the concerns often debated in Muslim public discourse and social circles.

Among the League's key objectives was the provision of religious education to Muslims, particularly Muslim youth. There was a strong push for instruction to be given in Urdu in schools and teachers were provided, for example, at the Methodist School in Toorak and the Sangam School in Nadi (Ali 1980). Although there were, in early 1900s, 'three or four [Muslim] schools and three buildings in country districts for worship', no such service or facility was available in the capital Suva, where around that time only 70 Muslims lived (Ali 1980: 109). When the League was established in 1926, a school already existed known initially as

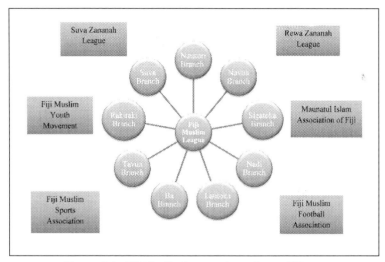

Figure 9.1: Fiji Muslim League branches, affiliates and non-affiliates (*Source:* By the author).

Islamic Girls School, but then it went through a name change to Suva Muslim Primary as it became co-educational. With its focus on religious education, the League managed to build from its own coffers numerous schools across the country over the years through its branches and in the last several decades amassed seventeen primary and five secondary schools of varying sizes and a tertiary institution Islamic Institute of the South Pacific (Hussain 2018).

The Muslim schools run by the League principally have Muslim students in them but there is also a small mixed student population comprising indigenous Fijians belonging to Christian faith, Hindus, and others. In 2000 there were 3,015 Muslim, 994 indigenous Fijian, and 455 others, including Hindu and Sikh students in the secondary schools and 5,243 in primary schools (Hussain 2018). The overall academic performance of the students is of high standard allowing an increasing number of students to pursue further studies at the tertiary level either locally or abroad. There is a steady growth in the number of diploma and graduate holders, some made possible through scholarships but most through the sacrifices and efforts of the students' own families. Apart from scholarships, the League

240   JAN A. ALI

provides assistance for tertiary studies for disadvantaged Muslim students through loans from its Education Trust and the Islamic Development Bank (Hussain 2018).

Besides education as its central focus, the League was committed to fulfilling the social and welfare needs of the community from the very outset. As such, to this day, it provides assistance to Muslims from its national headquarters and from the various branches across the country. Its welfare assistance keeps numerous Muslim families clothed, fed and housed and many children in school. There is a snapshot of the Fiji Muslim League's various branches, affiliates and non-affiliates as shown in Figure 9.1.

MUSLIM SUBGROUPS

Islam and Muslims in Fiji have always been represented by various Muslim organizations. They have emerged in direct response to the growth in the Muslim population and various social and religious needs of the Muslim community. Throughout the history of a permanent Muslim presence in Fiji, Muslim communities have retained a focus on establishing and maintaining local Islamic infrastructure with a particular emphasis on the construction of mosques, *markazes*, and schools. The Sunni-based Fiji Muslim League has been the principal representative body of Islam and Muslims in Fiji which is recognized by the Fijian government and other overseas state jurisdictions.

Although it seems that the Fiji Muslim League had the best of intentions, it never succeeded, as a peak body, in bringing together Muslim civic society organizations and Fijian Muslim communities into a single fold. The internal cracks in the Muslim community began to appear soon after the arrival of Maulana Mirza Muzaffar Beg in Fiji. Maulana Mirza Muzaffar Beg was an Ahmadi from the Ahmadiyya movement which originated in India in 1889 and has been considered by Sunni and Shia Muslims as a heterodox group. The Ahmadiyya doctrine makes numerous assertions which alienates it from mainstream Islam. Three assertions are worthy of mention. The first is that the Ahmadis believe that Jesus of Nazareth died a natural death. The second is that Ahmadis hold that Mirza Ghulam

FROM INDENTURED LABOURERS TO PERMANENT SETTLERS 241

Ahmad of Qadian who declared himself the Mahdi (Promised Messiah) and the founder of Ahmadiyya movement, deserves the appropriate reverence and honour when according to Muslim orthodoxy, the Messiah is Jesus, son of Mary, who will return from heaven at the 'right' time. The third is regarding the institution of revelation, which according to Ahmadis never ended with the death of Prophet Muhammad but continued and then finally ended with the passing away of Ahmad.

Sunni-dominated Fiji Muslim League issued a *fatwa* (religious edict) upon realizing this fact declared Ahmadis as non-Muslims and banned Maulana Mirza Muzaffar Beg and his followers from attending the Jame Mosque in Toorak. Maulana Mirza Muzaffar Beg and his followers subsequently registered their own association under the name of Ahmadiyya Anjuman Ishaat-i-Islam of Fiji in 1934 and started publishing the Paigham-e-Islam—a trilingual monthly magazine—and numerous circulars and tracts all in English, Urdu, and Hindi languages as part of its religious activity. Since then Ahmadis and Sunnis have remained two major separate religious groups in Fiji.

As time progressed and Muslims began to move in and out of Fiji and different Islamic knowledge and practices, often with roots in the Indian subcontinent, started to flow into Fiji, further division ensued particularly in the majority Sunni community. As early as the 1930s, Muslims in Fiji actively sought to establish separate sectarian practices as a marker of a separate Muslim identity. Thus, the Maunatul Islam Association of Fiji was formed officially in 1942 which, decades later, in 1982, was registered as the Maunatul Islam Association of Fiji. The organization is constituted by subscribers to the Shafi'i School of jurisprudence who are descendants of Muslim indentured labourers from Kerala in South India. The group is usually referred to as Maryala in Fiji, perhaps because of the link with Kerala where Malayalam is spoken (Ali-Chand et al. 2016). What is distinct about this group is what is claimed by it as a religious practice and that is the *ratib* (a practice which involves chanting and piercing the cheeks and body with needles) and chanting Darood-o-Salaam—Yaa Nabi Salaamu Alaika (praising and sending blessings upon Prophet Muhammad). The latter aspect

242 JAN A. ALI

of this is also a practice common among *Miladis* which will be discussed below.

Another organization which emerged within Sunni Muslim community was the Ahl-i-Hadith; a minority group in Fiji. The group is more of a subsect than a full-blown independent sect. It is a derivative of Sunnism. Ahl-i-Hadithis are descendants of the 'Wahhabi' movement of Sayyid Ahmad Shahid, which emerged in 1820s in the Punjab district in India in direct response to Sikhism (Ahmad 1966). Thus, the group is sometimes referred to as the Wahhabis. The founding of the Ahl-i-Hadith in Fiji is usually attributed to Maulvi Nur Ali who preached the Wahhabi/Ahl-i-Hadith creed actively in the 1920s. Ahl-i-Hadith was officially registered as the Fiji Anjuman Ahle Hadith in 1959 by Wahid Nur Ali, son of Maulvi Nur Ali and later the name was changed to Jamiat Ahle Hadith Fiji (Ali-Chand et al. 2016).

The first more prominent appearance of the activities of Ahl-i-Hadith in Fiji started in the late 1970s (Ali 2003). The Wahhabi movement has a strong theological and fundamentalist approach to Islamic practice and this is evident in the Fijian version of the Ahl-i-Hadith. The group vehemently opposes anyone indulging in *taqlid* (accepting authority without question on religious matters), that is, authority from sources not found in Islamic scriptures— *Qur'an* and Hadiths attributed to the first three generations of Muslims (Brown 1999), oppose everything introduced to Islam after the earliest time (Roy & Antoine 2007: 27), and denounces the act of veneration of saints and the worship of their tombs as *shirk* (polytheism) (Ali-Chand et al. 2016). Ahl-i-Hadith also reject *milad* (chanting Darood-o-Salaam-Yaa Nabi Salaamu Alaika-praising and sending blessings upon Prophet Muhammad), *ratib*, and the celebration of the birthday of Prophet Muhammad. Male adherents of Ahl-i-Hadith tend to have a particular style of untrimmed beard and in ritual acts of Islamic worship they noticeably differ from the Hanafi School of jurisprudence where the men hold their hands above the navel when offering *sala'at* (prayer), raise them up to their heads before bowing, and say 'ameen' in loud voice after the *imam* (prayer leader) finish reciting Sura Fatiha (the first chapter of the *Qur'an*) (Hewer 2006: 204).

FROM INDENTURED LABOURERS TO PERMANENT SETTLERS **243**

Miladis are another group in Fiji spread across the country but most active in the western parts of the main Fiji island of Viti Levu. The Miladis have a very obscure history both in India where the sect first originated and in Fiji. It is, however, a subsect of Sunnism who celebrate the birthday of Prophet Muhammad (*miladul-nabi*) (Shepard 2016) as a religious ritual and delight in loud chanting Darood-o-Salaam-Yaa Nabi Salaamu Alaika—praising and sending blessings upon Prophet Muhammad at every religious occasion or ceremony such as Eid-ul-Fitr (festival celebrating the end of the holy month of Ramadan) and social gathering such as weddings and birthdays. The practice is commonly called *mila'ad* in Fiji. They perform *niyaz* where participants sit around the food and make supplication. The supplication is to bless the food which participants subsequently eat. This is a Muslim version of the Hindu *prasad* (blessed food) that is offered to people following the *puja* (worship). Also the Miladis place particularly strong emphasis on the death rites, which entails *tija* (prayer for the dead after three days of burial), *chalisa* (prayer performed for the dead after 40 days), *chamai* (prayer performed for the dead after six months), and *salinna* (prayer performed on the anniversary of death). All these death rites mainly comprise the recitation of the *Qur'an*. For Miladis these various rituals and practices serve to affirm their communal identity and not only individual households but their extended families, relatives living close by. Neighbours actively participate in them collectively helping to cultivate what they consider as an Islamic identity and a sense of unity (Ali-Chand, et al. 2016).

Even though all these rituals are un-Islamic, it is not unusual to find some of these rituals practised by some mainstream Sunnis in Fiji as well. The boundary that divides the Miladis from the mainstream Sunnis, therefore, is porous and fluid. Miladis do not have their specific mosque or school and often share them with the mainstream Sunnis. Thus, what constitutes a Miladi and what constitutes a mainstream Sunni is a contentious and problematic issue. Briefly it may be said that the Miladis do consider themselves as a distinct and separate group and are vehement critics of the Tablighis.

The Tabligh Jama'at ('a group conveying the message of Islam') is an apolitical Islamic revivalist movement founded by Maulana Muhammad Ilyas in India in 1927. Its arrival in Fiji is not formally documented but some scholars note 1966 (Ali-Chand et al. 2016) and some 1968 (Ali 2018) to be the year the movement entered Fiji. Six Tablighis of Indian descent from Zambia arrived on a preaching mission and worked with some local Muslims in Nadi (a town on the main Fiji Island of Viti Levu). From there they moved to other urban centres on the island. After this first visit of Tablighis from overseas, more visits were organized by other Tablighis—particularly from India and Pakistan. By the 1980s, Fiji had become an important destination for Tabligh work and it continues to be so to this day.

Once the Tabligh Jama'at was firmly established in Fiji and Tablighi activity started to gain acceptance in the Muslim community, the movement began to make consistent progress and expanded to all main towns and cities on the two large islands of Fiji-Viti Levu and Vanua Levu. In all these areas, the Tabligh Jama'at has been able to exercise considerable influence over the Muslim population and paved the way for Islam to undergo a monumental trans-formation.

The principal aim of the Tabligh Jama'at is to reform nominal Muslims and turn them into 'proper' practising Muslims. It relies on its six basic principles to achieve this. They are drawn from the *Qur'an*, Hadith, and its two basic texts are *Bahishti Zewar* and *Fazaaile-Amaal*. The six principles are:

   (i) *shahadah* or the article of faith,
  (ii) five daily *sala'at* (prayer),
 (iii) *ilm* (knowledge) and *dhikr* (remembrance of God),
  (iv) *ikram-i-muslim* (dignity of Muslims),
   (v) *ikhlas-i-niyat* (amendation of intention and sincerity), and
  (vi) *tafrigh-i-waqt* (to spare time).

This constitutes the movement's basic platform. Based on this, Tablighis move from house to house and city to city inviting Muslims towards pristine Islam. In Fiji and elsewhere Tablighis are known for strict observation of *parda* (segregation of the sexes), maintaining

FROM INDENTURED LABOURERS TO PERMANENT SETTLERS **245**

strict Islamic dress codes, and educating nominal Muslims on the fundamentals of Islamic faith (Ali, 2018). Over the years it has successfully proselytized many Muslims and helped in the removal of syncretistic elements from Muslim religious practices. Tablighis in Fiji are easily identified if the men sport long beard, tie a white turban or wear a white cap and wear *shalwar* (trousers typically wide at the waist but narrow down to a cuffed bottom) and *kameez* (a long loose-fitting shirt) and women in *niqab* (face covering leaving the eyes uncovered) and *burqah* (loose garment covering the entire body from the top of the head to the toes) often black in colour.

MUSLIM-NON-MUSLIM RELATIONS AND THE GLOBAL IMPACT OF ISLAMIC REVIVALISM

As has been seen above, Muslims have established themselves firmly as permanent citizens in Fiji. They have their own community, religious infrastructure, and socio-economic and cultural networks with complex yet strong bonds with other groups of population including indigenous Fijians. After all, Fiji is a multi-faith and multicultural society and individual communities don't exist and operate in isolation from one another but in conjunction with each other and on the whole engage in cooperative interaction. Despite a level of fragmentation and mistrust between communities and maintenance of distinctive community identities characteristic of all societies, Muslim and non-Muslim communities in Fiji generally work collaboratively in terms of sharing important information such as shared development of member databases and e-commerce facilities, coordinate activities such as Fiji independence day, and cooperate in the delivery of services such as social welfare. An important positive benefit of all this is that complex community challenges and issues and even intercommunity discord are potentially resolved through joint engagement and development of common goals contributing to the greater worth of communities and individuals experience a sense of 'belonging together'.

In Fiji there is an Interreligious Peace Council of Fiji which was established in 2009 (Universal Peace Federation 2009). It is

246 JAN A. ALI

represented by three major religious groups namely Christians, Hindus and Muslims and various other minor faith-based organizations. Its purpose is to facilitate peace-building in Fiji and prevent the occurrence of political turmoil characterized by four coups d'état since independence in 1970 using faith-based resources and organizations. Religious leaders are encouraged by the council to work together in peace-building in Fiji and stress is placed on religious organizations to focus and work on not only its own members but members of other faith groups which can lead to a stronger united Fiji. Muslims have paid keen heed to the mission of Interreligious Peace Council of Fiji and various Muslim organizations have become very active in promoting and realising its course. In the year 2020, for instance, numerous Muslim youth groups associated with the Fiji Muslim League, participated in the interfaith youth forum in Fiji, discussing the practice of fasting organized by the Columban Interfaith Ministry desk, Fiji, in the capital Suva. The Muslim idea of fasting (Ramadan) has a strong nuance of peace, charity, and tolerance and occasions like this is a real evidence that Muslim and non-Muslim rapport is active and working with the potential to strengthen personal relationships further and build stronger national community. It also shows that Muslims not only have the willingness to work and cooperate with other non-Muslims but make concerted effort to contribute to the improvement of their entire society.

MUSLIM-HINDU RELATIONS

Contrary to popular belief and some academic polemics, religions through scriptural teachings and the threat of divine punishment, have been shown to play a pivotal role in encouraging normative and cooperative behaviour within the community and between communities. It is true that the cooperative and tolerant behaviour religions promote, can sometimes be highly parochial, where members may opt to work with and support the in-group rather than the out-group. However, when it comes to Muslim-Hindu relations in Fiji, despite occasional tension at social or personal level, co-operative interaction and behaviour is quite a commonplace.

FROM INDENTURED LABOURERS TO PERMANENT SETTLERS   247

Muslims and Hindus live in harmony in their neighbourhood, often visiting each other's homes, supporting and helping in one another's daily routines such as driving one for doctor's appointment, assisting each other during a wedding or funeral, men socializing particularly over *kava* drinking and children and adults take part in recreation with each other, for example, playing soccer in the local park or a makeshift ground. They work with each other in state departments, hospitals, police forces, the army, schools, private firms, stores, factories and farms. There are Muslim children who attend Hindu schools and vice versa, and Muslims and Hindus shop at each other's stores. Rai observes:

> I believe that the foundation of this strong Hindu-Muslim relationship was laid [long time ago]. I work with an equal number of Hindus and Muslims. . . . During the last 15 years, I have spent most of my time with a Muslim friend, a 5 time a day *namazi* and a Haji. My relationship with him and all my Muslim friends in India, UK, Fiji and other countries is based on very strong bonding that I had developed with my Muslim brothers and sisters in my village (Personal E-mail Communication, 16 October 2020).

Carmen Voigt-Graf in her research found 'that relations between Indo-Fijians of various backgrounds were amicable, sometimes stressing that marriages between partners of different religions or regional origins were fairly common' (2008: 7). In her work the following excerpt aptly summarizes the current Muslim and Hindu relations in Fiji,

> There is real good unity between the religious groups here in Fiji. During indenture, our ancestors all suffered together and people realised that they had to unite against the bosses if they were to reach anything. Since that time, there is good co-operation between Hindus and Muslims. I know a lot of Hindus who are married to Muslims. Basically we are all the same and that is how we treat each other (Voigt-Graf 2008: 7).

THE IMPACT OF GLOBAL ISLAMIC REVIVALISM ON MUSLIM-HINDU RELATIONS

Internally dynamic and multifaceted, Islamic revivalism is a global phenomenon that seeks the removal of foreign accretion in normative and ritualistic Muslim practices and promote greater religious

248

consciousness and piety. In Fiji, this mission is been generally carried out by the Tabligh Jama'at as discussed above. There is no research undertaken to gauge the impact of the process of Islamic revivalism on Muslim-Hindu relations in Fiji, however, anecdotal evidence demonstrates only marginal effect. Some Tablighis don't want to associate even with other Muslims who don't agree with them. They want to separate themselves from those with dissimilar views or values. Regarding Muslim-Hindu relations, often difficult and even impractical, some Tablighis might try to steer away from socializing and interacting with Hindus at social and personal levels based on their interpretation and understanding of the Islamic scripture or what may be described as the movement's world view and teachings. For instance, a Tablighi man may not attend a Diwali (Hindu festival of lights) invitation from a colleague or a Tablighi family may not invite the Hindu neighbour to an *aqeeqah* (Islamic tradition of the sacrifice of an animal on the occasion of a child's birth). Another example will be a Tablighi family refusing to send their children to a nearby Hindu school and instead send them to a public school several kilometres away from home, or Tablighis refusing to purchase cooked food from Hindu outlets or restaurants even if they display the *halal* (permitted) sign or certificate. These are only a few examples and provide mere glimpses into the effects of global process of Islamic revivalism carried out in Fijian context by the Tabligh Jama'at on Muslim-Hindu relations and not a comprehensive picture of the relationship. Important research is needed to gain better understanding of the impact of Islamic revivalism on Muslim-Hindu relations in Fiji.

POLITICS IN FIJI AND THE ROLE OF MUSLIMS

Muslims have been politically active since 1929 through the Fiji Muslim League seeking separate representation for Muslims in the Legislative Council. Except for a brief period of five years from 1932 to 1937, Muslims have had representation in Fiji's Parliament. From 1937 to 1963, out of five Indo-Fijians in the Legislative Council, at least one has always been a Muslim. The Muslim Political Front was formed to promote Muslim political interests

FROM INDENTURED LABOURERS TO PERMANENT SETTLERS **249**

and rights and in 1966 it allied with the newly formed Alliance Party.

Since the last quarter of the twentieth century, Muslim political activism has changed significantly. Secular educated nominal Muslims have stood as candidates for election to the parliament emphasizing the importance of secular politics and the distancing of faith from state. In the past, charismatic Muslim political leaders linked to Muslim organizations were able to rely on their support and their members' votes. These days communal voting is still relevant and Muslim organizations continue to have a sphere of influence but what counts the most is ordinary Muslims vote for those parties that have the highest levels of communal appeal with policies that seek to address every issue such as education, health and employment. In this regard, Prasad (2007: 324) notes that, 'While the leadership of religious groups, like the FML [Fiji Muslim League], may maintain high profile relationships with political leaders, it does not follow that the rank and file membership will follow.'

Considering this, what has become of Muslim political activism? One can suggest that if Muslim political activism is a process through which Muslim religious interests, rights, and institutions are being prioritized, promoted, and safeguarded, then there is no such thing in Fiji. Muslims in the Fijian parliament for instance, the likes of Aiyaz Sayed-Khaiyum with multiple portfolios and the *de facto* Prime Minister and Faiyaz Koya, the Minister for Industry, Trade, Tourism, Land and Mineral Resources, are political figures with secular political and social values and they represent secularism and not the faith of Muslims. They manage to hold power, legitimacy and popularity not because they represent Islam and its adherents in Fiji but through a policy of aggressive secularism.

CONCLUSION

Muslims initially came to Fiji as temporary indentured labourers between 1879 and 1916 as part of a larger group of Indian indentured labour force brought in by the British to work on the sugarcane fields. Muslims constituted and continue to constitute a

250 JAN A. ALI

minority group in Fiji and under the harshness and inhumanity of the indentured labour system they forged a close bond with fellow Indians who were majority Hindus. However, when the Arya Samaj launched its reform programme and attempted to mobilize the Hindu community against Muslims the Muslim-Hindu relations received a permanent blow and the two communities never united since.

When indenture came to an end in 1920, Muslim numbers increased, both through birth and migration. Muslims started to develop their community in earnest, became more organized and resourceful, and established their own identity in the Islands through the establishment of mosques and *markazes*, primary and secondary schools, *madrasas*, and civil society organizations. Muslim unity did not last too long though and the community was essentially divided into two groups—majority Sunnis and minority Ahmadiyyas. This schism led to the establishment of other separate organizations which exacerbated the situation in Fiji with now organizations competing against each other rather than complementing one another. This is very much the situation about the Muslims in Fiji today.

The journey for Muslims from indentured labourers to permanent settlers in Fiji has been inflicted with trials and tribulations but as a bunch of hardworking, tough, and resilient people they have made remarkable progress in maintaining their culture, heritage, and religion and secured their permanent membership in the Fijian multicultural society.

REFERENCES

Ahmad, Qeyamuddin (1966). *The Wahabi Movement in India*. Islamabad: National Book Foundation.

Ali, Ahmed (1981). 'Muslims in Fiji: A Brief Survey', *Journal Institute of Muslim Minority Affairs*, 3(2): pp. 174-82.

—— (1981). 'Fiji: The Fiji Indian Achievement', in Ron Crocombe (ed.), *Pacific Indians: Profiles in 20 Pacific Countries*. Suva: Institute of Pacific Studies, University of the South Pacific: pp. 22-32.

—— (1980). *Plantation to Politics: Studies on Fiji Indians*. Suva: University of the South Pacific and the Fiji Times and Herald Limited.

FROM INDENTURED LABOURERS TO PERMANENT SETTLERS **251**

—— (1979). *Girmit: The Indenture Experience in Fiji.* Suva: Bulletin of the Fiji Museum, No. 5.

—— (1979).'Indians in Fiji: An Interpretation', in Subramani (ed.), *The Indo-Fijian Experience.* St Lucia, Queensland: University of Queensland Press: pp. 3-25.

—— (1977). 'The Emergence of Muslim Separatism in Fiji', *Plural Societies La Haye, 8*(1): pp. 57-70.

—— (1976). *A Society in Transition: Aspects of Fiji Indian History 1879-1939.* Suva: School of Social and Economic Development, USP.

Ali-Chand, Zakia, Shazna Buksh and Afshana Anzeg (2016).'Islam in Fiji: Continuity, Adaptation and Change during the Indenture and Post-Indenture Periods', in Maurits Hassankhan, Goolam Vahed, and Lomarsh Roopnarine (eds.), *Indentured Muslims in the Diaspora: Identity and Belonging of Minority Groups in Plural Societies.* New York: Routledge: pp. 275-300.

Ali, Jan (2018).'The Tabligh Jama'at and Islamic Revivalism in Fiji', *Pacific Dynamics: Journal of Interdisciplinary Research, 2*(1): pp. 12-20.

—— (2003).'Islam and Muslims in Fiji', *Journal of Muslim Minority Affairs, 23*(2): pp. 413-26.

Brennan, Lance, John McDonald and Ralph Shlomowitz (1992). 'The Origins of South Indian Muslim Indentured Migration to Fiji', *Journal Institute of Muslim Minority Affairs, 13*(2): pp. 402-9.

Brown, Daniel (1999). *Rethinking Tradition in Modern Islamic Thought.* Cambridge: Cambridge University Press.

Burton, John (1909). *Our Indian Work in Fiji.* Suva: Methodist Mission Press.

Fiji Demographics Profile (2019). *Index Mundi.* Accessed on 2 May 2020. Retrieved from https://www.indexmundi.com/fiji/demographics_profile.html

Gillion, Ken (1977). *Fiji's Indian Migrants: A History to the End of Indenture in 1920.* Melbourne: Oxford University Press.

Hewer, Chris (2006). *Understanding Islam: The First Ten Steps.* London: SCM Press.

Howard, Michael (1991).'State Power and Political Change in Fiji', *Journal of Contemporary Asia, 21*(1): pp. 78-106.

Hussain, Mohammed (2018). *Fiji Muslim League (Sabeto Branch): 1936 and Beyond.* Auckland: M. Hussain.

Lal, Brij (2016). *Historical Dictionary of Fiji.* Lanham, Maryland: Rowman & Littlefield.

—— (ed.) (1998).*Crossing the Kala Pani: A Documentary History of Indian Indenture in Fiji.* Canberra: Division of Pacific and Asian History, Research School of Pacific and Australian National University: Asian Studies.

Miller, Kevin (2008). 'A Community of Sentiment: Indo-Fijian Music and Identity Discourse in Fiji and its Diaspora' (PhD thesis, Loss Angeles: University of California).

Prasad, Jonathon (2007). 'The Role of Hindu and Muslim Organizations during the 2006 Election', in Jon Fraenkel and Stewart Firth (eds.), *From Election to Coup in Fiji: The 2006 Campaign and its Aftermath*. Canberra: ANU Press: pp. 315-36.

Rai, Satish (2020). Film & TV Producer/Director/Writer/Actor/Community Development Professional, Raivision Academy of Film & TV, Sydney. Personal e-mail communication, 16 October 2020.

Ramesh, Sanjay (2017). 'Indo-Fijian Counter Hegemony in Fiji: A Historical Structural Approach', *Pacific Dynamics: Journal of Interdisciplinary Research*, *1*(1): pp. 66-85.

Roy, Olivier and Antoine Sfeir (eds.) (2007). *The Columbia World Dictionary of Islamism*. New York: Columbia University Press.

Sandhu, Kernial (1969). *Indians in Malaya: Some Aspects of their Immigration and Settlement (1786-1957)*. Cambridge: Cambridge University Press.

Shepard, William (2016). 'Muslims "in" New Zealand or "of New Zealand?"', in Erich Kolig and Malcolm Voyce (eds.), *Muslim Integration: Pluralism and Multiculturalism in New Zealand and Australia*. New York: Lexington Books: pp. 93-111.

Tinker, Hugh (1974). *A New System of Slavery: The Export of Indian Labour Overseas 1830-1920*. London: Oxford University Press.

Universal Peace Federation (2009). 'Interreligious Peace Council Inaugurated in Fiji', *UPF*, 21 March, Fiji. Accessed on 7 November 2020. Retrieved from http://www.upf.org/interfaith-programs/1784-interreligious-peace-council-inaugurated-in-fiji

Voigt-Graf, Carmen (2008). 'Transnationalism and the Indo-Fijian Diaspora: The Relationship of Indo-Fijians to India and its People', *Journal of Intercultural Studies*, *29*(1): pp. 81-109.

CHAPTER 10

The Muslims who Arrived in Trinidad, 1887-1891: A Preliminary Assessment

HALIMA-SA'ADIA KASSIM AND PERRY POLAR

INTRODUCTION

It is said that 'you *die twice*. One time when you stop breathing and a second time, a bit later, when somebody says your name for the last time.'[1] The existing historical records of indentured labourers documented the names and other social characteristics of individuals who traversed the 'kalapani' (black water). This allows descendants of indentured labourers to rediscover the names of their ancestors who have inadvertently been written into history and understand the 'complex and contested history' (Lal 2019, 81) that have forged their societies. These records take as their subjects ordinary people and foregrounds their names and social characteristics into 'the ever-growing pile of historical "debris"' (Hitchcock 2013: n.p.). It also permits the de-anonymizing of indentured labourers, ascribing to them an identity. Researchers are thus presented with an opportunity to rescue the 'lives . . . of people most in danger of being forgotten [and place it at] . . . the centre of our regard' and attempt to 'redress that most final, and

[1] The quote is credited to the graffiti artist Banksy, but the sentiment is not his alone and it can be attributed to several different people or cultures. For example, Irvin D. Yalom, *Love's Executioner and Other Tales of Psychotherapy;* David Eagleman, *Sum: Forty Tales from the Afterlives,* Egyptians, Jewish, etc.

254 HALIMA-SA'ADIA KASSIM AND PERRY POLAR

brutal, of life's inequalities: whether or not you are forgotten', by authoring their stories. These stories, be it oral family accounts, published research or statistical data, provide the basis for human beings to 'retain a curiosity about who they are and how they have come to be what they are, in other words, curiosity about questions of identity, purpose and place' (Lal 2012: Abstract).

The indenture project, as part of a global capital-labour nexus, emerged as a strategy to address the effects of the emancipation of slaves which led to labour shortages caused by the planters' insistence that wages in the colonies be kept depressed. It led to over 500,000 Indians being transported from India to the British Caribbean between 1838 and 1917.[2] This not only ensured the economic viability of plantations, but also altered the socio-political landscape of the colonies. Trinidad saw the arrival of over 147,000 Indians during this period, representing the plurality of religions, castes and districts, mainly in North India.

While the plurality of indentured immigrants is acknowledged, there is limited research on migrants disaggregated by variables such as religion, age, gender, caste and so on. Moreover, there have been no efforts to determine the exact number of Muslims that arrived, their social origins or other characteristics for Trinidad or determine how representative this subgroup was of the larger migrating population. Roopnarine (2014: 394) expressed frustration at the 'possibly inaccurate numerical statistics' on aspects of Indian indentured historiography in the Caribbean 'in published studies on the topic'. He noted this as a major flaw in Indian indentured historiography in the Caribbean and counselled on

---

[2] Indian indenture was introduced to Mauritius in 1834, British Guiana in 1838, Trinidad and Jamaica in 1845, small West Indian colonies such as St. Kitts, St. Lucia, St. Vincent and Grenada in the 1850s, Natal in 1860, Suriname in 1873 and Fiji in 1879. During the 82 years of indentured emigration, over one million Indians were introduced into these colonies (Lal 1996: 42). Roopnarine (2009, 71) noted that 'For over three-quarters of a century (1838-1920), British, Danish, Dutch, and French governments transported an estimated 500,000 indentured Indian labourers from the Indian subcontinent to the Caribbean'.

THE MUSLIMS WHO ARRIVED IN TRINIDAD, 1887-1891   255

the need for 'further analyses to ensure transparency and appropriate interpretation of results' so as to reduce/eliminate 'inconsistent and possibly inaccurate numerical statistics' (394-5).

This article seeks to rectify these gaps by mining the entries in the General Registers for the period 1887-91 and corroborating it with entries from the Ship Registers/Emigration Passes, where these are available.[3] The existing data on Muslims is analysed to establish trends and patterns regarding demographic characteristics, bodily marks, geographic origins, second time migration to Trinidad, family accompaniments, birth and mortality aboard ships, returnees to India, and the estates to which immigrants were assigned. The importance of historical demography has been well-articulated by Mercer (1995) who noted that,

reconstruction of the demographic features of a community through aggregation of individual and life histories built up from nominal sources: i.e. those in which an individual is named . . . offers a window on social history through the linkages which can be made between the individual and wider economic, social and cultural patterns: mobility economic and physical, occupation, educational performance, religious membership, family and community relationships support structures, social unity and divisions (cited by Munroe 2000: 10).

This article (re)constructs the demographic and social narrative of the Muslim indentured population for a select period. It adds to the corpus of work on indentured immigrants and in particular, the Muslim subpopulation, and thus ensures that they are part of the indenture immigration narrative.

While historians such as Smith (1959), Gillion (1959), Lal (1980, 2012), Bhana (1987) and Laurence (1994) investigated from a country specific view, the geographical and social origins of indentured labourers (with Muslims as part of the entire population) and presented statistical data, the analyses was completed at a macro-level. This study examines a specific group of indentured

---

[3] The authors are grateful to the staff of The National Archives of Trinidad and Tobago, which holds various registers of the Indian immigrants who arrived between the years 1845 and 1917.

immigrants, Muslims, recruited from India to a specific colony, Trinidad, in a specific time period. By framing this study in the context of micro-history, that is, 'the intensive historical investigation of a relatively well defined smaller object, or a single event, or a village community, a group of families, even an individual person.' (Carlo Ginzburg 1980 cited in Kisantal 2015, 513), it ensures that the similarities/differences of a subpopulation (community) will not be lost in the historical process or the larger historical narrative.

In the words of Geertz, a cultural anthropologist, micro-history allows for the formulation of a 'microscopic analysis as a means of generating conclusions that are applicable to a greater percentage of the general population' (cited by Levi 1991). By examining the social and geographical origins of the Muslim indentured labourers, it provides more precise statistics on Muslims. This article also contributes to a deeper understanding of the process of religious reconstitution in the society and the extent of plurality among the Muslims, especially, as they were culturally, racially, linguistically, and ethnically different, as documented by Vahed (2001: 195). Further, it places a more central focus on the development and evolution of the Muslims within the indentured labourer narrative.

GEOGRAPHICAL AND SOCIAL CHARACTERISTICS OF THE IMMIGRANTS

Indenture provided a source of labour for colonies in the British Empire for almost 80 years, assuring the economic viability of plantation agriculture. It led to the movement of over a million men, women, and children from India on ships bound for Trinidad, British Guiana, Mauritius, Natal, East Africa, Fiji, or other colonies to work mainly on sugar plantations. Historians have identified the push conditions for migration (see Mahmud 2013; Mahase 2012; Roopnarine 2011). While 'the total number of labourers who emigrated from India comprised a small percentage of the total population of the country' (Mahase 2012: 251), this out-migration from colonial India contributed to dramatic demographic and social changes within the receiving colonies.

With regard to Indian indentured historiography, as Lal (2014:

THE MUSLIMS WHO ARRIVED IN TRINIDAD, 1887-1891 257

394) noted that 'studies on indenture from India tend to concentrate on the emigration of Indians from that region' while on the Caribbean end emphasis is on the settlement, working conditions, and accommodation/resistance dichotomy, with little on cultural and religious aspects (see, for example, Roopnarine 2009; Mahase 2008; Roopnarine 2007; Seecharan 1999; Mangru 1996; Ramnarine 1987; Samaroo 1996; Mohapatra 1996; Laurence 1994; Shepherd 1994; Look Lai 1993; Samaroo 1987; Haracksingh 1987; Mahabir 1985; Tinker 1974; Vatuk 1964 and others). Historians have considered Indian indenture from perspectives such as labour mobility (Major 2017); a capitalist-imperialist framework (Mahmud 2013; Mahase 2012; Northrup 1995); the transformation of the Indians' social and economic structures and the impact of colonial rule on India (Batsha 2017; Major 2017; Kumar 2016; Meena 2015; Mahase 2012; Talbot 2011; Maddison 1971); and motivations for indenture (Green 1983; Kale 2010).

Considering the religious background of Indian indentured immigrants to various colonies, scholars generally agree that the proportion of indentured Muslims was approximately the same from the United Provinces (UP) and Bihar (Lal 1980; Jha 1973).[4] Gillion, who examined the causes, nature and effects of Indian immigration and settlement in Fiji, concluded that Muslims accounted for 14.6 per cent of total immigrants (1958: 496). In a 1980 study, Lal established that Muslims furnished 15.1 per cent of Indian emigrants to Fiji during the period 1879 to 1916 (1980: 209).[5]

[4] Jha (1973, 31) cites Comins who noted that in 1891, 85.9 per cent of the non-Christian Indians were Hindus and 13.44 per cent Muhammadans. Jha continues that according to the 1901 census of India, 85 per cent of the population in UP were Hindus and 14 per cent Muslims and in Shahabad (in Bihar) 92.7 per cent Hindus and 7.3 per cent Muslims. Lal (1980, 211) stated that the 'percentage contribution of the various groups to indentured emigration is greater than their proportionate strength in the UP.' In the case of Muslims, they represented 13 per cent of the population in UP from 1891 through 1911.

[5] Lal (1980: 209-10) notes that among the Muslims were high status groups such as Pathans, Sheiks, Saiyids, and Moghuls. He continued that the 'overwhelming majority clearly were ordinary Muslims, perhaps converts from Hinduism during the period of Moghul rule in India'.

In a subsequent study, Lal (1996: 172) concluded that 'of the indentured emigrating population between the 1880s and the end of emigration in 1916, . . . Muslims [comprised] 12 per cent.' From this, one can conclude that Muslims made up between 12 and 16 per cent of the indentured migrant population to Fiji.

Brennan et al. (1998: 71) noted that Muslims provided a steady annual stream of about 10 per cent to Mauritius, Natal, Fiji, Guyana, and Jamaica during the period of indenture. Bhana (1987: 122) suggested that Muslims comprised 3 per cent among the Madras group and 5.5 per cent of the Calcutta group of migrant to Natal. However, his sample covered 90,000 of the 150,000 migrants to Natal. Vahed (2001: 194), who studied all 150,000 emigration passes, found that in Natal indentured Muslims accounted for approximately 7 to 10 per cent of migrants.

With regard to the Caribbean, Laurence (1994: 110), specified that 14 per cent of the immigrants who arrived in Trinidad between 1874/75 and 1917 were Muslims. It is the range of 12 to 15 per cent that is often cited (including the work of the first author of this article) as a representative of the Muslims who arrived as indentured labourers in the Caribbean/Trinidad. This, therefore substantiates the call by Roopnarine (2014: 394) for more accurate numerical statistics on aspects of Indian indentured historiography in the Caribbean.

Indian immigrants' societies in the colonies were constructed along caste based *inter alia* on original territorial linkages/religious/occupational/functional/sectarian categories. Although Islam makes no caste distinctions, 'Muslims in India nevertheless tended to segment themselves in caste-like groups (e.g. Saiyids, Ashrafs, Ajlafs, Jolahas and Rajputs)' (Chetty, n.d.). To this caste-like group, Bal and Sinha-Kerkhoff (2007: 133) added Sheikhs, Pathans, Moghals, Fakirs, Ghosis and Hajam. Moreover, many Muslims were Hindu converts. For example, Manihir, Dhobi, Gaddi, and Teli are Hindu caste names which Muslims bore.

While the immigration records identified the immigrants as 'Muslims', this categorization is limited, and one cannot determine the sect, their *madhab* (school of thought), or the extent to which they were influenced or affected by the numerous Islamic

THE MUSLIMS WHO ARRIVED IN TRINIDAD, 1887-1891   259

reformist or revivalist movements which were a feature of their homelands in the second half of the nineteenth-century. Titus (1960, 31), writing on the religious history of India, avers that the areas where the immigrants originated, there were some Shia Muslims but that Sunni Muslims of the Hanifa *madhab* predominated. Bal and Sinha-Kerkhoff (2007: 133) also observed that most Muslims were from the Sunni Hanafi *madhab* although some were influenced by Shias and Sufis. It can be concluded from this that there was some level of faith homogeneity among Muslim immigrants.

Indentured immigration to the West Indies from Calcutta was regulated by Act XXI of 1844 and stipulated that a number of women should be recruited to emigrate. In 1868 the proportion of women was amended and fixed at a ratio of 40 women to 100 men. For Trinidad and British Guiana, the overall ratio was not met for the period 1874 to 1917 (Laurence 1994: 119, 123). Similarly, for Natal there was a shortage of women throughout the period (Bhana 1987: 23). Chatterjee (1997: 54) found that women comprised 12,303 out of a total of 37,991 migrants (32.38 per cent) who arrived in Trinidad between 1876 and 1892. Muslim women, numbering 2009, made up 16.3 per cent of this number (Chatterjee 1997: 50).

Most immigrants to Trinidad were from the United Provinces of Agra and Oudh in North India. In fact, 90 per cent of immigrants to Trinidad embarked from the port of Calcutta while just 10 per cent emigrated through the port of Madras (Jha 1973: 28). Historians writing on recruitment have argued that the migrants represented not only the approximate numerical strength of a society,[6] but that it was also a representation of other socio-economic characteristics of caste, language and economic status. Gillion (1959),

---

[6] While earlier than the period under consideration, Geoghegan in his investigation of emigration in India in 1870 showed that between 1842 and 1870, the indentured labourers came mainly from the north (64 per cent), south India (30 per cent) and to a much lesser extent from Bombay (6 per cent). He also noted that Muslim migration from Calcutta between 1842 and 1870 was 15 per cent (or 49,860 of 323,877). See Geoghegan 1873: 70-2.

260 HALIMA-SA'ADIA KASSIM AND PERRY POLAR

Perry (1969), Jha (1973), Laurence (1984), Bhana (1987), Lal (1996, 2012), Chatterjee (1997); Brennan et al. (1998), Vahed (2001) and Mahase (2015), amongst others, have examined the geographic origins/registration of Indian indentured labourers for Natal, Fiji, Mauritius, British Guiana and Trinidad. For Trinidad, Laurence (1994: 110-12) identified the following principal districts in North India where emigrants were registered—Northwest Provinces, Oudh, Bengal & Bihar, and Punjab[7]—which is consistent with findings for British Guiana, Jamaica, Fiji, Mauritius, and Natal. Mahase (2015: 2) identified that most of the labourers in Trinidad came from the United Provinces and Oudh, with smaller numbers from Bihar, Bengal, Madras and Bombay.

Bhana (1987) and Lal (1980: 330-2; 2012: 46, 109) have discussed the family/kinship of migrants for Natal and Fiji, respectively. They found that around two-thirds of migrants emigrated as composite social units from their villages; either as husband/wife, husband/wife/children, or parent/children. Chatterjee's (1997: 54) work on women's indentureship experience in Trinidad and Guyana noted that the percentage of married women emigrating to the colonies was significantly lower in the early years of indenture (fluctuating between 25.6 per cent and 36 per cent). However, between 1887 and 1891, the percentage of married women rose dramatically to a yearly average of approximately 74 per cent (Chatterjee 1997: 54).

Birth and death formed a natural part of the cycle of life and emigrants aboard the ships from India destined for Trinidad experienced both. Chatterjee (1997) discussed the presence of pregnant women aboard the ship, despite the 1860s government regulation to discontinue the embarkation of pregnant women and very young children. She noted that for Trinidad the average number of births at sea between 1871 and 1890 was about 15 per shipping season with the highest number of births (32) recorded in 1890 (1997: 108).

---

[7] Laurence (1994, 110-12) listed the following districts: Northwest Provinces (Agra, Allahabad, Azamgarh, Bareilly, Basti, Benares, Kanpur, Ghazipur, Gorackpur, Jaunpur, Mathura, Others), Oudh (Fyzabad, Gonda, Lucknow, Others), Bengal & Bihar (Burdawan, Calcutta, Darbhanga, Gaya, Patna, Shahabad, 24 Parganas, others), and Punjab (Delhi, others).

THE MUSLIMS WHO ARRIVED IN TRINIDAD, 1887-1891   261

Migratory behaviours of the immigrants were neither linear nor static. There were migrations and re-migrations within the British Empire as well as between the British and other European colonies. Roopnarine (2011: 174) noted that of the immigrants who 'crossed the Indian and Atlantic Oceans to work in the Caribbean, 175,000 returned home when their contracts expired while 350,000 stayed back in the Caribbean'. Roopnarine (2009: 75) also noted that 'in spite of the planters' determination to encourage Indian labourers to stay in their Karma Bhumi ("land of work"; the Caribbean), the average return rate was around 8 per cent per annum to migrants' Janma Bhumi ("land of birth"; India). However, around 40,000 to 50,000 of those who had returned to India re-indentured for a second and sometimes even third term in the Caribbean or other colonies. This second or even third term of indenture was complex but continuous.'[8] Although not precise, Roopnarine (2009: 87) calculated that re-migration began in the 1860s and continued until 1920, averaging around 200 per annum.[9] The estimated number of re-migrants was thus around 40,000 to 50,000. For Trinidad, Roopnarine estimated a yearly average of 42 (2009: 88).

METHODOLOGY

The geographical and social origins of Muslim indentured labourers are considered to (re)construct the demographic and social narrative of the Muslim indentured population for a five-year period, 1887-91. The short timespan allows for better management in

[8] For example, migrants would serve five to fifteen years in the Caribbean and return to India but would again return to the Caribbean, while others would after finishing their indenture in other British colonies (e.g. Mauritius, Fiji, and Natal) and chose the Caribbean instead of returning to their original indentured destinations.

[9] Using data from the 1881 Report of the Immigration Agent General, Roopnarine (2009) showed that for British Guyana showed that 247 labourers migrated for a second time under indenture from another colony, i.e. Demerara, Jamaica, Trinidad, Mauritius, St. Vincent, Reunion, and Suriname for the period 1872-81. Citing Comins (1893), Roopnarine (2009) identified 2,358 Indians who migrated from other colonies to Trinidad for a second time under indenture between 1877 and 1892. See Roopnarine 2009: 84, 88.

262   HALIMA-SA'ADIA KASSIM AND PERRY POLAR

the recording, interpreting and analysing the data. Two sources were examined—the General Registers[10] and the Emigration Passes—to develop this narrative.[11] Based on the General Registers one had access to a listing of the full details of the immigrants which began in 1886, but only partially covered the full calendar year. As such, documenting of the records began from February 1887. The General Registers of Indentured Immigrants, held at the National Archives of Trinidad and Tobago, were examined for Muslims immigrants who arrived on 24 ships originating from Calcutta during the five-year period 1887-91. The list of ships and dates of arrival are given in Appendix 1.

Approximately 14,000 records were scanned in the 'Caste' column for the main term 'Mosulman' but also for other groups known to be Muslims. Informed by the work of Lal (1980) and Bhana (1987) the registers were examined for the following caste groups: Behnas, Darzis, Dhunias/Dhuniyas, Fakirs, Gujars, Hajam, Hijra, Julahas, Kunjras, Moghuls, Momins, Muslim Rajputs, Nau-Muslims, Pathans, Qassais, Ranghbars, Rangrezs, Saiqilghars, Saiyids, Shaikhs and Sheiks. For the period under study there were no entries for Behnas, Darzis, Fakirs, Gujars, Hijras, Julahas, Kunjras, Momins, Muslims Rajputs, Qassais, Ranghbars, Rangrezes, and Saiqilghars. Although Hajams (Hajamin, Hajjam) are identified as

[10] The General Registers contain the ship number, the registration number of the immigrants, their sex, age, height, their father's name, their native place, the name of the plantation to which they were assigned, and from the late 1880s additional information such as caste, bodily marks, and date of exemption were included. Under the column 'Remarks', information such as birth of children, death of immigrant, illness, return to India, receipt of land is recorded. Relevant information about the migrants was entered into the General Registers of Immigrants (and various Plantation Registers) to keep track of the migrants' progress and whereabouts in the colony.

[11] The Emigration Passes contain the following information for each immigrant: immigrants' name, sex, age, caste, bodily marks, districts of origin and registration, town and village, father's name, name of next of kin, and marital status. It also identified the name of the ship on which they arrived in Trinidad, the depot number and immigration number of the emigrant.

THE MUSLIMS WHO ARRIVED IN TRINIDAD, 1887-1891   263

having Muslims only Muslim Hajim was counted as Muslim. The listing below shows the scheme for main 'Caste' categories under which variation on the spellings were encountered or possible conversions were classified.

- Muselman: Dosad (Muselman), (Muselman) Chamar, Dhopnia Muselman, Musl. Dhooman, Musleman, (now) Musleman, (Musleman) Mehtu, (Musleman) Mehter, Muselman Shaik, Mooselman, Now Muselman, Muselman Barbar, Shaik Muselman, Muselman (Syed), Mosulman/Moosulman, Musalmany, Mosleman.
- Dhuinya: Dhunia
- Mohamedan: Mahamadan, Mahamadan
- Pathan: (convert) Pathan, Paithani
- Syed
- Shaikhs: Shaik, Shaikh
- Sheikh: Sheikh (Teli), Muslim Shekh, Shekh, Shiek, Shikh, Seikh, Sheekh, Shukh.

Given the inconsistency in spelling and in the recording of native places and names of estates, secondary sources were consulted to corroborate the information from the Registers. For example, a native place had several different representations—Bar Barrielly/ Bas Barrielly/Babarielly/Bareilly—or an estate was recorded as Plan Paliais/Plain Palais. To resolve these inconsistencies, Bhana (1987), Laurence (1994), Lal (1980) and Jha (1973) were consulted to confirm the names of the native places identified in the Emigration Passes. For this dataset, native places where more than ten immigrants are identified, data are presented; otherwise it is recorded as 'Other'.

Deen (1994, 266), who identified 294 estates in Trinidad to which the immigrants were assigned, was consulted to substantiate the listing of estates to which the immigrants were assigned.[12] As such, names of some estates were reclassified, such as Bonne Aventure was changed to Bonne Adventure, or the names of estates

---

[12] The authors appreciate listing provided and reference identified by Dr. Bisham Ramlal, Faculty of Engineering, UWI.

were combined, such as Concord also includes Concord SN and Concord PAP. However, there were some estates listed in the registers that were not identified by Deen, for example Wellington. Challenges also existed for the allocation of individuals to a specific estate when two estates were combined, for example Orange Grove and Macoya. In such cases, this was treated as separate estates, for example Orange Grove Estate and Macoya Estate.

An Abstract summarizing arrival details was generally included in the General Registers for each ship.[13] These were used to calculate demographic data, distribution of the subpopulation, sex, births, and mortality. Volga (1889) did not include an Abstract, hence data from Deen (1994: 277) on the emigrating Indians for this ship was used. Still, this posed a challenge as infants were not isolated but possibly classified with boys and girls.

Emigration Passes which corresponded to these persons were examined either in hard copy or microfilm to verify information in the General Registers and provide information on family relationships and previous places of indenture. Given the deteriorating condition of some of the Emigration Passes (both hard copy and microfilm) only 81 per cent of the records were verified. This information was also recorded in the Microsoft Excel database.

Full geographic, social and personal data from the General and Ship Registers were recorded using Microsoft Excel. Data was then categorized by the specific variables and counted manually or with the use of software. Descriptive statistics were to present an analysis of these basic social characteristics. This followed the approach adopted by Lal (1980), who indicated that there was no need for inferential or advanced statistical analysis. No cross-sectional analysis is presented.

This study has certain limitations. While previous studies in receiving colonies (Natal, Fiji, British Guiana, and Trinidad) adopted

[13] The Abstract recorded the number of men (>12 years), women (> 12 years), boys (> 2 years-12 years), girls (> 2 years-12 years) and infants (< 2 years) in categories such as: distributed from depot, sent to hospital from ship, sent to hospital from depot, Sent to convalescent depot, paid passage at Calcutta, arrived in Trinidad, embarked at Calcutta, etc.

THE MUSLIMS WHO ARRIVED IN TRINIDAD, 1887-1891 265

a population-based approach to studying the characteristics of indentured labourers, this article examines a subpopulation for a five-year period, focusing entirely on indentured Muslims based on criteria outlined above. This is in line with the earlier research undertaken in Fiji and Natal by Bhana (1987) and Lal (1980). By focussing only on those self-identifying as Muslims and groups predominantly Muslim (based on the literature) it provides a clearer picture of the characteristics of the Muslim population and reduces the risk of data misrepresentation. It also only focuses on a five-year period thus, providing more manageability in analysing the data.

RESULTS AND DISCUSSION

LANDED IN TRINIDAD

An estimated 14,237 Indians left India between 1887 and 1891 and 13,969 (or 98.1 per cent) landed in Trinidad as indentured labourers. The difference between the numbers was due to a combination of deaths, births, and passengers (see Appendix 2 Table A).

MUSLIM DISTRIBUTION

The number of Muslims landed in Trinidad was 1,519 with 1,497 surviving the journey. The overall total percentage of Muslims who landed in Trinidad was 10.9 per cent of the total immigrants arriving (see Appendix 2 Table A). This correlates with the findings of Brennan et al. (1998: 71) for Muslims migrating to Mauritius, Natal, Fiji, Guyana and Jamaica during the indenture period. It remains to be determined if there was a reluctance among planters to employ Muslim indentured labourers in Trinidad, as in Natal, where employers asked that no Brahmins or Muslim would be recruited because their religious practices detracted from their labour (Vahed 2001, 198).

DISTRIBUTION BY SHIP

There were year-to-year and ship-to-ship differences that probably related to recruitment patterns and 'push factors' in India

266 HALIMA-SA'ADIA KASSIM AND PERRY POLAR

itself. As such, the yearly percentages of Muslims arriving to the colony decreased from 1887 (12.1 per cent) to 1891 (9.8 per cent). The ship Jura, which made three crossings during the period under review had the highest percentage of Muslims—17.1 per cent in 1888 and 15.3 per cent and 15.9 per cent in 1889—compared to other ships. This is probably a coincidence as no other factors can be discerned. The ships with the largest number of Muslims were *Jura* (1888) and *Main* (1891) with 96 and 94 Muslims respectively. Conversely, the ships with the lowest number of Muslims were *Rhine* (1891), *Jumna* (1889), and *Volga* (1889) which ranged from 37 to 38. Data on numbers of persons embarking is presented for information purposes (see Appendix 2 Table A).

POPULATION DISTRIBUTION

Looking at the difference between the distribution of Indians, and Muslims as a subgroup, it was found that the proportion of Muslim men was consistently less every year than the proportion of the overall Indian male population (-5.6 per cent for the period), while Muslim women were consistently higher every year than the proportion of women overall (5.2 per cent for the period). Muslim women, based on the evidence so far, came both as part of a family unit as well as single (unaccompanied) individuals. There was no clear pattern with Muslim boys, girls and infants as they were within 1 per cent of their respective Indian categories.

It suggests that Muslim women were arriving in Trinidad at a higher percentage than the norm for the female Indian population. This concurs with the observations by Chatterjee (1997: 51) that 'Muslim women formed a larger percentage of the female population emigrating than brahmins, artisans, and Christians combined' (see Appendix 2 Table B).

SEX DISTRIBUTION

Although the proportion of Muslim females was higher than the overall Indian migrant female population, the percentage of Muslim males over the five-year period was still greater (60.8 per cent)

THE MUSLIMS WHO ARRIVED IN TRINIDAD, 1887-1891

than that of the Muslim female population. This was the case in virtually every shipment. There was no clear trend of increasing or decreasing ratios (see Appendix 2 Table C). The results of this five-year period do not concur with the findings of Laurence (1994: 123) that overall that ratio of 60 : 40 male : female was not met for Trinidad. More research is required over a longer time span to determine whether this was the pattern throughout indenture and what the implications of this were.

CASTE

Approximately 84.9 per cent of the landed Muslims were classified as 'Muselman' (see Appendix 2 Figure 10.1). The remaining groups identified as Muslim included Pathans (7.2 per cent), Shaikh (0.9 per cent), Sheiks (3.8 per cent), Mohamadans (2.4 per cent), Momins (0.3 per cent), Dhuniyas (0.3 per cent), Syeds (0.1 per cent), Behnas (0.1 per cent), and a Muslim Hajjam (0.1 per cent). The other categories searched were not identified.

AGE DISTRIBUTION

The data suggests that Muslim males aged 21-5 comprised the majority group (331) and this was consistent across the years. The age categories 16-20 years (184) and 26-30 years old (179) were also high and these three categories accounted for 75.1 per cent of the Muslim males who came. A similar pattern was seen with women with the age group 16-30 years accounting for 71.6 per cent of Muslim females. The number of males aged 10 and under (139) was very similar to the number of females aged 10 and under (132). This is captured in Appendix 2 Table D. Generally, Muslims aged 21-30 years represented three quarters of the total Muslim immigrants (73.8 per cent), which was higher than the overall findings of Laurence (1994) for Trinidad (61 per cent). As with Natal (Bhana 1987: 25), for example, emigrants aged 21-5 years dominated for Trinidad, representing just over one-third (539 or 36 per cent). The predominance of this young group is not surprising since employers were looking for fit and able-bodied to work on plantations.

HEIGHT DISTRIBUTION

The heights of males and females were constant except for 1888 where there a minor drop, which the authors attribute to a mathematical anomaly due to lower sample size (only three ships arrived in 1888) rather than any other factor measured in the study. On an average, males were 161.3 cm (or 5'4"), while females were 147.8 cm (or 4'10") in height (see Appendix 2 Table E). Interestingly, the immigrants' height was on an average nine centimetres shorter than the those arriving in Natal whose heights varied between 156 cm and 170 cm (Bhana 1987: 24).

BODILY CHARACTERISTICS

There were 1,228 immigrants (80.2 per cent) recorded as having bodily marks. These included scars (53.1 per cent), warts (7.2 per cent), tattoos (4 per cent), moles (2.8 per cent), pock-marked face (9.2 per cent), inoculation mark (1.5 per cent), and others (2.5 per cent). The recording of scars as the highest category of bodily marks is consistent with the findings for Natal by Bhana (1997). However, it remains unclear what the reasons underlying these marking were, although Bhana (1987, 25) speculated that it may be from injuries but given the high number with bodily marks, this was more likely to have religious or caste significance.

NATIVE PLACES

The 1,519 Muslim immigrants who arrived were from 124 districts across nine known states/provinces including the princely states, Bombay Presidency and Madras Presidency. Punjab/United Province of Agra and Oudh (UP) yielded the most immigrants (989) followed by Bihar (287), which is consistent with the literature. Busti (Basti), Azimgarh, and Jounpur provided just over a third (36.6 per cent) of the immigrants from Punjab, while Gaya, Mozafferpur and Saran provided 57.1 per cent of the migrants from Bihar. For the period under review, the Central Provinces and Orissa provided the least immigrants (see Appendix 2 Table F1 and F2 and Figure 10.2).

THE MUSLIMS WHO ARRIVED IN TRINIDAD, 1887-1891

SECOND INDENTURE

Khunjhani (#77979), arrived in Trinidad in February 1887 aboard the *Bann* with her husband, Chamru; they were re-indentures of Trinidad. Hafizkhan (#84125) who arrived in Trinidad in November 1889 aboard the *Avoca* was a re-indenture from Natal. There were many such cases. The Emigration Passes revealed that there were 116 second time Muslim indentured immigrants representing 7.6 per cent of the Muslims who came to Trinidad. The majority of the second time indentured Muslims (88 per cent) came from a Caribbean territory (Guadeloupe, Guyana, Suriname, St. Vincent, and Trinidad) with the majority coming from British Guiana. The others were from non-Caribbean territories like Bourbon, Fiji, Natal, and Mauritius).

It is noteworthy that second time indentured migrants also came from French and Dutch colonies. Roopnarine (2011) identified the re-entry of previously indentured labourers from the Caribbean, but he made no mention of previously indentured labourers from non-Caribbean colonies re-indenturing in the Caribbean (see Appendix 2 Table G).

There were also eight indentured Indians who migrated to the Spanish Main and 26 left for Demerara. In both instances, passages were forfeited.

The instances of re-indenturing do raise critical questions about indentured migrants being fraudulently lied to by recruiters and not having any knowledge of what to expect in the colonies. Those who went to the colonies, returned to India and re-indentured, had a clear idea of what to expect. It is also likely that when they returned to India, they told family members and neighbours about conditions in the colonies and likely influenced others to follow. Further analysis is required to see whether those who re-indentured were accompanied by people they were familiar with.

FAMILY ACCOMPANIMENTS

The Emigration Passes reviewed (1,187) showed that approximately 45 per cent of persons on the ship were accompanied by a family member. This comprised 194 family units. The number of Muslim

270 HALIMA-SA'ADIA KASSIM AND PERRY POLAR

mothers with children was the highest category (62). The number of Muslim couples (56) without child/children was just over the number of Muslims couples with child/children (49). There were four instances of husbands with two wives and children; three cases where three generations were observed (a grandmother, her married daughter and her daughter's children); and three cases where there were siblings. The 'other' category included such examples as a couple (husband and wife) with a child but also the husband's brother; a case with an uncle and nephew, or more commonly where children were present, but it is not clear who the parents are (see Appendix 2 Table H).

The findings are similar to those of Lal (1980: 330-1; Lal 2012: 46, 109), who also found many instances of composite family units; however, the percentage of husband/wife families in Trinidad was lower (57.7 per cent) than that noted for Fiji (68.6 per cent). The number of single mothers accompanied by children (32 per cent) was higher in Trinidad than the 12.1 per cent identified by Lal (1980, 285). There were a few cases of single fathers with children (3.6 per cent) emigrating to Trinidad.

The number of single Muslim mothers is interesting and part of a pattern of single female migrants to the colonies. Many writers have interrogated the reason for this phenomenon and a recent work that sparked a great deal of debate is Gaiutra Bahadur's *Coolie Woman: The Odyssey of Indenture*, which is a biography of Bahadur's great grandmother who emigrated to British Guiana from Bihar in 1903. Bahadur points to such factors as caste and the Indian family structure as factors that may have induced emigration. Though a Brahmin, she adjusted to indentured labour and made a new home in British Guiana. More broadly, Bahadur examines feminist themes such as poverty, women's oppression, the sexual abuse of women, and violence against women. We know little about the Muslim women migrants to Trinidad, but it is fair to speculate that their experiences were similar.

BIRTHS ABOARD SHIP

Births aboard the ship were determined via the General Register and often, slips of paper inserted in the Emigration Passes. The

THE MUSLIMS WHO ARRIVED IN TRINIDAD, 1887-1891 271

records showed that Abdoolah, for instance, being born aboard the *Sheila* in November 1886 to Kony (#77356) from Alighur. There were 112 recorded births on the ship regardless of population subgroup with 1888 having the lowest value (8), possibly due to fewer ships arriving. It should be noted there was no data for four ships. This suggests that pregnant women were recruited contrary to the 1860s regulation. The data suggests that there were 22.4 births per shipping season, which was higher than the average number of births identified by Chatterjee (1997, 108) for the period 1871-90 (see Appendix 2 Table I). However, for the period under study there was only one Muslim birth aboard the ships, which could indicate that the practice of not having pregnant women on board the ship held for Muslims.

MORTALITY ABOARD SHIP

As with births, the mortality rate was identified from the entries in the General Registers and verified with the Emigration Passes. The total number of Indian deaths for the period was 261 with 43.3 per cent of these occurring in 1891 mostly on the Main and the Avoca. Further research may be required to determine if there were factors beyond the generally ascribed ones such as ill-treatment, under-nourishment/under-fed, poor sanitation and disease, that influenced high mortality on these ships. For Muslims, there were twenty-two (22) deaths over the five-year period, with six deaths occurring in 1891 aboard the aforementioned ships. The death rate for Muslims was 1.4 per cent, which was lower than the overall percentage of Indian deaths (1.9 per cent).

Proportionally, men (0.6 per cent) and women (0.8 per cent) died at a lower rate than boys (1.8 per cent), girls (3 per cent), and infants (19 per cent). The ships examined suggest that mortality rates of the Indians was higher than Fiji or Natal, where it was 1.9 per cent. The ships that had the most deaths docked between October and December with the exception being the British Peer which berthed in February 1891.

There was one particularly interesting case where both parents died, the mother, Koreemon, aged 30, on board the *Avoca* which

272 HALIMA-SA'ADIA KASSIM AND PERRY POLAR

docked in November 1889 and the father, Peerbokus, aged 38, died subsequently in June 1890. Their son, Hasan, aged 7 was sent to Belmont Orphanage in August 1890 (see Appendix 2 Table J). No record of what happened to Hasan is available.

ESTATE ASSIGNMENT

There were 101 estate categories identified from the records. The four most assigned estates for Muslims were Caroni (58), Saint Augustine (56), Waterloo (53), and Orange Grove (49) (see Appendix 2 Table K and Figure 10.3).

RETURNEES

Of the estimated 500,000 immigrants who arrived in the Caribbean, 175,000 returned to India when their contracts expired (Roopnarine 2011, 174). For the five-year period, there were 337 Muslim returnees to India. Based on the total number of immigrants who embarked—13,969—(and not taking into consideration those who died or left for other colonies or the Spanish Main), approximately 2.4 per cent returned to India. Of the immigrants who arrived in 1889 and 1891, 81 and 79 returned to India, respectively with only 43 of those arriving in 1888 returning (see Appendix 2 Table L).

CONCLUSION

The research for this article relied heavily on archival records to reconstruct 'the demographic features of a community' (Mercer 1995) with the intent to add to the corpus of work on indentured immigrants and, the Muslim subpopulation in particular, ensuring that they were part of the indenture immigration narrative. The meticulous recording system of the British allows for aspects of their story to be excavated. These records build a 'picture of the human capital which shaped the economy, demography and culture of' Trinidad and supports the understanding of 'the nature, dynamics, and consequences of a major modern human

THE MUSLIMS WHO ARRIVED IN TRINIDAD, 1887-1891

migration, the legacy of which continues to influence the lives of tens of millions of men, women and children in various parts of the world' (UNESCO).

The findings show that for the period under review, around 10.9 per cent of immigrants were Muslims, the male : female ratios (60 : 40) were generally met, the migrants were aged between 21 to 30 years of age, with an average height of 161.3 cm for males and 147.8 cm for females and were generally from Uttar Pradesh and Bihar. There were a small percentage of second time indentures, while family units made up a substantial portion of the migratory population, and a very small number returned to India. This is consistent with the patterns observed for the larger indentured Indian group as well as for indentured migrants to other colonies. This raises the question of whether recruitment strategies also operated at the level of caste/religion. Future work must examine the patterns of Muslim migration and settlement between 1892 and 1917 to determine the consistency of patterns.

By adopting a micro-analytical approach to the study of indenture records, the authors were able to provide greater details on a smaller subgroup of the indentured population. This research is important for the Muslim community, which is a minority in Trinidad, where it constitutes around 5 per cent of the total population. Such information may appear to focus excessively on the quantitative but it provides a connection between the past and the present by providing a sense of rootedness and connection to India. As Waet Jenand Vahed (2014: 72) noted, these written regimes can 'serve economic interests by harnessing global linkages' and be a mediating movement in the Indian diaspora. This is especially important in the context of continuing 'Arabization' of Islam in Trinidad, and 'Islamophobia' towards Muslims more generally. Such information on origins helps to dispel some of the myths peddled by reformist Muslims, as well as by those who are anti-Muslim by underscoring the contribution of Muslims to the development of Trinidad. They are as much Trinidadian as their Hindu and Christian counterparts of indentured ancestry.

REFERENCES

Bahadur, Gaiutra (2013). *Coolie Woman: The Odyssey of Indenture*. London: Hurst & Company.

Bal, Ellen and Kathinka Sinha-Kerkhoff (2007). 'Separated by the Partition? Muslims of British Indian Descent in Mauritus and Suriname', in Gijsbert Oonk (ed.), *Global Indian Diasporas: Exploring Trajectories of Migration and Theory*. Amsterdam: University Press: pp. 119-49.

Batsha, Nishant (2017). 'The Currents of Restless Toil: Colonial Rule and Indian Indentured Labor in Trinidad and Fiji' (Ph.D. dissertation, Columbia University).

Bhana, Surendra (1987). *Indentured Indians in Natal, 1860-1902: A Study Based on Ship's Lists*. Durban, University of Durban Westville: Promila/BSA.

Brennan, Lance, J. McDonald, and R. Shlomowitz (1998). 'The geographic and social origins of Indian indentured labourers in Mauritius, Natal, Fiji, Guyana and Jamaica', *South Asia: Journal of South Asian Studies, 21*(1): pp. 39-71.

Chatterjee, Sumita (1997). 'Indian women's lives and labor: the indentureship experience in Trinidad and Guyana: 1845-1917' (Ph.D. thesis, University of Massachusetts Amherst).

Chetty, Kishore (n.d.).'*Caste and Religions of Natal Immigrants', Gandhi-Luthuli Documentation Centre*. Retrieved from http://scnc.ukzn.ac.za/doc/SHIP/caste.html.

Deen, Shamshu (1994). *Solving East Indian Roots in Trinidad*. Bahamas, Freeport Junction: HEM Enterprises.

Geoghegan, John (1873). *Note on Emigration from India*. Calcutta: Office of Superintendent of Government Printing.

Green, William A. (1983). 'Emancipation to indenture: a question of imperial morality', *The Journal of British Studies, 22*(2): pp. 98-121.

Gillion, Keith L. (1958). 'History of Indian Immigration and Settlement in Fiji' (Ph.D. dissertation, Australian National University).

Hitchcock, David (2013). 'Why history from below matters more than ever', *the Many-headed monster Blog*. Accessed 22 July 2013. Available at https://manyheadedmonster.wordpress.com/2013/07/22/david-hitchcock-why-history-from-below-matters-more-than-ever/.

Jha, Jagdis C. (1973). 'Indian heritage in Trinidad, West Indies', *Caribbean Quarterly, 19*(2): pp. 28-50.

Kale, Madhavi (2010). *Fragments of Empire: Capital, Slavery, and Indian Indentured Labor in the British Caribbean*. Pennsylvania: University of Pennsylvania Press.

THE MUSLIMS WHO ARRIVED IN TRINIDAD, 1887-1891   275

Kisantal, Tamás (2015). 'What Is Microhistory? Theory and Practice', *Hungarian Historical Review*, 4(2): pp. 502-36.

Kumar, Nitesh (2016). 'Economic Impact of British colonial rule on Indian Agriculture: A Review', *International Research Journal of Social Sciences*, 5(2): pp. 56-8.

Lal, Brij V. (2019). *Levelling Wind: Remembering Fiji*. Acton, Australian Capital Territory: Australian National University Press.

—— (2012). 'Origins of the Girmitiyas', in Brij V. Lal (ed.), *Chalo Jahaji: On a Journey through Indenture in Fiji*. Canberra: Australian National University Press: pp. 99-119.

—— (1996). 'The Odyssey of indenture: fragmentation and reconstitution in the Indian diaspora', *Diaspora: A Journal of Transnational Studies*, 5(2): pp. 167-88.

—— (1980). 'Leaves of the banyan tree: origins and background of Fiji's north Indian indentured migrants, 1879-1916' (Ph.D. dissertation, Australian National University).

Laurence, Keith O. (1994). *A Question of Labour: Indentured Immigration into Trinidad and British Guiana, 1875-1917*. Jamaica, Kingston: Ian Randle Publishers.

Levi, Giovanni (1991). 'On microhistory', in Peter Burke (ed.), *New Perspectives on Historical Writing*. Pennsylvania, University Park: Pennsylvania State University Press: pp. 93-113.

Maddison, Angus (1971). 'The Economic and Social Impact of Colonial Rule in India', *Class Structure and Economic Growth: India & Pakistan since the Moghuls*. Available at http://www.ggdc.net/maddison/articles/moghul_3.pdf.

Mahase, Radica (2015). 'A brief look at the Indian Indentureship system in Trinidad', Speech to YATRA, East Indian Cultural Promotions, Claxton Bay, 30 May.

—— (2012). 'Imperialism, Labour Relations and Colonial Policies: Indian Indentured Labour in Trinidad, 1845 to 1920', *Man in India*, 92(2): pp. 247-61.

Mahmud, Tayyab (2013). 'Cheaper than a Slave: Indentured Labor, Colonialism, and Capitalism', *Whittier Law Review*, 34(2): pp. 215-43.

Major, Andrea (2017). 'Hill Coolies': Indian Indentured Labour and the Colonial Imagination, 1836-38', *South Asian Studies*, 33(1): pp. 23-36.

Meena, Hareet Kumar (2015). 'The Impact of British Rule on Indian Villages', *American International Journal of Research in Humanities, Arts and Social Sciences*, 12(1): pp. 94-8.

Munro, Doug (2012). 'Of Journeys and Transformations: Brij V. Lal and the

Study of *Girmit*, in Brij V. Lal (ed.), *Chalo Jahaji: On a Journey through Indenture in Fiji*. Canberra: Australian National University Press: pp. 1-23.

Northrup, David (1995). *Indentured Labor in the Age of Imperialism, 1834-1922*. Cambridge: Cambridge University Press Archive.

Perry, John A. (1969). 'A History of the East Indian Indentured Plantation Worker in Trinidad, 1845-1917' (Ph.D. dissertation, Louisiana State University).

Roopnarine, Lomarsh (2014). 'A critique of East Indian indentured historiography in the Caribbean', *Labor History*, *55*(3): pp. 389-401.

—— (2011). 'Indian migration during indentured servitude in British Guiana and Trinidad, 1850–1920', *Labor History*, *52*(2): pp. 173-91.

—— (2009). 'The Repatriation, Readjustment, and Second-Term Migration of Ex-Indentured Indian Laborers from British Guiana and Trinidad to India, 1838-1955', *New West Indian Guide/Nieuwe West-Indische Gids*, *83*(1-2): pp. 71-97.

Smith, Raymond T. (1959). 'Some social characteristics of Indian immigrants to British Guiana', *Population Studies*, *13*(1): pp. 34-9.

South African History Online (2016). *Areas indentured Indians came from*. Available at http://scnc.ukzn.ac.za/doc/SHIP/places.html.

Talbot, Ian (2011). 'The Punjab under colonialism: order and transformation in British India', *Journal of Punjab Studies*, *14*(1): pp. 4-10.

Tinker, Hugh (1992). *A New System of Slavery*. London: Hansib Publishing Limited.

Titus, Murray T. (1960). *Islam in India and Pakistan: A Religious History of Islam in India and Pakistan*. Madras: Christian Literary Society.

UNESCO (2012). *International Memory of the World Register—Indentured Immigration Records*. Mauritius. Retrieved from http://www.unesco.org/new/fileadmin/MULTIMEDIA/HQ/CI/CI/pdf/mow/nomination_forms/mauritus_Indentured.pdf.

Vahed, Goolam (2001). 'Uprooting, Rerooting: Culture, Religion and Community among Indentured Muslim Migrants in Colonial Natal, 1860-1911', *South African Historical Journal*, *45*(1): pp. 191-222.

Waetjen, Thembisa and Goolam Vahed (2014). 'Passages of ink: Decoding the Natal indentured records into the Digital Age', *Kronos*, *40*(1): pp. 45-73.

APPENDIX 1

TABLE 10.1: SHIPS AND DATES OF ARRIVAL
BETWEEN 1887 AND 1891

Ship Name	Date of Arrival
Bann	24 February 1887
British Nation	25 October 1887
Brenda	16 November 1887
Sheila	10 December 1887
Jura	29 January 1888
Rhine	2 October 1888
Hereford	31 October 1888
Jura	10 January 1889
Jumna	10 January 1889
Grecian	1 October 1889
Volga	21 October 1889
Avoca	2 November 1889
Jura	17 December 1889
Hereford	5 February 1890
Grecian	16 October 1890
Bruce	17 November 1890
Ganges	25 November 1890
Allanshaw	13 December 1890
British Peer	3 February 1891
Avon	1 March 1891
Rhone	9 October 1891
Main	31 October 1891
Avoca	14 November 1891
Rhine	13 December 1891

APPENDIX 2

TABLE A: MUSLIMS LANDED IN TRINIDAD RELATIVE TO OVERALL INDENTURED LANDED/EMIGRATING FROM INDIA BETWEEN 1887 AND 1891

Year	Ship	Muslims arrived	Total arrived	Muslims ship per cent	Muslims (end year) per cent	Total embarked
1887	Bann	80	586	13.7		589
	British Nation	43	511	8.4	12.3	515
	Brenda	73	537	13.6		540
	Sheila	72	546	13.2		557
	Jura	96	562	17.1		572
1888	Rhine	62	689	9.0		694
	Hereford	57	609	9.4	11.6	622
	Jura	81	531	15.3		534
	Jumna	38	458	8.3		464
1889	Grecian	46	548	8.4		569
	Volga	37	556	6.7	11.0	569
	Avoca	73	626	11.7		646
	Jura	82	515	15.9		528
	Hereford	74	600	12.3		606
	Grecian	56	561	10.0		563
1890	Bruce	73	514	14.2		516
	Ganges	60	571	10.5	10.6	580
	Allanshaw	47	668	7.0		672
	British Peer	67	608	11.0		634
	Avon	71	558	12.7		560
1891	Rhone	51	685	7.4		701
	Main	94	636	14.8	9.8	660
	Avoca	48	632	7.6		659
	Rhine	38	662	5.7		687
TOTAL		1,519	13,969	10.9		14,237

Note: For the Volga (1889), there were 18 deaths including 5 infants born on the ship, thus 13 persons were added to the 556 to get an estimate of the total embarked for Volga.

THE MUSLIMS WHO ARRIVED IN TRINIDAD, 1887-1891   279

TABLE B: PERCENTAGE OF INDIAN MEN, WOMEN, BOYS, GIRLS AND INFANTS LANDED IN TRINIDAD BETWEEN 1887 AND 1891

Year		*Men*	*Women*	*Boys*	*Girls*	*Infants*
1887	Indian Distribution	59.4	26.4	6.8	5.0	3.6
	Distribution of Muslims	48.3	36.4	6.7	4.5	4.1
	Difference	-11.1	10.0	-0.1	-0.5	0.5
	Percentage of Muslims	10.0	17.6	12.5	10.9	14.5
1888	Indian Distribution	56.4	23.5	8.0	6.3	5.7
	Distribution of Muslims	53.5	27.9	6.0	7.0	5.6
	Difference	-2.9	4.4	-2.0	0.7	-0.1
	Percentage of Muslims	11.0	13.7	8.7	12.7	11.3
1889	Indian Distribution	59.5	24.3	7.1	5.2	3.9
	Distribution of Muslims	52.8	29.8	6.7	5.1	5.6
	Difference	-6.7	5.5	-0.4	-0.1	1.7
	Percentage of Muslims	9.8	13.5	10.5	10.7	16.0
1890	Indian Distribution	58.2	24.4	6.4	6.0	5.0
	Distribution of Muslims	52.3	30.6	6.1	6.8	4.2
	Difference	-5.9	6.2	-0.3	0.8	-0.8
	Percentage of Muslims	9.6	13.4	10.2	12.0	9.0
1891	Indian Distribution	54.1	27.4	7.0	6.0	5.4
	Distribution of Muslims	51.8	28.2	7.9	7.6	4.6
	Difference	-2.3	0.8	0.9	1.6	-0.8
	Percentage of Muslims	9.3	10.0	10.9	12.4	8.3
TOTALS	Indian Distribution	57.3	25.3	7.0	5.7	4.9
	Distribution of Muslims	51.7	30.5	6.8	6.2	4.8
	Difference	-5.6	5.2	-0.2	0.5	-0.1
	Percentage of Muslims	9.8	13.1	10.6	11.8	11.1

TABLE C: PERCENTAGE OF MUSLIM MALES AND FEMALES BETWEEN 1887 AND 1891

Year	Ship	Males	Females	% Males ship	% Males (end year)	% Females (end year)
1887	Bann	44	36	55.0	57.1	42.9
	British Nation	24	19	55.8		
	Brenda	41	32	56.2		
	Sheila	44	28	61.1		
1888	Jura	61	35	63.5	61.9	38.1
	Rhine	42	20	67.7		
	Hereford	30	27	52.6		
1889	Jura	52	29	64.2	62.7	37.3
	Jumna	21	17	55.3		
	Grecian	29	17	63.0		
	Volga	24	13	64.9		
	Avoca	51	22	69.9		
	Jura	47	35	57.3		
1890	Hereford	40	34	54.1	58.8	41.2
	Grecian	31	25	55.4		
	Bruce	48	25	65.8		
	Ganges	35	25	58.3		
	Allanshaw	29	18	61.7		
1891	British Peer	41	26	61.2	62.3	37.7
	Avon	45	26	63.4		
	Rhone	33	18	64.7		
	Main	61	33	64.9		
	Avoca	28	20	58.3		
	Rhine	22	16	57.9		
TOTAL		923	596	60.8		

THE MUSLIMS WHO ARRIVED IN TRINIDAD, 1887-1891 — 281

TABLE D: AGE DISTRIBUTIONS OF MUSLIM MALES AND FEMALES

Age	1887	1888	1889	1890	1891	Total
			MALES			
>6	11	13	22	16	28	90
6 to 10	13	5	14	7	10	49
11 to 15	2	4	0	2	9	17
16 to 20	30	25	43	43	43	184
21 to 25	60	54	72	67	78	331
26 to 30	31	21	51	32	44	179
31 to 35	2	6	15	14	15	52
36 to 40	4	4	7	2	3	20
41 to 45	0	0	0	0	0	0
No data	0	1	0	0	0	1
TOTAL	153	133	224	183	230	923
			FEMALES			
>6	11	14	21	16	23	85
6 to 10	7	8	6	14	12	47
11 to 15	0	2	3	0	3	8
16 to 20	28	9	34	31	25	127
21 to 25	45	31	42	45	48	211
26 to 30	18	14	20	15	22	89
31 to 35	5	3	5	5	6	24
36 to 40	1	0	2	1	0	4
41 to 45	0	1	0	0	0	1
TOTAL	115	82	133	127	139	596

TABLE E: HEIGHT DISTRIBUTIONS OF MUSLIM MALES AND FEMALES

Height	1887	1888	1889	1890	1891	Total (cm)	Total (feet/inch)
Males	162 (n=121)	159.1 (n=107)	161 (n=181)	161.9 (n=157)	162.4 (n=182)	161.3	5'4''
Females	147.5 (n=93)	146 (n=57)	147.2 (n=99)	148.8 (n=97)	149.3 (n=100)	147.8	4'10''

*No heights were recorded for infants and a few immigrants.

282 HALIMA-SA'ADIA KASSIM AND PERRY POLAR

TABLE F1: NATIVE PLACES OF MUSLIM INDENTURED LABOURERS, 1887-91

States	Districts	1887	1888	1889	1890	1891	Total
Bihar	Durbanga/Darbhanga	13	4	6	5	0	28
	Gya/Gaya	22	5	14	14	8	63
	Monghyr	1	0	2	9	1	13
	Mozafferpur/ Mazafferpur	10	3	21	4	5	43
	Patna	8	8	27	12	3	58
	Sarun/Saran	9	4	6	15	4	38
	Shahabad	4	1	26	5	8	44
	TOTAL	67	25	102	64	29	287
Madras	Madura	0	0	0	0	11	11
Presidency	TOTAL	0	0	0	0	11	11
Rajasthan	Bharuthpur	4	2	5	0	0	11
	Mathura/Muttra/ Muthra	7	0	2	0	1	10
	TOTAL	11	2	7	0	1	21
Punjab/	Agra	5	9	3	1	1	19
United	Allahabad	2	7	12	7	8	36
Province	Azimghur/Azmagarh	16	30	20	32	24	122
of Agra	Ballia/Bullia	10	4	0	12	20	46
and Oudh	Baharaich/Bahraich	2	2	0	2	4	10
	Barabanki	7	3	7	3	16	36
	Bareilly/Barrielly/ Bas Bareilly	3	4	8	18	2	35
	Basti/Busti/Bustee	17	11	19	30	80	157
	Benares	10	4	2	3	9	28
	Cawnpore/Cawnpur	2	6	6	0	4	18
	Delhi	3	2	2	0	4	11
	Etah	2	0	7	1	0	10
	Faizabad/Fyzabad	3	8	9	13	7	40
	Ghazipur/Ghazeepur	10	15	25	9	16	75
	Gonda	6	1	7	14	16	44
	Goruekpur	4	3	5	9	6	27
	Hurdoi	1	0	9	2	0	12
	Jounpur/Jaunpur/ Gjaunpur	6	16	19	30	12	83

THE MUSLIMS WHO ARRIVED IN TRINIDAD, 1887-1891   283

Lucknow	4	6	8	3	4	25
Meerut	1	0	3	1	6	11
Mirzapur	4	5	0	3	5	17
Partabghur/Pertabghur	1	1	2	9	1	14
Rai Barrielly/Rae Bereilly	1	6	7	6	6	26
Shahjahanpur	1	2	3	1	10	17
Sitapur/Seetapore	7	2	1	2	0	12
Sultanpur	5	7	10	5	16	43
Unnao/Unao	3	1	1	1	9	15
TOTAL	136	155	195	217	286	989
Other*	48	32	51	29	39	199
Unknown**	6	1	2	0	2	11
Missing data	0	0	0	0	1	1
GRAND TOTAL	268	215	357	310	369	1,519

Notes: *'Other' includes districts with fewer than 10 arrivals for the period. These 199 districts are as follows: 24 Pergunnah, Aligurh/Aligarh, Ajmere, Amritsar, Arrah, Badaon/Budaun, Barow, Bankoria/Bancoorah/Bankura, Baksan, Banda, Begra/Bogra, Bhagulpur/Bhaguepore, Bhedeon/Bhadeon, Bihar, Birbhum/ Birbhom, Bombay, Bulansaher/Bulandshahr, Burdawan, Bheenbhoom, Calcutta, Champaran/Champarun, Dacca, Dholpur, Dumka, Etawah, Fatehpur/Fattehpur, Faranabad/Faradabad/Farrekabad/Farukhabad, Foridpur/Faridpur, Gangam/ Ganjam, Goorgaon/Gurgaon, Gowaliar, Gujrat/Goojrat, Goypur, Hazaribagh/ Hozaribagh, Howrah, Hydrabad, Jamonia/Jamunia, Jaloom/Jalaun, Jessore/ Jessorre, Jhansi, Jhelam, Jhulawar/Jhalawar, Jodhpur, Kopa, Kuttra, Kheri, Lahore, Lakhimpore/Lakhimpur, Ludihiana, Madras, Maghura, Mainpuri/ Mainipuri, Maldah, Manbhoom/Manbhum, Medinapur/Midnapur, Motihari, Murdabad/ Moradbad, Multan, Mursidabad, Mymensingh, Nagar, Nagode, Naintal, Nazepur, Narasingpur, Nasirbad, Orai, Panipat, Patiala, Peawo, Pilibith, Puraria/ Purreah, Purnea/Purnia, Rampur State, Rampur, Rohtok, (Ghusi) Sayna Darwaza, Sealkote/Sialkot, Sirbith, Siliguri, Sitamaree/Sitamarhi, Soolundshar, Tanighat, Touk, Ulwar/Alwar, and Umjolla.

**'Unknown' includes Barow, Bheenbhoom, Nagar, Peawo, Puraria/Purreah (2), (Ghausi) Sayni Darwaza, Sirbith, Soolundshar, Tanighat/Tarighat, and Touk.

TABLE F2: NUMBER OF STATES—DISTRICTS AND NUMBER OF PERSONS ORIGINATING, 1887-91

States/Provinces	Districts	No. of arrivals
Bengal	17	36
Bihar	19	317
Bombay Presidency	2	6
Central Provinces	1	2
Madras Presidency	2	12
Orissa	2	3
Princely State	5	11
Rajasthan	8	31
Unknown	11	11
Punjab/United Provinces	57	1,089

TABLE G: SECOND INDENTURE—FIRST PLACE OF INDENTURE FOR IMMIGRANTS TO TRINIDAD, 1887-91

Place	Nos.
Réunion/ *Île Bourbon* (Burbo)	1
Fiji	1
Guadeloupe	1
Guyana	47
Natal	11
Mauritius	1
Suriname	21
St. Vincent	1
Trinidad	32
TOTAL	116

THE MUSLIMS WHO ARRIVED IN TRINIDAD, 1887-1891   285

TABLE H: MUSLIM FAMILY ACCOMPANIMENTS, 1887-91

Category	Number
Number of Muslims unaccompanied on ships	657
Number of Muslims accompanied by family member	531
Number of Muslim family units	194
Number of Muslim couples (husband/wife) with no child/children	56
Number of Muslim couples (husband/wife) with child/children	49
Number of Muslim mothers alone with child/children	62
Number of Muslim fathers alone with child/children	7
Number of Muslim husbands with two wives and no child/children	0
Number of Muslim husbands with two wives with child/children	4
Number of Muslim family units with three generations	3
Number of Muslim Sibling Units	3
Other Muslim relationships	6

Note: Based on the data from emigration passes reviewed (1187).

TABLE I: BIRTHS ON SHIPS BETWEEN 1887 AND 1891

Year	Ship	Birth on ship		Additional information
1887	Bann	No data	15	No data
	British Nation	8		
	Brenda	2		
	Sheila	5		
1888	Jura	4	8	
	Rhine			No data
	Hereford	4		
1889	Jura	5	19	
	Jumna	5		
	Grecian	1		
	Volga	5		
	Avoca	3		
	Jura			No data
1890	Hereford	4	32	
	Grecian	6		One died
	Bruce	5		One died
	Ganges	9		
	Allanshaw	8		
1891	British Peer	12	38	
	Avon	7		
	Rhone			No data
	Main	8		
	Avoca	5		
	Rhine	6		
TOTAL		112		

THE MUSLIMS WHO ARRIVED IN TRINIDAD, 1887-1891

TABLE J: DEATHS ON SHIPS BETWEEN 1887 AND 1891

Year	Ship	Muslim	Men	Women	Boy	Girl	Infant	Total	Year
1887	Bann	1	2		1			3	21
	British Nation	0	3	1				4	
	Brenda	0	1		1		1	3	
1888	Sheila	2	6	2		1	2	11	29
	Jura	3	4	3		1	2	10	
	Rhine	1	2	1		1	1	5	
	Hereford	2	4	5		1	4	14	
1889	Jura	0					4	4	77
	Jumna	0	1					1	
	Grecian	2	1	ND	3	3	14	21	
	Volga	1	ND	2	ND	ND	ND	18	
	Avoca	1	2	1		2	13	20	
1890	Jura	2	4	1			8	13	21
	Hereford	0	3		1		2	6	
	Grecian	0					2	2	
	Bruce	0		1			1	2	
	Ganges	1	1			2	4	7	
	Allanshaw	0	2	1			1	4	
1891	British Peer	0	2	1	4	4	15	26	113
	Avon	0	2		1			2	
	Rhone	0	3	3	1	2	7	16	
	Main	3		2	3	2	19	24	
	Avoca	3	3	4	3	4	13	27	
	Rhine	0	2			1	12	18	
	TOTAL	22	48	28	18	24	125	261	
	Population	1,519	8,011	3,528	974	798	658		13,969
	Per cent deaths	1.4	0.6	0.8	1.8	3.0	19		1.9

288 HALIMA-SA'ADIA KASSIM AND PERRY POLAR

TABLE K: ESTATES TO WHICH MUSLIMS WERE INDENTURED BETWEEN 1887 AND 1891

	1887	1888	1889	1890	1891	Total
Adela	2	0	0	0	0	2
Aranguez	3	3	1	0	6	13
Barataria	0	0	0	5	0	5
Belle Vue	5	0	1	2	1	9
Ben Lomond	2	0	0	4	6	12
Bien Venue	8	0	0	0	10	18
Bien Venue & La Fortune	0	0	0	0	4	4
Bonne Aventure	0	3	5	0	1	9
Brechin Castle	22	5	5	6	5	43
Bronte	0	30	0	1	0	31
Buen Intento	0	1	4	8	0	13
Camden	6	2	8	1	14	31
Canaan	3	0	6	6	2	17
Cane Farm	0	0	0	1	4	5
Caroni	12	2	0	3	41	58
Cedar Grove	0	0	6	0	0	6
Cedar Hill	3	8	4	8	5	28
Chaguaramas	0	0	4	0	0	4
Columbia	8	0	0	5	0	13
Concord	9	8	3	3	17	40
Constance	4	0	0	1	0	5
Craignish	0	6	1	0	8	15
Dinsley	0	7	1	0	4	12
Edinburgh	0	0	0	0	2	2
El Salvadore	0	0	0	4	0	4
El Socorro	11	10	2	1	0	24
Endevour	0	1	0	3	1	5
Esperance	1	2	0	0	0	3
Esperanza & Phoenix Park	0	0	0	6	2	8
Esperanza	12	0	8	3	10	33
Exchange	0	0	0	3	0	3
Florissante	0	0	1	0	0	1
Friendship	1	0	1	0	0	2
Garden	0	0	13	0	0	13
Garden & Bon Aire	0	0	0	14	0	14
Golconda	1	0	10	0	0	11
Golden Grove	0	0	3	3	0	6
Guayacare	0	0	0	0	1	1

THE MUSLIMS WHO ARRIVED IN TRINIDAD, 1887-1891 289

Harmony Hall	7	3	17	1	6	34
Hermitage	1	0	2	2	0	5
Inverness	0	7	1	2	13	23
Jordan Hill	0	11	3	0	0	14
La Florrisante	0	0	3	0	0	3
La Fortune	6	3	2	22	7	40
La Plaissance	3	0	18	0	1	22
La Reunion	0	0	1	1	4	6
La Resource	0	0	0	0	1	1
La Soledad	0	0	1	2	0	3
La Vega	0	0	0	0	1	1
Laurel Hill	0	5	2	0	0	7
L'Emrieuse	0	0	8	7	0	15
L'Esperance	0	0	1	0	0	1
Lothians	0	0	11	0	2	13
Macoya	3	5	3	0	0	11
Malgretoute	1	5	5	0	13	24
Maracas Bay	1	1	0	0	2	4
Milton	0	6	0	0	0	6
Mon Desir	5	0	0	5	0	10
Mon Jaloux	0	3	2	0	1	6
Mt Plaisir	0	0	0	4	14	18
Mt Pleasant	2	3	10	3	4	22
New Grant	5	0	2	0	4	11
Orange Groove	0	4	17	22	6	49
Orange Grove & Macoya	0	0	0	1	0	1
Palmiste	4	0	6	7	5	22
Paradise	0	1	1	0	0	2
Perseverance	5	1	0	10	0	16
Perserverance (Ced)	0	0	5	3	2	10
Perseverence (Chag)	1	2	9	0	3	15
Pererverance (Cou)	0	0	0	7	9	16
Perseverence (May)	3	0	0	0	0	3
Petersfield	3	0	4	9	5	21
Petit Mourne	5	0	12	6	9	32
Phillipine	0	6	2	0	7	15
Phoenix Park	3	4	0	0	0	7
Picton	1	0	5	11	9	26
Plain Palais	0	0	4	6	0	10
Plaissance	4	0	0	0	5	9
Reform	2	10	0	2	6	20
Retrench	1	0	0	1	0	2

Contd.

290 HALIMA-SA'ADIA KASSIM AND PERRY POLAR

TABLE K (*Contd.*)

	1887	1888	1889	1890	1891	Total
River	0	7	16	0	0	23
Rivulet	11	0	3	4	0	18
San Juan	2	0	0	0	0	2
San Jose	0	0	0	0	1	1
San Pablo	0	7	0	2	0	9
San Rafael	0	0	1	0	0	1
Spring	0	0	0	12	3	15
St. Augustine	5	6	15	15	15	56
St. Claire	1	0	1	1	15	18
St. Helena	0	0	2	1	0	3
Ste Marie	5	0	0	3	0	8
Torouba	4	1	0	15	16	36
Trafalgar	1	0	1	1	0	3
Union Hall	13	2	6	2	7	30
Usine Ste Madeline	1	0	2	2	8	13
Valsayn	0	0	0	12	0	12
Waterloo	19	4	23	0	7	53
Wellington	11	3	9	2	2	27
Williamsville and Brothers	1	2	10	5	1	19
Woodbrook	0	0	0	1	0	1
Woodford Lodge	9	3	12	4	2	30
TOTAL	262	203	345	307	360	1,477

Note: Some spellings have been changed to match the listing by Deen (1994, 266). Chaguaramas, La; La Plaissance, L'Emrieuse, Lothians, San Rafael, Wellington are not on the list by Deen (1994, 266). Concord also includes Concord S.N., Concord P.A.P., Esperanza is a combination of Espernza SEO and Esperanza Mont, La Fortune is combined with La Fortunee. The difference between the number of Muslims who arrived (1519) and those who were sent to estates (1477) is due to deaths, a person who paid passage on arrival, a person who became a domestic servant and few persons not originally identified in the Register but detected from Emigration Passes.

THE MUSLIMS WHO ARRIVED IN TRINIDAD, 1887-1891 291

TABLE L: NUMBER OF RETURNEES TO INDIA BASED ON SHIP AND YEAR OF ARRIVAL IN TRINIDAD

Year	Ship	No. of returnees	Total
1887	Bann	26	
	British Nation	18	
	Brenda	12	63
	Sheila	7	
1888	Jura	23	
	Rhine	15	46
	Hereford	8	
1889	Jura	20	
	Jumna	5	
	Grecian	13	
	Volga	7	79
	Avoca	18	
	Jura	16	
1890	Hereford	12	
	Grecian	20	
	Bruce	13	68
	Ganges	12	
	Allanshaw	11	
1891	British Peer	20	
	Avon	15	
	Rhone	15	81
	Main	17	
	Avocat	9	
	Rhine	5	
TOTAL		337	337

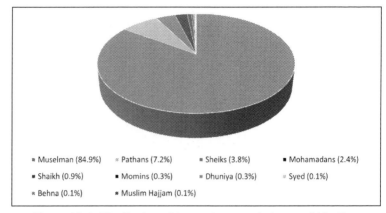

Figure 10.1: Distribution of 'castes' among indentured Muslims (*Source:* One Hajjam Musl. was included in the analysis. Although 26 additional Hajjams were identified, their names did not suggest that they were Muslims and were excluded from the analysis).

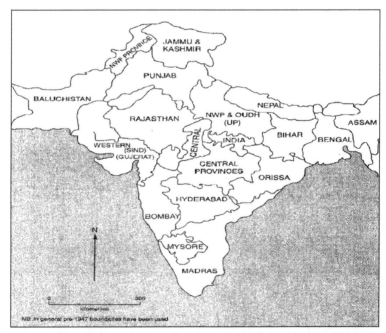

Figure 10.2: Map of native places of India (*Source:* Brij V. Lal, 'Maps'. In *Chalo Jahaji: On a Journey through Indenture in Fiji*, 399-400. ANU Press, 2012. http://www.jstor.org/stable/j.ctt24h3ss.27).

THE MUSLIMS WHO ARRIVED IN TRINIDAD, 1887-1891

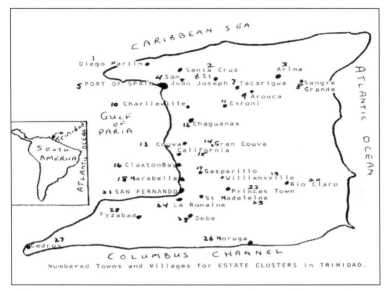

Figure 10.3: Location of estates in Trinidad (*Source:* Shamshu Deen, 1994. *Solving East Indian Roots in Trinidad*. HEM Enterprises).

PART III

INTERRELIGIOUS RELATIONS IN THE *GIRMIT* DIASPORA

CHAPTER 11

Interreligious Cooperation: Suriname and Guyana, 1950-2014

KIRTIE ALGOE

INTRODUCTION[1]

Among the people with a religious affiliation in today's world, Christians are the largest religious group (32 per cent), followed by Muslims (23 per cent) and Hindus (15 per cent) (Pew Research Center 2012: 9). Many regions with these religious groups faced extreme violence such as wars during conflicts (Reychler 1997). However, this is not the case in the Caribbean, where Christians, Hindus and Muslims comprise the vast majority of the population in three nations: Suriname, Guyana and Trinidad and Tobago. Insight in interreligious relations in these nations is necessary considering the increasing debates on the negative influence of religious groups on social stability in the world (Canetti, Hobfoll, Pedahzur & Zaidise 2010: 576). These debates do not entirely reflect the Caribbean experiences with religious groups. Barriteau (2006: 12), who describes the Caribbean as a 'zone of peace' in the confrontational world, rightly points out that its peace is overlooked. Therefore, this article pays attention to the interreligious relations of Caribbean nations. The focus is the evolution of interreligious cooperation between Christians, Hindus, and Muslims in Suriname and Guyana, two neighbouring nations, from 1950 to 2014.

[1] This article results from the author's dissertation (2017) on Hindu and Muslim Responses to Christian Dominance in Suriname and Guyana between 1950 and 2014.

Suriname and Guyana evolved from an initial indigenous religious landscape to a religious mosaic. Critical demographic changes occurred during European colonialism. With the arrival of European colonizers in the sixteenth century, the religious composition started to change in both countries. They introduced Christianity and Judaism. Later other people were brought to Suriname and Guyana. Major groups were enslaved as workers from Africa and Asian indentured labourers. Among others, these groups introduced traditional African religions, Hinduism, and Islam. In the course of time, Christianity, Hinduism, and Islam evolved as the three largest religious groups [Figures 11.1(a) and 11.1(b)].

Despite having in common three major religious groups, Suriname and Guyana differ in terms of religious denominations. In the 1900-1950 period major Christian denominations in Suriname were Moravians and Catholics. There were also smaller groups of Lutherans and Dutch Reformists. Guyana had members of all aforementioned Christian denominations, but the largest group were the Anglicans. It was also populated by a smaller number of Presbyterians and Methodists. With respect to Hindus, there were two large denominations in Suriname and Guyana: Sanatan Dharma

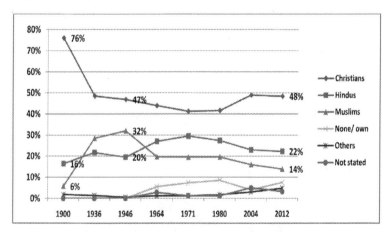

Figure 11.1(a): Population by religion in Suriname in the twentieth and twenty-first century (*Source:* Algemeen Bureau voor de Statistiek, 2007, 2013; Vernooij, 2012, compiled by author).

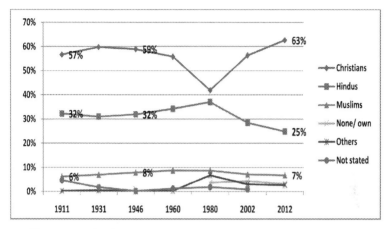

Figure 11.1(b): Population by religion in Guyana in the twentieth and twenty-first century (*Source:* British Guiana Population Census 1960. Volume 2, Part A, 1960, Census of the colony of British Guiana 1946, Part D, 1946; Bureau of Statistics Guyana, 2016; Guyana Bureau of Statistics, 2007).

and Arya Samaj. However, with regard to Islam, Suriname is more diverse than Guyana. Besides the denominations of Sunnis and Ahmadis in these two nations, Suriname also has a particular distinction of Muslims by ethnicity. Large ethnic groups among the Muslims are the Javanese and the East Indian people. The Javanese Muslims are further differentiated by east- and west-oriented prayers (Soeropawiro 2016: 236). The former are traditionalists who kept on to their religious practices as in Indonesia where they faced the west, oriented at Mecca, during prayers. The east prayers are reformists who believe in praying with the face to the east, since Mecca is located towards the east of Suriname.

Between 1900 and 2014 the religious demography changed in Suriname and Guyana. But for the purpose of this article the changes[2]

---

[2] 1950 is considered a turning point as from this year on Hindus and Muslims increasingly began to institutionalize their religions in Suriname and Guyana, nations that were historically dominated by Christians. They gradually established denominational schools. Hindu and Muslim religious holidays were also acknowledged between the 1960s and 1970s (Ramsoedh & Bloemberg

300 KIRTIE ALGOE

between 1950 and 2014 are addressed. The most remarkable change was that the share of traditional Christians dropped in both nations, much larger in Guyana. At the same time, the percentage of Evangelicals grew, however their relative increase was higher in Guyana (from 0 per cent to 28 per cent) than in Suriname (from 0 per cent to 11 per cent). This growth occurred at the cost of membership of other Christian denominations and non-Christians. It will be explained later that these demographic changes have implications for interreligious cooperation in the two nations.

THEORETICAL AND METHODOLOGICAL SCOPE

The concept of concerted diversity is the basis for conceptualizing interreligious cooperation. Concerted diversity is considered a form of interreligious relations (Algoe 2017: 29) that emphasizes the belief in and practice of equality, solidarity, and conflict-solving. It is the 'interactive combination of differences into a mutually beneficial synergetic force that does not destroy the singular characteristics of specific groups because it values them as powerful assets for harmony' (Sankatsing 2016: 395). According to concerted diversity, differences of social groups are harmonized. In this process their dignity is secured while finding ways to cooperate with each other in solidarity. Concerted diversity in practice refers to an ongoing dialogue where involved parties are open to accept a negotiated compromise for the time being. It is a process where the respective compromise respects the stakeholders, maintains their principles and supports their aspirations (ibid). There is solidarity rather than polarization.

1995: 17; Algoe 2017: 15). Addressing institutionalization of religions is necessary, as it can affect their power structures in the larger society as well as their interreligious relations (Algoe 2017, 26-33). 2014 is chosen as data collection for the dissertation, on which this article is based, was completed in this year to obtain insight in the most recent development of relations between religious groups.

INTERRELIGIOUS COOPERATION: SURINAME AND GUYANA 301

Interreligious cooperation in this article is an expression of concerted diversity that refers to the way religious groups build mutual relationships at an institutional level based on three core values: religious equality, solidarity and conflict solving (ibid.). Equality refers to the beliefs in the similar importance of religiously diverse groups. Solidarity emphasizes the beliefs in joint effort rather than competition and dominance. It has the ability to sympathize with others, even if they do not belong to their own group. Hence it can cope with diversity in a positive way. Social groups can have contradictory interests and needs with a material base, but as Sankatsing states (ibid.: 22) 'deliberation, persuasion or coercion cannot discursively erase differences between individuals or social groups, whenever divergent interests have a material base'. Conflicting parties can solve their tensions by deliberately accepting what is seen as the 'best available' solution for the time being, rather than forcing homogeneity, uniformity and consensus. 'Not consensus should be pursued, but rather harmony, the achievement of a negotiated outcome in a dialogue between diverse interests, that is accepted by all parties' (ibid.: 23). It is not the unification, but the respect for different needs and interests and the acceptance of diversity among the people that have solutions (ibid.).

Interreligious cooperation involves practices and the promotion of religious equality, solidarity and conflict solving within religious organizations and in the public spheres. It can take various forms and can emerge from within religious people, or from outside for instance during shared consultation about government policies. An example of the former is ecumenical services between religious groups. During such services, religious leaders attempt to express shared religious values.

This article focuses on the joint interactions by various religious groups with particular intentions such as community welfare, or improvement of interreligious relations (Weller 2013).[3] Four factors

[3] Interreligious cooperation should not be confused with the concept of interreligious dialogue. The latter departs from the view that religions do not approach each other based on superiority ideals, an argument with Christian influences (Karuvelil 2012, 57). Interreligious dialogue focuses on how common

are assumed to influence interreligious cooperation: religious demography, government policies, religious institutions, and religious leadership (Figure 11.2).

Religious demography may stimulate interreligious cooperation when there is no threatening change in the share of religious groups in the population. Bouma and Singleton (2004, 14) explain that such demographic changes may lead to tensions among religious groups. When religious groups face a significant decline in their 'market share' due to religious conversion, it becomes difficult for them to encourage ideals of religious equality and solidarity.

Government policies are official policies of governmental authorities to encourage, prevent or regulate certain activities in society (Bramadat 2008, 122) such as laws and ordinances on religious matters. Government policies can support interreligious cooperation by,

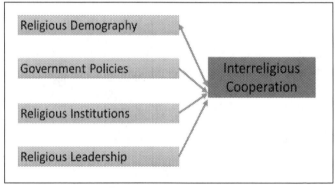

Figure 11.2: Factors of interreligious cooperation
(*Source:* By the author).

religious values such as the belief in one God encourage religious harmony (Hospital 2007: 358). An important common ground underlined by interreligious dialogue is that people perceive the 'Ultimate/God/Supreme' differently. While this perspective is important for creating mutual understanding, it excludes religious groups who do not believe in an 'Ultimate' such as Buddhists (ibid.). In other words, the concept of interreligious dialogue is limited in explaining peaceful interreligious relations *without* shared religious beliefs.

for instance, involving religious groups in the decision-making process. This involvement facilitates an on-going dialogue between religious groups in which they are encouraged to settle their own (possible conflicting) interests. Government officials can make the policies in a transparent way after listening to involved parties (Rose-ackerman 2008). In this way, policies translate the ideals of religious equality, solidarity and conflict-solving into deeds. Policies can fairly and equally allocate public resources to religious groups and thus 'prove' the practice of religious equality.

Religious leadership and religious institutions are crucial factors in interreligious cooperation. Both factors may promote ideals of religious equality and solidarity for they have a certain authority over individuals and thus influence their thinking. Religious leaders can be persons to whom people trust their secrets, sins, and dreams (Kane & Jacobs 2012, 60). They exercise moral leadership. Religious organizations are institutions that provide material resources such as religious buildings (mosques, churches, temples), schools and graveyards and that encourage shared values and norms among their members at the meso- and the national level. Due to these resources, religious institutions are able to influence the mind and behaviours of religious groups.

To understand how interreligious cooperation between Christians, Hindus, and Muslims in Suriname and Guyana evolved after 1950, this article used a mixed methods research design with focus on the comparison of cases. In particular, the explanatory sequential form of the mixed methods research design is selected. In this design quantitative analyses are followed up with qualitative analyses (Creswell & Clark 2011: 71). The nations of Suriname and Guyana are compared as a case based on their religious demographic similarities: Christians, Hindus, and Muslims are the largest religious groups. Both nations can be described as 'most similar cases' (Ragin 1987: 48). Guided by the mixed method design, a more or less similar set of qualitative and quantitative methods is used for the case study of Suriname and Guyana. This is required in comparative studies (Bryman 2004: 72). The major qualitative methods are oral history and documentary research, while the quantitative methods involve analyses of official statistics and secondary data.

304 KIRTIE ALGOE

INTERRELIGIOUS COOPERATION IN SURINAME

The national umbrella interreligious organization in Suriname, the Interreligieuze Raad in Suriname (IRIS), was founded in 1989. It has representatives of major religious groups (Marshall 2007: 69) as well as other small religious groups. With respect to the Hindus, both the Sanatanists and Arya Samajis are represented. The Muslim organization of East Indian descent of the Ahmadiyya denomination is a member of IRIS. The Javanese Muslims of both the Ahmadiyya and Sunni denomination are represented through the umbrella organization Madjilies Moeslimin Suriname (MMS). And with respect to Christians, the Catholics are participating in IRIS.

It can be argued that the membership of IRIS is influenced by religious demography. The major religious groups in Suriname, as mentioned before, are Christians, Hindus and Muslims [Figure 11.1(a)]. These groups are organized in bodies that are members of the IRIS. The respective members are Arya Dewaker, Sanatan Dharma, Madjilies Moeslimin Suriname (MMS), Surinaamse Islamitische Vereniging (SIV), and the Roman Catholic Church.[4]

In addition to religious demography, religious leadership also influences IRIS. Officially this organization aims at strengthening the interreligious cooperation on social, religious and ethical issues (Marshall 2007: 69-70). IRIS was a result of the negotiation between religious bodies, leaders and the state owned media for air time to present religious programmes on television (ibid.). In this process the religious organizations were in the frontline to formalize interreligious cooperation. Besides the need for joining forces in order to get air time, another factor was also of influence on the establishment of the IRIS, namely the political circumstances. Suriname had a military regime and during this period, in December 1982, fifteen prominent persons were killed which had a huge impact on the political climate as well as on foreign affairs. IRIS openly condemned the killings of the persons and began holding ecumenical

---

[4] IRIS also had a representative of the Moravian Church in the early years. But this Christian denomination is no longer a member of IRIS (Marshall 2007: 69).

INTERRELIGIOUS COOPERATION: SURINAME AND GUYANA 305

services for repose of the souls of these victims in 1989 (Algoe 2009: 47). These services were requested by the family of the victims. Here one sees that religious leadership of IRIS responded to the political circumstances.

Noteworthy is that the work of IRIS has been encouraged by government policies such as in the 1990s when the country suffered from an economic crisis. IRIS and other religious organizations were part of a committee that had to develop a national plan to recover from the crisis (Algoe 2009). This committee was supported by the government led by Jules Wijdenbosch. IRIS discussed this plan with the president, the labour unions, and the private sector. They all joined the committee called 'gestructureerd same nwerking sverband'. During the 1990s there were huge strikes and it is argued that due to the intervention of IRIS these strikes were stopped (ibid.). This case shows how interreligious cooperation intertwines with government policies.

Interreligious cooperation, as conceptualized earlier, includes the belief in and practice of equality, solidarity and conflict solving. The practice of religious equality ideals by IRIS is reflected in many activities. In the course of years, this organization executed programmes on religious education containing religious and ethical issues. An important contribution of IRIS was the broadcasting of the *Ramayana*, a Hindu religious epic, on television (ATV) in the 1990s. The head of IRIS, Nico Waagmeester, gave a commentary in Dutch explaining the moral and religious dimension of this epic for both Hindus and non-Hindus. This programme was meant to enhance the understanding of the religion to the general public.

An activity by IRIS that expresses the ideals of religious equality and solidarity are the ecumenical services. On World's Religious Day IRIS now has programmes regularly (Figure 11.3). Some ecumenical services were formally requested by the government. IRIS, for instance, held such services for people with AIDS and their family in the Moravian Church (Algoe 2009: 47). Here one sees how the government can encourage interreligious cooperation.

Another important activity of IRIS was the encouragement of solidarity ideals when the Christian holiday Good Friday and the Hindu festival Phagwa coincided in 2002. These are religious

Figure 11.3: Different religious groups on World Religion Day 2010 (*Source:* Tull, 2010).

holidays with contradicting religious principles. Christians usually celebrate Good Friday in a sober manner, while on Phagwa Hindus express enthusiasm. IRIS published articles in the newspapers asking the mass to respect and express solidarity for each other's religious beliefs. Hindus were requested to remain silent in the neighbourhood of churches (Waagmeester 2002: 6).

The religious institutions in IRIS do not only foster relationships between each other in the sphere of religion, but they also take a moral stance on practical issues in society. In 2005 IRIS participated in a health community project on HIV/AIDS organized by the PAHO. Two congresses about religion and health were organized. In 2006 it contributed to an exposition about Earth Day. It called Surinamese people across regions to express their bonding with earth in their own way such as painting, poem, craft picture, and donation to children (Waagmeester 2001). In 2010 speeches were delivered by Christian and Hindu leaders on biodiversity. They spoke against gold mining and logging because these activities cause environmental pollution which strikes tribal societies in particular (Tull 2010).

INTERRELIGIOUS COOPERATION: SURINAME AND GUYANA   307

IRIS is verbal on political issues. As mentioned before, in the 1980s it condemned the killings of the fifteen prominent citizens. The current president Bouterse, who is considered the main culprit, was Catholic (Evers 2011) and lost support of the traditional Christian churches who were in IRIS. In 1996 this organization wrote a piece named 'Hoe nu verder?' (How further?) with recommendations for the organization of the elections (Marshall 2007: 70). In 2012 it spoke against the amnesty law about the 'December killings 1980' passed by the government. It argued that this law severely opposed the legal case the families of the victims had filed against Desi Bouterse, and therefore recommended that the law should be withdrawn ('Iris: Amnestiewet is begin dictatuur', 2012). Here one sees that IRIS presents moral views on political issues.

The practice of religious equality, solidarity and conflict solving by IRIS is challenged by theological views and relations *among* religions groups. Illustrative is the role of the Moravian Church in IRIS. In the early years after its establishment IRIS had a representative of the Moravian Church. But this Christian denomination is no longer a member of IRIS (Marshall 2007: 74) and according to some scholars this was due to the theological views of other leaders in the Moravian Church. They did not subscribe to ideals of religious equality and therefore described the initial participation of the Moravian Church representative in IRIS as a personal action. In the meanwhile, the formal responsibilities of the respective representative of this Church had increased tremendously due to a new position and this compelled him to cease the participation in IRIS (ibid.). Here one sees how theological beliefs about religious equality affect religious leadership which in turn influences the participation of religious groups in interreligious organizations. This differs from the Catholic Church. Among the founders of IRIS was the Catholic bishop Zichem ('Monseigneur Aloysius Zichem bijgelegd', 2016). He was known for his personal ties with leaders of other religious groups. According to scholars, these ties strengthened the journey towards IRIS.

Another case that illustrates the complexity to maintain religious equality and solidarity in IRIS is the participation of the Sunnis,

308 KIRTIE ALGOE

the more conservative Muslim denomination. The main Sunni organization with predominant East Indian followers, the Surinamese Muslim Association (SMA), is not a member of the IRIS. It is argued that they do not participate in the activities of IRIS because of the membership of the Ahmadis (Marshall 2007). Sunnis and Ahmadis had theological conflicts which emerged in the early twentieth century (Hassankhan 2016: 203-6).[5] This suggests that religious relations among Muslims have implications for the working of IRIS.

A final case that shows the complexity to maintain religious equality and solidarity in IRIS is the role of the Evangelical and Pentecostal churches. They are not represented in the IRIS and the same may be explained by the relations between these churches and the so called traditional Christian denominations (Moravian, Dutch Reformed, the Roman Catholic, Presbyterian, Anglican and Lutheran Church). Internationally there is a difference between these two groups. The non-traditional Christian denominations involve the Protestant movements with emphasis on personal human spiritual experience that emerged since the late 1960s. Two forms

---

[5] Muslims of East Indian origin were represented by the Surinaamse Islamitische Vereniging (SIV). They believed that Mohammed was the last prophet. However, controversy emerged within SIV when Maulana Ameerali of Trinidad visited Suriname in 1934 (Hassankhan 2016: 203). He introduced the principles of a new theological school, the Ahmadiyya Movement that considers Mirza Ghulam Ahmad as a reformer in Islam. This theological difference in SIV led to the division between the Sunnis and Ahmadis. The former accuse for taking Mirza Ghulam Ahmad as the final prophet, while the latter deny that ('Al is de leugen nog zo snel, de waarheid (Al Haq) achterhaalt hem wel', 1975: 5-6). Ahmadis argue that they follow the principles of Mirza as long as these do not conflict with the *Quran*. Sunnis organized themselves in Khilafat Anjuman (1931), Anwar Islam (1931), and Hidayat Islam (1932) (Prins 1961: 23). In 1950 a Muslim leader from Pakistan encouraged Sunnis to bring various Sunni organizations together and organize themselves further. Consequently, various organizations including Khilafat Anjuman merged in the Surinaamse Moeslim Associatie (SMA) in 1960. Sunni and Ahmadiyya leaders had severe theological debates which often led to frictions within families (Hassankhan 2016: 206).

INTERRELIGIOUS COOPERATION: SURINAME AND GUYANA   309

of such movements must be distinguished:[6] Evangelicalism and Pentecostalism. In Suriname their population gradually increased; also, at the cost of the members of traditional Christian denominations, since the second half of the twentieth century. Traditional churches differ in beliefs and worship from the Evangelical and Pentecostal churches, which create a certain distance between them. This relationship can explain the non-participation of Evangelical and Pentecostal churches in IRIS. Another explanation is that these churches do not subscribe openly to beliefs in religious equality. On the contrary, some Evangelical pastors discourage interreligious interactions, arguing that these oppose their religious beliefs. 'We do not encourage our members to participate in the religious celebrations of others' (S, Personal Communication, 23 August 2012). Their main views are that salvation of nation comes only through Christ and that Evangelicalism is the only 'real' religion, thus other religious groups are not equal to this Christian denomination (ibid.). There are some cases where Evangelical leaders with political influence have publicly condemned other religious groups. In 2011, for instance, Steve Meye, the head of the umbrella organization of Evangelical churches, strongly opposed the request for formal recognition of

[6] The term 'Evangelical' dates from 1831. Throughout the years it has been defined in various ways and with diverse links with Christian denominations (Crossley 2016). In this study, the focus is on the renaissance movement of Protestant churches such as Pentecostal in Suriname and Guyana, since the second half of the twentieth century. In the same period, the North American Protestant movement emerged and it was called 'Evangelical' (ibid.). Evangelicalism is a denominational movement among Protestantism that emphasizes the authority of the Bible and the Holy Spirit (Woodhead 2002, 201). Two main beliefs of Evangelicals are that salvation comes through conversion where one develops a personal relationship with Jesus Christ and that the *Bible* has a unique authority in the life of humans (ibid.). Pentecostalism differentiates itself from Evangelicalism in the possession by the Holy Spirit. There is a main belief in 'baptism by the Spirit' (ibid.: 201), where the experiences mark the difference between those who are born again and saved by the Spirit, and those who are enslaved by the world, flesh and devil (ibid.). In this study both Pentecostal and Evangelical movements since the 1960s are hence referred to as 'Evangelicalism'.

310 KIRTIE ALGOE

Winti, a traditional Afro-Surinamese religion, as a religion in 2011 (Bauw 2011). Meye argued that Winti would bring bad luck to the country (ibid.). He referred to Haiti where according to him the large-scale practice of voodooism, another traditional religion of people from African descent, has led to poverty and natural disasters (ibid.).

INTERRELIGIOUS COOPERATION IN GUYANA

Guyana's national umbrella interreligious organization (IRO) was founded in 2003, much later than in Suriname. The founding of IRO was influenced by government initiatives. According to a Muslim informant former president Bharath Jagdeo was inspired to organize a harmony week in Guyana when he came back from a visit to the Middle East (F, Personal Communication, 14 September 2012). One of the ideas to promote harmony was to establish an inter-religious TV channel for all religious groups. The state supported this project and various religious organizations including Christian, Hindus and Muslims were involved in the decision-making (V, Personal Communication, 21 March 2014).

While founding IRO resulted from political initiatives to promote religious harmony, religious leadership played an important role in determining the nature of its activities. Involved religious leaders focus on the reduction of ethnic tensions during elections by encouraging shared religious morals (R, Personal Communication, 13 December 2013). Guyana has experienced political elections characterized by strong tensions between Indo-Guyanese and Afro-Guyanese people, the two major ethnic groups for many years. These tensions were once very violent in the 1960s, but now the two groups are colder, reserved and openly prejudiced about each other (ibid.). IRO believes that utilizing religious similarities in programmes can hamper ethnic tensions during elections. It pro-pagates ideals of mutual respect for religious groups. The following quote of a religious leader is illustrative:

Because we realize how the population is divided we still have to promote a culture of peace and harmony in the country. We have to respect each other religions and each others beliefs. Because in the past when there was not so much harmony or when the country was in conflict and we realize to eliminate this conflict, the religious community needs to lead the way. If the religious community can't find common ground on which to unite, how can we tell the politicians to unite? How can we inspire the politicians to work in harmony? If you do this, you believe in God. God is a god of love. As Christian we understand, we believe and accept that Jesus had said that the first thing in our life is to love God first, with all your heart, body and soul. When you finish doing that you love your neighbour as you love yourself. And these two commands are above all the others. So, in order bring anything to unite and to bring harmony, we got to love (N, Personal Communication, 13 December 2013).

The above citation illustrates the promotion of ideals of religious equality and solidarity by IRO. This organization also held a peace walk in January 2006, which was a year of elections (Figure 11.4). It is argued that until then it was the most peaceful general election in Guyana (N&R, Personal Communication, 13 December 2013). The walk was supported by former president Jagdeo who joined the mass of about 200 persons halfway. In 2006 with support of the UN, the IRO convinced political parties to sign a peace pact in the building of the Parliament. The IRO distributed 'peace buttons' with words of peace as used by different religious groups such as Salome, Ohm Shanti and Salam Alekum (ibid.).

Figure 11.4: Peace walk organized by IRO in 2006
(*Source:* Ramsammy 2006).

Other activities of IRO include peaceful intervention in violent conflicts where political influence did not succeed. Less than ten years ago some people were protesting, using guns in an area called Bartica. Politicians wanted to talk to these people, but they were rejected. Then the head of the IRO, Bishop Edghil, asked IRO members to intervene. The IRO was received by the people and it helped to solve the matter. This occurred outside the media attention. The following situation was described by an informant, 'When we got there, there was fire on the bridge. And the people cleared a path for us to walk through. We were able to talk to the people in that war who were dictating. Some were so fired up that they wanted to take this thing to the one ridiculous level to the next possible' (N&R, Personal Communication, 13 December 2013). While this case does not reflect a matter of interreligious relation at first sight, it illustrates how religious leadership of the IRO affects conflict resolution of social issues.

This interreligious cooperation in IRO can be explained by the religious leadership. Various Christian, Hindu, and Muslim leaders held and promoted views on mutual understanding. The following quote of a Hindu religious leader is illustrative:

Each person has their own vision, their own way of seeing God. Different perspective of seeing. Krishna may appeal to you, Shiva may appeal to you but to not me. Christ may appeal to another one. Allah may appeal to another. We don't tell people what to believe in, because we believe in the concept that we're all born divine. So your birth is divine. So a God exists in you and in me (P, 8 December 2013).

While IRO promotes mutual understanding between religious groups, its working is challenged by religious demography and linkages with politics. Initially IRO had representatives of traditional and Evangelical churches, Hindus, Muslims and other small religious groups (R, Personal Communication, 13 December 2013). Now IRO has members from the Evangelical Muslim, Bahai, Catholic, Anglican, and Rastafarian communities (N&R, Personal Communication, 13 December 2013). Hindus are no longer a member of the organization. They prefer to be independent and work on social issues (V, Personal Communication, 21 March 2014).

A possible explanation for the withdrawal of the Hindu organization is the large conversion of Hindus to Evangelicalism in the past years. There is an increase of Evangelicals among East Indians, who were historically predominantly Hindus.[7] According to LAPOP results, the percentage of Evangelicals among East Indians increased greatly from 4 per cent to 13 per cent between 2006 and 2014 (Figure 11.5). At the same time, according to the census of 2002 and 2012, the share of Hindus declined from 28 per cent to 25 per cent while that of Christians increased from 56 per cent to 63 per cent [Figure 11.1(b)]. These data suggest that religious conversion to Evangelicalism contributed to the declining share of Hindus and procentual growth of Christians between 2002 and 2012. A Hindu leader explained that it is difficult to strengthen interreligious

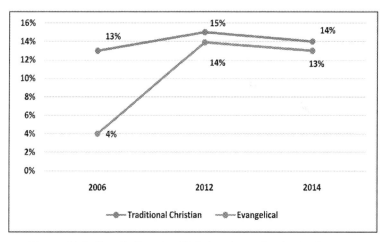

Figure 11.5: East Indians by Christian denomination in Guyana, 2006-14 (*Source:* 'The Americas Barometer by the Latin American Public Opinion Project (LAPOP),' 2006, 2010, 2012, 2014, compiled by author. Sig. 2006: 0.000; 2012: 0.000, 2014: 0.000).

---

[7] According to Omonhiomwan (1971: 57), the share of Hindus among East Indians fluctuated between 84 per cent in 1917 and 72 per cent in 1946. The Muslim population changed between 16 per cent and 18 per cent in the respective years (ibid.).

314 KIRTIE ALGOE

cooperation when involved partners attract each other's members based on convictions that the religion of the latter is inferior. Here one sees how religious demography influences practices of inter-religious cooperation, which is in line with Bouma and Singleton's (2004: 14) views.

IRO has perceived links with politics. According to an Evangelical informant, IRO was considered to be linked to the ruling party of Jagdeo to attract voters:

> IRO was a political something. It was president Jagdeo's brain child. Most Christian churches didn't support IRO. (. . .) And Jagdeo was trying, . . . you see religion was very powerful force in Guyana. And he was trying to bring the religions together with an organization that was politically larger with influence in there. You see the PPP has never had any Christian support, 'cause it was predominantly Indian. Some Indian people had a lot of reservations. (. . .) Though they had some prominent Hindus in PPP, but many Christians in the IRO were attracted by president Jagdeo to bring the religions together, whether it meant we were controlling them. So he said he would offer them a Christian television station. People saw that IRO was a political thing that Jagdeo himself started today, with the aims of controlling Christians, Hindus and Muslims and political gain. And use the churches' religious influence to support what the government was doing, right. So they never really got, most Evangelicals and Pentecostals don't have anything to do with (W, Personal Communication, 20 September 2012).

The IRO confirmed that it didn't have all the support of the political parties, particularly of the opposition. The perceived linkage of the IRO as a political instrument of the coalition restricted interreligious cooperation. Some Evangelical churches do not want to become member of this body because of this political alignment.

COMPARING SURINAME AND GUYANA

Having addressed the working of interreligious organizations in Suriname and Guyana, one now proceeds with the comparative analyses. One first looks at the participation of Christians, Hindus, and Muslims in the interreligious organizations in Suriname and Guyana (Figure 11.6).

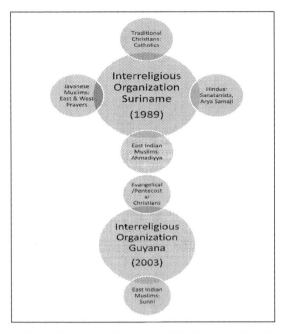

Figure 11.6: Christians, Hindus and Muslims in interreligious organizations in Suriname and Guyana (*Source:* Chart prepared by the author).

There are three major differences between the interreligious organizations in Suriname and Guyana. First, in Suriname the interreligious organization enables a larger participation of Christians, Hindus, and Muslims than in Guyana (Figure 11.6). The former nation has representatives of all three religious groups, while in Guyana, Hindus are no longer involved. Second, Suriname has traditional churches in the frontline of the interreligious organization, while Guyana has Evangelical churches. Third, the interreligious organization in Suriname is older than in Guyana. Each of these differences will now be explained in detail.

The first difference, the larger participation of religious groups in umbrella interreligious organization in Suriname, is explained by religious demography. In Guyana the share of Hindus dropped between 2002 and 2012 which seems to be influenced by their

316 KIRTIE ALGOE

religious conversion to Evangelicalism. This apparently discouraged them to participate in interreligious organization with predominantly Evangelical churches. In Suriname the Evangelicals also gained large demographic influence, but not at the similar cost of the Hindu share in the population. In this nation mostly Maroons and Javanese Muslims convert to Evangelicalism, which is discussed elsewhere (Algoe 2017: 55-6). In Suriname Hindu bodies do not experience this reservation in interreligious organization as in Guyana.

The second difference, which deals with the larger participation of religious groups in umbrella interreligious organization in Suriname, is related to government policies. This factor can help us understand why Guyana has a larger involvement of Evangelical Churches in the IRO, while Suriname has a significant contribution of traditional Christian churches. The founding of IRO in Guyana was an initiative of the government. As said before, former president Jagdeo sought to hold a harmony week in Guyana after visiting the Middle East. At that time the government had received requests of different religious groups for establishing a TV channel, but after the visit to the Middle East, the government suggested an interreligious channel rather than granting religious groups permission for their own TV channel. This suggestion became a major project under supervision of the IRO. The founding of the IRO also intertwined with party political processes. The ruling party led by Jagdeo had historical links with the major Hindu and Muslim bodies in the country, but later the Evangelical churches joined the party. An Evangelical bishop was even appointed as the minister of finance. He had huge influence on other Christian churches and maintained connections with the Hindu and Muslim bodies because of his alliances with the ruling party. In this context the bishop took the relationship with other religious organizations to the level of IRO. By doing so, according to informants, he was trying to attract Christian voters for Jagdeo's party.

In Suriname, on the contrary, the IRIS was an activity of traditional Christian churches and other non-Christian groups to negotiate with the state-owned media for getting broadcast time on television. The political climate also had an influence on the working of the IRIS. This organization held ecumenical services for persons who were killed during the military regime. From a comparative perspective it can be argued that in Guyana, government policies and underlying political processes contributed to the larger involvement of Evangelical churches in the national interreligious organization than in Suriname.

The third difference, including the earlier founding of the umbrella interreligious organization in Suriname (1989) than in Guyana (2003), is associated to religious leadership and religious organizations. These two factors influenced the umbrella interreligious organization in both nations, but 'operated' differently due to varying national political and social contexts. The circumstances of the founding of the interreligious organization in Suriname were different. The IRIS in Suriname began as an initiative of religious groups to have equal access to broadcast time on television. Later this initiative was broadened to social and religious matters (Marshall 2007, 70). Guyana on the contrary faced political struggles; it had a regime that weakened religious institutions as well as hampered their critical stance to the government. After the regime the country suffered from emigration and other economic problems that didn't seem to foster conditions for interreligious cooperation. As an informant said, 'I think in the past people were not so certain. They were suspicious of one another. In the past it wasn't ready yet. You know sometime you try to do something and you're struggling, you don't get it done on the right time. Right people come together and it just happens' (N&R, Personal Communication, 13 December 2013). This informant illustrates how the religious leadership for the umbrella interreligious organization in Guyana emerged in the 20s rather than in the 1990s due to the political context.

Suriname and Guyana have this in common that the umbrella interreligious organization strives for religious harmony. In both nations these organizations are also involved in social and political issues in which they utilize theological views and similarities. But at the same time the working of the umbrella interreligious organization in Suriname (IRIS) and Guyana (IRO) is challenged by religious demography and religious leadership. In Suriname

318 KIRTIE ALGOE

the opposing views on religious equality among Christian denominations and the theological differences between Muslim denominations are identified. In Guyana the religious conversion of Hindus to Christianity is hindering the adequate practice of religious equality in the IRO.

CONCLUSION

Both Suriname and Guyana have an umbrella interreligious organization in common that attempts to foster religious harmony, but there are differences in their contribution to the interreligious relations between Christians, Hindus, and Muslims. The major difference is that in Suriname all three religious are involved in the interreligious organization, while not in Guyana. Due to this fact the contribution of interreligious organization in Suriname is larger than in Guyana. Religious demography is perceived as the major explanatory factor for this difference.

Another critical difference is that the interreligious organization in Guyana is a more top-down initiative, while in Suriname a bottom-up one. In the former nation the government stimulated the interreligious cooperation, while in the latter nation it was a result of negotiation among religious groups and state-owned media for resources. Here the differences in significance of factors of establishment of the umbrella interreligious organization is identified: government policies in Guyana and religious leadership in Suriname.

A final difference is that unlike Suriname in Guyana the focus of the umbrella interreligious organization is the reduction of ethnic tensions during political elections. In Suriname the activities of this organization involve the promotion of religious harmony and engaging in social and political issues rather than hampering ethnic tensions. This difference is explained by the nature of the political climate in both nations.

By comparing Suriname and Guyana on interreligious cooperation, this paper obtained an insight into the impact of religious demography, government policy, religious institutions, and religious leadership by nation. While these factors are important in both

INTERRELIGIOUS COOPERATION: SURINAME AND GUYANA **319**

nations, they have different influences on interreligious cooperation due to the contextual factors. The most striking differences are the influence of religious demography and government policies.

REFERENCES

Al Haq Redaktie (1975). 'Al is de leugen nog zo snel, de waarheid (Al Haq) achterhaalt hem wel', *Algemeen Surinaams Islamitisch Maandblad Al-Haq*, 4(42): pp. 2-7.

Algemeen Bureau voor de Statistiek (2013). *Resultaten Achtste (8e) Volks—en Woningtelling in Suriname. Demografische en Sociale Karakteristieken, [Results Eighth (8th) Population and Housing Census in Suriname. Demographic and Social Characteristics]*. Paramaribo, ABS: Censuskantoor.

—— (2007). *Godsdienst/Geloofsovertuiging in Suriname. Werkzamen en werklozen in Suriname, 5(235) [Religion/Beliefs in Suriname. Employed and Unemployed People in Suriname, 5(235)]*. Paramaribo, ABS: Censuskantoor.

—— (2005). *Zevende Algemene Volks—en Woningtelling. Landelijke Resultaten. Volume I. Demografische en Sociale karakteristieken, 1 [Seventh General Population and Housing Census. National Results. Volume I. Demographic and Social Characteristics, 1]*. Paramaribo, ABS: Censuskantoor.

Algoe, Kirtie (2017). 'Hindu and Muslim Responses to Christian Dominance, Interreligious Relations in Suriname and Guyana 1950-2014' (Doctoral dissertation, Paramaribo, Anton de Kom University of Suriname).

—— (2009). *Suriname: schip van diversiteit met een boeg van saamhorigheid. De invoering van Holi en Id-ul-Fitr als nationale feestdagen in Suriname [Suriname: Ship of Diversity with a Bow of Togetherness. The Introduction of Holi and Id-ul-Fitr as National Holidays in Suriname]*. Paramaribo: Stichting Wetenschappelijke Informatie.

Barriteau, Violet E. (2006). 'The relevance of black feminist scholarship: a Caribbean perspective', *Feminist Africa Diaspora Voices*, (7): pp. 9-31.

Bauw, Josta (2011). 'Belijders Winti geloof vinden dat Meye respect moet tonen', *Starnieuws*. Retrieved from http://www.starnieuws.com/index.php/welcome/index/nieuwsitem/4443.

Bouma, Gary D. and Andrew Singleton (2004). 'A Comparative Study of the Successful Management of Religious Diversity: Melbourne and Hong Kong', *International Sociology*, 19(1): pp. 5-24.

Bramadat, Paul (2008). 'Religion and public policy in Canada: An itinerary', *Studies in Religion/Sciences Religieuses*, 37(1): pp. 121-43.

320 KIRTIE ALGOE

Bryman, Alan (2004). *Social Research Methods*. New York: Oxford University Press.

Bureau of Statistics Guyana (2016). *The Census Road. Compendium 2. Population Composition*. Guyana. Retrieved from http://www.statisticsguyana.gov.gy/census.html#comp

Canetti, Daphna, Stevan E. Hobfoll, Ami Pedahzur and Eran Zaidise (2010). 'Much ado about religion: Religiosity, resource loss, and support for political violence', *Journal of Peace Research, 47*(5): 575-87.

Creswell, John W. and Vicky L.P. Clark (2011). *Designing and Conducting Mixed Methods Research* (2nd edn). Los Angeles: Sage Publications.

Crossley, Samuel (2016). 'Recent Developments in the Definition of Evangelicalism', *Foundations: An International Journal of Evangelical Theoloy*, (70): pp. 112-33, May.

Dagblad Suriname (2016). 'Monseigneur Aloysius Zichem bijgelegd', *Dagblad Suriname*, 21 November, Paramaribo. Retrieved from https://www.dbsuriname.com/2016/11/21/monseigneur-aloysius-zichem-bijgelegd/

Evers, Ivo (2011). 'Velen schreven Bouterse af, wij hebben hem omarmd', *Trouw,* 23 June. Retrieved from http://www.trouw.nl/tr/nl/5091/Religie/article/detail/2456637/2011/06/23/Velen-schreven-Bouterse-af-wij-hebben-hem-omarmd.dhtml

Guyana Bureau of Statistics (2007). *The Co-operative Republic of Guyana. Population and Housing Census 2002. National Census Report*. Guyana.

Hassankhan, Maurits, S. (2016). 'Islam and Indian Muslims in Suriname: A Struggle for Survival', in M. S. Hassankhan, G. Vahed and L. Roopnarine (eds.), *Indentured Muslims in Diaspora: Indentity and Belonging of Minority Groups in Plural Societies*. New Delhi: Manohar: pp. 183-22.

Hospital, Clifford G. (2007). 'Towards Maturity in Inter-faith Dialogue', *Cross Currents, 57*(3): pp. 356-64.

Jamaica Department of Statistics (1949). *Census of the Colony of British Guiana 1946, Part D*. Kingston: Central Bureau of Statistics.

Jap-A-Joe, Harold, Peter Sjak Shie and Joop Vernooij (2001). 'The Quest for Respect. Religion and Emancipation in Twentieth-Century Suriname', in R. Hoefte and P. Meel (eds.), *Twentieth Century in Suriname. Continuities and Discontinuities in a New World Society*. Kingston, Jamaica: Ian Randle Publishers: pp. 198-219.

Kane, Michael N. and Robin J. Jacobs (2012). 'Perceptions of the Humanness of Religious Leaders Among University Students', *Journal of Spirituality in Mental Health, 14*(1): pp. 59-81.

Karuvelil, George (2012). 'Absolutism to Ultimacy: Rhetoric and Reality or Religious "Pluralism"', *Theological Studies, 73*(1): pp. 55-82.

INTERRELIGIOUS COOPERATION: SURINAME AND GUYANA   321

LAPOP (2014). 'The Americas Barometer', *The Latin American Public Opinion Project (LAPOP)*, Vander Bilt University. Retrieved from www.Lapop Surveys.org.

—— (2012). 'The Americas Barometer', *The Latin American Public Opinion Project (LAPOP)*, Vander Bilt University. Retrieved from www. LapopSurveys.org.

—— (2010). 'The Americas Barometer', *The Latin American Public Opinion Project (LAPOP)*, Vander Bilt University. Retrieved from www.Lapop Surveys.org.

—— (2006). 'The Americas Barometer', *The Latin American Public Opinion Project (LAPOP)*, Vander Bilt University. Retrieved from www.Lapop Surveys.org.

Marshall, Edwin K. (2007). *De interreligieuze dialoog in Suriname. Ala kerki bun? [The Interfaith Dialogue in Suriname. Ala kerki bun?]*. Utrecht: Utrecht University.

Omoruyi, Omonhiomwan (1971). *Social Communication and the Plural Society: an Inquiry into the Process of Integration in a culturally fragmented Society (Guyana)*. Buffalo: State University of New York.

Pew Research Center (2012). *The Global Religious Landscape. Pew Research Center Report* (vol. 1). Retrieved from http://www.pewforum.org/files/2012/12/globalReligion-full.pdf

Porterfield, Amanda (2013). 'Religious Pluralism in Religious Studies', in C.L. Charles and R.L. Numbers (eds.), *Gods in America: Religious Pluralism in the United States*. New York: Oxford University Press: pp. 21-4.

Prins, Jan (1961). 'De Islam in Suriname: een oriëntatie', *Nieuwe West-Indische Gids/New West Indian Guide, 41*(1): pp. 14-37.

Ragin, Charles C. (1987). *The Comparative Method. Moving Beyond Qualitative and Quantitative Strategies*. England, London: University of California Press Ltd.

Ramsammy 'Sunhealthy relationship (2006). 'Will Elections = Peace? A prayer for peace', *Guyana 360*. Retrieved 7 January 2016. Retrieved from http://guyana360.blogspot.com/2006/01/will-elections-peace.html

Ramsoedh, Hans and Lucie Bloemberg (1995). *Surinaamse Verkenningen. The Institutionalization of Hinduism in Suriname and Guyana*. Amsterdam, the University of Amsterdam: Department of Human Geography; Paramaribo: Leo Victor.

Reychler, Luc (1997). 'Religion and Conflict. Introduction: Towards a Religion of World Politics?', *The International Journal of Peace Studies, 2*(1): pp. 19-38.

Rose-Ackerman, Susan (2008). 'The voluntary sector and public participation:

322 KIRTIE ALGOE

The case of Hungary', *Annals of Public and Cooperative Economics, 79* (3-4): pp. 601-23.

Sankatsing, Glenn (2016). *Quest to Rescue our Future.* Amsterdam: Rescue Our Future Foundation.

—— (2007). 'Development and society in the Americas', *Caribbean Reality Studies Center,* 8th International Meeting on Education and Thinking, Aruba: 1-11, 2-5 May. Retrieved from www.crscenter.com.

—— (2004). 'People's Vote Compatible with People's Fate. A democratic alternative to liberal Democracy', in J. Menke (ed.), *Political Democracy, Social Democracy and the Market in the Caribbean.* Anton de Kom University of Suriname: Democracy Unit, Faculty of Social Sciences: pp. 1-27. Retrieved from http://www.crscenter.com/

Soeropawiro, Stanley (2016). 'Development of Islam among Javanese Muslims in Suriname', in M.S. Hassankhan, G. Vahed and L. Roopnarine (eds.), *Indentured Muslims in Diaspora: Indentity and Belonging of Minority Groups in Plural Societies.* New Delhi: Manohar: pp. 229-74.

Starnieuws (2012). 'Iris: Amnestiewet is begin dictatuur', *Starnieuws,* 22 March. Retrieved from http://www.starnieuws.com/index.php/welcome/index/nieuwsitem/9897

Surinaamse Moeslim Associatie (2000). *50 jaar Surinaamse Moeslim Associatie 1950-2000 [50 years Surinamese Muslim Association 1950-2000].* Paramaribo.

Trinidad Central Statistical Office (1963). *British Guiana Population Census 1960. Volume 2, Part A.* Trinidad and Tobago: Population Census Division, Central Statistical Office.

Tull, Stefano (2010). 'Kerkleiders: Goudwinning moet stoppen'.Retrieved on 28 May 2012, from http://suriname.wedd.de/print.php?sid=537.

Vernooij, Joop (2012). *De regenboog is in ons huis. De kleurrijke geschiedenis van de r.k. kerk in Suriname [The Rainbow is in our House. The colorful History of the Roman Catholic Church in Suriname].* Nijmegen: Valkhof Pers.

Waagmeester, Nico (2002). 'Van multiculturele naar interculture samenleving', *De Ware Tijd, Kompas.*

—— (2001). 'Een bijdrage van de Interreligieuze Raad in Suriname (IRIS). Aan: alle Surinamers in de gehele wereld. Verbondenheid met de aarde'. Retrieved 2 July 2015, from http://www.ivisep.org/index.php? option= com_content&view=article&id=153:aardedag-2001&catid=21: milieu-artikelen&Itemid=31.

Weller, Paul (2013). 'Interreligious Cooperation', in D. Cheetham, D. Pratt and D. Thomas (eds.), *Understanding Interreligious Relations* (1st edn). Oxford, United Kingdom: Oxford University Press: pp. 365-89.

INTERRELIGIOUS COOPERATION: SURINAME AND GUYANA 323

Woodhead, Linda (2002). 'Christianity', in L. Woodhead, P. Fletcher, H. Kawanami and D. Smith (eds), *Religions in the Modern World: Traditions and Transformation* (1st edn). London, New York: Routledge, Taylor & Francis Group: pp. 154-81.

APPENDIX 1

TABLE 11.1: POPULATION BY RELIGION IN SURINAME AND GUYANA FROM 1950 TO 2012

(figures in per cent)

Religion	Sur	Guy	Sur	Guy	Sur	Guy	Sur	Guy
	1946	*1946*	*1980*	*1980*	*2002*	*2004*	*2012*	*2012*
Christians	46.8	58.9	41.6	41.9	49.0	56.3	48.4	62.6
Hindus	19.5	31.9	27.4	37.1	23.0	28.4	22.3	24.8
Muslims	32.0	7.9	19.6	8.7	16.0	7.2	13.9	6.8
None/own	–	1.0	8.5	3.7	4.0	4.3	7.5	3.1
Others	0.5	0.1	1.7	6.8	3.0	3.0	4.8	2.7
Not stated	–	0.2	1.2	1.9	5.0	0.9	3.2	–
TOTAL	100.0	100.0	100.0	100.0	100.0	100.0	100.0	100
TOTAL ABSOLUTE	173,404	369,678	355,240	758,619	492,000	751,224	541,638	746,955

Source: Algemeen Bureau voor de Statistiek, 2005, 2013; Bureau of Statistics Guyana, 2016; Census of the colony of British Guyana 1946, Part D, 1946; Guyana Bureau of Statistics, 2007; Jap-A-Joe, Sjak Shie, & Vernooij, 2001; Vernooij, 2012.

CHAPTER 12

Fasting Practices of Religiously-mixed Families in Trinidad: Evaluation of the Social-Psychological Impact

SHALIMA MOHAMMED

An 'ethnic ghost' embedded into the subconscious of the East Indian (EI)[1] community in Trinidad and Tobago (T&T) owing to its collectivist origin, is the importance of the family unit and acceptance of the view that familial bonds are formed through the culturally recognized union of marriage. It was highlighted in 2003 in a study done on 'Major Trends Affecting Families in Central America and the Caribbean' that Trinidad[2] was exceptional among countries in the Anglophone Caribbean because, '. . . substantially greater proportions of women were involved in formal marriage due mainly to its EI subpopulation' (St. Bernard 2003: 3). The number of females of EI descent in the total population in the year 2000 was 251,716. That number had decreased by 2011, to 234,260, a decline of 6.93 per cent, despite the fact that the population grew by 5 per cent (UNDP, 2013).[3] Since EI women

---

[1] The words Indian and East Indian are used interchangeably to refer to descendants of Indian indentured immigrants who are nationals of Trinidad and Tobago.

[2] Although Trinidad and Tobago form a twin island republic, Trinidad was distinguished by St. Bernard because of the disproportionately higher number of persons of EI descent on the larger island (Trinidad 37.01 per cent, Tobago 2.54 per cent in 2011) (UNDP 2013: 16).

[3] Persons of East Indian descent constituted 40 per cent of the total population in 2000 but, had declined to 35.4 per cent by the year 2011 (Central Statistical Office: 2012).

preferred marriage to unmarried and common law status, then of the 181,990 unions (136,326 marital unions and 45,664 common law unions) among the total population in 2011, a large proportion should have been with women of EI descent. Unfortunately, the official National Statistics does not differentiate between the number of married persons in T&T by ethnicity, religion, or other demographic indicators. For this reason, the number of interreligious unions and by extension, the number of persons in interfaith families cannot be ascertained. But the lack of statistics does not suggest that they do not occur. In fact, the significant disproportion in the number of persons ascribing to different religions among the EI population in T&T, increases the likelihood of selecting spouses who follow different doctrines.

Pike (2017) estimated that roughly half of the EI population followed Hinduism while the other half followed mainly Islam, Presbyterianism and Catholicism.[4] Between 2000 and 2011, there was a decline in the number of adherents to Hinduism (-4.3 per cent), Presbyterianism (-10.2 per cent) and Catholicism (-1.4 per cent) but a nominal increase in Islam (1.6 per cent). While the precise factors accounting for the change in religious affiliation are unknown, one likelihood is religious conversion because of the appeal of a particular faith or, due to marriage.[5]

Disapproval of marriage to a person of a different religion and race is another 'ethnic ghost' in the traditional EI community. Each religious group seeks to increase its number of followers and in the cases of Christianity and Islam, are guided by stipulations within the holy books which espouse the view that marriage should

---

[4] According to the 2011 population census, of the 1.3 million people living in Trinidad and Tobago (T&T), Christians constituted the largest religious group (55 per cent = 726,000), followed by Hindus (18 per cent = 240,000) and then Muslims (5 per cent = 66,000) (UNDP 2013). This unique society also comprises of several minority religious groups such as Jehovah's Witnesses, Baha'is, Jews, and others (21 per cent = 268,000).

[5] The official population statistics also showed a tremendous increase of 108.4 per cent in the number of persons identifying as Pentecostal/Evangelical/Full Gospel and 22.7 per cent increase of Seventh Day Adventists.

FASTING PRACTICES OF RELIGIOUSLY-MIXED FAMILIES 327

be to one with shared religious beliefs, values and practices (Bible Corinthians 6:14, Deuteronomy 7:3; *Qur'an Al-Nisa* 4:25). Hinduism purports that spouses should be selected from those whose hearts are pure and clean (*Rig Veda*: 2/35/4). This cultural belief has transcended time and is gaining wider acceptability in T&T, largely because of the challenges in finding marriage partners in one's own religious group among the small number of Muslims, Presbyterians and Catholics in the total EI population. Despite the fact that the number of males of EI descent is on par with females, the significant disparity between the number of Hindus compared to Muslims, Presbyterians and Catholics has resulted in interreligious marriages.[6] This situation begs one to look closely at the process of interaction which has been evolving in the interreligious families.

It is difficult to identify any EI clan in T&T in which every single member observes the practices of one single religion. While the number of interfaith unions could not be ascertained, the Judiciary Annual Report (2017) showed over the six-year period 2009-15, the number of divorces in T&T increased and impacted 23,558 families. In response to the statistics, Canon John Rohim, an Anglican priest remarked to the Guardian newspaper, 'For some institutions marriage is a business, but, as a marriage officer you have a responsibility to spend time with [the engaged couple] preparing them for this very important move, and I don't think that is happening in a lot of cases' (Gordon 2012). Whether or not there is guidance from faith-based marriage officers, family members or knowledgeable friends; or failure to heed their advice, interfaith couples, though they may be in the minority, confront both opportunities and obstacles and effectuate solutions based on their unique circumstances. In those unions in which spouses retain religious loyalty according to the tenets of their respective faith systems, there are some commonalities including: (a) belief in a Supreme

---

[6] For the purposes of the current research, 'interreligious marriage' refers to any marital union in which the spouses are of EI descent and follow different doctrines. The terms 'religiously-mixed', 'interreligious' and 'interfaith' are used interchangeably.

Creator, (b) different forms of worship, and (c) fasting to fulfil their religious obligations.

Religious fasting is multidimensional, comprising spiritual, communal and personal aspects. It is the concept under investigation so that inferences can be made concerning its impact on behavioural changes which occur in EI interfaith families, as they strive to achieve cohesion as a family unit. Religious fasting requires discipline and demands denial of self-indulgent behaviour. Most learning theorists agree that the behaviour one exhibits is dependent upon what one learns from certain experiences (Olson & Hergenhahn 2008). It is logical that interfaith family members might be constrained to observe the various fasting protocols which are outside of their realm of experience, owing to their differences in practices according to the faith of origin. Fasting is learned rather than instinctive and so just as not every member of every single-faith family fasts, so too, not every member of every interfaith family fasts. A fasting person might experience some aversion to avoidance of pleasurable habits such as eating or drinking or engaging in spousal intimacy. But in an interfaith family, avoidance requires cooperation from the spouse and/or children who follow a different religion. It is also logical that he or she might be resistant to modifying his or her own behaviour, albeit temporarily, while other family members are fasting. Naturally, there will be some effect on the relationships within the household.

The focus of the current study is to determine: (a) what the effects of religious fasting on relationships are and (b) how do members of interreligious families manage to retain their faith in each other and the tenets of their respective religions when obstacles arise in the fasting period. These questions will be addressed by investigating how fasting is negotiated between couples when spouses are of a different religion; and between members of families in which children have changed religions or married and brought a spouse of a different religion into the household where only one faith was followed.

Religious fasting practices, in terms of their impact on the family and on society at large, have been marginally explored. Previous research has focused largely on how fasting impacts physical health (Mir & Sheikh 2010), and to a lesser extent, on the theological basis for the practice (Mathews & Eck 2013). It has been found to have pragmatic appeal as a vehicle to nurture communal and familial ties and responsibilities (Talukdar 2014). In terms of the effect of religion on the social system of the family, the research findings have been contradictory. Religion can be intrusive to the familial social system (Dean & Carlson, 1984), but it has also been found to have a compensatory function in marital relationship satisfaction (Hansen 1987).

The main goal of this study is to determine the impact of the demands of fasting on the social relationship between spouses, as well as among members of the family who are of different faiths. This issue will be addressed by considering the degree of participation in observance of the fast by members of the family of a different belief system and the impact of that participation on family relationships. The findings will be analysed, based on the theory of reasoned action (TRA) postulated by Fishbein and Ajzen (1975).

According to Fishbein and Ajzen (1975), reasoned action occurs because of the interrelationship among beliefs, attitudes, intentions and overt behaviour. The basis of the interrelationship is belief. Most beliefs are influenced by prior information available to an individual and in turn affects attitude. Attitude is related to the totality of an individual's beliefs rather than any particular belief he or she holds. Similarly, a person's attitude is related to the totality of his intentions and not necessarily to any single intention. Intentions serve as the primary determinants of overt behaviour. For change in beliefs, attitudes, intentions and behaviour, there must be active participation and persuasive communication.

The TRA has been shown to predict intentions and behaviours accurately in diverse research studies. Support for the propositions of the TRA were found in studies on sports coaches' use of exercise (Burak, Rosenthal & Richardson 2013); mobile phone usage (Azam & Lubna 2013); paramedic use of fluids and drugs (Banerjee, Siriwardena & Iqbal 2010); Wireless Application Protocol (WAP) technology (Suki, Ramayah, Loh Mun & Amin 2011) and job application decisions (Hooft, Born, Taris & Flier 2006). To the best of one's knowledge, the current study will be the first to use TRA to explain fasting behaviour.

330 SHALIMA MOHAMMED

OPERATIONAL DEFINITIONS OF
RELIGIOUS FASTING

According to Christianity and Islam, fasting is abstinence from food and drink. In the *Old Testament*, Queen Esther asked her uncle Mordecai to request of others that they fast, and do not eat nor drink for three days, night or day so she could obtain favours from the king (Esther 4: 16). The *Qur'an* states clearly, eat and drink until the white thread of dawn appear to you, distinct from its black thread [of night] then complete your fast [by not eating or drinking] till the night [sunset] appears (*Al Qur'an* 2: 183). The definition of 'fasting' in Hinduism is less clear. There are guidelines as to why one should fast, but not specifically on how to conduct the fast and when to do so. A Brahmin is advised to never eat the food of a king, Sudra, goldsmith, leather cutter, artisan, washerman, and unchaste woman, among many others. If he has unwittingly eaten the food of one of those, he must fast for three days (*Manu Smriti* 4: 222). One can only assume that the fast requires that he gives up what he had taken, which is food.

The reason for fasting differs according to which religious text is consulted. The earliest Biblical account of fasting was of Moses' stay on Mount Sinai for 40 days and 40 nights in which he neither ate nor drank but reportedly received the 10 Commandments (Exodus 34: 28). It is possible that fasting was one of Moses' laws because it was a common practice among the people who came after him. But fasting was done in combination with prayer. Both practices were observed when mourning someone who died by violence (Samuel 1: 12); prior to leaving for a challenging work assignment abroad (Acts 13: 2); prior to meeting with an official in authority to seek an immense favour (Esther 4:16); giving thanks for blessings from the Almighty (Luke 2: 37), when seeking redress from injustice (Psalms 35: 1-3); when seeking forgiveness to atone for unfair treatment to others (Daniel 9: 3-5) and as a form of penitence to increase humility (Kings 21: 25-7).

In Islam, the extrinsic motivation to fast is the promise of 'reward' from the Creator. According to Abu Huraira, good deeds are rewarded by being multiplied 10 times (*Sahih Bukhari*, Book# 31, *Hadith*

FASTING PRACTICES OF RELIGIOUSLY-MIXED FAMILIES 331

#118) and on the Day of Resurrection, the gate in Paradise called *Ar-Raiyan* will be opened only for those who have fasted (Narrated by Sahl, *Sahih Bukhari*, Book# 31, *Hadith#* 120). But most importantly, fasting is purported to be a shield or protection from the hellfire and from committing sins (Abu Huraira, *Sahih Bukhari* Book# 31, *Hadith#* 128), primarily because it praises the creator and teaches self-restraint (*Al Qur'an* 2: 183).

Hindus follow the laws outlined in the Dharma text of *Manu*, which delineates why one should fast and how the fast should be observed. Fasting is viewed as an act of penitence. For instance, to decrease feelings of guilt, one should, controlling his organs during three months, continuously perform the lunar penance by subsisting on sacrificial food or barley gruel, in order to remove the guilt of violating a Guru's bed (committing adultery) (*Manu Smriti* 11: 107). By means of these penances, men who have committed mortal sins (*mahapataka*) may remove their guilt, but those who committed minor offences, causing loss of caste (*upapataka*) can do it by various other penances (*Manu Smriti* 11: 108). For a person who has committed the minor offence of slaying a cow (or bull) the penance lasts three months. During the first month he must drink a decoction of barley grains, shave all his hair, cover himself with the hide [of the slain cow], and live in a cow house (*Manu Smriti* 11: 109). During the following two months, he should eat a small quantity of food, without any factitious salt at every fourth meal time and bathe in the urine of cows, keeping his organs under control (*Manu Smriti* 11: 110).

Of all the penances decreed for the removal of guilt, not necessarily for adultery, modern Hindus in T&T adhere mainly to the mandate of eating small, salt-free meals. It is likely that living in a cow house and bathing in cow urine is abhorrent and impractical. Hindus in T&T more commonly abstain from alcohol, intimate contact, and food (such as meat, fish, and eggs) as a form of physical purification of themselves in preparation for spirituality in *puja* (devotional worship) and Diwali. However, documented evidence of this fasting protocol remains elusive.

In the multi-religious T&T, it is quite common for the auspicious period of fasting for Christians, Hindus and Muslims to coincide. Some Christians fast during *Lent* (the span of time in the Church calendar between Ash Wednesday and Easter Sunday) by abstaining from food and drink only on one day of the week (Rau 2012). For most, the fast constitutes abstaining from a favourite food such as meat on Fridays or desist from a pastime such as smoking cigarettes or going to the movies. But Christians voluntarily fast at any time as a form of penance or to focus their hearts and minds on the Supreme Being. This mode of fasting departs from traditional practices mentioned in the *Bible* and the origin of this contemporary innovation of the Church is unknown.

Hindus choose to fast on specific days to pay homage to a particular deity but the majority fast on Thursdays which is dedicated to Lord Vishnu. They eat yellow coloured food and fruits on this day. Additionally, some Hindus fast in the week preceding a special *puja*; in observance of rites for deceased relatives; and yoga instructors fast for 40 days preceding *Guru Purnima* to commemorate their spiritual and secular enlightenment.

Muslims fast throughout the ninth month of the Islamic calendar (*Ramadhan*) because the *Qur'an* stipulates that everyone present during the month should spend it in fasting. Muslims who were ill or on a long journey during *Ramadhan,* fast in the following days (*Al Qur'an* 2: 185) and women in particular, are often found to be fasting in the tenth month—*Muharram*, because they are exempted from fasting while menstruating during *Ramadhan.* Fasting is also recommended in the last month of the Islamic calendar—*Zul Hijjah when* the annual *Hajj* pilgrimage is performed in Mecca. The guidelines require those who are unable to go to Mecca due to ill-health or financial incapacity to fast or feed the poor. Those who go to *Hajj* and cannot make an offering, fast for three days during the *Hajj* and seven days after return, making 10 days of fast in all (*Al Qur'an* 2: 196). Some Muslims also fast during the 'white days' of the Islamic months (thirteenth, fourteenth and fifteenth) to gain the benefits of a full month of fast (*Al-Bukhari* and *Muslim*).

Ramadhan occurs at varying times in the Gregorian calendar

FASTING PRACTICES OF RELIGIOUSLY-MIXED FAMILIES   333

because Islamic months are determined by the lunar cycle. *Lent* and *Ramadhan* sometimes occur simultaneously and within those weeks, Hindus observe the scheduled weekly fast. Due to the overlap in prescribed periods of fasting, it is natural that challenges will arise for members of interfaith families because they will be abstaining from different things. Muslims avoid food, drink and marital relations during the daylight hours of the fast. However, the *Qur'an* is specific that one can eat until the next dawn and is permitted on the night of the fasts, to have marital intercourse (*Al Qur'an* 2: 187). Like Muslims, local Hindus avoid marital relations while fasting but if the fast is for a week, they avoid marital relations even at night. How does this affect the marriage between a Muslim man and a Hindu woman? If a Hindu man is observing the weekly fast and can eat only *sattvic* (vegetarian) food but his Christian wife is observing *Lent* and she chooses to eat fish, will one party be offended by the other's choice? Further, what is the case in families where the husband is a Muslim, the wife is a Hindu, and the children are Christians?

METHOD

PARTICIPANT CHARACTERISTICS

To determine how interfaith families negotiate the various fasting protocols, case studies were done using five participants: one male and four females. The single commonality among all was that they are descendants of Indian indentured labourers. The single, unmarried male participant was born into a Hindu family and followed Hinduism, but he converted to Islam in early adulthood. The four female participants, three of whom were Muslims and one, an Anglican, all married Hindu men. To appreciate the diversity fully among the participants, demographic information about each participant is presented in tabular format in Appendix I and participant characteristics which are topic-specific and which may have a bearing on the interpretation of the results, are presented in Appendix II as Cases A to E.

334 SHALIMA MOHAMMED

SAMPLING PROCEDURES

Social media was used to solicit participants for this study. It was expected that the notices circulated via Facebook, e-mails and through word of mouth, would have elicited many participants. Unfortunately, this was not the case. Only five participants selected themselves into the sample by consenting to share their experiences. The data were collected through lengthy recorded interviews with the participants at their homes. They willingly shared information without any expectation for compensation. Out of the five informants, only two were specific about safeguarding their identities. However, in keeping with research ethics, the names of the five persons have been modified to protect their privacy. The thematic and affective elements of the dialogue with them were analysed to probe how fasting was negotiated in their interreligious families.

RESEARCH DESIGN

Since the sample size is small, the case study approach has been deemed most appropriate for this investigation, as it allowed for documentation and conveyance of the diverse experiences of the five participants. From this invaluable record, the reader can glean a clear picture about what is most interesting about the fasting behaviours of the participants. It is factual and chronicles the religious life of the participants and their family members, in their own voices. Participants were interviewed in the comfort of their homes and later contacted by telephone and e-mail, to clarify vague points. The reason for the natural setting is that it served to put the participants at ease and it prompted their memory. Facts which would otherwise have been lost were openly discussed because they were in a comfortable environment.

RESULTS AND DISCUSSION

All five participants fasted habitually. Four of them observed the fast as prescribed by their own and their family members' belief system. One habitually observed the fast according to her husband's

FASTING PRACTICES OF RELIGIOUSLY-MIXED FAMILIES   335

faith instead of her own. In all cases, there were elements of disagreement in the relationships, but not related to fasting. The dominant themes which emerged from the analysis about fasting and the social implications to family life were mutual concession, religious tolerance, and behavioural change. Preference for fasting in the Hindu tradition by non-Hindu participants was an unexpected finding.

MUTUAL CONCESSION

For Zyad, choosing Islam over Hinduism was a big disappointment for his family, especially his mother. This was because the family practised all aspects of the Hindu faith and as they resided close to a *mandir*, they spent a lot of time there and were heavily involved in the related activities. But during his first *Ramadhan* as a Muslim, he fasted for the entire month and his mother's attitude softened. He advised,

She did not really give many arguments once she realized that I am fasting and I go to mosque, everyday. She realized that it was a change for me, and it was something better, so she began to slowly accept it. Some days she would [go out of her way to] selectively prepare meals that I wanted to break the fast with, and I would always appreciate it.

Like Zyad, Zamina faced opposition to being a Muslim, but that was while residing with Hindu in-laws for the first three years of married life. She said, 'My mother-in-law was difficult to deal with and I did not want to create any conflict, so I did little by way of observing Islam. The compromising part of it was important to life'. Years later, she and her husband Kameel moved into their own house, and he started to practise Hinduism for the first time in the marriage while she was practising Islam. Did he fast according to the Hindu tradition? She replied, 'Yes, we both did. We just abstained from meat: no flesh, no eggs or whatever and we just continued to do whatever he wanted to do for peace and quiet.'

This admission to doing whatever he wanted seemed that she was the only party compromising. However, while he was performing more Hindu prayers and observing Hindu fasts, he also fasted

336   SHALIMA MOHAMMED

during *Ramadhan*. Zamina confirmed that, 'Kameel was always interested. During *Ramadhan*, he [a Hindu] would fast, not during the whole month, maybe a week.' But this was more than she was doing for *Ramadhan* because she had to take a long, arduous journey from work to home. How did that make her feel? 'Good!' she exclaimed. She paused here and replied thoughtfully, 'It was a joy that he was doing the Muslim fast and was comfortable doing that.'

Jassine's situation was different. She admitted, 'I practised my religion all the time. I had no difficulty being married to a person who was Hindu.' But neither her Muslim mother, nor his Hindu mother was pleased with the religious persuasion of their children's spouses. She explained,

Although Vic would never fast with me [for *Ramadhan*], he never complained or used negative words because he respected that it is a religious belief and just as I used to put importance to the situation, he did too. He was not into fasting in the Hindu manner either but while we were [residing] in Barbados, we came back to Trinidad on two occasions for *Diwali* and he would fast for *Diwali*. I did too. We would not eat meat then, because we knew we [were] going by Ma (his mother) for *Diwali* so we wanted to make sure that we did nothing to pollute it.

Was being deprived of meat an inconvenient compromise for her? She explained,

No, I did not feel deprived. I think it was good thing to do! Again, because it was a religious custom and we are a part of a Hindu and Muslim family, so we wanted to make sure that we observed it as well. Just because of that. It was not a pressure, sometimes I am glad not to eat meat.

Sherry, a Muslim, expressed a similar preference for avoiding meat while joining her Hindu husband in his fast, going so far as to say if she were not already so wiry, she would consume vegetarian meals on a full time basis. In terms of fasting as a Muslim, she said,

As a child I remember fasting six or seven days [each *Ramadhan*] and eventually maybe none, and after marriage, I started back fasting. He used to drink [alcoholic beverages] heavily and that was a problem for me. In the beginning, I had hoped he would stop drinking during *Ramadhan* while I fasted, but he continued.

FASTING PRACTICES OF RELIGIOUSLY-MIXED FAMILIES 337

When I got married, I made sure we kept fast on a Thursday. I would make sure and prepare a vegetarian meal so he would fast. As far as I am aware, [his family] did not [fast]. But I wanted him to do it just for him to be a little bit on the religious side. I feel religion grounds you and I wanted that for him, because he did not come from too much of a religious background. He was one hundred per cent okay [with fasting].

Rona, who is an Anglican, makes a limited concession for Dev's Hindu fast saying,

I respect my husband's religion and I do not have any problems fasting and doing preparation for the *puja*. I try not to cook any meat at home [while he is fasting] but I eat it outside. However, in the week leading up to *Diwali* and for his annual *puja*, I fast like him because I have to help with the preparation like cleaning, cooking, and making of sweets. I fast because I want to show support to my husband.

Dev compromises too. Rona explained,

My husband tries not to eat meat when I fast for Easter. He does it for health purposes and [finds it easy as] he is still able to eat fish. If he has to prepare meat, he will prepare something else for me to eat. He fasts two days weekly; on a Tuesday and a Friday, because of his *Patra* (religious character). I do not fast the two days of the week when he fasts, but if we are home and not working [on his fasting days], we cook food that all of us (they have two children) can eat; most of the time it is vegetarian.

RELIGIOUS TOLERANCE

For all the participants, fasting required patience and acceptance while living with a number of family or spouse who came from a different religious tradition. Zyad's mother teased him from time to time. Grinning here, he said,

So throughout *Ramadhan*, I would be at work and get home close to the time to break the fast [sunset]. Sometimes when I complained that I am hungry, she would exaggerate a little bit and she would say, 'Well I am not telling you to starve yourself'! I took it in stride. We have to deal with the criticisms from time to time.

338   SHALIMA MOHAMMED

The Islamic fast is commonly derided by non-Muslims for being a form of starvation but, his mother's tolerance, which Zyad interpreted as acceptance of his choice, was reflected in her response to his requests for preferred meals. He said,

Mom works but is at home before I am. Most days during the month of fasting, she would prepare dinner by the time I got home. You do not always get her to make what you want so I utilized it [her tolerance] when I could. I craved Mac and Cheese during *Ramadhan* for some strange reason, so she prepared that for me whenever I asked.

Zamina and Kameel were similarly very tolerant toward each other's fasting practices. She said,

At *Diwali*, we [she and their two children) light the *deya* (earthen lamp) together with him; everybody fast together with him; whatever day he wanted to fast, everybody fast! There was no difficulty, no displeasure, nothing. As soon as *Ramadhan* was coming around, he would do whatever needed to be done . . . clean up the place and get everything ready. He grew up next to the mosque, so he knew what to do [in preparation] more than me!

For Sherry, tolerance to Hindu fasting and practices was necessary. She said,

Normally every year, we would do a Hindu prayer, so we would fast about two weeks for that and then for Diwali. We are always fasting I think, about a week or so, and recently we started back fasting on a Thursday because I feel he is more grounded [when he fasts]. I never liked *Ramadhan* fasting to be honest with you. I think it is very difficult. I fast [for *Ramadhan*] but not very often. In the Muslim way, I have never kept a whole month of fast, but I try to keep at least 10 days. Now as a result of my medical issues, I travel for treatments and am not able to fast [for *Ramadhan*].

Like the other four participants, Rona and Dev had never had any conflicts about fasting. She said,

My husband never forced me to fast and neither had I forced him to do so. I respect my husband's religion and I do not have any problems fasting and doing preparation for the *puja*. I sit behind him and listen to what is being done at the *puja*. He never attended church but when I have [Christian] functions at home, he assists me in every way.

FASTING PRACTICES OF RELIGIOUSLY-MIXED FAMILIES 339

CHANGE IN BEHAVIOUR

Several of the participants expressed a positive change in the relationship they shared with members of the family as a result of fasting.

In the month following *Ramadhan*, Zyad admitted that he and his mother did not have any formal conversation about the experience of fasting according to Islam. But he explained,

I have heard people say that she has seen a change in me, and she likes that, and she is more appreciative of the things I do, work wise. I have spoken at numerous Islamic events throughout *Ramadhan* and she was really proud of that. She realized I was really committed to it.

Their relationship changed from one in which Zyad was threatened with eviction to 'peaceful co-existence' because of his commitment to religion and persistence at fasting.

For Zamina and Kameel there were several changes over the years in their religious and secular life. Some 25 years into their marriage, Kameel performed *puja* regularly and she would assist by making the food and sweets for the offerings. But she did not sit in *puja* with him and insisted that there would be no *jhandi* (symbolic bamboo pole with coloured flags) erected. She performed her daily *namaaz*, but he did not join her.

Fasting was the one thing they did together, irrespective of religion. However, a few years before his death when his affliction with a chronic illness began to take a toll on him, the unity in fasting inspired a change in his choice of religion. Zamina disclosed:

He of himself; sat down one day and asked to go and see the Imam. So we carried him. Although he took *Shahadah* (prayer to revert to Islam) at the very beginning [of our marriage] when we took *Nikah* (Muslim marriage ceremony), he asked to do it [again 25 years later]. I went to the Imam and I said, listen, ask him exactly if he want to do this; if he accepts this; I do not want to be responsible. I told the Imam that. Do not let me be accountable [for him taking *Shahadah*]. So the Imam sat down and asked him three times . . . are you sure this [accepting Islam] is what you want? Each time he replied yes! We had witnesses. He sat down and everything the Imam told him to recite, he recited, everything, like before [when they got married]. And with that we were okay. The only thing is that he wanted to have a big prayer [*Qur'anic* reading] before he died and I did not get around to doing it. I did not get to do the prayers that he wanted to do. He died and I did not get to do that. Inside here (with tears streaming down her face, she pointed to her heart), still hurts that I did not get to do it.

For Jassine who was married to Vic for just five years and who practised Islam, she intended to perform the last rites for her Hindu mother-in-law who outlived Vic, but ultimately, she performed a Hindu fast for him, some thirty-one years after his death. On hearing all that a Pandit had said, 'about the different stages and the prayers that you are supposed to offer', she realized that 'what a Hindu soul has to pass through before they reach to Heaven is serious and I don't know if all the rites were done for Ma (Vic's mother)'. When she consulted with the Pandit he instead advised her to, 'Do a prayer for your husband, but we will mention Ma as well.' That required her to fast according to the Hindu protocol for one month. About the experience, she said,

On the Sunday that we went to the temple; we had to prepare seven bags of *seedah* [gift] to give to different people, which was clothing and foodstuff. For the Pandit, we had to have a little piece of gold as a gift. For some reason I was told to buy a white towel, so I bought a beautiful white towel, and we went to the mandir. After everyone had left, it was our turn. It is not something I would do all the time, because I pray every day according to Islam and I ask God to bless them but I felt really, really good that we did that on that occasion.

Irrespective of religion whichever type of fast was required and how ever varied the associated rituals, the participants willingly engaged. Ishan was also willing to fast in the Muslim manner to honour his commitment to his wife Sherry, their relationship, and the Supreme Creator. Sherry disclosed:

Being Hindu, he drinks alcohol. After a couple years with me going through depression and taking medication, I was not able to fast at all. He was actually fasting for me during the month of *Ramadhan*. It was just something he wanted to do. I would get up and cook for him and he would fast.

FASTING PRACTICES OF RELIGIOUSLY-MIXED FAMILIES   341

PARTIALITY TO HINDU PROTOCOL
IN FASTING

The Hindu fast was practised in much the same way by all participants. There is abstinence from meat of all kinds, fish, eggs, alcohol and intimate relations. To begin the fast, according to Sherry, Ishan would offer water in the morning at the *Jhandi*. It ends either at 6 p.m. on the same day of the fast or the next day. About rituals to end the fast, Zyad advised that there was none, 'If you wanted to, you just go back to eating meat.' At his house, members of the family would, 'dread the Thursdays because you could not eat meat.' But Zyad compared fasting in both Hinduism and Islam and concluded that 'fasting in Hinduism is much easier'. 'Usually we fasted about two weeks before the actual *puja*.' 'Some people go a month, but the fast is pretty easy.' Sherry, who is a Muslim, said, 'Aww . . . it [fasting as prescribed by Hinduism] is really easy, compared to the Muslim way. I enjoy it because it is easier and sometimes, I forget I am fasting. I feel like if I had more weight I would do it every day.'

ANALYSIS

From the fasting behaviours examined, it is evident that maintenance of the social relationships within the family structure took precedence over differences in religious practices. This outcome reflects an interrelationship among changed beliefs, new attitudes, new intentions and overtly different fasting behaviours (Fishbein & Ajzen 1975).

According to Fishbein and Ajzen (1975) empirical evidence suggests that most beliefs are formed because of probabilistic inferences according to syllogistic reasoning. The married couples reasoned that the state of marriage effectively changed the social relationship which existed between them. Further, just as their social and physical environments (new home) changed, so too the bond between the partners must change. The probabilistic inference was that it is necessary to change a belief to facilitate the establishment of a unique social identity as a new and interfaith family unit (Tajfel 1970, cited by Breckler, Olson & Wiggins 2006).

The empirical research showed that a person's attitude toward any issue or event is determined by his salient beliefs linking the issue or event to various attributes, and by his evaluation of those attributes. The issue or event in all cases, which was linked to the married couples' belief in the desirability of a unique social identity, was that they did not heed their parents and relative's initial persuasiveness against interreligious unions.

Four women married Hindus, three of whom did not consecrate the unions as prescribed by their faith. Adherence by the women to Islam and Christianity rather than conversion to Hinduism, may have been a form of resistance against patriarchal orders (Avishai 2008). Four Hindu men married women without the customary *puja, vivahhavan* (lighting of the sacred fire) and *mangalphere* (circling of the sacred fire). In Zyad's situation, a Hindu young man chose to independently follow a different religion from his immediate family and the clan. He bonded with members of the *jamaat* (congregation) at the *masjid.* The attributes of the spouses and *jamaat* members were evaluated to be positive and more valuable than religious rituals and patriarchy. A new attitude was created based on the totality of beliefs that strengthening and protecting the new interfaith family unit was the means to proving that it was the right choice.

Fishbein and Ajzen (1975) found that the intention to perform a given behaviour is related to attitudes toward the behaviour and subjective norms concerning performance of the behaviour. The attitude toward strengthening the interfaith union emerged because relatives told them interfaith marriages were not acceptable. The intention was made to deliberately keep the interfaith family unit together. In the final analysis, a person can form new beliefs only by performing some behaviour. In the respondents' homes, while each spouse continued to pray according to his/her respective religion, there was assimilation of each other's fasting protocols into individual religious behaviours. The fasting behaviour was the single commonality adopted by the interfaith families. They did not pray like, other although they witnessed the other person praying. The

FASTING PRACTICES OF RELIGIOUSLY-MIXED FAMILIES 343

sacrifice required focus, empathy and efficient regulation of social emotions, for which there is a biological basis.

Processing information about social emotions is associated with activity in the dorsal medial prefrontal cortex of the brain (Heatherton 2011). This cortex allows one to restrain one's emotions and the distractions in one's life.

Social neuroscience suggests that one can strengthen this internal restraint mechanism by activating it regularly. Fasting challenges the brain and in turn, the fasting person develops adaptive stress responses (Mattson cited in Sugarman 2016). The will power necessary to inhibit the fasting person's basic desire to eat and drink during the daylight hours for days, combined with the will power to clear the mind for regular prayer, serves to slowly develop restraint. It allows the fasting person to regulate emotions more efficiently. Fasting viewed from this new perspective provides a means toward creating the best environment in one's brain for overt behaviours of kindness and empathy which engenders spiritual kinship within the home and society (Radecki 2017).

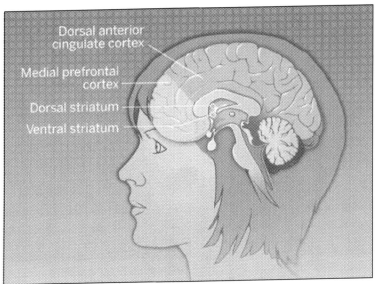

Figure 12.1: Processing Information (*Source:* Based on heatherton, 2011).

Social emotions aid successful relationships by two pathways. First, they provide incentives in the form of feelings of affection and love. Second, they increase the likelihood that people will adhere to the societal norms that are necessary for group living. By marrying someone of a different faith, the participants risked social exclusion. But the experience of negative social emotions in the forms of feelings of guilt, embarrassment or shame subsequently encouraged them to act within the bounds of socially acceptable conduct in their own homes. Positive social interactions were therefore strengthened within the home.

CONCLUSION

This study examined the social impact of fasting in interreligious families. From the experiences of the four women who participated in the study, it is apparent that fasting according to the faith adhered to by one's spouse, is a form of relationship maintenance that enhances marital satisfaction. There is assimilation of each other's fasting practices and etiquette into one common, familial custom. This was true in the experience of the single male participant, whose choice to follow a different religion converted his single-faith family into an interfaith one. The negotiation which takes place, creates a unique understanding and cohesive force which serves to strengthen the family unit. Additionally, observing the several periods of fasting required by the different religions augments the God-consciousness of numbers of the family. There is an overall intensification of spirituality as opposed to religiosity, among fasting persons.

Interreligious fasting also results in positive social benefits to the family unit and the wider society. Preparing for the fast and sacrificing together creates a sense of camaraderie and cooperation within the home. Having knowledge about different religious beliefs and fasting protocols makes family members of the more relatable, across a wider cross-section of the population.

IMPLICATIONS

Strong restrictions on interfaith marriages in Eastern countries result in honour killings, violence, and clandestine weddings. But in T&T, despite the different value systems of the members in religiously-mixed families, harmonious co-existence prevails. Here is a model for the future. Given the current rate of globalization and the expansion of plural societies, the phenomenon of inter-faith families is inevitable. By 2050, interfaith unions are likely to be in the mainstream. Children will increasingly choose to follow the spiritual or religious path which gives meaning to their lives rather than follow paths out of tradition. The form of negotiation which takes place between spouses and other members of the family belonging to different faiths in T&T, can be emulated to engender harmony among interreligious families.

An increase in the number of adolescents and young adults presently living in interreligious families presents an area for further investigation. Interreligious families have taken a personalized approach to traditional fasting practices. Members of the family unit learn from each other and translate that learning into a unique modus operandi. It is of interest because, to establish a firm religious identity, this unique group could create new religions in which the new practices would be acceptable. In the pluralistic societies which exist in the Caribbean, the children of interreligious families could possibly engage in 'cultural fasting' rather than religious fasting because of its constructive value to the maintenance of social bonds.

REFERENCES

Ali, A. (2004). 'Al-Baqarah', in *The Qur'an*. Valsayn, Trinidad and Tobago: IQra: p. 16.

Ali, Riad Hassan (2013). 'Jhandis', *Impact on Hindu Iconology in Trinidad and Tobago Blog*, University of the West Indies. Retrieved from https://tnthinduhistory.wordpress.com/chapters/jhandis/.

Avishai, Orit (2008). 'Doing Religion in a Secular World: Women in Conservative Religions and the Question of Agency', *Gender & Society, 22*(4): pp. 409-33.

Azam, Muhammad S. and N. Lubna (2013). 'Mobile Phone Usage in Bangladesh: The Effects of Attitude towards Behavior and Subjective Norm', *Annamalai International Journal of Business Studies and Research*, 5(1): pp. 25-34.

Banerjee, Smitha C., A.N. Siriwardena and M. Iqbal (2010). 'What influences

346 SHALIMA MOHAMMED

pre-hospital cannulation intentions in paramedics? An application of the theory of reasoned action', *Journal of Evaluation in Clinical Practice, 17*(1): pp. 84-90.

Bible Study Tools Staff (2018). 'King James Version—KJV Bible'. Retrieved from https://www.biblestudytools.com/kjv/1-kings/21.html.

—— (2015). '40 Top Bible Verses About Fasting—Read Scripture Guidelines'.Retrieved from https://www.biblestudytools.com/topical-verses/bible-verses-about-fasting/.

Bible Study (2015). 'What does the Bible say about fasting?' Retrieved from http://www.biblestudy.org/basicart/what-is-fasting-and-why-should-we-do-it.html

Buhler, George (1999). 'Manusmriti. The Laws of Manu—Part 1 (tr. Buhler G.)', *Hinduwebsite*. Retrieved from http://www.hinduwebsite.com/sacredscripts/hinduism/dharma/manusmriti_1.asp.

Burak, Lydia J., M. Rosenthal and K. Richardson (2013). 'Examining attitudes, beliefs, and intentions regarding the use of exercise as punishment in physical education and sport: An application of the theory of reasoned action', *Journal of Applied Social Psychology, 43*(7): pp. 1436-45. doi:10.1111/jasp.12100.

Central Statistical Office (2012). *Statistics*. Retrieved from https://cso.gov.tt/statistics/

Dean, Dwight G. and Robert S. Carlson (1984). 'Definitions of Life Situation and Marital Adjustment', *Journal of Comparative Family Studies, 15*(3): pp. 441-8. doi:10.3138/jcfs.15.3.441

Fishbein, Martin and I. Ajzen (1975). *Belief, Attitude, Intention, and Behavior: An Introduction to Theory and Research*. Reading, Massachusetts: Addison-Wesley Publishing Company.

Gordon, Zahra (2012). 'Divorce on the rise', *Trinidad & Tobago Guardian*, 6 December. Retrieved from http://www.guardian.co.tt/lifestyle/2012-12-06/divorce-rise.

Gosine, Mahin, N.K. Mahabir and D. Malik (1995). 'East Indian Food Culture in the Caribbean', in M. Gosine, N. Kumar Mahabir and D. Malik (eds.), *The Legacy of Indian Indenture: 150 years of Indians in Trinidad*. New York: Windsor Press: p. 178.

Griffith, Ralph T.H. (2015). *The Rig Veda*. Retrieved from https://sacred-texts.com/hin/rigveda/

Hansen, Gary L. (1987). 'The Effect of Religiosity on Factors Predicting Marital Adjustment', *Social Psychology Quarterly, 50*(3): pp. 264-69. doi:10.2307/2786827.

Heatherton, Todd F. (2011). 'Neuroscience of Self and Self-Regulation', *Annual*

Review of Psychology, 63: pp. 363-90. Retrieved from https://www.ncbi.nlm.nih.gov/pmc/articles/PMC3056504/.

Herring, Bert (2013). 'The Mystery of Fast-5 and D.I.E.T.', *YouTube*, January 22. Accessed on 7 April 2018. Retrieved from https://www.youtube.com/watch?v=xHQbg4xH9lw.

Hooft, Edwin A., M.P. Born, T.W. Taris and H.V. Flier (2006). 'Ethnic and Gender Differences in Applicants' Decision-Making Processes: An Application of the Theory of Reasoned Action', *International Journal of Selection and Assessment, 14*(2): 156-66. doi:10.1111/j.1468-2389.2006.00341.x

Judiciary Annual Report 2014-15 (2017). 'Newsroom: Annual Reports'. Retrieved from http://www.ttlawcourts.org/index.php/newsroom-69/annual-reports.

Mathews, Steven and E. Eck (2013). 'Fasting, justification, and self-righteousness in Luke 18: 9-14: A social-scientific interpretation as response to Friedrichson', *HTS Teologiese Studies/Theological Studies, 69*(1): pp. 1-9. doi:10.4102/hts.v69i1.1957.

Mattson, Mark (2014). 'Why fasting bolsters brain power', *You Tube*. Retrieved 7 April 2018, from https://www.youtube.com/watch?v=4UkZAwKoCP8.

Mir, Ghazala and Aziz Sheikh (2010). 'Fasting and prayer don't concern the doctors . . . they don't even know what it is': Communication, decision-making and perceived social relations of Pakistani Muslim patients with long-term illnesses', *Ethnicity & Health, 15*(4): pp. 327-42.doi:10.1080/13557851003624273.

Naved, Zia (2009). 'Ramadan: Fasting in the Hadith', *A Muslim's Quest for the Truth Blog*. Retrieved from http://navedz.com/2009/07/29/ramadan-fasting-in-the-hadith/.

Norazah, Mohd S., T. Ramayah, Y. Loh Mun and H. Amin (2011). 'An Empirical Investigation of Wireless Application Protocol (WAP) Services Usage Determinants', *International Journal of E-Business Management, 5*(1): pp. 2-15. doi:10.3316/ijebm0501002.

Olson, James M., S.J. Breckler and E.C. Wiggins (2006).*Social Psychology Alive*. Belmont, California: Wadsworth Publishing.

Olson, Matthew H. and B.R. Hergenhahn (2008). *An Introduction to Theories of Learning* (8th edn.). New York, Prentice Hall: Pearson.

Pike, John (2017). 'Trinidad and Tobago-Religion', *Global Security.org*. Retrieved from https://www.globalsecurity.org/military/world/caribbean/tt-religion.htm.

Radecki, Dan (2017). 'The Neuroscience of Fasting', *Bahai Teachings.org*. Retrieved from http://bahaiteachings.org/neuroscience-fasting.

Rau, Andy (2012). 'What is Lent?', *Bible Gateway Blog*. Retrieved from https://www.biblegateway.com/blog/2012/02/what-is-lent/.

Selwyn, Ryan D. (1999). *The Jhandi and the Cross — The Clash of Cultures in Post-Creole Trinidad and Tobago*. St Augustine, University of the West Indies: Sir Arthur Lewis Institute of Social and Economic Studies.

Sinclair, Upton (2001). *The Fasting Cure*. New York: Chet Day's Health and Beyond Online. Retrieved 6 April 2018, from http://apache2.pum.edu.pl/~fasting/upton.pdf.

St. Bernard, Godfrey (2003). *Major Trends Affecting Families in Central America and the Caribbean*. New York, United Nations: Department of Economic and Social Affairs. Retrieved from https://www.un.org/esa/socdev/family/Publications/mtstbernard.pdf

Sugarman, Joe (2016). 'Are There Any Proven Benefits to Fasting?', *Johns Hopkins Health Review*, 3(1): pp. 9-10. Retrieved from http://www.johnshopkins healthreview.com/issues/spring-summer-2016/articles/are-there-any-proven-benefits-to-fasting.

The Editors of Encyclopaedia Britannica (2015). 'Manu-smriti. Hindu law.' Retrieved from http://www.britannica.com/topic/Manu-smriti.

UNDP (2013). *Trinidad and Tobago 2011 Population and Housing Census Demographic Report: UNDP in Trinidad and Tobago*. Retrieved from https://www.tt.undp.org/content/trinidad_tobago/en/home/library/crisis_prevention_and_recovery/publication_1.html.

Zaha, Web (2015). 'Hadith Collection'. Retrieved from http://www.hadith collection.com/.

APPENDIX I

TABLE 12.1: DESCRIPTION OF RESPONDENTS

Name	Zyad	Zamina	Jassine	Sherry	Rona
Gender	Male	Female	Female	Female	Female
Age	26 years	64 years	60 years	35 years	32 years
Religion	Islam-Converted from Hinduism to Islam on 16 April 2015	Islam	Islam	Islam	Anglicanism
Marital status	Single	Widowed for 10 years	Widowed for 33 years	Married	Married
Religion of spouse	–	Hindu	Hindu	Hindu	Hindu
Duration of marriage	–	30 years	5 years	17 years	10 years
Family characteristics	Resides with widowed mother and younger sister who are Hindus.	Resides in her own home with her 50-year-old daughter and 2 grandchildren. Her daughter is divorced from a Hindu.	Resides in her own home with her 39-year-old daughter who is unmarried.	Resides with her 46-year-old husband in their own home.	Resides with her 38-year-old husband and 2 children in their own home.
Number of children	0	2	1	0	2
Occupation	Part time clerk. Student of Business Management	Retired legal secretary	Retired human resource manager	Accounts clerk	Teacher

350 SHALIMA MOHAMMED

APPENDIX II

CASE A

Zyad's initial name is A. Maharaj. He converted to Islam against his mother's wishes although he lives with her. He said he was influenced by close association with the Muslim teachers at the primary school which he attended from the age of five years. Noting his attendance at Islamic classes, Zyad's mother, prohibited him from going; he went so far as to tell that he would not be able to live in her house should he become a Muslim. His initial response was to bypass it as a joke, but he admits there were many serious arguments. As a Hindu, he fasted every Thursday and during the week preceding *Diwali* and *puja*. His extended family were all Hindus, and his mother would consult the Pandit for all important decisions. They live close to a *Mandir* but Zyad admitted he hardly went there. When he accepted Islam in April of 2015, he fasted for two months. He prepared for *Ramadhan* by fasting for the entire preceding month. He then successfully fasted during the entire month of *Ramadhan*.

CASE B

Zamina was born into a Muslim family in which attendance to *masjid* and fasting for *Ramadhan* was the norm. She was pursued by her best friend's Hindu brother whom she married in 1974, at the age of 24 years. A *nikah* (Muslim marriage ceremony) was performed at her parents' house and he accepted Islam and the Muslim name, Kameel. The couple lived with Kameel's Hindu family who, three months later, encouraged him to perform the Hindu marriage ceremony. Zamina reluctantly agreed saying, 'I am into it [the marriage] already, where do I go, you understand? So I said ok. There were lots of people doing Hindu and Muslim marriages together [at that time] so I went ahead, and I thought it would be ok.' She admitted however that her married life was filled with ups and downs. She has two adult children who each have two children of their own. Her daughter, who is divorced from a Hindu, lives with her. They all fast during *Ramadhan*.

CASE C

Jassine was born into a Muslim home in which fasting and attendance to *masjid* during *Ramadhan* was the norm. Her mother spent her evenings at the *masjid* teaching children how to read the Arabic *Qur'an*. Jassine married Vic, a Hindu, who died five years after their marriage in a tragic plane crash in 1983. They had

FASTING PRACTICES OF RELIGIOUSLY-MIXED FAMILIES   351

a civil marriage ceremony because it was inexpensive and they wanted to use their money for an apartment. Religiosity in the wedding extended to having their friend who was a Presbyterian priest, bless the rings. Members of the family did not attend because their widowed mothers, who were the authority figures in the respective households, both opposed the interreligious union. Although Vic's mother and family were Hindus, he did not practice any religion on account of him being, 'a good person who does good things for other people' but over the course of the marriage, Jassine continued her Islamic practices, including fasting.

CASE D

Sherry's Muslim family prayed but fasting was hardly practised. Yet her marriage to Ishan, a Hindu was initially opposed by her family. Their marriage ceremony was a simple registration at Ishan's parent's home in which a Pandit recited a Hindu prayer and her uncle recited a Muslim prayer. Ishan was willing to get married under Muslim rites, but Sherry was against it because he would have had to convert to Islam, and she did not believe in people changing their religion. The couple's parents and immediate family members reluctantly witnessed the marriage. Sherry works as an accounts clerk from her home for the car parts business owned jointly with Ishan.

CASE E

Rona is an Anglican whose marriage to Dev was a simple registration under the Hindu Marriage Act. They had a priest and a pandit at the wedding but did not have either one recite any prayer. Religion was discussed before the marriage only to the extent that future children should choose which faith to follow. They exposed their two children to Anglicanism and Hinduism. Rona attends church regularly, fasts for *Lent,* and belongs to Anglican lobby groups. Dev, by contrast, attends neither church nor *mandir* but he fasts weekly on Tuesdays and Thursdays. Rona takes the children to church with her while Dev prays at home and the children pray with him. Rona, however, does not pray with them.

Contributors

KIRTIE ALGOE is a researcher and lecturer at the Anton de Kom University of Suriname. In particular, she works in the Interfaculty of Graduate Studies and Research. She holds a bachelor's degree in Sociology, a master's degree in Development and Policy, and a PhD degree in Social Sciences. Her publications focus on religious diversity in the Caribbean, especially the role of government and the underlying political processes. In 2022, she published the book Religion, Power, and Society (Routledge). She has also contributed to a biographical history of Christian-Muslim relations 1500-1900 (Brill). She currently works on religious healing and biomedicine, sport and gender, qualitative methods, and political elections in Caribbean countries. Email: kirtie.algoe@gmail.com

JAN A. ALI is a religious sociologist specializing in Islam. He is a senior Lecturer in Islam and Modernity in the School of Humanities and Communication Arts and the Founding Convenor of WSU Postgraduate Islamic Studies Network in the Graduate Research School at Western Sydney University. Currently, Jan is working on two separate research projects. His first project is a sociological study of Islam and Muslims in Australia. In his second project Jan is studying different aspects of Muslim terrorism particularly its causes and consequences. E-mail: jan.ali@westernsydney.edu.au

FREEK L. BAKKER was assistant professor in Hinduism and Buddhism, comparative religion and interreligious dialogue at the Department of Philosophy and Religious Studies of the Faculty of Humanities of the Utrecht University until his retirement on 1 February 2017. In 1995 he started his research on Caribbean Hinduism. He wrote many books and articles, the most important of them being the book *Hindoes in eencreoolsewereld* (Hindus in a Creole World, 1999). Later he also did research on Dutch

354 LIST OF CONTRIBUTORS

Hinduism, which resulted in the book *Hindus in the Netherlands* (2018). E-mail: f.l.bakker51@hotmail.com

MATHIEU CLAVEYROLAS is senior research fellow at the CNRS (Paris) and member of the *Center for South-Asian Studies* (EHESS/ CNRS). As an anthropologist specialized in religions, he first focused on Indian Hinduism through temples, pilgrimages and practices, before studying Mauritian Hinduism. He is now starting a new research among Guyanese Hindus in New York City. Among his main publications are: *Quand le temple prend vie. Atmosphèreet-dévotion à Bénarès* (2003, CNRS edn.) and *Quandl'hindouismeestcréole. Plantation etindianité à l'île Maurice* (2017, EHESS edn.). E-mail: mathieu.claveyrolas@laposte.net

KARTHIGASEN GOPALAN currently serves as senior lecturer in History for the Department of Social Sciences at Sol Plaatje University in Kimberley, South Africa. Prior to this, he worked at the University of Fort Hare where he served as lecturer (2016-20) and Deputy HOD (2019-20) for the Department of History. He completed his Doctoral Degree in Historical Studies at the University of KwaZulu Natal in 2017, where he assisted in teaching for the History Department, History Education Department and for the Access Programme. E-mail: karthigasen.gopalan@spu.ac.za

PRASHNEEL R. GOUNDAR a lecturer in language at Fiji National University, Lautoka, Fiji. His books include *Pursuing Divinity in Paradise* (2020), *In Simple Words* (2017) and *Writing and Publishing in Fiji; Narratives from Fijian Writers* (2018). He is currently working on his Doctor of Philosophy (Linguistics) and has an M.A. in *Teaching English as a Second Language.* He serves on the Editorial Board of *Language Teaching Research, English Language Teaching,* and the *Journal of Applied Research in Higher Education.* E-mail: prgoundar@gmail.com

FARZANA GOUNDER is a linguist and Deputy Head of School (Research) at IPU New Zealand Tertiary Institute. Her research interests include oral narratives of indenture and their role in collective memory formation, and discourses on health, human security

LIST OF CONTRIBUTORS

and migration. She is the author of *Indentured Identities: Resistance and Accommodation in Plantation-Era Fiji* (2011), and co-editor of *Women, Gender, and the Legacy of Slavery and Indenture* (2020) and *Social Aspects of Health, Medicine, and Disease in the Colonial and Post-colonial Era* (2020). E-mail: fgounder@ipu.ac.nz

MAURITS S. HASSANKHAN is a historian and senior lecturer/researcher at the Anton de Kom University. He is also Chairman of the National Archives Council in Suriname and President of the International Scientific Committee of the Indentured Labour Route Project. His research interests include indentured labour, migration, diaspora and development, ethnic relations and ethnocentrism, including ethnicity and politics. He has organized several international conferences on slavery and indentured labour, migration and diaspora. Collaborating with Sandew Hira, he created the data bases on indentured labourers from India, China and Indonesia to Suriname (1998-2000). E-mail: mauritshassan@gmail.com.

HALIMA-SA'ADIA KASSIM holds a Ph.D. in History from the University of the West Indies (UWI). She has previously held teaching, research, development, and management positions nationally and regionally. She is currently employed at the University Office of Planning, UWI. Dr. Kassim has published several articles on the Muslim community related to education, religious organizations, gendered identities, cultural retention and negotiation in Trinidad and Tobago and on issues related to higher education administration and education and gender. E-mail: Halima-Sa'adia.Kassim@sta.uwi.edu.

VINAY LAL is a professor of History at UCLA. He is a member of the editorial board of such journals as *Culture, Theory, and Critique* and *South Asian Diaspora* and writes regularly on a wide variety of subjects for periodicals in the US, India, and Britain, including the *Economic and Political Weekly* (Mumbai), *The Little Magazine* (Delhi), and *Social Scientist* (Delhi). He has authored/edited seventeen books. His works have been translated into French, German, Spanish, Finnish, Hindi, Urdu, Kannada, Korean and Persian. E-mail: vlal@history.ucla.edu

356 LIST OF CONTRIBUTORS

RADICA MAHASE is a Senior Lecturer in History at the College of Science, Technology and Applied Arts of Trinidad and Tobago (COSTAATT). She has a Ph.D. in History from UWI, St. Augustine and a MA in Indian History from Jawaharlal Nehru University, Delhi. She is the author of, *Why Should we be called 'Coolies': The End of Indian Indentured Labour* (2020). Email: radica.mahase@gmail.com

SHALIMA MOHAMMED is an educator and independent researcher. She holds a M.Sc. Degree in Business Psychology, B.Sc. Degree in Psychology (Cum Laude), and a Diploma in Business Management. Her main research interests are ethnicity, religion, culture, multiple intelligences, positive psychology, and the business of education. She is a member of the National Trust of Trinidad and Tobago. E-mail: shalimamd@gmail.com

NARINDER MOHKAMSINGH studied Indian philosophy, Sanskrit and Hinduism at the KERN Institute of Leiden University. From 1988 to 2004 he was associated with CODARTS, the former Rotterdam's Conservatory as a lecturer of Hindi, Indian Cultural History and History of Indian Music. In 2004 he migrated to Suriname where he worked for Culture Studies until 2009. In between, he conducted research for Bidesia, an international Bhojpuri & Diaspora Project from 2004 to 2007. From 2009 to 2013 he was back in the Netherlands as assistant professor in Hinduism and Indian philosophy at the Leiden Institute of Religious Studies (LIRS). In 2013 he returned to Suriname and has since then been connected to the University of Suriname. Mohkamsingh regularly publishes in the field of Indo-Caribbean culture, religion and music. E-mail: mohkamsing@gmail.com/ narinder.mohkamsing@uvs.edu

SATYENDRA PEERTHUM is a historian at the Research Unit of the Aapravasi Ghat Trust Fund (AGTF) which manages the Aapravasi Ghat World Heritage Site in Port Louis, Republic of Mauritius. He is a member of the Secretariat of the International Indenture Labour Route and of the Centre for Research on Slavery

LIST OF CONTRIBUTORS 357

and Indenture and a part-time lecturer in history at the University of Mauritius and a Mauritian writer. Over the past seventeen years, he has published and co-authored on the above-mentioned themes in academic articles, conferences, and books. E-mail: satyendra-peerthum@gmail.com

PERRY POLAR holds a Ph.D. from the University of the West Indies (UWI). He has worked extensively in several areas including agriculture, environment, and the urban sector. He is engaged in film making, and examining the relationship between culture and development. E-mail: perrypolar@gmail.com

BRINSLEY SAMAROO graduated from Delhi and London Universities after which he had a long career in research and teaching at the University of the West Indies and at the University of Trinidad & Tobago. His area of interest is the Indian Diaspora. He was also a member of Parliament from 1981 to 1991 serving first as leader of the opposition in the senate and from 1986 to 1991 as a minister of the government. E-mail: bsamaroo40@gmail.com

SHERRY-ANN SINGH is a lecturer of Indian Diaspora Studies and Indian History and Head of the Department of History, University of West Indies, St. Augustine, Trinidad and Tobago. She has held fellowships at the Centre for the Study of Culture and Society in Bangalore, India and at the University of Warwick, UK. She has earned the Young Caribbean Scholar of the Year Award from the George Bell Institute of Queen's College, Birmingham (UK), 2004. Her monograph *The Ramayana Tradition and Socio-Religious Change in Trinidad, 1917-1990* was published in 2012. E-mail: sherry-ann.singh@sta.uwi.edu

GOOLAM VAHED is Professor in the Department of History, University of KwaZulu Natal. He received his Ph.D. from Indiana University, Bloomington. His research interests include the history of identity formation, citizenship, ethnicity, migration and transnationalism among Indian South Africans and the role of sport and culture in South African society. He has published widely in

358   LIST OF CONTRIBUTORS

peer-reviewed journals and his co-authored books include *Schooling Muslims in Natal: Identity, State and the Orient Islamic Educational Institute* and *The South African Gandhi: The Stretcher Bearer of Empire.* E-mail: vahedg@ukzn.ac.za

Index

African-Creole cultural hegemony 80
Ahl-i-Hadith in Fiji 227, 242: opposes
    anyone indulging in *taqlid* 242;
    reject *milad* 242
Ahmadis 208, 227, 237, 240-1, 299,
    308
Ahmadiyyas 207-8, 250
Akhil Bharatiya Hindu Mahasabha 92:
    Bhawani Dayal 93-4; Natal
    Indian Teachers Society 99;
    Pandit Rishiram 97; S.R. Naidoo
    97; Syllabus Committee 98-9;
    third South African Hindu
    Conference 96; Y.M. Naidoo
    97-8
Ambedkar, B.R. 79
American Aryan League 138, 140,
    149: Forbes Burnham 149; sided
    with PPP 149
Apartheid period, 1948-94 65-72:
    Arya Samaj movement 66; de
    facto segregation 65; Group
    Areas Act 65; important trends
    among Hindus 65-6; monastic
    vows (*sannyasa*) under Swami
    Purushottamananda 66; National
    Party (NP) government, 1948,
    paradoxical consequences for
    Indians 65; Neo-Vedanta
    reformist movements 66;
    Ramakrishna Centre 66;
    reformist movements 66;
    reformist tendencies in India,
    influenced local practices in
    South Africa 66; Sanskritization,
    process of 65-6
Areas Reservation Bill 93

Arian Benevolent Home 70
Arya Dewaker 137-8, 139, 146, 304
Arya Pratinidhi Sabha (APS) 93-4,
    139; of Trinidad 151
Ārya Samāj 17: Bhāi Parmānand 134;
    destabilized the caste system
    134-5; founded by followers of
    Swāmī Dayānanda Saraswatī 134;
    Hinduism, reformation of 135;
    impact on Caribbean Hinduism
    133-55; in the Caribbean 133;
    marriage system 134; Pandit
    Hariprasad Sharma 134;
    promoted a better position for
    women 135; taught monotheism
    135
Ārya Samāj in Carribean 153-5:
    debates about religious and
    political themes 153; ethnic
    Hindustani political parties 154;
    focused on education, on
    establishing schools 153;
    importance of contents and holy
    formulae of the Vedas 153; in
    Trinidad, rich Hindustanis
    constructed *koutias* 153-4;
    orthodox Hindu *pandits* started
    to recite Vedic mantras 153; role
    in politics 154; Sanātanī *pūjā*-
    ceremony 153
Arya Samaj Association in Chaguanas
    138
Arya Samaj missionary movement
    90-1: Maharishi Dayananda
    Saraswati 91
Arya Samajis 20, 133: in Guyana 138,
    140; in Trinidad 133-5

360 INDEX

Aryan Seereeram Memorial Primary School in Chaguanas 151
Asian indentured labourers from India and Indonesia 22-3

Basispartijvoor Vrijheid en Democratie (BVD—Base Party for Freedom and Democracy) 149
Berbice Central Arya Samaj 140, 150
Bethesda Movement (Pentecostal Christianity) 67
Bhāi Parmānand 92, 134, 136
Bhojpuri Mauritians 51
Broader Hindu Community Business Network South Africa 74-9: Facebook account 74

Canadian Presbyterian Mission 136: Annie School of the Moravian Brethren 136; James Basnett Cropper 136; John and Sarah Morton 136
Caribbean Hinduism 20, 134, 353
Caribbean Hindus: knowledge of the Vedas among 141
Caribbean nations, interreligious relations 297
Caribbean, Ārya Samāj in evolution of Hindustani political parties 146-52: Bhadase Sagan Maraj 12; democracy in Suriname 147; ethnic Hindustani political party 152; in Guyana and Suriname 152; in Trinidad and Suriname 152; Jagernath Lachmon 152; Jagesar Persad Kaulesar Sukul 146; orthodox Hindu Brahmins 148-9; Roman Catholic background 147; Round Table Conference of 1948 147; Sanātanīs 149; Surinaamse Hindoe Partij (SHP—Surinamese Hindu Party) 147

Caribbean, first schools for Indians 136: Ārya Samāj associations 136; Bhāi Parmānand 136
Carribean, Hindu marriage, struggle for recognition of 144-6: 1930s, Legislative Council of Trinidad, debates about recognition of Hindu and Muslim marriage 145; Aryan Pandit Hariprasad Sharma 144; Hindu Marriage Bill 145; in Guyana 145-6; in Suriname 145; in Trinidad 144-5; numerical decline of the Ārya Samāj in later years 144
Carribean, new temples in 142-4: havan-ceremonies 143; Hindu temples, rectangular shape of 143; koutias 143; Sanātanī temples in Guyana 143; Suriname, Ārya Samāj built temples in the 1930s 143
Cato Manor in Durban 70
Christian theology 208: St. Augustine 208
Colonial Born and Settlers India Association (CBSIA) 95-6
Conquistadores 209

Das, Bhai Mati 92
Dauka Puran 113
Dayānanda Saraswatī 91-3, 141-2: recited Vedic mantras in their rituals and added the havan-offering to pūjā-ceremony 142; replaced the pūjā by the havan 142
Dayal, Bhawani 93, 101-2
de Kruijf, Hans 149
Desiré Delano Bouterse 149
Dharamsingh 159-60, 167-71: established several baithaks in southern Flacq district 169-70
distant diasporic communities 80
Divine Life Society 66, 67
Draupadi firewalking festival 76

INDEX

361

Dravidian orthodoxy 44-8: *bonhommelapaille* 45; Brahmin-Aryan-Sanskrit association 46; evolution operates at two levels 45; *gardienlakour* 45; *gramadevangal* 45; Maduraiviren 45; *mandir* or *shivala* 45; Mauritian Bhojpuri culture on the Mauritian Tamils, influence of 46; Mauritian Tamil Hinduism 44; *Minis Prince* 45; MTTF exclusively promotes Tamil prayers 46; new learned traditions, authoritative representative of 46-7; *panjangam* 47; Selven is respected for his knowledge of Tamil 46; Selven's *kovil*, fire-walking ceremony organized by the priest in-charge 47; Tamil community in Mauritius, vitality of 46; Tamilization 45; Tamilize, overall temptation to 45; *Tirrukural* 47; *traiteur* specialists, practices of 47; *Witchcraft and Black Magic* 47

Easter festival 76
Era of segregation, 1914-1948 64-5: 1940s, growing tension between Indians and Africans 65; departure of Gandhi from South Africa 64; Hindus in Natal 64; Indians in Durban 64; Indians in South Africa, religion as less divisive 64; Indians in South Africa, unemployment and low pay 64; National Party (NP), 1948 65; white minority government, focus on repatriating Indians 64

Fiji 225: Arya Samajists formed the Maha Sabha in 1926 101; multicultural society 225-6

Fiji Hindi 113: Radio Mirchi from the Fiji Broadcasting Corporation (FBC) 113-14
Fiji Hindu ritual calendar 63
Fiji Hindus, challenges and issues to consider 125-8: attention to health, especially at a young age 126; engaging the youth, taking interest in their activities and preserving culture 125; issue of alcohol and sexual abuse 127; live-in-relationships or sex before marriage 126; migration 126-7; social media 127; Westernization 125
Fiji Hindus, COVID-19 relief works 123-5: ISKCON organizes free food distribution on Saturdays 124-5; non-governmental organizations, concept of 'service for humanity' 125; Sanatan Dharam Pratinidhi Sabha of Fiji 124; TISI provides lunch to students 124
Fiji Hindus, in business sector 122-3: Flour Mills of Fiji 123; Prouds Fiji Limited 123; R.B. Patel Supermarkets 123; R.C. Manubhai Group 123; Shop N Save Supermarkets 123; Tappoos 122-3; Vinod Patel Group 123
Fiji Hindus, political participation 122: 2013 Constitution of the Republic of Fiji 122; Arya Pratinidhi Sabha of Fiji 122; National Federation Party (NFP) 122; Sanatan Dharam Pratinidhi Sabha 122; TISI 122
Fiji Holi 63
Fiji Indians: Holi and Muharram festivals 63; social life of 79
Fiji Muslims 226-7: Deobandism 227; Hanafi school of jurisprudence 227; mosques and *markazes*

362 INDEX

(Islamic centres), establishment of 226; Mosques and *markazes* 226; Shafi'i school of jurisprudence 227; Sunni 226-7

Fiji Muslim League, establishment of 237-40: committed to fulfilling the social and welfare needs 240; key objectives 238-9; Muslim schools run by the League 239; provides assistance for tertiary studies 239-40; succedent of *Anjuman-e-Islam* (1919) with fundamental objectives 238; Suva Muslim Primary 239

Fiji Muslims, as indentured labourers 229-33: discouraged from permanent settlement 231; hierarchical and diverse social order in India 232; imposition of a special tax on free Indian residents 231; indentured system, hierarchical structure of 231; labourers were left recourse-less 231; living conditions 232; Muslim indentured labourers 229; Muslims found practising their faith extremely difficult 230; pull factors 230; women, recruitment of 231

Fiji Muslims, indentured system 227-9: abolished in 1920 228; Agreement of Indenture 228

Fiji Muslims, initial Muslim-Hindu cooperation and co-existence 233-5: 1930s, relations showed signs of fracture 234; *da'wah* (preaching) efforts 235; few minor disputes either over women or religious values 233; Indians human rights and freedom 234; Muslims and Hindus stood in solidarity 233; Muslims countered with intense proselytization 235; Sangathan

Movement 235; shortage of women 233

Fiji Muslims, Muslim community building, and Muslim organizations and subgroups 235-7: Anjuman Ishait El Islam 237; Anjuman-e-Islam 237; Anjumani-Hidayat-ul-Islam 237; *da'wah* missions 236; educated Muslims versed sufficiently in Islamic theology and law 236; fear of loss of identity amongst Muslims 237; Islamic Code of Conduct 236; Muslims distributed written materials on Islam and Prophet Muhammad 236; organized as a group and embarked on preaching missions 236; Toorak Jame Masjid 237; Vunimono Islamic School in Nausori 237

Fiji, books and publications on Hinduism 120-2: *Fiji Sun* 121; *Pursuing Divinity in Paradise* 120; specific books on Sri Krishna 121; Sri Ramakrishna Mission, Nadi, sells books 121-2; Swami Vivekananda College 122; *The Fiji Times* 121

Fiji, conferences on Hinduism 119-20: Vishva Hindu Parishad (Fiji) 119-20

Fiji, important *poojas* and festivals 107-12: annual *taipusam pooja* 107-8; *bhajans* and *kirtans* in the name of God 107; *Chautaal* 110; Diwali or Deepawali 111-12; firewalking 107-8; Ganesh Chaturthi 110; Gujaratais, *dandiya* 109; Holi 109; *mandalis* 107; men dress in *kurtas* 112; *patraasi pooja* 108; Raksha Bandhan 110-11; Ram Navmi 107; Sri Krishna Janmashtami

INDEX 363

107; Sri Subramaniam Temple 107; TISI Sangam 107; women wear a *sari* or *salwar kameez* during Diwali week 112

Fiji, Muslim-Hindu relations 246-7: live in harmony in neighbourhood 247

Fiji, Muslim-Hindu relations, impact of global Islamic revivalism 247-8: carried out by the Tabligh Jama'at 248; Interreligious Peace Council of Fiji 245-6; Muslim idea of fasting (Ramadan) 246

Fiji, politics and the role of muslims 248-9: Aiyaz Sayed-Khaiyum, *de facto* Prime Minister 249; Faiyaz Koya, Minister for Industry, Trade, Tourism, Land and Mineral Resources 249; Muslim political activism 249; Muslim Political Front 248-9; Muslim political leaders linked to Muslim organizations 249; Muslims in the Fijian parliament 249

Fiji's Hindus 79: their egalitarianism 79

Fiji's language 112-14: *girmityas* 113; Hindu community uses Fiji Hindi 112, 113; mother tongues such as Tamil, Gujarati, standard Hindi also practiced 113; *Shanti Dut* 114; Taukei and Fiji Hindi languages 114

Fijian Muslim communities 240

free migrants 90

Funeral customs 118-19: Arya Samajis, death ritual lasts for three days 119; *chhamaasi* 119; Hawan Yajis 119; Hindus in Fiji 118; *kava* 119; *Mundan* 118; North Indian families, two grand *poojas* after thirteen days of mourning 119; North Indians, thirteen-day mourning period 118-119; *saleena* 119; South Indian funeral ceremonies 118; South Indians, *teen maina* 119; Suva in Fiji, modern cremation furnace 118

Gandhi Memorial Vedic School 138

Gandhi, Manilal 95

Gandhi, Mohandas K.: played a crucial role in transcending religious difference 63; work in promoting 'Indianness' 102

General Registers: for the period 1887-91 24

Gengaiamman festival 76

Girmit 20

Girmit Diaspora, interreligious relations in 24-5: indentured labourer narrative 24

Girmitiyas in Fiji 128

Global Hindu Foundation 100

Goodlands 31-2

Group Areas Act 1950 70

Guyana Arya Pratinidhi Sabha 140

Guyana Central Arya Samaj 140, 150: Satyadeow Sawh 150; sided with PPP 150; Vishwa D.B. Mahadeo 150

Guyana, interreligious cooperation 310-14: interreligious organization (IRO) 310

Guyana, interreligious organization (IRO) 310: ideals of religious equality and solidarity 311; interreligious cooperation in 311; peaceful intervention in violent conflicts 311; perceived links with politics 314; promotes mutual understanding between religious groups 312

Guyanese Ārya Samājīs 140

Hadith 208, 209, 210, 218, 242, 244

Hajj pilgrimage 208, 332

Hare Krishna beliefs 68

364   INDEX

Hare Krishna Temple, public festivals
68: Ratha Yatra 68-9
Hindi schools (*patha-shala*) 17
Hindiusm in South Africa: large scale
and highly visible public festivals,
resurgence of 76; Shri
Mariamman Temple in Mount
Edgecombe 76
Hindoestaans-Javaanse Centrale Raad
(HJCR- HJCR—Hindustani-
Javanese Central Council) 147:
Jagernath Lachmon 147
Hindu Dharma Association of South
Africa (HINDASA) 78
Hindu diaspora discourse 17
Hindu Mauritians 18
Hindu missionaries from India 17
Hindu organizations: ineffective in
preventing conversions 99
Hindu practices: heterogeneity of 85
Hindu Sabhas 138
Hinduism 16: in a Creole society 16
Hinduism in Fiji, pivotal
developments 19-20, 105-28:
Arya Pratinidhi Sabha of Fiji 106;
Arya Samaj, esatbalished in Fiji,
25 December 1904 106; Fiji Sikh
Society 106; Gujarat Society
106; The India Sanmarga Ikya
(TISI) Sangam 105-6;
International Society for Krishna
Consciousness (ISKCON) 106;
many Sanatan schools operating
in Fiji 106; religious
organizations 105; Sanatan
Dharam Pratinidhi Sabha 106
Hinduism in Natal 85
Hinduism in South Africa, 1860-2020
55-80: Apartheid era (1948-94)
56-57; Colonial period (1860-
1914) 56; European imperial
expansion 56; Hinduism,
transformation of 56; Hindus to
South Africa, movement of 56;

hundred *jatis* or subcastes 55;
KwaZulu-Natal 55; Natal
government 55; Orange Free
State 55; period of Segregation
(1914-48) 56; post-Apartheid
period 57
Hinduism in the diaspora:
transformation of 16-17
Hinduism: definition of 87-8;
diverging religious practices
originating in the Indian
subcontinent 87; reification of
18-19; religious diversity of 16;
survival in a foreign land 85;
within the local Mauritian
context 29
Hindu-Mauritian religious authority
32-44: *Arulmigu Mariammen
Tirrukovil* 34; Astoria road *kovil*
34; essential role of Tamil priests
in today's Mauritius 40; Hindu
temple priest in Mauritius 40;
Hinduism in Varanasi 33;
kodimaram 34; Mariammen *kovil*
in Goodlands 35; Mauritian Tamil
authorities, desire for recognition,
visibility and community union
38; Mauritius Tamil Temples
Federation (MTTF) 35;
Mauritius' current religious
evolution 40; National Temples
Federations 40; priest's status in
Hinduism 37-44; prologue 32-5;
Selven Adukhan, life story of
35-7; traditional Mauritian
association of the Brahmin 39;
traditionally carnivorous goddess
Mariammen 40
Hindus United 108 Project of the
Hindu Mahasabha 75
Hindustani community 17

Iberian Islam 209-10: *Qur'an* 210
Iberian Muslims 210

INDEX

Immigrant Viramen or Veeramen 170-1

Indentured immigrants, plurality of 254

Indentured labourers 85: de-anonymizing of 253; of Mauritius 227

Indentureship: diaspora of 16

Indian orthodoxy 48-52: apparitions of Hindu deities on the Mauritian soil 48-9; assimilating to the caste system 50; barbaric' India 49; caste and renunciation 50; Mauritian Hindu influence 50; Mauritian low-caste priests 50; Mauritian Tamil Hinduism 49; Mauritian Tamil practices and individuals, ethnography of 48; Mauritian-made Hindu-ness 49; self-manifested images (*svarup*) 49

Indo-Trinidadians, historiography of 23-4

International Hindu missionaries 85

International Society for Krishna Consciousness (ISKCON) 68: Bengali Bhaktivedanta Swami Prabhupada 68; Chaitanya Mahaprahu 68; Hare Krishna Temple, near the Phoenix Plaza 68; Phoenix, township established for Indians in 1970s 68; Sri Sri Radha Radhanath Temple in Chatsworth 68

Interreligieuze Raad in Suriname (IRIS) 304-5: Evangelical and Pentecostal churches 309; Evangelicalism and Pentecostalism 309; non-traditional Christian denominations 308; participation of the Sunnis 307-8; political circumstances 304; political issues 307; practice of religious equality, solidarity and conflict solving 307; religious equality and solidarity, ideals of 305; religious institutions in 306; solidarity ideals, encouragement of 305; World's Religious Day 305

intricate relationship Muslims 23

Islam 208: acquisition of knowledge for personal and social development 209; comprehensive skein guided by Five Pillars 208; emphasis on education 209

Islam and Muslims in Fiji, Muslim subgroups 240-5: Ahl-i-Hadith 242; Ahmadis 240-1; Ahmadiyya doctrine 240; Darood-o-Salaam—Yaa Nabi Salaamu Alaika 241; Maulana Mirza Muzaffar Beg 240; Shafi'i School of jurisprudence 241; Wahhabi' movement of Sayyid Ahmad Shahid 242

Islam in the non-Hispanic colonies 210-15: Abu Bakkar al Siddiqui 211; African survivals in Tobago 214; Anglo-American War of 1812 213; British conquest of Jamaica 211; Bryan Edwards 211; Bush Negro society 214; enslaved Africans, batches of 211; Jonas Mohammed Bath 212; Mandinga 213; Mandingo priests 213; Mohammedu Sisei 212-13; (pre-British) Spanish administration 210; Suriname and Guyana, African Islamic presence 214; Trinidad, Islamic African presence 212

Islam in West Africa, Caribbean origins of 22

Islamic missionaries from Asia 23

Islamic School in Nausori 237

Islamic traditions, diversity of 23

366 INDEX

Jamaica-based Democratic Labour Party (DLP) 151

Javanese in Suriname 219-21: 1920, end of indentureship 219; Abul Hasan Isphahani 220; Anjuman Sunnat al Jamaat Association (ASJA) 219; Caribbean Muslims 220; Egyptian Revolution of 1952 220; Islamic Guardian Association 219; Muslim Committee of the West Indies, created under leadership of Wahid Ali 220; Queenstown Jama Masjid (JMQ) 219; Rahaman Gajraj (of Guyana) 221; Tackvee Yatul Islamic Association 219; Trini/Guyana Islamic leadership 220; Wahid Ali 221

John Francis Rowlands 70: Indianized his version of Christianity 70

Kavadi 61-2, 76
Kirtie Algoe 24
Kovil 38

Las Casas 209
Global Hindu Electronic Network (GHEN) 78

M.D. Naidoo 66: returned to South Africa in 1953 as Swami Nischalananda 66; took final monastic vows (*sannyasa*) under Swami Purushottamananda 66

Maha Sabha in South Africa: differed from its counterparts in the diaspora 101

Mahdi 208

Mariamman 'Porridge' prayer 76

Maritius, Indian Old Immigrants 167-8

Mathieu Claveyrolas 18

Maunatul Islam Association of Fiji 241

Mauritian culture 30

Mauritian Hindu institutions 52

Mauritian Hindu religious authority 32

Mauritian Hindu religious specialists 18

Mauritian Hinduism 18, 50-1: contemporary evolution of 31; evolution of 30-1; Mauritian discourse and realities 51; Mauritian specificities 51; renovations serve 51; socio-economic situation 51

Mauritian indentured labourers 31

Mauritian *kovils* 41

Mauritian landscape 31

Mauritian plantation 18

Mauritian priests: relational competence 44

Mauritius

Mauritius: Hindu deities in 38; immigrants in, promoted Ram Leela and Ramayana consciousness 171-2; nation-building processes 52; redundancy of places of worship 40; social and economic relations which the old immigrant entrepreneurs 163-4

Mauritius Tamil Temples Federation (MTTF) 35, 41: Mauritian priest as an employee 41; priest, prerogatives and obligations of 42; priest's office, professionalization of 42; salaried priest 41-2; salaried status 42; social work 44

Metaphor of exile 17

mila'ad 243

Miladis 243: Darood-o-Salaam-Yaa Nabi Salaamu Alaika 243; Fiji island of Viti Levu 243; various rituals and practices serve to affirm communal identity 243

INDEX

367

Mirza Ghulam Ahmad 207-8
Moeslim Partij (Muslim Party) 148
Muharram: Hindus in Natal,
  celebrated by 90
Muslims in the Indentured Diaspora 22

Natal: religious practices of indentured
  migrants 89-90
Natal and Fiji: family/kinship of
  migrants for 260
Natal Education Department (NED)
  98
Natal Indian Congress (NIC) 63, 95
Natal Tamil Vedic Society (NTVS) 75
Neo-Vedanta 66
New World possessions 209
Nineteenth century Protestantism 71

Oeday, Bharat 137

Pandit Ayodhyā Prasād 138
Pandit Mehta Jaimini 95
Pather, P.R. 98
Paramaribo 137
Pentecostal Christianity: grew because
  of ignorance of Hindu convertees
  71; reasons for spread of 71
Pentecostal churches 69
Pentecostal expansion, from the 1960s
  72
Pentecostalism 18, 67, 70, 71-2, 309:
  group participation 71-2; among
  Indians, rise of 70
People's National Congress (PNC)
  149-50: Cheddi Jagan 149;
  Forbes Burnham 149
plural Fijian society: Muslim
  community, evolution and
  development of 23
Poosari 38
post-apartheid African National
  Congress (ANC) led government
  72

Post-apartheid period 72-4; 1990s,
  growth of Hindu organizations
  and temples 73; Bengali Hindu
  Community of Cape Town 2014
  73; demise of Apartheid in the
  context of globalization 72;
  Hindu presence, visible in larger
  cities 73; Hindus, assertive in
  laying criminal charges against
  whites 76-7; Johannesburg,
  establishment of the Chinmaya
  Mission in the Midrand in 2015
  73; Kali Amman Temple opened
  in Malvern, Johannesburg 73;
  onset of democracy in 1994, new
  pressures facing Hindu leaders
  87; PIO (Person of Indian
  Origin) cards 73; post-Apartheid
  Telegu-speaking migrants 73;
  South Africa, influx of migrants
  from the Indian subcontinent 73;
  Valliama Social Justice Interim
  Committee 74; witnessed many
  Hindus and Muslims moving
  into former white areas 76

Qur'an 208-11, 214, 218, 242-4

Ram Leela 21: enactment of 21;
  Ramayana consciousness and
  heritage 21
Ram Leela and *Ramayana* in
  Mauritius (1870-1950), history
  and symbolism of 159-76:
  Aapravasi Ghat World Heritage
  Site or the Immigration Depot
  161; Beekrumsing Ramlallah
  Interpretation Centre, Aapravasi
  Ghat World Heritage site 162;
  collective group actions between
  the early 1860s and the early
  1880s 160-1; Indian indentured
  labourers 161; Indo-Mauritian

368 INDEX

popular culture and intangible values 174-5; Jean-Francois Rouillard 159-60; Kaithi and Devanagari scripts of northern India 162; Protector of Immigrants 159; Protectors of Immigrants between 1883 and until the end of indenture in 1910 160; Ram Leela being enacted on some of the sugar estates, hamlets and villages 164; Ram Leela or 'Ram's Play' 161; Ram Leela, important form of entertainment among majority of the non-literate immigrants 165; Ramayana Centre Act 176; Ramayana consciousness, entrenchment of 176; second half of the 1960s, process of community formation 161

Ram Leela and reading of the *Ramayana*, village/estate camp culture in twentieth century 172-4: 1870s and the early 1900s, the enactment of Ram Leela 172; 2010, importance of Ram Leela for the villagers of Cottage 172; between the 1920s and the 1960s 173; Chubylall Mathur 173; early 1900s and 1950s, historical figures encouraged Hindu Indo-Mauritians to become educated 173; Late Balram Narsimooloo of the village of Cottage 172; mid-twentieth century, Ram Leela performances, common in the Mauritian villages and estate camps 173-4; Pandit Bissoondoyal and the Jan Andola, encouraged the enactment of the Ram Leela, *Ramayana* and *Gita* 174

Ram Maharaj of the South African Hindu Dharma Sabha 99-100

Ramayana 17: consciousness nurtured through the reading and chanting 173; forebears narrated stories of 168-169

Rashtriya Swayamsevak Sangh (RSS) 78: aim to transform India into a Hindu state 78; idea of a Vedic Golden Age 78

Represented Communities 62

ritual oriented Hinduism 89-90

Saiva Sidhantha Sungum 67: Guru Subramaniya Swamikal 67; Siva Kumara Prathanay 67; South African Tamil Federation 68

Sanātanī Hindus 147

Sanātanī 141

Satya Sai Baba 68, 69

Selven Adukhan 35-52

Shias (Party of Ali) 207

Ship Registers/Emigration Passes 24

Shree Benoni Gujarati Hindu Samaj Shree Radha Krishna Mandir 74: 108 Shree Hanuman Chalisa, reital of 74

Sirdar Ramdhuny Nundall 165: established a *baithka* 165; helped to establish the tradition of the *Ramayana* 165

Sirdar Ramdhuny Nundall, immigrants Servanin and Rungassamy 163-7: *avenues of socioeconomic mobility* 163; Crispin Bates 163; early pioneer Indian indentured workers 163; established different *baithaks* on the sugar estates of Union Vale, St. Hubert and Beau Vallon 166; *intermediaries* with the plantation owners/employers 163; Marina Carter 163; Old Immigrant entrepreneurs 163

social investment 44

Social or collective memory 16

INDEX

369

South Africa, colonial period in 57-63: Abrahamic faiths 58; canonical authority 59; Colonial ethnographers 57-8; *Devi Puranas* 58; Draupadi (fire walking) festival 61; financial constraints 60; first generation Hindus 57; Hindu practices in nineteenth-century India 57; Hindu's attachment to the philosophy of *bhakti* 59; Hinduism and Islam, religious boundaries between 58; Hinduism practiced in Natal 59; Hinduism required thorough reformation 58; Hinduism, fundamentals of 59; Hindus in South Africa 59; Husaini Brahmins 58; indentured workers participated in the Muslim festival of Muharram 60; Indian nationalists in late nineteenth-century India 58; Kavadi 61-2; lower caste Tamil-speaking Hindus 62; Mariamman 'Porridge' festival 61; Mariamman and Draupadi as South Indian goddesses 62; Muharram celebration 60-1; Muharram massacre of 1884 60-1; Munisvaran and Koterie, subsidiary deities of Mariamman 62; Protestant Christianity 59; *Saivite Puranas* 58; sectarianism, idea of 58; Shree Temple 61; simple structures allowed Hindus to practise ritual and engage in sacrificial worship 60; Sunday school patterned after Christianity 60; temples and religious rituals 57; *Vaishnava Puranas* 58

South Africa: Hinduism in 18; Indian population, Christian composition of 69

South Africa, Indentured labourers and Hindu practices in 88-99: Free migrant Hindus 88; homogeneous Hinduism 91; international Hindu missionaries 90; migrants brought traditions to Natal 89; religious practices between North and South Indians, broad differences 89; traditions evolved separately 89

South African Hindu Maha Sabha 86-7: B.D. Lalla 86; coordinate the affairs of more parochial Hindu institutions 86; critics feared sectionalism 86; encompassed various strands of Hinduism 86; formation of Union in 1910 86; leaders, aimed to promote a purely religious identity 86; unitary Hindu identity, purpose to establish 86

South African Hindu Mahasabha (SAHMS) 74: change in the embracing approach 78; current Maha Sabha president Ashwin Trikamjee to label Maharaj a 'maverick' 100; language or regional affiliation as the basis for ethno-religious identity 75; National Council of Hindu Priests (NCOHP), creating and managing of 74; Shudda logo 74; South African Qualifications Authority (SAQA) for priests' training 74; South African Tamil Federation, suspended membership in Mahasabha 75

South African Hinduism 19

South African Hindus 77: Hindutva ideology and organizations transported to many diasporic communities 77-8; not immune

370 INDEX

to emergences of expansive
Hindu consciousness 77
South African Indian Congress (SAIC)
96
South African Red Cross 75
South African Tamil Federation
(SATF) 75: organized a World
Tamil Federation conference in
South Africa in 2001 75
Spain: Amerindian population 209;
colonial dilemma 209
St Clement's Vedic School in
Barrackpore 151
state aided schools 136
Sugirtharajah 91: reform movements
in India 91
Sunni-based Fiji Muslim League 240:
Ahmadiyya Anjuman Ishaat-i-
Islam of Fiji 241; issued a *fatwa*
(religious edict) 241; Paigham-e-
Islam 241
Surinaamse Hindoe Partij (SHP—
Surinamese Hindu Party) 147:
Jagesar Persad Kaulesar Sukul
147
Suriname and Guyana, between 1900
and 2014, religious demography
changed 299-300
Suriname and Guyana, 1950-2014,
interreligious cooperation 297-
318: between Christians, Hindus,
and Muslims 303; concerted
diversity 300; conflict solving
301; equality 301; government
policies 302-3; religious
demography 302; religious
leadership and religious
institutions 303; solidarity 301;
theoretical and methodological
scope 300-3
Suriname and Guyana, 1950-2014,
interreligious cooperation,
comparison of 314-18:
government policies 316-17;

major differences 315; religious
demography 315-16; religious
leadership and religious
organizations 317
Suriname and Guyana, African Islamic
presence 214-15: Islamic *dawah*
encouraged by North American
Islamic practices, revival of 215;
post-slavery period, influx of
Indians and Javanese 215;
religious observances, for Africans
in South American colonies 215;
slave registers 214-15
Suriname, Ārya Samājīs in evolution of
Hindustani political parties 146-
52: legislative council 146;
Koloniale Staten 146; Staten van
Suriname 146-7
Suriname, Indian and Javanese Islam
215-17: Hindus and Muslims
lived in relative harmony 216;
Imams and Moulvis 216; Munshi
Rahaman Khan 215; Muslims
came in small numbers to the
Caribbean before 1857 216
Suriname, interreligious cooperation
304-10: Interreligieuze Raad in
Suriname (IRIS) 304-5; Javanese
Muslims of Ahmadiyya and Sunni
denomination 304; Madjilies
Moeslimin Suriname (MMS) 304
Surinamese Aryans 139
Swami Dayananda 91-2: inherent
weaknesses in Hindu practices 91
Swami Nischalananda 66-7
Swami Sahajananda 67: influenced by
Swami Sivananda's book *Practice
of Karma Yoga* 67; opened
Sivananda International Cultural
Centre (SICC) 67
Swami Shankaranand 62-3, 92:
established Hindu youngmen's
associations in major urban
centres of Natal 63; established

INDEX

South African Hindu Mahasabha in 1912 63; instrumental in motivating local Hindus to establish reform oriented Hindu bodies 92; lectures on Hinduism 95; political agenda of Mohandas K. Gandhi, created dissension among Indians 63; print capitalism fostered nations 62

Tabligh Jama'at 244: *Bahishti Zewar* 244; *Fazaaile-Amaal* 244; principal aim 244

Tablighis 244-5

Tamil side, monumental temples 31: Dravidian model 31

The Arya Pratinidhi Sabha of Trinidad 138

The British Colonial World and *The Indian Ocean World* 164

The Indian Muslims 58

The Indian Sanmarga Ikya (TISI) Sangam 106-7

Theory of Reasoned Action 25

Transnational Hindu Movements 17

Trikamjee, Ashwin 70, 100

Trinidad: People's Democratic Party (PDP) 151; People's National Movement (PNM) 151; Sanatan Dharam Maha Sabha 151

Trinidad, 1945, universal suffrage introduced 150: Afro-Trinidadians 150; Brahmin Bhadase Sagan Maraj 150; Ranjit Kumar, president of the East Indian National Congress (EINC) 150

Trinidad, immigrants: age distribution 267; births aboard ship 270-1; bodily characteristics 268; caste 267; distribution by ship 265-6; Emigration Passes 264; estate assignment 272; family accompaniments 269-70; General Registers and the Emigration Passes 262; General Registers of Indentured Immigrants 262; geographical and social characteristics of the immigrants 256-61; height distribution 268; immigration records identified the immigrants as 'Muslims' 258-9; indentured immigration to the West Indies from Calcutta, Act XXI of 1844 259; Indian immigrants' societies in the colonies 258; methodology 261-5; migratory behaviours of the immigrants 261; mortality aboard ship 271-2; Muslim distribution 265; native places 268; population distribution 266; Presbyterian schools in 136; religiously-mixed families in 25; results and discussion 265; returnees 272; scheme for main 'Caste' categories 263-4; second indenture 269; sex distribution 266-7; Sunni Muslims of the Hanifa *madhab* 259; United Provinces (UP) and Bihar 257; women's indentureship experience in Trinidad and Guyana 260

Trinidad and Tobago (T&T), East Indian (EI) community in 325-9: demands of fasting on the social relationship between spouses 32; disapproval of marriage to a person of a different religion and race 326-7; EI women preferred marriage to unmarried 325-6; number of females of EI 325; religious fasting 328; religious fasting practices 328-9; theory of reasoned action (TRA) 329

Trinidad and Tobago (T&T), East Indian (EI) community, religious

372 INDEX

fasting, operational definitions 330-3: adherence by the women to Islam and Christianity 342; analysis 341-4; annual *Hajj* pilgrimage 332; change in behaviour 339-40; earliest Biblical account of fasting 330; extrinsic motivation to fast 330-1; fasting behaviours 341-3; Hindu protocol in fasting, partiality to 341; Hindus choose to fast on specific days 332; Hindus follow the laws outlined in the Dharma text of *Manu* 331; *Muharram* 332; Muslims fast throughout the ninth month of the Islamic calendar (*Ramadhan*) 332-3; mutual concession 335-7; participant characteristics 333; penances decreed for the removal of guilt 331; period of fasting for Christians, Hindus and Muslims 331-2; religious tolerance 337-8; research design 334; results and discussion 334-5; sampling procedures 334; social emotions aid successful relationships 343; subjective norms concerning performance of the behaviour 342; *Zul Hijjah* 332

Trinidad Hindu Maha Sabha 138

Trinidad Hinduism 21-2, 181-201: 1945-90, tremendous economic and political change 183; being and belonging, balance between 201; Carnival 198-200; caste 187-9; change and continuity, diametric pull between 200-1; development of 182; diaspora communities, fundamental processes in the formation of 183-4; double diasporic condition evoked by the migration and settlement 201; Hindu socio-religious development 183; Hinduism from India to Trinidad, relocating of 183; Indo-Trinidadians, eventual movement of 22; Shakti traditions, concentration of 181-2; social and geographical diversity 181; trying conditions experienced under the indenture system 182; Vaisnavite 181; *vanvaas* of indentureship 200

Trinidad Hinduism, Carnival 198-200: annual Carnival revelry 198-9; Calypsoes 199-200; Gods and Worshippers of India 199; Hindus in Carnival activities 199; Vishnu's Kingdom 199

Trinidad Hinduism, caste 187-9: non-Brahmin priesthood 188; numerous *jatis* or subgroups, restrictions and boundaries of 187; Sanatan Dharma Maha Sabha (SDMS) 188

Trinidad Hinduism, cremation 196-7: Cremation Amendment Act of 1976 197

Trinidad Hinduism, marriage 198: Marriage Bill 198

Trinidad Hinduism, negotiating ideology 195-6; Christian missions and schools, dialogic influence of 196; *Dharmachaarya* as the Hindu Archbishop 196; Hindu community's extended and intricate contact with; Hindu observance of Sunday services 196; multicultural societies, conflict among different religious denominations 195; structural pressure generated by the Christian Holy Book 196

Trinidad Hinduism, negotiating landscape 191-5: annual *Phagwa*

INDEX

festivities 195; *Baal Vikaas Festival, 1986* 193; *Divali Nagar,* initiation of 193; Green Street Hindu Temple in Tunapuna 192; Hindu Prachar Kendra 195; Hindu religion and culture, growing appetite for transporting elements 194; *Kartik Nahaan,* observance of 193; *lota* and *thali* used in *pujas* 192; national *pradakshina,* 1987 193; *Phagwa* festival 194-5; pilgrimaging tendency 192; *pitchkaaree* form 195; religious observances, individual and communal Boundaries 194; SDMS and non-SDMS schools 193; Secondary Schools' *Sanskritic Sangam,* 1979 193

Trinidad Hinduism, negotiating practice 184-7: 1935, introduction of Hindi films into Trinidad 186; Indian Renaissance 184; La Divina Pastora into the Hindu pantheon, inclusion of 187; Little (folk) tradition in India 185; *Madrassis* (and non-Madrassis) of smoking *ganja* (marijuana), common practices by 185; non-Hindu elements and observances, inclusion of 187; *Sipari Mai* (Mother of Siparia) 187; standardization of the many strands of 184; temple-based collective worship 185-6; Trinidad idea of religion 184

Trinidad Hinduism, Ramayana 189-91: Derek Walcott 191; Indo-Trinidadian society 190; People's National Movement 191; Ram Leela 190; *Ramayana* tradition 189-90; *Ramcharitmanas,* diasporic appeal of 189; social, religious and

political leaders 191; Western elements, negative impact of 190

Trinidadian Aryans 139

Trinidadian politics 152

Trust and Reconciliation Commission (TRC) 70

Ummah 22

Ummah in contemporary Caribbean, challenges 221: division of the faith into ethnic/racial moulds 221; neo-Sufi movements, rise of 221; reformist tendencies, arrival of 221

Ummah in the Caribbean 217: African and Asian Origins of Caribbean Islam 207-21; languages spoken by the *girmityas* 217; Mazar Khan 217; Munshi Rahman Khan 217; Raymond Chikrie 217; Rose Hall uprising of 1913 217; significant role played by the Pathans 217

United National Congress (UNC) 151

Vanvaas 18

Vedic Dharam Arya Sabha of Trinidad 139

Vedic Mission 139

Vedic Mission of Trinidad and Tobago 139

Vedic Mission School 137; established by Ārya Samājīs in Chaguanas 137; Pandit Hariprasad Sharma 137; Seereeram Maharaj 137

Verenigde Hindoestaande Partij (VHP—United Hindustani Party) 148

Virendra Callee 170-1

Vishwa Hindu Parishad (VHP) 78

Wahhabi movement 227, 242

Wedding customs, of Indo-Fijian communities 114-18: concept of dowry, does not exist 118; Hindus and Muslims, Indian and Native Fijians, marriages between 117-18; legality of the marriage 116-17; North Indians and South Indians, marriages between 117; photography as an integral feature 116; readymade costumes 115; Sanatan and Arya Samaj weddings, main differences between 115-116; three 'days' events 114; traditional wear for the grooms 114-15

white Afrikaner National Party 86-7

Willie Cumberbatch 138

Young Men's Vedic Society (YMVS) 75